HOME AND AWAY

HOME AND AWAY

The Rise and Fall of Professional Football

on the Banks of the Ohio, 1919–1934

Carl M. Becker

OHIO UNIVERSITY PRESS   ATHENS

Ohio University Press, Athens, Ohio 45701
© 1998 by Carl M. Becker
Printed in the United States of America
All rights reserved

Ohio University Press books are printed on acid-free paper ⊗ ™

02 01 00 99 98   5 4 3 2 1

Frontispiece: Glenn Presnell: Tank, Spartan, and Lion (in Detroit Lions uniform, c. 1934) *Courtesy of Glenn Presnell*

Book design by Chiquita Babb

Library of Congress Cataloging-in-Publication Data
Becker, Carl M.
    Home and away : the rise and fall of professional football on the banks of the Ohio, 1919–1934 / Carl M. Becker.
        p.   cm.
    Includes bibliographical references (p.) and index.
    ISBN 0-8214-1237-X (cloth : alk. paper). — ISBN 0-8214-1238-8 (pbk. : alk. paper)
        1. Football—Ohio—Ironton—History. 2. Football—Ohio—Portsmouth—History. 3. Football—Kentucky—Ashland—History. 4. Football teams—Ohio—Ironton—History. 5. Football teams—Ohio—Portsmouth—History. 6. Football teams—Kentucky—Ashland—History.   I. Title
    GV950.B43 1998
    796.332'64'0977187—dc21   98-23470

To Marilou, who walked the sidelines with me,
and Glenn Presnell, All-American halfback, All-American man

"We played for the crowd and the hell of it."

A Tank

Contents

List of Illustrations		xi
List of Figures		xiii
Preface		xv
Prologue: Three American Cities		1
1	Its Players Perform Not Like Heroes	6
2	An Ancient Rivalry as Pert as Ever	16
3	All Bill Did Was Blink His Eyes and Throw a Blank Stare	34
4	Poor Old Portsmouth	54
5	He Must Choose	81
6	It Isn't Whether You Win or Lose, It's How You Play the Game	114
7	Knock the Tanks and You Knock Ironton	137
8	Turn the Town Upside Down with a Really Good Team	159
9	Portsmouth Is Football Crazy	182
10	Portsmouth Is in the Big League	212
11	Football Is the Salvation	247
12	If We Had Scored Then	269
13	The League Wants Larger Cities	289
Epilogue: Three American Cities and Their Paid Football Teams		304
Appendix: Seasonal Records of Teams, 1919–1933		307

Contents

Abbreviations	319
Notes	321
Bibliography	351
Index	359

Illustrations

Glenn Presnell: Tank, Spartan, and Lion (in Detroit Lions uniform, c. 1934)

frontispiece

following page 140:

Downtown Ashland, c. 1926

Downtown Ironton, c. 1930

The Selby Shoe Company, Portsmouth, c. 1925

Tanks, 1922

Bill Brooks, c. 1922

Armco Park grandstand, c. 1925

Tanks, 1925

Beechwood grandstand, 1926

Virgil Perry, Armcos coach, 1927

Armcos, c. 1927

Armcos game at Armco Park, c. 1927

Portsmouth Shoe-Steels and Coach Jim Thorpe, 1927 (mural on Portsmouth floodwall)

Tanks, c. 1928

Tanks fans at Redland Field (Tanks vs. Guards, 1928)

Carl Brumbaugh, a Spartan in 1929, Chicago Bears quarterback in 1930

Earl "Greasy" Neale, Tanks coach, 1930

Tanks defeating Bears at Redland Field, 1930

Glenn Presnell, c. 1930

Earl "Dutch" Clark, Spartans back, 1931–32

Grover "Ox" Emerson, Spartans lineman, 1931–33

Illustrations

George "Potsy" Clark, Spartans coach, 1931–33

Spartans tryouts, 1932

Spartans, 1932, at Ebbets Field, Brooklyn

Spartans-Packers ticket, 1932

Spartans vs. Packers, 1932 (mural on Portsmouth floodwall)

George Halas, Chicago Bears coach, 1932

Playoff game, Spartans vs. Bears, Chicago Stadium, 1932

Harold "Red" Grange

Spartans ready to board bus for trip to Chicago, 1933

Figures

1. The Tri-State	3
2. Single Wing	13
3. Double Wing and Notre Dame Box	14

Preface

You can walk onto the football field at the Tanks Memorial Stadium on the east side of Ironton, Ohio, and, giving free rein to imagination, hear the sounds and see the sights of a football game played there on a Sunday in the 1920s. Men attired in the red jerseys and brown duck pants of the Ironton Tanks will be groaning and grunting as they block and tackle against their foe, perhaps the Spartans of Portsmouth. The white-shirted officials will be meting out penalties for rough play and other infractions of the rules. Scanning the crowd in the stands—two or three thousand — the viewer will see men waving their caps—straw hats if the day is warm and sunny—as the Tanks near the enemy's goal line. Occasionally, several will furtively slip a flask out of their overcoats and take a "snort" of white lightning or some other product of a still operated by local men in defiance of the Volstead Act. The women will root for the Tanks with equal passion; a few, the flappers of the new age, will smoke a cigarette or even share the flask with their escorts. Children will also be at the stadium, roaming around and near the stands, paying little heed to the game.

Historians of professional football, even those worthies in the Professional Football Researchers Association, have given little attention to the semiprofessional and independent professional teams of the 1920s like the Tanks and their opponents in the Ohio Valley—and with good reason. They played before small crowds, seldom ventured many miles beyond their home fields, rarely developed any reputation beyond their communities, and presaged no great changes in professional football. Yet for hundreds of communities they were a source of entertainment and pride.

In the following pages, I have attempted to chronicle the origins and play of the several semiprofessional teams in the 1920s representing three cities on the Ohio Shore—Portsmouth and Ironton in Ohio and Ashland in Kentucky. They engaged in vigorous competition with one another and with other elevens in Ohio, often manifesting both admirable and deplorable levels of play. At times, they aspired to reach

Preface

a higher rung in the ladder of professional football, sometimes unrealistically. At any level, though, the men in the togs wished to play for pleasure and for the crowd.

I have also attempted to tie the teams to their communities. Each team had a different provenance and a different meaning for its community. And each community had a different memory of the team or teams playing in its name.

I have narrated the progress of the several teams season by season—their history occurred that way—not in any thematic way, except insofar as I drew conclusions from their play and place in a community over the course of a season or several seasons. I should offer a word of explanation or apology to readers for the organization of my narrative describing the teams' play through a season—for the movement back and forth among the teams as they played through their schedules. Had I followed one team game by game through its entire schedule, I would have then had to repeat the description of games as I followed the second and third teams or to ask the reader to flip pages forward and backward to trace the progress of a team.

The research made me aware of the interdependence of a historian's labor. Because newspapers of the 1920s were my primary source, I had to beat a constant path to the office of interlibrary loan at Wright State University, where Rita Johnson and her staff cheerfully hunted down and procured the microfilms I needed. On my numerous trips to Portsmouth, Ironton, and Ashland, the librarians offered me unstinting assistance. Especially going far beyond the second mile was Thomas Adkins at the Portsmouth Public Library. Naomi Deer at the Briggs Lawrence County Public Library also was helpful. Joe Horrigan, the curator at the Pro Football Hall of Fame, gave me invaluable information about the National Football League in the 1920s. Archivists at the Ohio Historical Society, the Pro Football Hall of Fame, and the Dunbar Library at Wright State University provided important assistance, too. Several men who had seen or played for the teams of the cities gave me a wealth of information that no newspapers could have yielded. I have particularly in mind Dr. Louis Chabody, Jim Secrist, Russell Burns, and James Thuma of Portsmouth; Harold Nicholson and Louis Ware of Ashland; and Lincoln DeLong, Harold Rolph, and Glenn Presnell of Ironton.

For grants defraying costs of travel and preparation of the manuscript, I am indebted to several persons at Wright State University: Robert Sumser, chair of the Department of History; Perry Moore, dean of the College of Liberal Arts; Lillie Howard, associate vice president for academic affairs; and Harley Flack, president of the university. Linda Kauppila in the office of the Department of History at Wright State University kept me supplied with the notepads, pens, stationery, and other items necessary to my work. I must also extend my great appreciation to Mindy Greene for preparing the diskettes.

Finally, I owe a great debt of gratitude to my wife, Marilou; she accompanied me on my numerous research trips throughout Ohio and did much of the "grunge" work in libraries and archives. Hers was a labor of love.

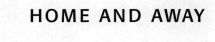

PROLOGUE
Three American Cities

IN THE SOUTHERNMOST segment of the Ohio River where it defines the southern boundary of the state lie three cities where semiprofessional and professional football teams sought to earn repute and dollars in the 1920s. Ashland, on the lower shore in Kentucky, fronts the river about six miles from the point where it turns northward at the boundaries of West Virginia and Kentucky. The villages of Catletts-burg, Kenova, and Ceredo, located to the east of Ashland, had social and economic ties to the city. Downstream about six miles across the river in Ohio is Ironton, stretching along the river in a two-mile band. The small communities of Coal Grove, a few miles to the east in Ohio, and Russell, just across the river in Kentucky, also fell within its social and commercial domain. The city had occasional social and economic communication with the towns of Jackson and Wellston, thirty and forty miles to the north. Downstream about thirty miles from Ironton, also in Ohio, where the river turns to the southwest, is Portsmouth. At its eastern outskirts is the town of New Boston. Almost due north twenty-five and forty miles are Waverly, a small town, and Chillicothe, a small city.

The communities were similar in their history, economic life, and demographic

Prologue

composition. All three derived recreational and commercial benefits from their common waterway, but all occasionally suffered the wrath of its springtime flooding. They lay in an expanse encompassing parts of Ohio, Kentucky, and West Virginia, the so-called Tri-State. They were all small urban centers surrounded by farms and villages; the population of the Tri-State probably was less than four hundred thousand in 1920. Though social gradations existed in all the cities, the gap among classes was not substantial, certainly not enough to cause bitterness or envy.

Ashland, settled in 1786, grew slowly in the first half of the nineteenth century. An iron and coal company was about the only source of vitality.[1] After the Civil War, an iron furnace, a foundry, and other small "manufactories" led to growth, and the population numbered nearly seven thousand by 1900. During World War I, the Ashland Iron and Mining Company expanded its operations, and by 1920 the population had risen to 14,729. Largely descendants of Kentuckians, Virginians, and Marylanders, the people of the city were nearly all native whites. Only about five hundred blacks—489, or 3.3 percent of the population—lived there.[2] The "new immigration" of the twentieth century barely touched the community. The foreign-born numbered only 220, the largest contingent 61 Germans. The city saw a surge of growth in the 1920s, when the population nearly doubled to reach 29,074 by 1930.[3] New industrial concerns spurred much of the growth. The American Rolling Mill Company, headquartered in Middletown, Ohio, purchased the mill of the Ashland Iron and Mining Company in 1921 and built facilities for an innovative continuous steel mill. Soon the mill was the principal employer in the city with a work force of 3,600. The Ashland Refining Company, founded in 1924, also employed several hundred men and women. "Spin-off" growth resulted from both firms. The population, about 95 percent native whites in 1930, remained in composition essentially as it was in 1920. As never before in its history, civic, social, and fraternal societies flourished. At the western doorstep, in Bellfontaine, affluent executives of new companies built fine houses, making that place the architectural showcase of the area. The Chesapeake and Ohio Railroad connected the community with the east and west. For news of Ashland and the outside world, residents read the *Ashland Independent,* a daily evening newspaper.

Like Ashland, Ironton owed its founding and early growth to iron. Settlers, many of German ancestry from Pennsylvania or Scotch-Irish from Virginia and Pennsylvania, and native Ohioans had come in the 1830s into the Hanging Rock area overlooking the floodplain where Ironton would be built. Using deposits of coal, iron, and limestone and stands of timber, they built more than a dozen pig iron furnaces.[4] Needing a river wharf where railroad cars could unload iron on boats, ironmasters

Figure 1. The Tri-State

Prologue

raised a pig iron port on the flood plain; here they could load a "ton of iron"—thus Ironton. Soon a foundry, a sawmill, several retail houses, and a hotel were in business. By 1852 the population was 1,751, and churches, newspapers, and other emblems of civilization were in place. After the Civil War, the pig iron industry flourished, with Big Aetna, the largest furnace in the world, its principal adornment. Other manufacturing concerns also were at work, including a large lumber company, fire brick companies, and a stove foundry. By the turn of the century the approximately twelve thousand residents of the city were served by telephones, electric lights, and electric street cars, but the iron industry around Ironton was in decline, few new manufacturing concerns were locating in the city, and growth was nominal.

At the opening of the 1920s, the population of Ironton was 14,007, descendants largely of the nineteenth-century pioneers. They had become ethnically homogeneous, Americanized with little concern about their roots. Only 300 whites, 131 of them Germans, were natives of foreign countries.[5] Blacks, accounting for 3.3 percent of the population, numbered 846. Commerce and manufacturing grew slowly in the 1920s. Probably the largest infusion of industrial employment came when the Selby Shoe Company of Portsmouth built a factory in the city. The Norfolk and Western Railroad, passing through the city, gave employment to many Ironton men. A station of the Chesapeake and Ohio was located at Russell. Local newspapers included the *Ironton Register,* an evening daily with a Sunday morning edition, and the *Morning Irontonian,* a morning daily. They merged in 1926 as the *Ironton Tribune,* an evening daily. The *Ironton News,* which began as a weekly early in the 1920s, became a morning daily by the end of the decade.

Responding to what they saw as economic stagnation, middleclass Irontonians, according to a historian of the city, "engaged in a cosmopolitan search" for a way to make their community a "sophisticated and progressive place."[6] In 1930, the population had risen to 16,821, an increase of about 2,800.[7] The number of foreign-born whites fell by nearly a hundred during the decade, and the number of blacks remained about the same. More than before, Ironton was a demographically uniform community.

Portsmouth was an older community than Ironton and Ashland and had risen on a different economic base, but its growth was also supported by iron. Settled in 1805, mostly by Virginians, at the confluence of the Ohio and Scioto Rivers, the village became a trading center for the settlers living along the Scioto River. Flatboats coming down the Scioto with corn, pork, flour, and whiskey for reshipment down the Ohio and Mississippi Rivers gave it a flourishing commerce.[8] As the southern terminus of the Ohio and Erie Canal, which opened in 1830, the area saw more trade.

Iron furnaces erected to the east of Portsmouth provided more commerce. Railroads built into the community in the 1850s doomed the canal but quickened economic life. After the Civil War, iron and steel mills and several other metalworking shops began production, but shoe factories soon became the principal employer in the community. By the end of the century, a dozen shoe firms were manufacturing shoes or parts of shoes. At that time the population was about seventeen thousand. The iron and steel industry grew appreciably early in the new century. Especially important was the Whitaker-Glessner plant, which the Wheeling Steel Corporation acquired in 1916; it proceeded to erect a large open blast furnace and to enlarge the old Glessner mills.

By 1920 Portsmouth was one of the largest cities in the Ohio Valley. Its population had nearly doubled since 1900 and stood at about 33,000. Like Ashland and Ironton, it was not a polyglot city. Only about 700 residents, nearly 300 of them Germans, were foreign-born. Blacks were relatively few, numbering 1,160.[9] Growth was rapid through the 1920s, owing largely to the shoe factories and steel mills. Shoe companies employed more than four thousand workers, the Whitaker mill five thousand. Additionally the Norfolk and Western and Baltimore and Ohio Railroads had together a work force of three thousand in their terminals. Optimism was the currency of the day in the civic clubs and in the two local newspapers, the *Portsmouth Times,* an evening daily, and the *Morning Sun,* a morning daily. By 1930 the population had risen to 42,560. But the number of foreign-born whites had fallen by about 60. The black population had increased by about 800 and, as a percentage of the whole population, from 3.5 percent to 4.4 percent.[10] Portsmouth remained, nonetheless, essentially a white community with little ethnic diversity.

In these small industrial cities, American football found expression in the 1920s in a form that was at once materialistic, idealistic, and egalitarian. Originating out of varying circumstances, the teams playing the game met different responses in their communities, but all eventually fell before a common foe—but not before they gave their fans seasons of great expectations, exhilaration, and disappointment.

1

Its Players Perform Not Like Heroes

A LITTLE MORE THAN fifty years after Princeton and Rutgers played the first intercollegiate football game (more nearly a soccer match) in 1869, representatives of ten professional football teams meeting in Canton, Ohio, organized the American Professional Football Association, the first national professional organization. In the intervening years a succession of rapid changes occurred in the rules governing the play and form of football and in its reach into American life.[1]

In the Princeton-Rutgers game, a descendant of a violent folk game that English villagers had played as early as the fourteenth century, the teams adhered to rules laid down by the London Football Association in 1862. Players on offense, the "bull dogs," could not run with the ball but advanced it by batting it with their hands, feet, or heads.[2] Five years later, employing rules of the Rugby Union of England, "backs" of the football clubs from McGill and Harvard Universities carried the ball toward the opposite goal line. By 1876 the rules of rugby or running with the ball prevailed in American collegiate football.

Its Players Perform Not Like Heroes

But Americans in the next three decades gave scant attention to either association or rugby rules of football, developing their own distinctive approach to the game.[3] Various collegiate bodies, often guided or dominated by Walter Camp, the principal engineer of modern American football, adopted rules on the scoring of points, the number of players on a team, the down yardage system, the number of players on the offensive lines, passing, and other aspects of the game so that by about 1912 the essential framework of the game was largely in place. Such changes, though originating in collegiate football, would long govern the play of semiprofessional and professional teams.

Profound changes evolved. A safety, once worth one point, counted two points by 1912; a field goal came down from five points to three points; a touchdown, once worth two points, became six points. Eleven men, not fifteen as at one time, constituted a team. Teams once could hold "undisturbed possession" of the ball in scrimmage; by the yardage system, they surrendered the ball if they did not gain ten yards in four plays. The rules did not adequately govern the disposition of players so teams developed "mass momentum" formations—linemen moving into the backfield ran interference for the ball carrier, often resulting in carnage; by 1910 seven men had to remain on the line of scrimmage. Once prohibited, the forward pass was in use, but with restrictions; the passer, for instance, had to throw the ball from at least five yards from behind the line of scrimmage.

In the initial decades of play, the game was the preserve of the eastern schools, Harvard, Yale, Princeton, Columbia, and others. But late in the century, midwestern universities—Michigan, Chicago, and Illinois, among others—were playing and soon organized the Western Conference, which attempted to promulgate rules governing eligibility of players. In the opening decades of the new century southern and western schools entered the lists and organized conferences. A "profusion of power" followed as latecomers such as elevens at the Universities of Pittsburgh, Minnesota, and Nebraska emerged as titans of the gridiron. In the second decade, the names of coaches at the large schools—Bob Zuppke at the University of Illinois and Glenn "Pop" Warner at the University of Pittsburgh, for instance—were becoming household words. Small colleges across the nation were also fielding teams. The collegians were about to enter a golden age of play in the 1920s.

High schools in the East and Midwest were also taking up football in the 1890s. In large cities teams developed intense intercity rivalries. At Dayton, Ohio, as in many other communities, the annual game between the leading schools, Stivers and Steele, a major social event in the community, became the occasion for parades, parties, and pranks. High school teams in small towns also engaged in vigorous competition with teams from neighboring communities. At whatever level, the elevens received impassioned support from adults, who, whether alumni or not, became their loyal fans.

 Outside the scholastic setting, Americans were playing football in the 1880s and 1890s under the auspices of athletic clubs. Ironically, though these clubs seemingly were sanctuaries of elitists committed to amateurism in athletic competition, they opened the door to the rise of professional football. The New York Athletic Club, founded in 1866, organized track and field competition among young men of elite social standing.[4] Similar clubs appeared in Baltimore, Chicago, and other large cities in the 1880s, and clubs sprang up in smaller cities throughout the nation in the 1880s and 1890s. In the large cities they built large clubhouses with gymnasiums, swimming pools, and bowling alleys. Even as they celebrated ideals of "fair play" and amateurism, members of athletic clubs, often men who had been ruthless business figures lionized by a society extolling the acquisitive values and winning at any cost, were willing to subsidize athletes who could give them dominion over other clubs. Though originally organized to advance competition in track and field, athletic clubs gradually gave increasing attention to football, forming teams for interclub competition, especially in the 1890s.

Out of this rivalry professional football took root. In 1889 six athletic clubs in New York, Baltimore, Boston, and Orange, New Jersey, formed a football league to vie for the "amateur title of America."[5] As they played in the 1890s, they compromised their amateurism slightly, awarding trophies or watches to outstanding players, who then converted them into cash at pawnshops. Inevitably, the athletic clubs went beyond modest subterfuges. Early in the 1890s, the Pittsburgh Athletic Club and the Allegheny Athletic Club, already intense rivals, organized football teams that met each other with doctored lineups.[6] In their first game in 1892, which ended in a tie, 6–6, the Pittsburgh club used its physical director as a player, paying him an increased salary during the football season, and also employed a "ringer," one "Stayer," who was, in fact, A. C. Read, captain of the Penn State college team. Despite recriminatory charges, the Allegheny club persuaded William "Pudge" Heffelfinger, who was then playing for the Chicago Athletic Association, to enter its lineup for a second game with Pittsburgh. Two of his teammates from Chicago also joined the Allegheny squad. Pittsburgh enlisted two players from the Pennsylvania Club of Steelton. After the game, played before a crowd of three thousand, which the Allegheny eleven won 4–0, Heffelfinger received $500 for playing and $25 for expenses.

Its Players Perform Not Like Heroes

Controversy over professionalism in football appeared in the Pittsburgh press for weeks.

Subsequently, the game spread into larger and smaller communities in western Pennsylvania, New York, New Jersey, and Ohio. In Ohio athletic clubs in Dayton, Cleveland, Cincinnati, and other cities began to pay men playing for them. Some semblance of order arrived in 1896, when the clubs began to name state champions. Then in the opening decades of the century, football enthusiasts in Massillon, Canton, Akron, Columbus, Dayton, Shelby, and other communities in Ohio, usually acting independently of athletic clubs, created such teams as the Massillon Tigers, the Akron Indians, the Canton Bulldogs, and the Columbus Panhandles. An era of colorful competition ensued.[7] The teams met in games turning on controversial, even bizarre, plays that determined mythical championships of the state. The Tigers, Indians, and Bulldogs each dominated play for two and three years in a row.

With the entrance of the nation into World War I in 1917 and the subsequent draft of young men into military service, the Ohio teams had difficulty building their rosters. Attendance at games fell off, and the teams did not play through the season. When the War Department tightened its policy governing conscription in 1918, the teams found it even harder to sustain their rosters. Employees in defense industries were working longer hours and could not attend games, and wartime restrictions rendered travel for the teams more difficult. All the elevens played abbreviated schedules or no games at all.

Nearly all the Ohio elevens resumed play in 1919 at war's end. Though they gave the fans exciting football through the season, nearly all took a bath in red ink. Two interrelated problems were at the heart of the problem. Salaries for players were constantly increasing, in large part because the gridders could jump from team to team, and managers, eager to win, were willing to shell out large salaries. But ticket prices and the size of football facilities did not provide the revenue to meet accelerating costs. Managers also did not serve the best interests of professional football when, as they often did, they hired a man who had played for his collegiate team on Saturday to play for the professional team under an assumed name on Sunday. The public saw such a practice as unethical, and college administrators damned professional football as an interloper in American athletics and a saboteur of higher education.

For a decade or so, proprietors of the Ohio clubs had talked about forming an official league with the authority to rationalize scheduling and clearly define championships. More important, such a league could adopt rules restricting the movement of players from team to team and the use of collegians. As support for a league grew among fans and sportswriters, representatives of the Ohio clubs began exploratory talks in 1919. They met in Canton in August of 1920, formed the American Professional Football Conference, and decided to invite representatives from other leading professional clubs to attend another meeting in September. Representatives from ten clubs in New York, Ohio, Indiana, and Illinois attended that meeting, renamed the league the American Professional Football Association, and came to agreements on the use of collegiate players and players' contracts. The league, renamed the National Football League in 1922, had miles to go to give order to professional football, but it had taken the first steps.[8]

At one time or another, the men playing for these teams—whether for the athletic clubs, the Ohio elevens, or the league squads—represented different degrees of pay for play. Probably the vast majority were semiprofessional players.[9] Typically they held full-time employment in the community and received a share of what their team garnered from passing the hat or from the gate. Men coming into a community from out of town to play a game at a fixed stipend, if they earned their living in some other setting, remained semiprofessionals. Even when players in a community received a salary per game or season and were fully employed in some other occupation, they were more nearly semiprofessionals. If players held full-time employment related to football—say as school coaches—they were at the edge of a full professional career. But only when they depended almost wholly on their play for a living did they become professional football players. Often observers of the football scene made little distinction between the semiprofessionals and the professionals.

 The men who organized the American league had to take seriously the strictures of college administrators and coaches even if their practices often contradicted their rhetoric. The collegians and millions of Americans subscribed to an ideology that enshrined amateurism as a great virtue in sports and scorned commercialism as a virulent infection. At the same time, though, their belief was fragile.[10] It did not stem from an established body of custom and was vitiated by the force of capitalism that emphasized winning at any cost. Men engaged in competitive sports, they argued in moments of pure idealism, had to be gentlemen eschewing material gain and vulgar and brutal behavior in their comportment. In 1921, the student editor of the *Yale Daily News* insisted that "organized brutality" might have become synonymous with football, but men whose "clean" and "fair" play had kept it a gentleman's game. Professional players afforded no such protection, indeed invited the lowering of standards: "The growth of professional football has not, fortunately, been rapid. Most college men recognize the risk of its

Its Players Perform Not Like Heroes

degeneration and refuse to take it up. The exceptions that go into the football business are rewarded by the loss of respect of their colleges."[11] In a widely publicized statement, the renowned coach Amos Alonzo Stagg declared in 1923 that collegiate football developed "character and manhood" and shaped men who were "right-minded" and patriotic; professional football, he feared, would destroy the intercollegiate game.[12]

Stagg had in mind particularly the professionals' use of collegiate players as ringers—men who played under assumed names. The ringers came on to the field for varying purposes. Because administrators in their institutions disapproved of professional football, collegiate and high school coaches used noms de guerre when playing for professional teams. Earle "Greasy" Neale, the head football coach at West Virginia Wesleyan, for instance, played as "Foster" for the Canton Bulldogs in 1917.[13] Collegians wishing to protect their status as amateurs also concealed their real identities. Pete Calac, a halfback at Wesleyan, was in the Bulldogs' lineup as "Anderson" that year. Teams or their boosters paid the ringers simply because they wanted to win or to cover bets. Stagg noted specifically the infamous and wholesale use of ringers in 1921 when ten Notre Dame men played for a semiprofessional team in Carlinville, Illinois, against nine regulars from the University of Illinois varsity pretending to be a team from Taylorville, Illinois.[14] Supposedly fans in each community wagered $50,000 on the game. Ringers entered the lore of American football in the period, investing the game with a tainted but picaresque mythology.

When Harold "Red" Grange left the University of Illinois to sign a contract with the Chicago Bears just after playing his last collegiate game in 1925, the administrators of collegiate football attacked professional football for staining amateurism in their game. John Griffith, the athletic commissioner of the Western Conference, denounced the professionals for tempting collegians with their offers but was certain that collegiate football would never become decadent "through spoliation by professionalism."[15] At the annual convention of the National Collegiate Athletic Association (NCAA) in 1925, held less than a month after the great defection, the Committee on Resolutions drafted a statement urging college and university administrators not to employ any coach, trainer, or official who gave "service to professional football."[16] After all, history had shown that healthful, recreational, and competitive sports died when "afflicted with professionalism." The American Football Coaches Association, the college coaches' organization, took a similar position.

Writing in the 1920s, a historian of American sports saw professional football as ersatz, a poor imitation of the collegiate brand, which turned men into menial workers: "Players are recruited from the ranks of college stars; as far as possible the

11

atmosphere of the intercollegiate contest is reproduced. The result has not been a particularly happy one from the standpoint of either spectators or players. The professional game is usually a sorry counterfeit of the great spectacle of the campus. Its players perform not like heroes, but like hired men. For the emotional basis of the scholastic sport has been substituted the gain impulse of the world of business." The promoters of professional football, he believed, still hoped that they could commercialize the game without losing the appeal that drew "thousands of dollars into the treasuries of the college athletic associations."[17]

Citing these "thousands of dollars," the professionals could have asked the collegians to remove the mote from their eyes. And in fact the collegians denouncing professional football for its "gain impulse" engaged in a debate among themselves and with outside critics throughout the decade over commercial and other aspects of football in academe: over the large expenditures for football programs, recruiting practices, training schedules for student athletes, eligibility rules, and other subjects.[18] Educators who argued that ventures in commercial amusements fell outside the legitimate function of colleges and universities nearly always found themselves on the losing side. The Carnegie Report of 1929 condemning the overemphasis on and commercialism of football in American schools drew little support from the general public or from collegiate administrators. University presidents could not scorn commercialism in sports, much less excoriate entrepreneurs in professional football, when they approved the construction of huge stadiums that created revenue for use in other athletic programs for students. They could not look askance at wealthy alumni who wanted more victories in football and who might contribute large sums to endowment programs. For faculty members who wanted to reduce the role of football at their institutions, *Liberty*, a mass-circulation magazine, expressed a popular view: "The problem is not the elimination or restriction of football but how long it will be before red-blooded colleges demand the elimination or restriction of those afflicted with an inferiority complex."[19] Perhaps as much as the professional football men, the professed amateurs in the game kept afloat the notion that men could play football for fun and money.

If the professional teams and collegiate squads in football did not share a common ideal of their game, they did employ similar rules and methods of play. They moved the ball from various formations in the 1920s, but easily the dominant formation was the single wing. Created by Warner early in the century, the single wing featured the use of a double-team block at trap block at

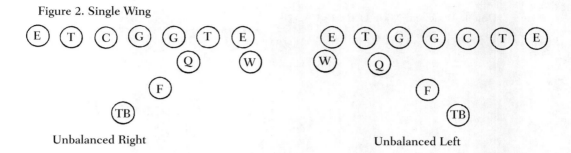

Figure 2. Single Wing

Unbalanced Right   Unbalanced Left

the point of attack.[20] To effect such blocking, the single wing resorted to an unbalanced line, with four linemen positioned to the left or right of the center. The tailback was the pivotal figure in the backfield. Lining up five to six yards behind the center or slightly to the left or right, he would handle the ball much of the time as a runner, passer, and kicker. The fullback, a yard or so closer to the line, blocked and ran smashes into the interior of the line. Positioned behind the guard and tackle on the strong side of the line, the quarterback, primarily a blocking back, called the plays. If the tailback called the plays, as sometimes was the case, sportswriters and coaches called him the quarterback. The wingback, usually at a position outside the end, blocked, was a pass receiver, and ran inside reverses. The single wing would long remain the staple of offensive formations. As late as 1940, when a renovated T was about to take center stage, Fielding Yost, one of the "grand old men" of American football, argued that "there was only one formation that's any good and it is the single-wing."[21]

The double-wing formation, another of Warner's creations, had some adherents but stemmed out of the single wing. In it the fullback moved to a position outside the left end and opposite the wingback. Knute Rockne used his own formation, the Notre Dame box, which was similar to the single wing. He lined up the fullback at nearly the same depth as the tailback, thus creating a boxlike pattern of the backs. What gave distinction to the Notre Dame box and offensive plays that coaches Henry Williams and John Heisman developed was the use of shifts in the backfield. The backfield men would shift from one formation to another and then would move rapidly from their second positions into the play. So rapid was that movement that the play became, in effect, one of momentum. The shifts were the subject of bitter dispute because they seemed to be a means of evading the prohibition against the use of momentum formations. In 1924, the NCAA rules committee decreed that players had to come to an absolute stop in the second position and remain station-

Home and Away

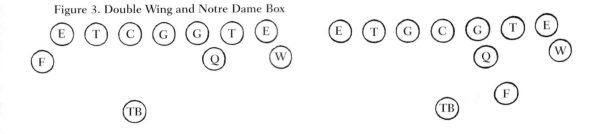

Figure 3. Double Wing and Notre Dame Box

ary momentarily.[22] The problem was the meaning of "momentarily." The committee defined it as one second in 1927 and then "at least one second" in 1931; thereafter, until the advent of the T, shifts became less popular.

Teams at all levels, perhaps especially professional elevens, played a conservative game. Defense marked the course of play.[23] A team would lie back on offense, waiting for the opponent to make a mistake to open the door to a score—a fumble or a blocked punt, for instance. The offensive team, moreover, faced many impediments. If a runner was knocked out of bounds, the next play began one yard from the sideline, with the result that the defensive team knew fairly well where it was going—to the middle of the field. The offense thus gave up a down. Calling out signals at the line of scrimmage—the huddle was not in general use until midway through the 1920s—the quarterback usually called a safe play on the first or second down—a smash into the middle. With several yards to go for a first down on a third down, the quarterback often called for a punt—sometimes on second down. On a muddy field the punt might come on first or second down, and then the receiver, if fielding the ball deep in his own territory, might punt the ball back. The team on offense could retain the ball if it recovered its blocked or botched punt on any down before fourth down. Good field position could result from a punt on an early down because the defensive safety would not retreat far for fear that the tailback might throw a pass in front of him or skirt the end for a first down. Though rules discouraged passing, a team might pass ten or twelve times in a close game, but coaches typically did not integrate passing into the offensive game, the quarterback calling for passes only in desperation. A team could expect to score no more than two or three touchdowns when it played a squad nearly equal to it. Scoreless ties were commonplace.

Collegiate and professional teams used similar equipment and uniforms in the 1920s.[24] The football, made of leather, was relatively fat with rounded ends, its long axis twenty-eight inches, its short axis twenty-three inches. Pants, usually made of duck, had pockets on the inside for the insertion of thigh and knee pads. Jerseys were made of cotton and wool. In the 1920s, a manufacturer added "grip-sure cloth" to them to help the ball carrier hold on to the ball, but the new feature did not readily catch on. Players who wore helmets—most did but not all—used a leather helmet with interior straps designed to cradle the skull away from the leather. All wore high-top shoes, usually with permanent rectangular cleats; interchangeable cleats came into some use after 1921. Shoulder pads were fragile contraptions resting on the crown of each shoulder. Ordinarily three men officiated a game. The referee had general control of the game; he saw that the ball was properly put in play and was the "final authority" on downs and the score; the umpire had jurisdiction over equipment and action of the players on the line of scrimmage; the head linesman called offside penalties and supervised the chain gang.

Semiprofessional elevens from three small American cities would enter a game whose keepers distrusted professional teams seeking a niche in it, whose rules finally became somewhat stable, a game wedded to one offensive structure and its variants, conservative in its strategic play but capable of great change.

2

An Ancient Rivalry as Pert as Ever

Following World War I, the people of Ironton and Portsmouth, as in thousands of communities across the land, could pursue their work and leisure. And young men organized football teams for competition in the Ohio Valley. They had no grand designs in mind, no thoughts of winning glory beyond their community, certainly none of earning gold. They simply wanted to play football and win games for themselves and earn recognition from their townspeople.

In Ironton the high school teams, eventually known as the Tigers, played those from Portsmouth, Ashland, and other nearby communities late in the 1890s.[1] Sandlot elevens in the town played one another in the 1890s and in the following two decades, appearing for a season or so and then disappearing. As early as 1893, the Irontonians were meeting town teams in the valley, developing a particularly intense rivalry with the Portsmouth Cycle Club for a few years.[2] The Middies were playing in 1914, and a few years later the Lombards, young men from the south side, were on the field. The Irontonians, Middies, and Lombards were, marginally at least, semiprofessional players, fully employed in various trades and receiving a few dollars from the gate receipts of their games. Spectators in the early days, paying a quarter or fifty cents for admission to games or dropping coins into a passing hat, never numbered over two or three hundred, except for the games between the Ironton and Portsmouth high school teams.[3] None of these teams, even the high school elevens, earned any special claim on the life and loyalty of the community; none became a source or symbol of civic pride. Taken together, though, they nurtured an interest in football in Ironton, creating an athletic environment certain to give rise to new ventures in football.

The team that became the "town team," the "famous Tanks," first played in 1919, almost exactly one year after the war ended. Through the ensuing decades, local analysts gave varying accounts of their origins and name. According to one story, the team was the creation of former high school stars seeking to regain their "old true form."[4] A program for a game in 1922 described their organization as a casual occurrence. A "band of youthful athletes," several of them returning from military service, had been meeting evenings to sing, to try out "glycerine tenors or basso profoundos"; one evening, they began talking about forming a football team.[5] Among them were Clarke Haney, Clarence "Concrete" Poole, and Ralph Mittendorf. A childhood fan of the Tanks recalled decades later that returning veterans organized the team because they "just wanted to play football."[6] Thirty years after the Tanks began play, Jack Coins, a reporter for the *Ironton Tribune*, asserted that he knew the "true" story about the team's origins.[7] His history was consistent with earlier and later accounts. Some Ironton boys from the north end formed a "pick-up" team to play the Norfolk and Western eleven in Portsmouth; though the game fell through, the "boys" continued as a team and a few days later met with some Lombard players and a "few others" and effected a merger. Thirty years after Coins set forth his "true" story of the Tanks' midwifery, an academic historian offered a similar version. The Tanks, he said, came out of an "amalgam of talent of two cross-town rival sandlot teams, the 'Irish Town Rags' and the 'Lombards,'" a union of "returning World War I veterans and younger athletes."[8]

Nearly all the chroniclers ascribed the founding of the Tanks to men returning from military service. They did not identify the veterans or give primary credit to one or two of them for organizing the team. Certainly former soldiers were important figures in the venture. Of the eleven men in the Tanks' starting lineup in their first game, at least five—William "Bill" Brooks, Ernest Clark, Clarke Haney, Waldo Mittendorf, and Clarence "Concrete" Poole—had been in the army during the war, but none had seen combat in France.[9] Perhaps one or more had played on army teams. Since late in the nineteenth century, the United States Army and Navy had been integrating competitive sports, including football, into their training programs to prepare men emotionally and physically for battle, and during the war the Commission of Training Camps called on the army and navy to organize baseball, football, and boxing teams at their training centers.

Clearly the Tanks were Ironton men to the bone. In their early twenties, nearly all had played football for Ironton High School, and all were living in Ironton or its environs.[10] Only one or two had attended a college or university. By occupations, they were blue-collar men epitomizing an industrial community: a shipping clerk at a slag plant, a machinist in a foundry, an electrician in a coke plant, a packer in a stove foundry, a pipefitter in a railroad yard, a postal worker, an installer of telephones, a municipal street worker, a painter in an automobile repair shop, an operator of a soft drink stand.[11]

No journalist, historian, or fan of the Tanks ever tied down the specific circumstances in the provenance of their name, perhaps one of the most appropriate athletic nicknames of the period, one that evidently no other team in the nation adopted. Obviously, the tank of World War I, with its implications of innovation and power, inspired the use of the name. As noted by one historian of the Tanks, the name also was fitting in a community dependent on the iron industry.[12] Down through the years, local lore offered few definitive details on the first use of the name. According to one popular story, the players may have adopted it after reading a headline in the *Irontonian* about a victory over the Norfolk and Western eleven: "Ironton Runs over Portsmouth Like Tanks."[13] But that was hardly so. The *Irontonian* had been calling them the Tanks for at least a month before they met the Portsmouth team. One tale had an anthropomorphic twist. Supposedly at the first game, Haney looked at Bill Brooks, a hulk of bone, muscle, and fat, and said, "Let's call this team the Tanks."[14] A similar account, one probably closer to the truth, had Haney proposing the name at the initial meeting of the choristers. Clearly taking pride in their sobriquet, sometime in 1919 the players purchased sweaters, probably solid brown, and had large Ts sewn on them.

As the Tanks were organizing, men in Portsmouth were taking steps to form a team. High school elevens, the Trojans, had been on the gridiron since the 1890s, and in the "good old days" of 1909 and 1910, an adult team had played elevens in the valley.[15] But neither that team nor others had won a special place in the annals of sport in the city, and apparently no squad bearing a Portsmouth name had been playing in the years immediately preceding 1919.

Then in September of that year, led by August "Gus" Putzek, an engineer in the large classification yard maintained in the city by the Norfolk and Western Railroad, men playing baseball in an industrial league decided to organize a football team. They had no question about finding "good" teams to play from Ashland, Ironton, Columbus, Chillicothe, and Camp Sherman, a large training center of the United States Army near Chillicothe. They were concerned, though, about raising money for uniforms and offering guarantees to visiting teams and could not decide whether to field a team representing the entire league or one bearing a separate identity. After receiving some material support from the Norfolk and Western, they chose to organize the team under the name of the railroad company, selecting Putzek as manager, Walter Dodge as coach, and Bob Quinn, a former halfback at Portsmouth High, as captain.[16]

Ordinarily, sandlot and semiprofessional teams elected their captains, coaches, and managers informally, often by acclamation. The captain, who sometimes also served as the coach, made decisions on the playing field. Usually the quarterback, but sometimes the tailback, called the signals, that is, the plays (prevailing rules prohibited a coach on the sidelines or a substitute coming into the game from calling plays); the coach directed the team in practices, determined the nature of offensive and defensive strategy, selected starting lineups, and, along with the manager, recruited players; the manager, sometimes a player, arranged the schedule, negotiated terms on the site of the games and the team's share of the gate, conducted ticket sales, sought publicity for the team, and joined the coach in recruiting players.

Putzek and Dodge soon "rounded up a hard fighting bunch of players" and were putting them through "dandy" practices at a lot at Sixteenth and Findlay Streets. Like the Tanks, the players were homegrown. All were living in or near the city. At least six, probably more, had played high school football in Portsmouth. As many as eleven had been members of service elevens while serving in the army and navy during the war.[17] Only one had collegiate experience in football. They were largely industrial workers. No fewer than five were machinists employed in the railroad yard or steel plants. One was a yardmaster, another a foreman at the classification yard. Four were working in shoe factories. One player was a catcher in a steel mill. Among them were a "car repairman," a butcher, a teacher, and two "laborers."[18] If any had established reputations in local football, they were Quinn and Dudley Molster, who had been outstanding players for the Portsmouth high school. Because of its newness and identification with one company in the city—because it was hardly a "town team"—probably the N. & W. squad, as it was generally known, could expect, at least at the outset, only a limited following in the community.

Home and Away

As portrayed in contemporary and later accounts, the Tanks of 1919 practiced and played under conditions hardly promising for their survival. Their coach was Hubert "Doc" Stewart, a halfback, who, also serving as their manager, was responsible for scheduling and arranging terms of games. They practiced early in the evening, probably twice a week, at the intersection of Eighth and Lombard Streets under an arc light. When the light failed, as it often did, the players moved a block to Seventh and Lawrence Streets; they could not easily practice there, though, because a car track ran through the middle of Seventh.[19] Their equipment by way of pads and helmets limited, the players had little protection against the hard-surfaced streets. But they did not run through full-scale scrimmages.

If practice was jerry-built, so, too, was the season's abbreviated play. The Tanks played four games in a schedule that Stewart arranged week by week. They did not play their first game until early in November, when they met the New Boston Tigers, a team from a small community at the eastern edge of Portsmouth. Played at Beechwood Park, the high school athletic field on South Seventh Street, where no stands were in place, the game attracted fewer than three hundred paying spectators. Admission was twenty-five cents, and as many as two hundred small boys jumped the fence encircling the field. Their defense prevailing in a "hard fought" game, the Tanks emerged victorious 9–0. The game gave them some attention in the city, the *Irontonian* providing its readers with a story of the contest, but the *Register* took no note of it. Next, playing before a "huge" crowd at Ashland, the Tanks lost to the Ashland Playhouse 7–0 in a "slow" game. According to a recapitulation of their record in 1919 compiled in 1983, the Tanks then played a scoreless tie with the N. & W. squad.[20] But the *Register* and *Irontonian* similarly reported that the Tanks and Playhouse battled to a scoreless tie at Beechwood only a few days after their first game. Perhaps the Tanks were developing a following. A "good" crowd, about a thousand, saw the Tanks outplay the "heavier" Playhouse eleven.

An increase in attendance did not, of course, signify that the Tanks were becoming the football team of the city through which residents might assert pride in their community. Even though the *Irontonian* was calling them the "first" team in Ironton, the Lombards, an older eleven, might contest their primacy. Various barriers, largely of their own making, however, prevented them from enlisting wide support in the city. They could hardly offer a convincing claim to represent the entire community while calling themselves "South Siders." They had little continuity in organization, patching themselves together year by year as a pickup team. They stained themselves, moreover, in 1919 in the scheduling of a game with the Norfolk team. As the season began, Putzek challenged the Lombards to a game. The Lom-

An Ancient Rivalry as Pert as Ever

bards accepted the challenge immediately, the game to be played in about two weeks. Applauding the Lombards' decision in an editorial as an act of civic virtue, the *Irontonian* declared that "Ironton again refused to take her hat off to Portsmouth in any line."[21] But then the Lombards decided not to play the Portsmouth team, explaining that the Norfolk men had been playing "big" teams and were superior to them. Though the *Irontonian* did not reproach the Lombards for their decision, certainly they lost face in the community.

With two teams in the city, ineluctably one had to challenge the other to a game. Well into the season, in November, the Tanks called on the Lombards to meet them for the championship of the city, baiting them with the allegation that they were afraid to play. Undaunted, the Lombards accepted the call, derisively retorting that the Tanks were "full of prune juice and rainwater."[22] Comparative scores and records, the Lombards argued, proved their superiority: they had played and won four games, outscoring their opponents eighty-eight to six; the Tanks had won but one, lost one, and tied one and had scored but nine points. Supposedly, the teams intended to meet on the Sunday before Thanksgiving. Both practiced hard for the encounter, but for reasons never explained, they did not take the field. Cancellations and postponements of games in football at all levels were endemic in the period owing to conflicts in scheduling, disputes over sites of play and selection of officials, inclement weather, and other factors.

Meanwhile, the N. & W. men were also experiencing problems in scheduling but were doing well on the field. Putzek had fixed eight dates for games with teams from the Ohio Valley and southern Ohio, among them elevens from Dayton, Cincinnati, and Columbus. (One Columbus team was the famed Panhandles, which had seven brothers, the Nessers, playing for it at one time or another.) Four were to be home games played at Millbrook Park, on the east side of the city. Fans could purchase a season ticket for one dollar or general admission tickets for fifty cents a game (women could buy a ticket for twenty-five cents). For one reason or another, his schedule proved a will-o'-the-wisp. Of the teams on his original slate, the N. & W. eleven met but two, Camp Sherman and the Columbus All-Stars. Eventually, Putzek arranged games with teams from Columbus—other than the All-Stars—Chillicothe, Ashland, Fort Thomas (Kentucky), Wellston, and Ironton—the Tanks.

The "River City Railroaders," as fans sometimes called them, posted a good record. After opening the season at Millbrook with a victory over Camp Sherman, 12–0, a "banner" crowd in attendance, they lost 14–0 to the Columbus Chippewas in Columbus. When they again defeated Camp Sherman at Millbrook, 6–0, Portsmouth now had a team to uphold the honor of the city in professional football.[23] For the first time, the *Times* gave considerable coverage to the local team's coming game, one of two scheduled against the Columbus All-Stars, taking particular note of reports that the teams were strengthening their rosters. Supposedly, the All-Stars were adding several college stars to their team, among them Ray Eichenlaub, who had played a conspicuous role at fullback for Notre Dame in its celebrated victory over Army in 1913. Briefly joining the N. & W. were the Pope brothers, Virgil and Harry, big linemen, "professional shiners" from Wellston. And reportedly Bill Friel, a good running back from Huntington, sent word to the railroaders that he would be on hand for the game.

What the teams were doing was "loading up," which meant they were recruiting new players for an important game. Unless a club had agreed not to use new players or had exchanged "eligibility" lists with an opponent limiting its roster to men playing in previous games, usually it opened itself only to some derisive comment. Such a practice could enhance interest in a coming game, but it could diminish the stature of a team, suggesting that winning was everything and that local players were not up to snuff. Less venial, of course, was the use of ringers, which entailed deception. Loading up and the use of ringers alike stemmed from team's thirst for a win, whether out of pride or to accommodate fans betting on a game. A team could conveniently complain about ringers. If it lost to a club accused of using ringers, it had explanations ready at hand; if it won, it found victory all the sweeter.

The game between the All-Stars and the N. & W. did not come to pass. Only a day or so before the day it was scheduled, the All-Stars, without offering any explanation, said they could not play.[24] Then the N. & W. players worked their way through Putzek's schedule. They defeated the Ashland Playhouse 6–0, easily beat a shorthanded All-Star squad 18–0 in a rescheduled game, played a Chillicothe eleven to a scoreless tie, and then overwhelmed a team out of Fort Thomas, 40–0. None of the games, all played at Millbrook, drew crowds of more than five hundred. The N. & W. men played their first game of any significance against the Wellston Eagles. Declaring that the Eagles, the Pope brothers now anchoring their line, were one of the strongest teams in southern Ohio, Putzek touted the contest as one that would decide the semiprofessional championship of southern Ohio.[25] Played on a wet, slippery field late in November, the game did not settle the issue, neither team managing any score; the N. & W. players made a dubious claim to the title on the grounds of having outplayed the Eagles.

The N. & W. eleven and the Tanks concluded the season in a Thanksgiving game at Beechwood that had great meaning for both teams. By winning, the N. & W. men, losers of but one game, could strengthen their claim to the mythical championship

An Ancient Rivalry as Pert as Ever

of southern Ohio; in beating such a team, the Tanks could substantially improve their record and reputation. The victor would bask for a moment in the civic sun. Virtually no observers offered any predictions on the outcome of the game. The *Times* said little about the Tanks. But the *Irontonian* saw the railroaders as a formidable opponent "cleaning up" adversaries with a "higher brand of football than high school teams have been putting up this year as mostly all the players are former high school stars."[26] Besides high school stars, Portsmouth was loading up with players from Syracuse University, Lafayette College, and other colleges and universities. Evidently the Tanks had added several players to their roster from the Lombards and the Playhouse. Of greater import for the game—and for years to come—they also acquired Charlton "Shorty" Davies. A hometown boy, Davies had just completed a season's play at Ohio State, lettering as a shifty halfback behind the great Charles "Chic" Harley. As his nickname implied, Davies was short, about five feet, seven inches, but he packed 160 pounds on a solid frame. He would provide the Tanks with "some class." Perhaps he also gave them a decisive advantage over the railroaders. Before a "record-breaking" crowd, including three hundred fans from Portsmouth, he became almost instantly the bellwether of the Tanks' offense, his spectacular fifty-yard touchdown run early in the game paving the way to a victory for Ironton by the score of 12–0.[27] Davies won repute but no share of the gate because he wished to preserve his eligibility for collegiate play. Sharing laurels with him was Brooks, who dominated the line of scrimmage on defense.

The play of Davies and Brooks was a substantive portent of things to come for the Tanks in the next several years. Davies was an omnipresent back on offense, ever capable of running hard for a few crucial yards or bursting into the secondary on a long, broken-field run. He would also serve as the coach for several years. Brooks was a mountain of a man at 250 pounds, and he anchored the line with imperious control. Playing for the Tanks for nearly a decade, he was a fount of emotion. He became noted for crying on the field when a game was not going well; nearly seventy years after seeing Brooks play, a Tanks fans recalled that Brooks "would cry when the Tanks were loosing [*sic*]."[28] Opponents often alleged that he engaged in dirty play. Besides leading the Tanks to numerous victories in the coming years, Davies and Brooks were colorful figures illuminating the Tanks' success and eliciting support for the team throughout the community. No one from the N. & W. eleven commanded attention in Portsmouth.

After the Tanks and the N. & W. eleven met, their managers attempted to finish the season with games that might attract fans. Putzek called on the Tanks to come to Portsmouth for a return game, saying that he would guarantee $100 for their expenses and give them a share of the gate.[29] When Stewart refused the offer, Putzek began negotiations with the "crack warriors" of Wellston for a game, but his proposal foundered over the issue of the site for the game. Meanwhile, Stewart accepted a challenge from the Lombards to play for the city championship. Again the Lombards cited comparative records to prove their superiority. But they proved their argument only on paper, not on the gridiron. For again the teams did not play. The players stored their togs, and fans had to ponder the question of which eleven was better.

At season's end, the Tanks were floating in the horse latitudes, materially and in the mind of the community. Surely they were not absolute amateurs, as they shared or expected to share in gate receipts from their games. If they saw themselves as semiprofessional players, they had to satisfy themselves with a few moments of glory but virtually no spendable treasure. For the only game for which the local newspapers provided an estimated attendance—the Ashland game at Ironton—probably they received a pittance. The thousand fans there, if paying an admission fee of twenty-five cents, accounted for gross receipts of about $250. The Tanks had to pay at least one official and a rental fee to the owner of Beechwood, the local Board of Education. They had to pay the travel expenses incurred by the Ashland team and its share of the gate, probably 40 percent. With each team carrying fifteen or sixteen men on its roster, a player could barely earn more than $8 or $9, a sum hardly commensurate with the mauling and mortification his flesh endured.

If the Tanks had not struck gold, neither had they touched the heart of their community. Continuity was difficult for baseball and football teams in small communities, and little that the Tanks did in 1919, except perhaps their purchase of lettered sweaters, promised that they would continue to play. They had played an abbreviated schedule, winning two of four games, scarcely an indication of success ahead. Despite receiving some praise from the Ironton newspapers, they had not captured the public's imagination by their play or personalities—though Davies and Brooks had such potential. They had not become the "town team" any more than had the Lombards. Neither team, in fact, had staked a claim to the community's loyalty or had elicited strong support from any influential group or institution. The people of the city would not offer emotional and material assistance until a team proved itself worthy on the scoreboard.

Measured by their record—five wins, two losses, and two ties—the N. & W. players might have expected their community to take a proprietary interest in them. Their position in Portsmouth, though, was similar to that of the Tanks in Ironton.

Fans paying their way into the park, however, seldom numbered much more than five or six hundred; their patronage was hardly sufficient for the N. & W. team to pay reported guarantees of $500 and $1,000 to visiting elevens. The N. & W. men could not readily commend their team to the community for several reasons. Their very name implied singularity in the community, but that was not a crucial problem, as the Packers proved in Green Bay. Of far more importance, fans could not easily sustain interest in any impending game or develop rivalries with other communities because scheduling was uncertain and extemporaneous. Fans found play to be rather antiseptic, too, devoid of any real excitement or controversy that might carry forward to the next season. No players manifested the speed and power—and personality—that Tanks fans found appealing in Davies and Brooks. The N. & W. eleven, in short, had not built surety for continuation.

As the season opened in 1920, the Tanks and Lombards prepared to play football again, each seeking to win repute inside and outside the community. The Tanks especially had a vision of preeminence, of becoming the representative football team of the community. Beginning to take up their cause was Pete Burke, the sports editor of the *Ironton Register*, who was giving them more space in his column, "Fumes," a collage of local and national sports commentary. As he understood it, Davies and Brooks, assuming the leadership in the reorganization of the team late in the summer, had resolved to build a football team that would be the "equal if not the peers of any team in the Ohio Valley."[30] They intended to recruit the "best material of this vicinity" and train such players to become a team that would "truly represent the entire city" and "furnish a brand of football of which Ironton [would] be proud." They expected to arrange games with some of the strongest teams in the state that would draw record crowds to Beechwood.

Soon Davies and Brooks sent notices to twenty-five "football men" in the community, calling them to a meeting to reorganize the team. At the meeting, the prospective players named Davies their coach and captain, Brooks their manager. Nearly all the men who played in 1919 were present. Brooks announced that he had games underway with elevens from Portsmouth, Wellston, Huntington, and Jackson and was seeking contests with the Cincinnati Celts and Columbus Panhandles, two premier clubs of Ohio. Echoing Davies and Brooks's sanguine reports, the *Irontonian* said that the Tanks might become a "leader" in gridiron circles in Ohio, the *Register* that the team would be "thoroughly representative" of the city and one of the best in the region.

Meanwhile, the Lombards, unwilling to concede the field to the Tanks, were readying themselves for play. At their organizational meeting, twenty men were in attendance. They chose Nate Ball, a former high school player in Ironton, as their coach and Wilbur "Squimby" Hughes, a railroad employee, as their "business and advertising" manager; Hughes announced that he would take a trip through the Tri-State booking games. Linking themselves to the war as had the Tanks, the players changed their name to the "Lombard Submarines" and declared that they would ignite an "explosion" on the gridiron.

Late in September, only about ten days before their first scheduled game, twenty-two candidates for the Tanks team assembled for their first practice. Employed during the day in various occupations, they practiced in the evenings, three to four times a week. They worked out on a field adjacent to the Semet-Solvay plant, which threw off a "brilliant flare," affording almost as much light as daylight. They went through calisthenics, worked on blocking techniques, and ran their offense—the single wing—in signal drills. Because two men were not available at each position, they did not engage in the hard knocks of scrimmages, instead walking through their plays.

As the Tanks practiced, Brooks was negotiating terms for games with the Lombards and other "good" teams in the region. He believed that he might more easily induce the good teams to come to Ironton now that the Board of Education was erecting bleachers at Beechwood. Seating about a thousand spectators, they did not accommodate all the crowds, and two years later, the board raised a grandstand of sorts seating another thousand spectators. Still, for big games, the Tanks brought in temporary bleachers.

Sporting new uniforms, the Tanks opened their season against Morris Harvey College in West Virginia. Evidently, the collegians viewed the Tanks as amateurs or felt no taint in playing paid men. The uniforms did not help. "Rangy" halfbacks leading the way, Morris Harvey defeated the Tanks 14–0. The Tanks made a credible showing, considering that they had not yet had a scrimmage and were playing a team that had recently held the "famous" Centre squad to a low score (in fact, though, Centre had defeated Morris Harvey 66–0). And by their "great play," Davies and Brooks gave promise of coming victories.[31]

Nevertheless, the Tanks were hardly off to an auspicious start, and waiting for them were men of a Portsmouth team eager to avenge their loss at Ironton in 1919. But they were no longer members of the N. & W. squad, which now was the Smoke House team. The Smoke House, operated by the Smoke House Company, was a tobacco shop on Chillicothe Street specializing in the sale of "Good Cigars in Perfect Condition," cigarettes, and candies. It was a popular hangout for men playing pocket billiards and engaging in small talk. Obviously, the owners had taken up sponsor-

An Ancient Rivalry as Pert as Ever

ship of the old N. & W. team in some way. Nearly all the players of the old team were on the new team, and Putzek and Dodge continued respectively as their manager and coach. So imperceptible was the change that for a while they were dubbed the N. & W. Smoke House. Very likely the team owed its inception to Harry Doerr, a longtime football enthusiast and secretary-treasurer of the tobacco company.

Newness in its denomination did not spell success for the Smoke House squad. The community paid little attention to it at the outset of the season. Initially, Putzek was unable to secure Millbrook for games and expected his team to play most of the season on the road or at the lot at Sixteenth and Findlay Streets. The Smoke House eleven hardly warranted much support in its early play. Literally with only eleven men, the team traveled to Columbus for its first game, meeting the Jungle Imperials, the "Imps," one of the stronger elevens in the capital city. The Smoke House men made a poor showing, the Imps "romping" over them 24–0. They then lost 9–0 at home to a "fast" Chillicothe Athletic Club. They raised the interest of fans and their own confidence when in their next game at Millbrook, with a crowd of about six hundred on hand, they won 13–7 over a "heavier and faster" American Legion club from Catlettsburg, supposedly the semiprofessional champions of Kentucky in 1919.

Buoyed by victory, the men of the Smoke House looked forward to meeting the Tanks at Millbrook in their next game late in October. The Tanks had not played since their opening loss, but the *Times* mistakenly said that they had won three games and that Davies was "running wild."[32] Newspapers in both communities nearly always exaggerated the strength of the local team's opponents, usually embellishing the abilities of individual players. By such puffery, they hoped to increase attendance for the home eleven's games. Neither team appeared to be strong, but each knew that a victory would enhance its status and attendance at games to come.

A "large" crowd at Millbrook, swelled by a substantial delegation of Tanks fans, saw a "furiously" fought game replete with "thrill after thrill" as play swayed between the thirty-yard lines. Rooters for the Tanks were quiet until Davies, slightly injured and standing on the sidelines in the first half in street clothing, entered the fray in the second half and, Frank Merriwell–like, ran eighty yards with an intercepted pass in the fourth quarter, enabling the Tanks to come off the field with a tie, 6–6. Officials had to stop the game once because the players became entangled as they "exchanged compliments." Obviously, one good game called for Brooks and Putzek to begin arranging a second one.

Meanwhile, Brooks struggled in his jerry-built scheduling. A day or so after the fray at Portsmouth, he made final arrangements for the Tanks to meet the Legion team from Catlettsburg. The Kentuckians, evidently fearing a "severe drubbing," canceled the game at the last moment.[33] In their stead, Brooks attempted to arrange a game with the Ashland Bulldogs but could not do so. He then scheduled a game with Marshall College. The Tanks defeated the collegians 13–0 and then demolished the New Boston Tigers 77–0, prompting the *Irontonian* to declare that they could make a "real showing" against any other team in the nation. Some fans, though, were disappointed by the one-sided contest and were grumbling about the caliber of the Tanks' opponents. Placating them, Brooks scheduled, on short notice, a game with a "big" team of former collegians in Nitro, West Virginia, an eleven then laying claim to the semiprofessional championship of the state. Arriving late in Ironton, not an uncommon failure of semiprofessional teams of the day, the Nitro eleven could not turn its collegiate players and a heavier line into a victory and were defeated by the Tanks 13–0 in a game that ended early in the fourth quarter because of darkness.

Because the Tanks were winning, Brooks was able to schedule two important games, one with the Lombards, the other with the Smoke House, to close off the season late in November. The Lombards, though receiving little publicity in the Ironton sports pages, were still playing and recently had posted several victories over area teams, including one over the Catlettsburg eleven. Early in the season, Brooks had unsuccessfully sought a game with the Lombards, but later, perhaps seeing an opportunity to recover their position in the community, they approached him and agreed to play the Tanks on Thanksgiving Day.

With fans looking forward to the big game, the championship of the city at stake, at first both teams practiced hard and predicted victory. The *Irontonian* viewed the Lombards as a threat to the Tanks, noting that they had produced "stars" in the past and had added new men to their roster. Certainly the Lombards appeared confident. Advertising their impending clash with the West Side Athletic Club of Charleston, West Virginia, a week before meeting the Tanks, the Lombards called themselves and the Charlestonians the "best [teams] in their locality."[34] Nonetheless, the Tanks slacked off practice, believing that they needed little preparation to ensure a victory. One Tank dismissed the Lombards as a second-rate squad pretending to play football: "The Lombard eleven is merely whistling to keep up its courage. That crowd of jazzers on the South Side is praying for the snow to stay on the ground until after Thanksgiving so they will have something to be thankful for one week from Thursday. They couldn't beat a carpet with a spring housecleaning." If the Lombards had the courage to face the Tanks, he said, they would not be able to show themselves in town for a year.[35]

The contest seemed to create interest in the community. From twelve to fifteen hundred spectators paid their way into Beechwood at fifty cents a ticket. If the

An Ancient Rivalry as Pert as Ever

Lombards did possess the advantage in speed, it meant little. The Tanks easily won 26–0 and could have scored more but "held back" in anticipation of their coming game with the Smoke House; the Lombards fought "pluckily" and, said the *Ironton-ian,* suffered no loss of reputation—an unlikely consequence. Brooks invited three of the Lombards to join the Tanks for the game with Portsmouth. One of them, Bill Heald, did come over and would remain as a stalwart on the Tanks' line for several years.

Putzek, meanwhile, had the Smoke House players fitfully working through a chaotic schedule. They played to a "thrilling" tie with the Wellston Eagles, posted yet another tie with the Columbus Maroons, and then overwhelmed the Ashland Bulldogs. Attempting to line up an opponent for a game on Thanksgiving Day, Putzek ran into one frustrating problem after another, at least one of his own making. Apparently he had scheduled the Mark Greys of Zanesville for a game at Millbrook after turning down their offer to play the Smoke House at Zanesville. Finding that he could not use Millbrook, he agreed to go to Zanesville. Then when Millbrook unexpectedly became available, he canceled the game with the Greys and arranged, he believed, a contest with the Wagner Pirates of Columbus. A "fast, clever" team, the Pirates had recently defeated the West Side Athletic Club to claim the championship of the city. Putzek was looking for a large crowd at Millbrook, as many as twenty-five hundred. But the Pirates backed out of the game only a day before Thanksgiving. Hurriedly, Putzek booked a game with the Oakwoods, a nondescript team in Columbus. The Smoke House men and their fans became parties to a charade at the game. As the hour for the kickoff neared, only five Oakwood players were in uniform on the field. They had taken a train from Columbus, but the remainder of the team had left by automobile and had not arrived—and never did. After delaying the kickoff for nearly an hour, the Smoke House players eager to play a game and their fans willing to pay to see it, Putzek and Dodge loaned the Oakwoods six men. Then the home team beat the "visitors" 48–0.

If Brooks and Putzek found scheduling games with Columbus, Zanesville, or Catlettsburg teams vexatious, as they surely did, they could have become exasperated in negotiating the second game of the season between their elevens. They did manage to arrange a game, but not before they and journalists in their communities engaged in a war of words over the past and future conditions of play. Especially the sportswriters roiled the waters. Controversy began when the Smoke House team canceled the return game scheduled at Beechwood, forcing the Tanks to arrange on short notice the date with the Nitros. According to the *Register*, the Smoke House men were simply fearful of the Tanks. Many observers had expected them to "crawfish" out of the game. It would take a steam donkey to pull the "yellow crown" of the Smoke House team. Putzek and the *Times* had a different version of what stood in the way of the game. They insisted that the Smoke House men would not play at Beechwood because the crowd always came onto the field when the visiting team showed signs of winning.[36] More than that, said the *Times* in language exacerbating the dispute, Portsmouth teams always had trouble in Ironton: boys and men there played an "unclean brand" of football, and it was "not in Ironton to be sportsmanlike even if it should come down to tiddledywinks." Responding to the *Times* in a vitriolic column, the *News* said that the Smoke House crowd simply had cold feet and would resort to all kinds of excuses to wear their "doll rags."[37]

As the sportswriters squabbled, Brooks and Putzek discussed terms for a game, often in a labored and disputatious way, and finally reached an agreement. Their teams would meet at Beechwood late in November, on the Sunday following Thanksgiving, the winner to take all the gate. Should the Tanks win, they would pay the traveling expenses of the Smoke House eleven. Two representatives of each team could stand at the gate to count the number of people paying for tickets. The teams would bear equally the costs of "extensive" advertising for the game. They agreed not to use "outside" men—ringers—or to load up and to exchange eligibility lists. To assure impartiality in the officiating, the managers said that they would attempt to procure "outside" officials. Putzek called on Brooks to post a bond of $500 as a guarantee against spectators coming on to the field; evidently not wishing to give credence to Putzek's earlier complaints on that count, Brooks refused but promised that he would have fifteen policemen on hand who would see that no fans could "invade one foot . . . of [the] playing field or end zone."[38]

Residents in both communities heard stories and read reports in their newspapers, often exhortative in nature, about the coming of the great clash. They learned that Don Hamilton, Ray Eichenlaub, and Vic Salt, all prominent professional officials outside the valley, would govern the game. Heretofore, amateurs from the area had served as referees, umpires, and head linesmen. Fans in Portsmouth received word of a special Norfolk & Western train to take them to "Cannonville"—the round trip fare was $1.70. The paper called for six hundred fans to board the train; if they accompanied the team in such a number, "you can bet your Adam's Apple that it will bring home the bacon." Later, the newspaper reported that the Smoke House men wanted a thousand fans from Portsmouth to be at Beechwood rooting "like H——." At Beechwood, they would find one side of the field entirely reserved for them.[39] In a lengthy editorial, the *Irontonian* counseled local fans on their responsibilities. Whether the Tanks won or lost, their rooters should be "good sports" and extend

An Ancient Rivalry as Pert as Ever

courteous treatment to the visitors. Portsmouth fans should be able to return home believing that they had received a "square deal." Whatever the outcome, the editorialist was pleased that an "ancient rivalry as pert as ever" would continue.[40]

Wanting a good gate and a dry field, the Tanks looked for fair weather, and fortunately, all was clear at Beechwood. A steady stream of automobiles poured into the streets around the park, causing numerous parking problems. An immense crowd, the largest in the history of Ironton football, jammed into the stands and stood on all four sides of the field. For the first time at any game in Ironton, women—"fanettes"—were standing in large numbers along the sidelines. All trades, professions, and classes were represented—preachers, priests, social leaders, churchgoers, and plain garden variety fans were all there.[41] As many as a thousand Portsmouth rooters were on hand, as well as six or seven hundred fans from Huntington, Ashland, and other nearby communities. Estimates of the crowd ran as high as four thousand, the gate receipts $2,500 to $3,500.

Before the game began, the Tanks protested that the Smoke House had players in uniform who were not on the eligibility list but finally decided not to press the issue. The game was grueling, a "regular bearcat" of a battle, with the teams playing their "heads off." Davies gave the Tanks the decisive touchdown early in the first quarter when he skirted an end for thirty-five yards on a play variously known as an old Army play, a crisscross play, and a run from the Illinois shift. He scored again in the second quarter; the game was scoreless thereafter, the Tanks winning 14–0. Davies and Brooks proved to be too much for the opposition. Despite the intensity of play, the teams did not engage in any serious verbal conflict or, noted an official, in roughhouse tactics. After the game, the Tanks ribbed the Smoke House players, who accepted their defeat graciously, offering no alibis for their failure. One observer thought that the game had all the elements of a college contest. The crowd, though enthusiastic, was orderly and "good-natured." Bettors in the crowd wagered $100 to $300.[42]

The Tanks, their season concluded, came out of the game with lumps and rewards. They were "generally limping," their wounds badges of honor. Davies reinjured a rib but was able to return, albeit gingerly, to his desk at the Portland Cement Company. The *Register* and the *Irontonian* proclaimed the Tanks the undisputed champions of southern Ohio, and the *Times* acknowledged their primacy, taking special note of Davies as "some bear."[43] Certainly the Tanks had posted a good record after opening the season with a loss and a tie, winning five games in a row without yielding a point.

The Smoke House players returned to Portsmouth to lick their wounds, with no man or boy who stood "cheering by," their play or labor not at an end. Putzek, after failing to negotiate a game with the Lombards, arranged, on one day's notice, a meeting with the Wellston Eagles. The crowd was good, considering the sudden announcement of the game. Using some kind of shift that confused the Smoke House, the Eagles won 10–0. Many spectators believed that the Eagles could give the Tanks a hard tussle. Putzek, ever the promoter, then attempted unsuccessfully to arrange another contest with the Eagles on Christmas Day. Now the Smoke House could review a distinctly mediocre season of three wins, four losses, and three ties, a record not brightened by a victory over any strong team.

At season's end in 1920, the Tanks had gathered momentum as an athletic institution that could become a prominent landmark in the life of Ironton. The newspapers of the community were giving them increased coverage, sometimes front-page columns. As in other cities where semiprofessional or professional football teams took root early in the century, the Tanks were becoming a shield for the community's prestige and honor.[44] After their conquest of the Smoke House, the *Register*, proposing a public banquet for the players, spoke of the fame and glory they had brought to Ironton. Reporters were beginning to characterize them as heroes, as "brave and splendid" men symbolizing and advertising the virtues of the community. The local elite would have been justified in viewing the Tanks as an institution promoting the city in the outside world, especially throughout the Tri-State. But blue-collar workers and manufacturing workers saw the team as an internal force representing them in a personal way, not as an engine of economic progress.[45] They likely were the fans who regularly came to all of the Tanks' games.

From their success and enhanced reputation, the Tanks had accumulated some capital to sustain themselves in a season of losses. One swallow, of course, did not a summer make. But with each year of vitality, a team might create additional support in the city. The Tanks could not afford, though, constant improvisation in scheduling, canceling games on short notice, and playing games extemporaneously. Such a course would cut fans adrift in a sea of uncertainty. Nor could they appear at the opening of a season as though they had yet to decide whether to play; by policy or pronouncements at the conclusion of a season, they had to assure fans that they would play the next year. Obviously, they had to win—and win with a few colorful, personable players. Their reputation among local fans depended, too, on their status outside of Ironton; if fans in Portsmouth or Ashland accorded them praise, they reinforced local pride in them. If business leaders saw the Tanks thus "advertising" the city and if they were looking for signs of progress in the city, they were likely to support them.

An Ancient Rivalry as Pert as Ever

In contrast with the Tanks, the Smoke House players had earned little status in Portsmouth. Only when they met the Tanks, or were about to meet them, did the *Times* increase coverage. The business community did not see them as a medium for promoting the city. No one proposed public banquets for them or called them heroes. No players of distinct personality had captured the attention of fans. Far more than the Tanks, the Smoke House team seemed to be a ragtag outfit, one bereft of continuity and a sense of permanency. Already the players had gone through a change of name. Putzek's scheduling was an exercise in scrambling improvisation, leaving fans uncertain about where, when, and whom the team would be playing one week after another. But winning could open the door to support, especially if the Smoke House players could number among their victories one over an Ironton team.

3

All Bill Did Was Blink His Eyes and Throw a Blank Stare

IN THEIR THIRD YEAR of play, the Tanks and the Smoke House men moved at a different pace. The Tanks were on the rise, winning and on their way to regional supremacy and distinction in their community; the Smoke House players were limping along, earning little success on the gridiron or recognition in the community. But out of a bitter dispute between the teams, one illustrating a perennial problem in their brand of football, the Smoke House men emerged with their hands clean, their integrity intact.

The season of 1921 did not begin on an auspicious note for the Tanks. Even before organizing and beginning practice, they learned that Davies and Brooks, their gazelle and bull, intended to play for West Virginia Wesleyan. In the face of their departure, the Tanks looked like a wreck, with no "parts to apply" for repair.[1] Fans would have to pin their hopes on the Lombards with their "bright array" of collegiate stars. At their first meeting of the season, held at the Elks Club, the Tanks learned of the loss of two more players from the squad of 1920—

All Bill Did Was Blink His Eyes

"Dutch" Mohr and "Pick" Progler. They believed, though, that they could obtain several men with collegiate experience who were working for the Wisconsin Bridge Company on the construction of a bridge across the Ohio River near Ironton. At a subsequent meeting, the players selected Frank Wieteki, a former high school player in Ironton and a real estate man, to replace Davies as coach, "Concrete" Poole as temporary captain, and Bill Schachleiter as temporary manager in the stead of Brooks.[2] Despite the dreary outlook, the Tanks were bravely facing the new season.

Conversely, with the local Chamber of Commerce taking the lead, businessmen had raised $1,000 for the purchase of "natty, nifty" uniforms for them. According to one reporter, the Tanks would be the greatest team ever in the Tri-State; they would have the unanimous support of Ironton fans; the famous team had "already established itself in the hearts of the fans" and would "rumble loud and long on Ironton and other gridirons this year."[3] A report on one of the Tanks' organizational meetings, a reporter for the *Irontonian* found that "football was in the air and the fine bunch of men present were confident of getting across a winning tradition of the Iron City."[4]

Good news abounded, too, about the local competition, the Lombards. After the Lombards played the Ashland Tigers in September, all the players intended to offer their services to the Tanks. With the infusion of the erstwhile Lombards, the Tanks would become a great gridiron machine, one to "boost to the skies" for a city deserving a great team. As the Tanks began practice, they and the community could rejoice in the return of several players to the fold. Davies had broken his leg at Wesleyan and was returning to Ironton to assist Wieteki as a coach. Also coming back after once deciding that he would not play was Progler. And Bill Brooks, having decided not to become a collegian but now momentarily living in Steubenville, expected to join the team, "to blow" in weekly after the season was under way. Nonetheless, Schachleiter looked for additional players, particularly for fast backfield men. Supposedly, he found one among the men from the bridge company, one Russell, who had been with a good team in Wisconsin in 1920.[5] Fans could also take encouragement in reports of the players, new and old, engaging in hard practices.

As they girded their loins, practicing and strengthening their roster, the Tanks hardly had even a tentative schedule before them. Schachleiter, scouring the region, declared that the Tanks would play only strong teams. They would not meet the Jackson Bearcats or the Ashland Tigers, a "heavy" but "awkward" team that had recently beat the Lombards, because they were weak and would not draw good crowds and thus not a good draw. The Tanks' reputation growing, fans could expect to see the strongest teams of Columbus, the champions of Cincinnati, and, if patronage was good, one of the "big elevens" from upstate—presumably the Canton Bulldogs. As it turned out, the Tanks played no teams from Columbus or Cincinnati but did meet the Ashland Tigers and Jackson Bearcats.

A week before Schachleiter spoke of meeting only good teams, he scheduled the Lombards, even as players on the older team talked about going over to the Tanks following their opening game with the Tigers the next day. At the announcement of the game, Burke, often choleric, complained that it was "poor stuff" for two "mediocre" elevens to meet but acknowledged that the fans wanted a "get together."[6] Something went awry, though, and the teams did not do as planned. A problem with the Lombards, a stubborn group still seeking status in the community, had to be resolved. Both teams wanted to play Sunday games at Beechwood so the Ironton Board of Education had to allocate division of its use. To the chagrin of the Lombards, the board, evidently viewing the Tanks as more nearly the town team, gave seven dates to the Tanks, three to the Lombards.[7] The Lombards thought the decision was unfair, all the more so because they had to cancel a game scheduled with the Smoke House at Beechwood.

Early in the season, the community had the opportunity to assess the teams by relative scores. In their opening game, the Tanks met the Jackson Bearcats, expecting "no trouble," even though they believed that the Bearcats were loading up. "All dolled up in new uniforms," an "array of bright red sweaters" (Burke described the jerseys as brown and called the team "Big Brown"), and playing before a "fair-sized" crowd, the Tanks met strong resistance from the Bearcats, edging them 6–0, the victory secured by Brooks's tackle at a crucial moment. A week later the Lombards, two new players strengthening them and Captain Nate Ball infusing them with all "kinds of pepper and ginger," met the Bearcats at Beechwood, determined to defeat them more decisively than had the Tanks.[8] Emotionally and physically prepared, the Lombards won 20–7 in an "exciting" game. The scores indicated that the Lombards were better than the Tanks.

If the Lombards had won a skirmish, they had hardly won a battle, much less a war. As the season moved beyond opening games, the Tanks were the clear victor in image. They mustered substantial support from businessmen, the Lombards none; and much more than the Lombards, they continued to strengthen their roster with new players. The Tanks' dominance in print and support presaged and hastened the Lombards' decline and eventual demise.

All Bill Did Was Blink His Eyes

Clearly, important institutions in Ironton were beginning to assume a proprietary interest in the Tanks, seeing in them an adornment, an advertising instrument for the community. Midway through the season, the community learned that the Tanks, though providing the Ohio Valley with "wonderful football," were in a "deep financial hole" and, noting that the Chamber of Commerce had "endorsed" them, called on fans in the city to help them if they wanted a "first class" team.[9]

No one measured the "deep financial hole" in public print. Surely few Tanks dug it. Nearly all were local men with full-time employment in the city. Semiprofessional in the fullest sense of the word, they practiced in the evenings and received a share of the gate after their team met its operating expenses—rental of Beechwood, payments to officials, and so on. Still a Tank or so may have burdened the budget. Reportedly, Wieteki was receiving a "handsome sum," and Brooks, who was traveling to Ironton from Steubenville each weekend, was not doing so "for his health."[10] The Tanks occasionally recruited men for a game or so. Link DeLong, who played for the Tanks in 1922, recalled years later that such players usually earned $50 a game.[11]

Despite their financial problems, early in October, the Tanks temporarily acquired two players from outside the community and Nick McMahon, a local theater entrepreneur who had been a "terror" of a halfback at Ironton High School in 1916. Besides players, the Tanks secured a trainer, H. R. "Doc" Scott, who had taken courses in physical education at Syracuse University and had served as an athletic director at Fortress Monroe during the war. A volunteer receiving no pay, he intended to put the Tanks through a "very thorough and systematic course" to improve their conditioning. He had the squad running a mile from the Elks Club to the practice field each evening. Playing their first game after he began his program, the "great Tank machine" defeated a "strong" team of "collegiate stars," the Charleston West Side Athletic Association, 34–0 without "tiring and blowing"—thanks to Scott.[12]

Whatever the depth of the financial cavity, the Tanks had to look to an important business institution in the community that would declare them worthy of support. Apparently the Chamber of Commerce was moving in that direction early in the season when it persuaded businessmen to give the Tanks $1,000 for the purchase of uniforms. As the Tanks faced a fiscal emergency, the day after their victory over Charleston, with only four hundred paying fans at Beechwood, the Chamber announced that it would take up a campaign for the sale of tickets to the game on the following Sunday against the Ashland Tigers, the day to be a "Boosters Day." The Charleston game seemed to call for heroic measures. The Chamber was looking beyond what it might achieve for one game. Appointed by officers of the Chamber,

Home and Away

eleven members of a special committee intended to canvass the community for funds to give Ironton a "brand of football of which the city may well be proud."[13]

The week preceding the game, the Chamber pushed sales of tickets throughout the city, and urged the citizenry to support the good work. A "squad" of representatives called on civic and social clubs to purchase tickets.[14] If the fans wanted a first class team for the city, they would have to pull the Tanks out of the hole; at least three thousand people needed to attend the Ashland game and subsequent games. Fans and people not interested in football were called on to support the Tanks, one of the "best advertising plans" in the city. At Portsmouth, the *Times* expressed amusement at the use of a boosters' day to shore up the Tanks: "It was up to Ironton to pass the hat. They are original, if nothing else, for Boosters Day for a football team is a novelty. Ironton has had so many Booster days for [base] ball teams that it simply has the habit and can't get away from it. You tell 'em gasoline, you auto."[15]

For all the canvassing, on the eve of the game, sales of tickets, running about five hundred according to one report, were far below what the Chamber and the Tanks wanted. Still, a larger crowd—a "record" crowd, many from Ashland—was predicted at Beechwood. Besides supporting the Tanks as an "advertisement" for the city, the fans could expect to see a hard-fought game.

The Tigers were still smarting over the Tanks' scorning them as a weak opponent early in the season. Moreover, Ironton fans believed, they had added some "prominent" collegiate stars from Kentucky to their roster, among them James "Red" Weaver, who had starred as a center at Centre College in 1920 and won acclaim that year as one of Walter Camp's All-Americans. Though Weaver decided at the last minute not to play, the Tigers still had a lineup "full" of college men, notably Ashby Blevins, an outstanding tackle from Centre, and gave the Tanks fierce resistance before falling 7–0.[16] Paid admissions numbered about fifteen hundred, hardly as many as hoped for, but, with tickets selling for a dollar, the Tanks had a gate of about $1,500, enough to meet all expenses.

As important as the game with Ashland was, it lacked the emotional intensity built into any contest between Ironton and Portsmouth teams. Victories for either community in the historic rivalry were sweet. For the Tanks to forge loyalty in Ironton, they had to dominate Portsmouth teams. If they could perpetuate the legend of success, the Tanks could strengthen their claim to roots in the community. Unlike established institutions in the city, they could not depend on ideological beliefs, religious tenets, ethnic ties, or other shared values or experiences for the creation of a constituency. Their fans and prospective fans would assay them by one test: winning touchdowns over Portsmouth teams. The Tanks had their first opportunity in 1921 to turn the "ancient rivalry" to good account when the Smoke House team appeared at Beechwood only a week after the Ashland Tigers left the field.[17]

 Despite organizational changes and an optimistic outlook, the Smoke House players were moving through an ordinary season, in some respects a copy of the preceding one. They had a new manager in Harry Doerr and a new coach in Dan Fries, who had played tackle for West Point in 1914. All of the "stars" of 1920 had returned to the team, and the roster included several new "notable" men. Old and new, they made a "clever fast team," the strongest ever to represent Portsmouth. Fries put them through rigorous practices, and Doerr worked on an attractive schedule for them and their fans—a "delectable football menu."[18]

Doerr, though, was building a schedule catch-as-catch-can, and from the beginning of the season it was hardly delectable. He thought he had an opening game ready with a good team, the West Side Athletic Club of Columbus. Unable to close negotiations for the game, he settled for the Ashland Tigers. Playing before a banner crowd at Millbrook, the Smoke House men could manage only a scoreless tie against the Tigers. Then, before meeting the Tanks, they narrowly lost to a team from Circleville, 3–0, defeated the Jackson Bearcats 6–0, and crushed the Chillicothe Majestics 50–0.

Going into the game against the Tanks, the Smoke House appeared to be facing a better team. The Tanks had won all three of their games, allowing their opponents no points; the Smoke House men had won but two of their four games. Against common opponents, the Tanks had a narrow edge. They had defeated the Jackson Bearcats 6–0, as had the Smoke House; the Tanks had won over the Tigers 7–0, and the Smoke House had tied the Tigers.

In the several days before the game, sportswriters in Portsmouth and Ironton kept veritable diaries on the teams' preparations for the game. They told of the Tanks and Smoke House men engaging in long, vigorous practices and planning new tactics—aerial attacks, sweeping end runs, flanking plays, and more. The Smoke House players were especially concerned about handling Brooks—his name was "ever on their lips."[19]

Many fans were laying bets on the outcome; the *Morning Sun*, a new newspaper in Portsmouth, told of a "large amount" of money that would change hands. There were predictions of a record attendance at Beechwood, with as many as eight hundred Portsmouth fans planning to invade Cannonville, three to five hundred by a

Norfolk and Western excursion train, several hundred by automobile. Fans were also coming from Huntington, Ashland, Catlettsburg, and other nearby communities. The contingent from Ashland intended to root for the Smoke House. Presumably, the only disinterested spectators would be the officials, Don Hamilton, Ray Eichenlaub, and an "able" man from Columbus. Both teams expected to receive a "square deal" from the crew.[20]

Notwithstanding the expenditure of newsprint, the crowd numbered only about eighteen hundred, not nearly as many as at the Tanks–Smoke House game at Beechwood in 1920, and despite the stories on end runs and passing, the play on a muddy field resulted in few thrills and no scoring. Reaching the Smoke House fifteen-yard line in the first quarter, the Tanks mounted the only drive that came close to a touchdown. Slowing down the Tanks' offense and the pace of play were numerous penalties, 145 yards against the Tanks, 45 against the Smoke House. The game was as exciting as a "croquet match."

More entertaining were the controversy and commentary after the game. In lengthy reports, sometimes three and four columns long, reporters argued about what had happened at Beechwood. A reporter for the *Register* thought officiating had cost the Tanks a victory. The disproportionate yardage in penalties, he believed, took the fight out of the Tanks. At the Marting Hotel after the game, explaining the disparity in yardage, supposedly Hamilton and Eichenlaub told Brooks and Scott that probably they had "watched [Ironton] more closely than Portsmouth." By that admission, said the reporter, they had made themselves ineligible to officiate any game in which the Tanks played. Hamilton, snorted the editor of the *Register*, should have sat on the bench in a recent hunting case in Portsmouth—he meted out more severe penalties than did the judge in that case.[21] Burke did not agree with his editor, saying that Hamilton and Eichenlaub, who had been "hurt" by the Tanks' criticism, had been "fair and square." Though taking note of the yardage in penalties, the *Irontonian* described the officials' work as satisfactory.

At Portsmouth, Pete Minego, an acerbic young sports columnist for the *Times*, took obvious delight in finding fault with the Tanks' play and behavior: the Tanks had lost their "pepper" when the Smoke House smothered their famous line plunges; they "fussed" among themselves; they "sneaked" off the field after the Smoke House players gave them a cheer at game's end.[22] Now the famous Tanks could give up their talk of playing the Canton Bulldogs. The referees, he was certain, had handled the game in a "perfect manner." A column head dismissed the Tanks' grumbling as a "Cheap Squeal Too Disgusting to Talk About," but the paper did talk about the grumbling: the Tanks had "clamored" for Hamilton and Eichenlaub to officiate the game and now complained about them. Their wailing revealed the "small town stuff" of Ironton: "Now if this isn't Ironton's calibre we will quit. That is one potent reason why it never has gotten out of its swaddling clothes. As one rooter said Sunday, they have a courthouse, a new bridge and a real hotel and the rest you can give to the Indians."[23] Football was becoming a metaphor for a community's failure to progress.

 Their record marred by the tie, the Tanks could no longer make an easy claim to dominance in semiprofessional football in the Tri-State. And the Lombards, perhaps taking heart from the Tanks' slippage, leaped at the opportunity to contest their primacy in Ironton. The South Siders were having an unhappy season. They had received the short end of use of Beechwood Park. They had posted an ordinary record at two wins and three losses; only fair-sized crowds attended their games. Only their win over Jackson by a larger margin than the Tanks' had given them an hour of pride. They were fast and played an open game but always had to overcome their handicap of small size. In that respect, the Lombards were "one of the classiest little football organizations in the Ohio Valley."[24]

The Tanks would sail between two dangerous rocks in a game with the Lombards. They would gain little stature in a victory but would lose status if they did not play them. Schachleiter had been talking to the Lombards about a game since the one scheduled early in the season had fallen through—but at arm's length. Now circumstances moved the teams to a contest. When the Asheville (Ohio) Athletic Association canceled a game with the Tanks on short notice because of injuries to its players, the managers of the Tanks and Lombards, acting with unwonted dispatch, agreed to a game. Their decision, facilitated by the looseness of scheduling, embodied what seemed wise and practical: the teams might draw a fairly good crowd; the game would settle the question of the city championship; and the fans had "risen from their hunkers" demanding a game.

The teams, their sights set on crowing in the community, prepared for the game; the Tanks developed new plays, and the Lombards worked on their end runs. Illuminating the fluid nature of semiprofessional football, "Hootie" North, a good running back for the Lombards, joined the Tanks before their game scheduled against Asheville and then, learning of the coming encounter, returned to his old team. On a soggy field before a disappointingly small crowd, the teams played a "thrilling" game. Their line dominating the Lombards, the Tanks won 21–7. Though hardly gaining a great victory, the Tanks could not have afforded a loss to a team still in place in Ironton. The defeat hastened the Lombards' demise; they played the season out and then disappeared from football in Ironton.

As the Tanks prepared for the Lombards, Schachleiter and Doerr were arranging a second game between their teams. They and sportswriters wrangled over selection of the officials. Doerr wanted Hamilton and Eichenlaub to serve again, but Schachleiter, his Tanks still complaining about penalties, refused to accept them, insisting that their work in the earlier game had not been "credible."[25] Portsmouth people then accused the Tanks of double-dealing: when in 1920 Hamilton and Eichenlaub officiated the Smoke House–Tanks game won by the Tanks, Irontonians praised them as the "best ever." The Tanks prevailing in the dispute, the managers selected as referee Herman Beckleheimer, the football coach at Morris Harvey; as umpire W. C. Thomas, an Ohio Conference official living in Wellston; and as head linesman Benton Salt of Columbus. Perhaps now, said the *Sun*, the Tanks would stop their "crying."[26]

The controversy that eventually developed had little to do with the officials. Early in the week preceding the game, the Tanks were contemplating the use of Lombards and other "outside material"—players from Ashland, Cattletsburg, Huntington, Ceredo, Kenova, and Marshall College.[27] Portsmouth was moaning and groaning about North and other Lombards joining the Tanks but said nothing about the Smoke House's sending a fake eligibility list to Ironton the previous year, one that did not include Red Williams or Red Selby "no more than a rabbit." Ironton did not complain then and still did not care whether the Smoke House went to the end of the football domain to find players. Without explaining its position, the *Register* simply stated that the first eligibility list could not apply now and that the Tanks would add the Lombards as they had in 1920.

Meanwhile the Smoke House and Tanks played and practiced. The Sunday following their tie with the Tanks saw the Smoke House men meeting the Asheville eleven at Millbrook. They beat the Asheville team 27–7, presaging, fans had to believe, a good performance against the Tanks. Fries had his men practicing long, hard hours, particularly working on opening holes for backs. Probably no defense, declared the *Sun*, could halt that attack. The Smoke House men were bent on winning, on giving the "highly touted" Tanks a "big surprise." At Ironton, after defeating the Lombards, the Tanks held "snappy" practices, often working on new plays. Probably more for publicity than for practice, the Tanks ran a signal drill on the eve of the game in the middle of the street in front of the Elks Club.

Meanwhile, the fans were preparing and being prepared for the game. Interest was mounting in both communities, created and sustained in part by the newspapers, with their daily accounts of what was happening and what might happen. Probably no other athletic contest in the history of the cities had become such a staple of everyday intercourse. Even persons only remotely interested in football, though recognizing the hyperbole in the sportswriters' language, had to discover something in it to stir them. They could read that the game would be a "terrible battle," a "titanic struggle," the "greatest pigskin scrap," the "greatest conflict ever on this part of the map," one of the "greatest struggles ever in the Ohio Valley."

Sports columnists, players, and fans all looked for a great crowd at Millbrook. Spectators would become part of the "largest crowd" in the history of sports in the Ohio Valley. All the newspapers ran display advertisements for the clash. Anticipating a large crowd, Doerr ordered three thousand tickets printed. Smoke House players worked the city, selling tickets at a dollar each to fans, who could also purchase them at the Smoke House and other retail establishments.[28] About eight hundred Irontonians, many of them the "fair sex," bought tickets at several downtown locations, the Red Cross Drug Store and the Elks Club among them. They intended to journey to Portsmouth by a special Norfolk and Western train, by traction cars, and by automobiles. A "hundred or so" fans from Ashland and Huntington expected to go to Portsmouth.

Whatever mode of transport they chose, the fans were moving in an electrifying atmosphere, akin, some thought, to what the loyal alumni of Yale or Princeton experienced when their teams played a crucial game. The "civilian population of Ironton were following their warriors to the bloody battleground to see them do their best in the conflict."[29] Once at Millbrook, they would see the colors of the "Big Red" draped on one goal post, the blue and white of the Smoke House on the other. They would also hear the forty-piece Elks band, which expected to strike up a victory march after the Tanks crushed the Smoke House and then to play a funeral dirge for the Smoke House players and the groaning Portsmouth crowd. They knew, though, that a Portsmouth band awaited them at Millbrook, prepared to draw from a similar repertoire. Smoke House fans were less imbued with rah-rah but, like college students at the bonfire on the night before the game, longed for "the sound of the whistle reverberating across picturesque Millbrook."

The game proved less interesting than the anticipatory rhetoric and the subsequent controversy. The Tanks arrived late, and play did not begin until well after 2:00 P.M. Played before a crowd of about four thousand on a "springy" field rendered wet by a recent rainfall, the game was devoid of daring strategy and sensational plays. Nor was it "ze battle royal" forecast by the *Irontonian*. After an evenly contested first quarter, the Tanks, their defense impenetrable, "completely outplayed, out ran, out fought, and out classed" the Smoke House team. They were leading 14–0 and threatening to score again with four minutes to play when, at Fries's threat to refuse to continue play on the darkening field, Thomas, with Beckelheimer concurring, ended the game. The Tanks had no great quarrel with the decision to halt play but vigorously protested the officials' declaration that Portsmouth had forfeited the game by a score of 1–0 and that all bets were off. They argued that the score of 14–0 should stand, alleging then and later that besides distorting reality the forfeited score especially accommodated gamblers who had bet on the Smoke House and who now repudiated their wagers. Perhaps more exciting than the game was the fighting among fans during and after the game. About a dozen fights occurred during the game, provoked by jubilant Ironton fans who insulted Smoke House partisans. After the game, a "big scrap" in East Portsmouth broke out among adherents of the teams, with "considerable blood spilled."[30]

The Tanks had much more to complain about than a forfeit. At the conclusion of play, Doerr refused to give them their share of the gate, 40 percent of which had to be a healthy sum. In their initial stories on the game, neither the *Register* nor the *Irontonian* offered a clear or detailed explanation for Doerr's action. But they condemned it in harsh language. Commenting on the day at Millbrook, the *Register* asserted that "the cheapest, rankest low-downed, crawfishiest, most childish, utterly despicable trick of the whole affair was the action of the Portsmouth team management in withholding the forty percent share of the gate receipts promised the Ironton club. This marks the Portsmouth football team as a bunch of quitters, too unsportsmanlike for words."[31] The *Irontonian* hinted at the problem, saying that the Smoke House men "kicked" at the appearance of Art Hall at quarterback—an implication that the Tanks had used an ineligible player. In withholding the Tanks' share of the gate, the Smoke House had pulled the "cheapest trick ever known in what can be called CIVILIZATION."[32] Both newspapers arraigned Portsmouth as "poor losers," as a community that could never stand defeat, an "outcast city athletically." Not surprisingly, Ironton fans were crying, "Scratch them off the list."

The *Herald-Republican,* a newspaper published in Waverly, also attacked the Smoke House eleven and Portsmouth. The *Herald* reporter subjected the Smoke House men to a scurrilous assault: "Then showing a streak of yellow the entire length of their backbones, the Portsmouth bunch quit playing when the ball was within a yard of Ironton's [Portsmouth's] goal and only four minutes to play." After the officials forfeited the game to Ironton and called off all bets, the Portsmouth "gang," demonstrating their sportsmanship, withheld the Tanks' share of the gate. It was a "cheap squeal from a cheap bunch of sports and only reflects the character of the city. It is the same dirty tactics that were used against Waverly the past ball season."[33] What else could one expect, he asked, of a community where a sportswriter slurred the Waverly high school football and baseball teams?

Only hours after the game, the Tanks secured what they considered to be a satisfactory resolution of the dispute over whether the officials could declare a forfeit of a game halted by darkness and the consequent refusal of a team to continue to play. Scott sent telegrams to Dr. Henry L. Williams, renowned coach at the University of Minnesota and a member of the NCAA rules committee, and to Paul H. Tobin, secretary of the committee, asking them whether the decision at Millbrook was correct: "Kindly wire at my expense your decision on the following: Team scored twice in three quarters, 14 to 0 score. Referee calling game account darkness, four minutes to play. Has referee right to give decision 1 to 0 after losing team refuses to finish game?" Both Williams and Tobin found the forfeiture to be incorrect.[34] Tobin's response read, "Losing Team Refuses To Finish. Score Stands 14 To 0. Referee Out of Jurisdiction To Declare Game Forfeited To Winning Side 1–0." The Tanks sent the "word" to Portsmouth, but as the *Irontonian* saw it, "the howling birds" there were not likely to hear or heed it.

The real issue, though, was not the forfeit but the Tanks' share of the gate. Through their newspapers, fans, players, and journalists in Portsmouth and Ironton fought a battle of words over the issue, often impugning one another's honesty and integrity. Anyone reading only the Ironton newspapers might have concluded that the Smoke House had acted as bandits, simply seizing the receipts and withholding the Tanks' share without any pretense of justification. The Ironton sportswriters gave their readers hardly any inkling of what moved Doerr to his seemingly spiteful decision.

One bare-boned account of the game from Portsmouth called attention to the Tanks' apparent use of players not on the eligibility list, specifically Art Hammond, Earle "Red" Shannon, and Ashby Blevins. Early in the first quarter, the Smoke House captain, Lonnie Chinn, realized that Hammond, playing quarterback, was not on the Tanks' eligibility list, that he was playing under an assumed name, that of Art Hall. Then the Smoke House discovered that Shannon and Blevins were also playing as ringers. Doerr took up the issue, meeting with Schachleiter for about fifteen minutes as the crowd sat waiting for play to resume. Finally, he consented to the Tanks' use of the three men. What made the behavior of the Tanks reprehensible to some was not so much that they had brought in ringers but that they had sullied competition between locals of each community, turning a game between two communities into one between insiders and outsiders. Accordingly, the Tanks had no right to call themselves the Ironton Tanks.[35]

Even more distressing was the report that four well-known Ironton men had engineered a deal for Hammond, Shannon, and Blevins to play for the Tanks. As soon as the ringers were working out with the Tanks, the four men sent $5,000 to Portsmouth to bet on their team. The Tanks, mere figureheads, had allowed gamblers, feathering their own nest, to revamp the lineup. "Why we have a hammerlock on you," a "leading citizen" of Ironton reportedly boasted on the day of the game, "or we would not be down here. We are not taking any chances whatever. Why everyone in Ironton knew that Hammond, Blevins and Shannon were to play." He explained that solicitors for the Tanks had passed the hat throughout the community, raising enough money to pay all the players before they went to Portsmouth. All in town, willing as they were to empty their weekly pay envelopes to beat Portsmouth, "kicked in." Learning of the purported contributions to the Tanks and the alleged use of ringers, a Portsmouth fan expressed dismay: "The Tanks pulled off a regular White Sox stunt yesterday and got away with it. They would use any kind of trick to win." But neither the *Times* nor Doerr believed that the Tanks "got away with it." Their crowing about the victory would not give them their share of the gate, said the *Times*. Doerr, insisting that the Tanks had willfully violated a written contract, swore that he would not give them one red penny; he had engaged an attorney and would resist payment to the last ditch. The receipts, in the meantime, were in a big safe at the Smoke House.[36]

Hammond, Shannon, and Blevins did, in fact, play under fictitious names.[37] Hammond was a quarterback who was currently playing at Marshall and had played for Ashland teams; he used the name Art Hall, an old-line Tank, and replaced Progler. A halfback, Shannon was then at Morris Harvey; his name in the lineup was Ball, apparently for Nate Ball, the former Lombard who had joined the Tanks. Blevins, who had once been with the Tanks, had recently been playing as a guard for the Ashland Tigers; his name for the game was that of a Tank, Howard Fritz. In none of the published lineups for the game did any one of real names of the unholy trinity appear. Though supposedly aware of the Tanks' intention to use the men, at the appearance of Shannon and Hammond on the field, Ironton fans exclaimed, "Who are those guys in the backfield?" The Smoke House players, not as gullible as the Tanks believed them to be, soon knew that something was wrong. The Tanks had arrived late at Millbrook, purportedly to make it more difficult for anyone to identify the players. Early on, though, Chinn had seen that the Tank playing as Hall was a ringer; a little later, he and other Smoke House men realized that the two other

All Bill Did Was Blink His Eyes

Tanks were Tanks in uniform only and were indeed ringers. The Smoke House team could have refused to continue the game until the ringers left the field. The referee, Thomas, had erred, too, in not declaring that all bets were off as soon as Chinn told him that ringers were playing for the Tanks. Chinn, explaining the Smoke House decision to play after he recognized Hammond as a ringer, said that Hammond had not "shown much" when he had played for an Ashland eleven. Had Chinn and Doerr known then that the Tanks had two more ringers, the Smoke House would not have played on; but Schachleiter assured them that he had no more—"All Bill did was blink his eyes and throw a blank stare."

For Portsmouth, the game revealed essential differences between the teams and even the communities. The Smoke House men, all local residents playing for the honor and love of the game and the city, had not received one cent during the season. In turn, the community was delighted that they played for Portsmouth. In contrast, instead of giving local players a chance, the Tanks, fearing that the Smoke House might beat their regular players and acting out of an "anything to win" spirit, had recruited high-priced collegiate stars, paying them as much $300. Thus they had ended up hopelessly in debt, constantly in need of boosters' days. If Irontonians wanted a professional team, they should invite the Dayton Triangles of the NFL to play for them.

As the Portsmouth newspapers mounted an attack on the Tanks and Ironton, bluster and obfuscation reigned in Ironton. Within hours of leaving Millbrook, the Tanks retained Edgar Miller, a Portsmouth attorney, as their counsel and instructed him to initiate a civil action, a breach of contract, to claim the purse.[38] Apparently Miller never filed suit, but probably the Tanks saw the threat to do so as a sword of Damocles hanging over the Smoke House. Ironically, soon the Ironton papers were admitting, by implication, that the Tanks had indeed employed ringers. According to one editorial, when the Smoke House squad came to Ironton in 1920 with thirty-three men, many not on the eligibility list, the Tanks had consented to their playing. Another took a similar line, rebuking the Smoke House for using fictitious names for Red Williams and Red Selby in one of the games in 1920 between the teams; that transgression gave the Tanks the right to sin, too.

The Ironton newspapers denounced Portsmouth in other ways, often irrelevant but good for use in a cat fight and portraying the city as the pariah of the valley. Saying that Portsmouth was a den of thieves and welchers, the editor of the *Register* called on all in the area to boycott teams there. The *Irontonian* declared that the city could not stand defeat. At Waverly, the *Herald-Republican* joined in the chorus of condemnation, portraying Portsmouth as a community wishing to lord its athletic

Home and Away

power over the entire Ohio Valley. Schachleiter, muddying the waters, asserted that he had the name of a Portsmouth man who had offered Hammond $200 to deliver the Tanks' signals to the Smoke House.[39] Perhaps listening to the Irontonians, the Jackson Bearcats canceled a scheduled game with the Smoke House at Millbrook supposedly because of Doerr's "rotten tactics" in denying the Tanks their money.[40] Apparently censuring Doerr and the Smoke House, Duke Ridgley, the popular sportswriter at the *Huntington Herald Dispatch,* feared that semiprofessional football in the valley had been damaged by the "petty larceny stuff."[41]

Despite the bitter rhetoric, Schachleiter went to Portsmouth a week after the game to confer with Doerr, confident that he would return home with the Tanks' share of the gate.[42] Rehearsing the course of the game, Doerr would not give an inch: the Tanks had deliberately and flagrantly violated the contract for the game by using Hammond; the Smoke House had "graciously" consented to his playing; Schachleiter, after saying that he had no more ringers in the lineup, proceeded to use two more. And that was why the Tanks had gone home penniless after the game and why he would now return to Ironton without the purse. Schachleiter's counter-accusation, that a Portsmouth man had tried to bribe Hammond, hardly germane, proved of no avail. Schachleiter departed Portsmouth vowing to pursue legal action—and not to "be long about it." For the moment, though, there was no move to resolve the dispute. If eligibility lists were more than ritualistic documents blinking at or tolerating deception, the Smoke House men had reason to complain. Soon after the meeting, the *Register* acknowledged that Shannon had recently played for Morris Harvey. The Tanks had placed themselves in a moral bind, at an impasse not easily resolved in their favor by legal action.

While the dispute continued with no settlement in sight, the Tanks were playing out their season. After a heavy downpour brought about cancellation of a Thanksgiving Day game scheduled against Morris Harvey, they met the Wellston Eagles. Playing for the unheralded Eagles were the Pope brothers, Harry and Virgil, who led their team in a fierce battle ending in scoreless tie. The Tanks then met Morris Harvey in a rescheduled game. At once it was a showcase of the Tanks' place in the athletic sun and standing in the community. Obviously anticipating a good crowd against an eleven packed with "speed merchants," including Earle Shannon the ringer, the Tanks offered to share the gate with the Ironton high school athletic association, which was attempting to liquidate a debt of $480; to that end, the Tanks gave a large block of tickets to high school students to sell for the association.[43] In the most "spectacular and brilliant game" ever played at Ironton, the Tanks, determined to treat college teams as they did all other elevens, defeated Morris Harvey 19–14. The

All Bill Did Was Blink His Eyes

Morris Harvey players praised the Tanks' line as the best that they had ever faced. Though supposedly numerous fans attended the game, the net gate was only about $150, reported the *Times* as it ridiculed the Tanks' effort to wipe out the high school debt.[44]

The Tanks concluded their season amid both controversy and success. Schachleiter saw Wellston, which had just defeated the Smoke House 14–0, as a good draw for a return game that ostensibly would decide the mythical championship of the Ohio Valley. Schachleiter and E. O. Hughes, the manager of the Eagles, haggled over financial terms. Finding in Schachleiter an intransigence tantamount to refusal to play the game, Hughes, said Minego, saw "a yellow streak running down the Tanks' back."[45] The managers, though, finally reached an agreement for the game. Because a championship of sorts was at stake in the "greatest game of the season," the Tanks practiced overtime, and the Eagles came to Ironton with two or three new players, including Walter Essaman, the line coach at Ohio State. The teams engaged in "much slugging" and many arguments. They played on virtually even terms, a blocked punt leading to a Tanks victory 7–6 and the "Southern Ohio Championship."[46] The Tanks thus ended the season undefeated, with seven wins and two ties, and defeated in return games the two teams that tied them. In celebration, they hosted a dance for the public a day at the Elks Club a day after the game, there shaking a "wicked boot on the floor."

Perhaps the Tanks' and the dancers' celebration was tempered by the *Times's* account of incidents occurring during and after the game, which said the Tanks had played in a disgraceful manner. They kept the officials busy trying to stop their slugging, and one Tank tried to provoke a fight with Essaman to get him out of the game. The Wellston players had no doubt about it: the Smoke House players were gentlemen, and they would not hesitate to play them again—but not the Tanks. The Tanks fans exhibited equally reprehensible behavior at the end of the game, coming on to the field threatening and manhandling Wellston players, one fan even brandishing a gun. Harry Pope, captain of the Wellston eleven, believed that he had to break all relations with Ironton: "When fans start flashing guns in the faces of our players and then beat them up, I think it is time to quit." A few minutes later, about twenty Irontonians attacked four Wellston men in front of the Eagles Club, "roughly handling them" and brandishing guns. Ironton men had also stopped Wellston men in an automobile, called them vile names, and struck one. Arrest might follow. So said the *Times*.[47]

The *Register* dismissed the complaints out of hand.[48] What fighting occurred during the game arose from the tension of battle, not malice. The only penalty for rough play came against Essaman. Countering the *Times*'s charges against the Ironton fans, the *Register* quoted a letter from Hughes, who said that they had treated the Wellston team courteously. But the *Register* virtually admitted that local fans had attacked Wellston people as he exculpated them in an odd way: Ironton men had not held the Portsmouth crowd responsible for attacks on them after the recent game at Millbrook. The Tanks did announce that that they would not admit anyone to games who had engaged in fights or quarreling along the sidelines.

The Smoke House team concluded play for the season a week before the Tanks did, also meeting the Wellston eleven at Millbrook. Unlike the Tanks game, the Smoke House–Eagles contest occasioned little commentary in newspapers or among fans, before or afterward. Several regulars on the Smoke House squad did not play for some reason, and the "well-balanced" Wellston team won handily 14–0, the Smoke House players taking some solace in Hughes's praise of their conduct. Thus the Smoke House ended the year with a record of three wins, three losses, and two ties, barely improving that of 1920. The team did not hold a dance or banquet to mark the end of the season.

As the Tanks and Smoke House closed off play, the dispute over the gate at Portsmouth was coming to a salutary end. Paradoxically, if anyone cut the strands in the Gordian knot that the Tanks and Smoke House had tied, he was Harry Taylor, editor of the *Times,* which in its sports pages had assailed Ironton and the Tanks for their behavior. Early in December, Schachleiter and Brooks, reportedly needing money to pay the Tanks and finding Doerr adamant on sharing the gate, went to Portsmouth to meet with Miller the attorney, saying that they intended to press the matter through legal channels. A few days later, in a lengthy editorial, Taylor called on the teams to settle their dispute and go on to "better feelings," to "better sportsmanship."[49]

In measured prose yielding little of the high ground for the Smoke House and scolding the Tanks and the Ironton newspapers, Taylor reviewed the controversy. The *Times* had refrained editorially, he said, from commenting on the dispute because feelings had been running high, but now that the season was over, the time had come for a settlement. Clearly, the Tanks had come on to the field with three collegiate players entered on the eligibility list under fictitious names. At the discovery of the "star" ringers, the Smoke House could have refused to play but had remained on the field, played, and lost. Though legally the Smoke House might withhold the Tanks' portion of the gate, "rightly" and "morally" and in the good name of the game, Doerr should pay the Tanks. Because the Tanks management put over

All Bill Did Was Blink His Eyes

a "wretchedly crooked deal," why, asked Taylor, should the Smoke House enter the "crooked sweepstakes"? He trusted the Portsmouth manager to act accordingly and the Ironton fans and the Ironton newspapers, which had countenanced the Tanks' use of ringers, to condemn their management. Then better feelings, better sports relations might ensue.

At Ironton, the *Register* and *Irontonian* published Taylor's editorial in full.[50] The editor of the *Register*, saying that he would not quarrel with "good old Harry Taylor," scoffed at his column and justified the Tanks' recourse to ringers. Had teams ever paid heed to eligibility lists in semiprofessional football? Did Portsmouth remember using ringers against the Tanks in 1920? Yet what happened in 1920, he argued, was not the point. The issue was that the Smoke House had taken the field for a game that they had agreed to play and would not have received any gate if the Tanks had not played. The Tanks had shared in the creation of the receipts and were entitled to their share. Would the Smoke House men have denied the Tanks their share of the gate had they won? Their jubilance at winning would have been so great that they would have increased the Tanks' share. Concluding, he advised Ironton teams to sever athletic relations with Portsmouth, which would always sulk at a loss.

For all the harsh language, the Tanks and Smoke House were moving to a settlement of the dispute; Taylor's editorial may have been a decisive factor in breaking the impasse. Only days later, payment was at hand, even for the men who had laid bets on the game.[51] Schachleiter and Brooks journeyed to Portsmouth and conferred with Raymond Saddler, momentarily replacing Doerr as manager—a face-saving maneuver for him—Captain Chinn, and several other players. Echoing Taylor, they all subscribed to the view that the Smoke House, having played the game after learning of the Tanks' violation of the eligibility list, should make payment. Saddler computed expenses of the game and wrote out a check for $725 for the Tanks, payment in full of their share of the gate.

What had poisoned the well, all the newspapers agreed, was gambling, which often led teams to the use of ringers and incited fans to unruly behavior. In another long editorial, Taylor called for the suppression of gamblers. They had brought about conditions discrediting the game and both communities:

> There was a coterie of men in Portsmouth who were at each game, flashing rolls of bills, offering to bet, and there was a similar coterie from Ironton just as eager to cover the bets offered. These men did not care about the game of football. They were interested in making money, and they were not choice about how they made it, so long as they won. It is not necessary to mention names; everybody who cares to know, in either town, is familiar with them.

51

Home and Away

> If we are to have professional football next year, these gambling followers of the game must be suppressed. . . . Football is too fine a game to become the plaything of gamblers.[52]

For once, the *Register* did not argue, saying, too, that the gamblers had to be suppressed and that the police of Ironton would do so.

 With their season completed, the Tanks could look back on a record of success and forward to bright prospects. They had finished play undefeated, vanquished their local foe, the Lombards, consigning them to oblivion, and turned aside the team from Portsmouth, the community of "ancient rivalry." They could claim supremacy in semiprofessional football in the Tri-State and the championship of southern Ohio. Though inclement weather and extemporaneous scheduling probably had cut attendance at their games, the Tanks seemed to be in reasonably sound fiscal condition at season's end. Even before receiving payment from the Smoke House, they had spent $1,000 for equipment and had $800 in the bank for distribution to players.[53] They received Christmas checks for all that was due them—whatever that was. Their "togs" were in good condition, and a "handsome" sum was still available for purchase of additional equipment. Believing that nearly all players on the roster would return in 1922, they could see another winning season looming on the horizon. Besides victories, a degree of fiscal health, and good prospects, they had attained something less tangible but equally significant. They had become increasingly the "town team," an established institution in, of, and for the community. The "best of feelings" existed between players and fans, and the community was latching on to them as its common property. Giving them material assistance signifying an element of emotional loyalty was the business community—the Chamber of Commerce purchasing equipment and selling tickets for them. Businessmen were beginning to regard support for them as a capital investment, as an "advertising instrument" yielding dividends of some sort. Municipal authorities also saw them in that light, willing as they were to use police to suppress gambling at the Tanks games and thus protect the name of the team and the city. The *Register* and *Irontonian* continued to give them full-throated, sometimes mindless, support. The Tanks, in turn, were commending themselves to the community—attempting to reduce the debt of the high school athletic association, holding a public dance. At the same time, though, as local elites were shaping the Tanks as a source of civic pride and as an instrument of boosterism, they were compromising the ideals of the original founders of the Tanks, the goal of playing football for sheer pleasure.

Unlike the Tanks, the Smoke House team had little standing in their community

All Bill Did Was Blink His Eyes

and commanded little loyalty there. They had no record of victories, none over the Ironton team, to point to. Their helter-skelter schedule did not serve them well, giving them the appearance of a ragtag, a sandlot eleven. No player among them—no Brooks or Davies—had risen appealing to fans as a dynamic and colorful personality. They had no identification in Portsmouth as an institution and received scant sustenance from any institutional group. What support they had from the *Times* and *Sun* came because they provided a medium through which to attack the imperious Tanks and Ironton. Among business firms, only the Smoke House company gave them any nourishment, though evidently of small consequence. Certainly no one viewed them as an advertising instrument for the city. Yet the Smoke House men had fans in the community. As many as eight hundred had followed them to the enemy's lair in Ironton, and several thousand had come out to Millbrook hoping to see them beard the Tanks. Their fortune depended, perhaps, on untracking the Tanks. They had to play to win, not for the intrinsic pursuit of play.

4
Poor Old Portsmouth

Entering the season of 1922 having lost only one game in two years, the Ironton Tanks had won acclaim in their community but had not yet gone far beyond its corporate boundaries in play and repute. They had but one opponent at the core of their schedule, the Portsmouth team, which they met six times over the three years of their existence, winning four games and tying two. Their victories over Portsmouth, though pleasing to Irontonians, did not give them greater visibility outside the Ohio Valley, nor did their unbroken success against other nondescript teams in the valley, which, with few exceptions, constantly changed names and organization. But beginning in 1922, the Tanks gradually widened their schedule geographically and developed a new rivalry with a valley community, supplanting in intensity, for the moment, the old competition with Portsmouth.

At the same time, the Smoke House squad was improving its record slightly but otherwise was moving along its old course. Scheduling remained inchoate, regional teams continued to be the primary opponents, and the community still had no abiding interest in semiprofessional football. And if the Smoke House men were on the

54

side of the better angels in the dispute with the Tanks in 1921, they and their allied sportswriters consorted with the lesser angels in a bizarre attempt to defeat the Tanks in 1923 and thus squandered what loyalty fans had accorded them.

The Tanks began the season of 1922 on a new note. At their organizational meeting, they selected Davies, now the football coach at Ironton High School, as their coach and captain, James "Jimmy" Lambert, an auditor for the Chesapeake and Ohio railroad, as their manager.[1] Several new men, two or three with collegiate experience, were candidates for the team, as well as nearly all those who had played in 1921, the graduates of "Tank University." Davies had more than thirty men out for the team at the opening of practices. Large crowds came out for the practices. The outstanding new back to survive Davies's cuts was John Andrews, who had played at Purdue and was working as an electrician at a local plant; he would play for the Tanks through 1927. Another fledgling making the team—but without experience as a collegiate player—was Theodore "Yabble" Abel, who played well at guard for the next five years. Ashby Blevins of Ashland also joined the Tanks. Viewing the workouts, Burke was effusive in his praise for the Tanks; the players were "wonderfully representative" of the community, and Ironton could be proud of them.[2]

The Tanks were soon ready to play, but Lambert was thrashing around in his search for teams to play. Failing to book clubs from Chillicothe and Lancaster, he was able to arrange an opening game with the Columbus Olympians at Beechwood. The first team that the Tanks had met from outside the Ohio Valley and from a large urban center, the Olympians were an "All-Collegiate 11," reputedly the best team in Columbus.[3] Though playing for a guarantee of $300, the Olympians were eager, the players said, to spread the ideals of amateurism. Sportswriters in Ironton gave the coming game considerable coverage. They affected a measure of cosmopolitanism in reporting that Lambert had selected "qualified" officials from outside of Ironton. But they also gloried in localism, in pride in their community, depicting the Tanks as a team indigenous to Ironton, as virtually an "All-Ironton affair." All but one lived in the city. They were happy to report, too, that the team represented the entire community, five or six former Lombards having a spot on the roster; thus, one said, there would "not be that sectional feeling that has done much to injure the game here in the past."[4]

Expecting a record crowd for the game, with fans from throughout the Tri-State descending on Ironton, Lambert prepared for a "grand rush." He hired guards to

Home and Away

stand sentinel along the fence surrounding Beechwood to forestall the "fence thieves." Because one end of the park was on private property, they could not restrict fans from gathering there to see the game. A large crowd saw a game played in extreme heat and thick dust. Especially the Tanks' line played well, with Brooks in on nearly every play; and the Tanks, though a "trifle ragged," won 12–0 or 13–6, the *Irontonian* and *Register* reporting different scores.[5] Symptomatic of the laxity of semiprofessional football, one of the Tanks' new linemen did not play because he did not have his equipment.

The crowd, reported as "large," numbered 781, 626 adults paying one dollar for admission, 155 students paying twenty-five cents. Altogether, gross receipts were $664. The Tanks evidently realized a profit. Lambert paid out $67 in the federal war tax, $25 to rent Beechwood, $45 for guards, $45 for officials, $7.80 for newspaper advertising, and smaller amounts for miscellaneous services. The Olympians took home at least $300. Net receipts thus were in the neighborhood of $167. At the time the balance in the Tanks treasury was $457.[6]

Showing great improvement and "brilliant and flashy play," the Tanks had little trouble at Beechwood beating their next opponent, a team from Athens with many former players from Ohio University in the lineup. They struck the Tanks as a "fine bunch of athletes." The writer for the *Irontonian*, though, did not spare the visitors and their community from ridicule, portraying Athens as a backward city: the players "came, they saw, and they got defeated. This was the story that the Athens boys carried back to the bughouse town. Of course they didn't have any intentions of defeating the Tanks when they left the trolleyless town."[7] He gave vent to a kind of paranoia common among Tanks fans, who believed that teams in the Tri-State especially recruited collegians to defeat the blue-collar players of Ironton. Of course, the Tanks themselves increasingly sought out collegians for their roster. Whatever its emotional or social import, the game had an unpleasant financial meaning for the Tanks. The small crowd in attendance did not enable them to cover expenses, the balance in their treasury falling by about a $100.

Even after the second game, Lambert had only a tentative schedule in place, many of the games still pending. He expected his team to meet, among others, the Nitros, Jackson, the Smoke House twice, and Huntington twice. Fans especially looked forward to the games with Portsmouth and Huntington. The contests with the Smoke House represented the continuation of the old rivalry with Portsmouth, the games with Huntington prospectively the advent of an interesting new competition in football with a larger city. No semiprofessional or professional football team

Poor Old Portsmouth

had come out of the city for years and because of Sabbatarian laws, no football team had played there on Sunday for several years.[8]

The Tanks played the Huntington eleven, the "Boosters" or "Independents," at League Park in Huntington a week after they met Athens. Ironton fans knew little about the Boosters, but their men seemed capable of giving the Tanks a battle. On their roster were seven or eight college stars. Brad Workman, their coach, had been a stellar halfback at Marshall, another back had played for Ohio State, and several men had once played for the Canton Bulldogs. Their line averaging nearly two hundred pounds, the Boosters believed themselves to be "invincible," and their fans were wild about them, praising them on street corners throughout the city.[9]

Even if the Tanks and their fans discounted the rhetoric, they anticipated a close game at Huntington and recognized it as one signifying primacy in the Tri-State. The Tanks, practicing vigorously, were confident of victory. Lambert and local sportswriters expected as many as two thousand Irontonians to swell a "monster" crowd at League Park, gave them detailed instructions on traveling the twenty-five miles to Huntington, and kept them apprised of the Tanks' condition. About six hundred Irontonians, not two thousand, traveled to Huntington to become part of a crowd estimated at from twelve hundred to two thousand.[10] All of Ironton was at the game, sitting in the grandstand or standing along the sidelines, wearing cards on their coats reading "TANK BOOSTER." The Tanks dominated play through much of the game. Davies made several sensational runs, giving the Tanks the victory 18–7. He was, said Ridgley, the inventor of the "pigskin shimmy," displaying more fancy steps than Charlie Chaplin could have. Ridgley also saw Burke, who used eight tablets and three lead pencils painting the story for the folks back home. As they praised the Tanks, the Boosters predicted a victory over them if the teams met in a return game. The Tanks had to be willing to play them again. Receiving 50 percent of the gate at League Park, they took home over $600 to raise their treasury to over $800.

The Boosters began dickering with Lambert for another game as the Tanks moved through a vagarious schedule. Failing to arrange dates with teams from Nitro, Chillicothe, and Wellston, he finally settled for games against Williamson in West Virginia and the Jackson Bearcats. Reports had both elevens studded with collegiate stars, but they proved easy prey for the Tanks. After flattening Williamson 76–0, they rolled over the Bearcats 40–0. The Tanks moved the starting time of the Jackson game back forty-five minutes so that Catholics could observe Cemetery Day at Calvary Cemetery and then reach Beechwood in time for the kickoff.[11]

Overpowering regional opponents and undefeated since their opening game in

1920, the Tanks were building their reputation and, as a consequence, were reshaping their schedule. Fans and local sports columnists saw them as a "superior machine," a team capable of giving any college team in Ohio a battle. Good guarantees notwithstanding, nearby teams in Chillicothe, Wellston, and elsewhere shied away from playing them. Besides, the Tanks were looking for big city teams to play, seeing victories over them as emblems of status, and teams in Cincinnati and Columbus reportedly were seeking out the Tanks for games.

But the Smoke House eleven, perhaps increasingly wary of the Tanks, were not looking for a game. Unrestrained by a contract, Dick McKinney, a salesman and the new manager of the Smoke House, canceled a game with the Tanks less than a week before its scheduled date. Supposedly, McKinney declared that "such bitter feeling exist[ed] between the teams that we deemed it advisable to not play the Tanks this season" and that the "rivalry [was] too strong for the game."[12] For Ironton writers, the Smoke House men simply recognized the superiority of the Tanks and wished to avoid a defeat. The *Register* denounced the decision as reflective of the execrable spirit animating Portsmouth for years. What would Portsmouth say, asked its editorialist, if the city built a good team that others would not play because it was too good? The Tanks ought to sever relations with the River City until "good sports" appeared in that city.[13] At Portsmouth, the *Times* dismissed the comments a "cheap chirp from Cannonville."

When the Smoke House vacated a date on short notice, Lambert, already discussing terms with the Boosters for another game, hastily reached an agreement with them. The Tanks, foreseeing a good crowd at League Park and appreciating the Boosters' ready agreement to a game, would return to Huntington. Among the players reportedly joining the Boosters was Iolas Hoffman, an All-American tackle from Ohio State. Brad Workman, the Boosters' coach, insisted that he would use the same lineup as he had in the first game, saying that he could do without ringers.[14] The Tanks, signifying their confidence in receiving a fair shake at Huntington, willingly permitted the Boosters to select officials for the game.

Embroidering the theme of cordiality, Ironton writers and players, too, portrayed the game as a showcase for the collegiatelike spirit and sportsmanship possible in semiprofessional football. Semiprofessional and professional football had then only a modicum of respectability in the American sporting world. It was often compared invidiously with the amateurism, the purity of spirit, the honest of purpose, and the wholesomeness found in collegiate play. Writers seldom vindicated it in its own right, much less comparing it favorably with the intercollegiate game, which, in

Poor Old Portsmouth

fact, was hardly free of grubby play and acrimonious rivalries. But the Tanks and Boosters expected to set a high standard at Huntington. They intended to play the game in a better style than in the collegiate game. They would not engage in any "rag chewing" against the officials, indeed would say nothing to them except through their captains, and had agreed to refrain from all "rough stuff" and "other features" of professional games. The players were "clean, intelligent fellows," nearly all collegiate or high school graduates, "good sports," who, playing in the "collegiate style," would elevate the stature of semiprofessional football in the valley.[15] Moreover, fans could enjoy all the thrills of a college contest for a dollar instead of the three dollars that they had to pay to see collegiate players in action. Ironically, even as writers and players employed the language of purity, many Tanks fans were going to Huntington "with several truck loads of jack to wager that the Tanks again [would] roll over the Boosters."

At Huntington, fans learned throughout the week of the Boosters' prowess, of their great improvement since the first game with the Tanks. The *Herald-Dispatch* ran advertisements publicizing the game and stories quoting Boosters players as they prepared for it. It would be the "greatest football game ever staged" in the city. It became the staple of everyday conversation: "On the street corners, and every place you go, you hear or see a group of fans discussing the game. It is the topic of the day and will continue to be until the final whistle has sounded Sunday afternoon at the Eighth street yard and the scorekeeper has announced the verdict of the day."[16] Three to four thousand fans were expected to crowd into League Park for the "greatest game" of the season. The Boosters had temporary bleachers erected to accommodate a thousand fans.

The crowd, estimated at about twenty-five hundred, five hundred or so from Ironton and other communities, had a varied, sometimes dynamic aspect. Fans jammed into the west end of the grandstand, bulged out of the bleachers on the south side of the field, roamed the sidelines, and milled around at a wall.[17] They saw a game as closely contested as could be, ending in a tie at 7–7. All agreed that it was the "best game" played in the Ohio Valley in years. The teams had promised to conduct themselves in a sportsmanlike manner, and evidently did so. After the game, the officials commended the Tanks for their "clean and aggressive play." The Huntington club, said the *Register*, "was clean and composed of gentlemanly fellows who lived up to their promise to the officials to speed play and avoid all 'rag chewing.'"[18] In consonance with the players' comportment, the crowd behaved much the same as a collegiate gathering. Fans applauded players on both sides, and the "jeering, catcalling, baiting of officials, etc., which formerly made up a professional football crowd's repertoire . . . was altogether lacking." The fans had made the game a "pleasurable event," one that could make for a good intercity rivalry. The game had scarcely ended before the Tanks' and Boosters' managers were negotiating terms and reaching an agreement for their teams to meet again on Thanksgiving Day, this time in Ironton.

In the intervening fortnight, the Tanks won two games, sandwiching between them an antic experience in scheduling. After easily beating an eleven from Lancaster that local scribes touted as a "strong" team, they expected to meet the Smoke House at Beechwood, Lambert and McKinney apparently having closed the breach between their teams. Then five days before the game, dissatisfied with the stipulation calling for the winning team to take 60 percent of the gate, the Smoke House canceled the date.[19] The *Times*, justifying the cancellation, complained that Lambert had sent the Smoke House a contract with "more holes than the prosaic family sieve." The Tanks affected satisfaction with the decision, saying that they did not want to play a "patched up, weak team." For the *Register*, the cancellation proved that "poor old Portsmouth" was "down and out athletically," that teams there objected to playing opponents if they were not certain of winning. Responding, the *Times* scouted the accusation as "sputterings from a Two-Story Town."[20]

Lambert, ringing the long-distance operator, called around for an opponent on brief notice. One after another, over the course of four days, three elevens agreed to play the Tanks at Beechwood only to beg off. The Columbus Eagles "dropped their feathers" because of injuries to several players; a team from Murray City also pled injuries; and the Zanesville Greys feared losing money on the game.[21] The skein of cancellations was the stuff of a comic opera.

What several Tanks did then was an amusing but telling commentary on the state of semiprofessional football. With no game to play Sunday in a Tanks uniform, Brooks, Blevins, and Schachleiter joined the Jackson team in Portsmouth meeting the Smoke House. They did not enter the game until the fourth quarter, but at one point all the Tanks planned to go to Millbrook in their uniforms, warm up on the sidelines, and then withdraw to the grandstand. Fearing that the Smoke House men would not appreciate their "little joke," they aborted the proposed hoax.[22] The *Times* took pleasure in reporting that the Smoke House players, besides defeating Jackson 13–6, pushed Brooks around as though he were a one-hundred-pound man. Clearly, argued the *Times* in a long stretch of inference, the game proved that the Smoke House had no fear of the Tanks. Perhaps taking instruction from the Tanks, a year later the Smoke House turned the planned hoax into a wild reality.

Poor Old Portsmouth

His Tanks already idle one Sunday, Lambert cast a wide net for an opponent for the following Sunday. Turned down by a "vaunted" Chillicothe eleven and the Lockland Athletic Club, he found in the Washington Court House Independents a team not "frightened" by the Tanks. Asserting that they had "nerved" themselves for the shock of combat, they arrived late at Beechwood short of shoes and strength and lost 45–0 before a crowd held down by inclement weather.[23]

The Tanks, becoming known as the "Big Red," now had to turn their attention to their Thanksgiving Day game against the Boosters. They had little time to "inly ruminate" but knew that the Boosters offered a serious challenge to their supremacy in the Ohio Valley. They had lost but one game, that to the Tanks, and a victory would give them an identical record, as well as a standoff in direct play at one win, one loss, and one tie. Moreover, a win at the end of a season counted more with fans and sportswriters than one early in the season because they imputed great meaning to apparent improvement.

As the teams briefly prepared for their encounter, they appeared to be evenly matched. Since the tie three weeks earlier, the Boosters had bolstered their lineup, adding the ringers Hammond and Shannon and Art Rezzonico, an outstanding quarterback who was still playing for Morris Harvey.[24] Of the eighteen men on the Tanks roster, nine had played at colleges, nine only at Ironton High School. Nearly all the Tanks were local men. In contrast, nearly all seventeen Boosters had experience in collegiate play, seven at Marshall. Many lived outside of Huntington. Irontonians were called on to give the hometown boys a large crowd. Noting that the Tanks might be playing their last game of the season, the *Irontonian* urged readers to go to Beechwood even though they might not gain admission: "Every man, woman and child of Ironton want[s] to see the Tanks wind the season up in a blaze of glory. Think it over football fans."[25] The *Register* argued that a large crowd was a just tribute to a team serving as a "good promotional force" for the city.

The Tanks and Boosters played a game that the *Register* described, with some justification, as the "greatest" football game in the history of the Tri-State. Ridgley used similar language, his column punctuated with superlative words such as "greatest" and "most sensational."[26] A crowd of about three thousand, six hundred sitting in temporary bleachers, saw a contest decided in the last minute when Andrews of the Tanks drop-kicked a field goal from the Boosters' thirty-yard line, giving his team a paper-thin victory, 12–10. A scribe for the *Irontonian*, though praising the entire team, singled out Shorty Davies and Bill Brooks for accolades: Davies had run like "Old Man Wellington at Waterloo," and Brooks, who threatened to injure all the Boosters if they did not "cut out the scoring stuff," played a "whale of a game." The

Home and Away

Boosters acquitted themselves well as a team and as sportsmen. They were, wrote Burke, a "splendid bunch of clean, square footballers who are in the game chiefly for the pleasure they derive from the sport." The crowd, though orderly, was often emotional, tense, and excited from play to play. Said Burke, "There were moments in that game when the sedate businessmen threw away their hats and petite maidens hugged the men next to them be they friend or foe, and the shower of hats resembled a convention of about two thousand Williamjay Bryans making ready for a political rally." The Ironton fans, of course, felt special elation at the end, their Tanks remaining undefeated and claiming the championship of the Ohio Valley. The Tanks could also pick up over $700 derived from the advertising notices of 120 merchants in the souvenir programs.[27]

Lambert was still attempting to round up games at Beechwood for the Tanks after they beat the Boosters. He could not, though, reach agreement with any of the teams that he sought out—the Columbus West Siders, a team from Chillicothe, the Wellston Eagles, and the Lockland Athletic Club, the issue of guarantees nearly always the sticking point. He had especially wanted to meet the West Siders, believing that if the Tanks won they would earn greater repute outside of southern Ohio. His negotiations with the Eagles occasioned a quarrel between the *Wellston Sentinel* and the *Register*. According to the *Sentinel*, the Eagles had challenged the Tanks four times to a game in recent weeks. By their silence, the Tanks had proved that they did not have the nerve to play the Eagles.[28] Burke ridiculed the notion that the Eagles could beat the Tanks: "All of which is to laugh, and then laugh some more." Besides, the Wellston boys were asking far too much at four hundred "simoleons" as a guarantee—a "hungry meat hook"—to come to Ironton.[29] The Tanks could get a big city team for that figure. A hundred dollars would be more realistic. Later, explaining the financial realities, he pointed out that the Tanks would take in about $800 from a crowd of eight hundred. The war tax and cost of insurance would reduce receipts to $670, leaving the Tanks with $270. Why, he asked, should the best team in the region take the short end of the deal?

Lambert failed to find an opponent, and the Tanks' play ended for the season. For the second straight year, the Tanks were undefeated, only one tie marring their record, and that with a team that they beaten twice. Their unbeaten streak, reaching back to the first game of 1920, was now at twenty-four games, and they could lay claim to two mythical championships—for whatever they were worth. Lambert had the Tanks moving in a new direction. He had them playing a Columbus eleven, had attempted to schedule other Columbus teams and a Cincinnati squad, and had opened an important new rivalry with a larger city in the Ohio Valley. Burke believed that the

American Rolling Mill Company—Armco—in Ashland would soon sponsor a team to compete with the Tanks and Boosters, one that would make the valley even stronger in semiprofessional football.

Off the field, seemingly the Tanks had planted themselves more firmly in the community. They had drawn large enough crowds to remain in the black—though apparently not by much. At season's end, they agreed to a distribution of $135 to each of the eighteen men on the roster and to Lambert, or about $15 a game.[30] They retained an undisclosed sum as a "nest egg" and appeared financially ready to play in 1923. They had at least the rhetorical support of the business community and the press. They could take satisfaction from special recognition given them in the community. The Knights of Pythias sponsored a public dance in their honor, the Melody Boys providing music. Making good on her promise to give them a banquet if they had an unbeaten season, Ola Henry "inflicted defeat" on them "by viands," setting a table for them that groaned with food; by the end of the repast, Davies had forgotten his signals, and Brooks could not budge from his chair.[31]

As the Tanks burnished their record and reputation, the Smoke House players were passing through a mediocre, indeed a disappointing, season. They prepared for play in the way typical of semiprofessional elevens. At an organizational meeting, the players, all from the team of 1921, chose Dick McKinney as their manager, Dan Fries as their coach, and Orville Montgomery as their captain.[32] Beginning their practices, they had but vague knowledge of their prospective schedule, knowing only that they might meet the Boosters and Tanks twice. McKinney, who was soon sharing his managerial duties with Russell Haley, president of the Smoke House company, arranged the schedule virtually week by week.

At the outset of their play, the Smoke House men showed little offensive strength, prompting Pete Minego to complain more than once that they needed more practice. After defeating the Washington Court House Independents 19–0 in their opening game, they could not manage any score in their next three games. They played to a scoreless tie with the Chillicothe Sunnybrooks, lost to the Independents in a return game 6–0, and fell to the Boosters 9–0. Playing two of the games at Millbrook, apparently they drew crowds of less than a thousand.

At this point—and about to face the Chillicothe eleven again—the Smoke House men attempted to strengthen their team. The players, turning out for a "splendid" practice, replaced Montgomery as captain, electing in his stead Sam Ackroyd, who had once played at Ohio State. Haley signed two players from the Wellston team, one Harry Pope.[33] Undefeated, the Sunnybrooks came to Millbrook as a "hard fighting, grim visaged crew" with the "malicious intent of victory." But they also came with a revamped, crippled lineup owing to injuries. With about five hundred fans in attendance, the Smoke House players ran over the Sunnybrooks 44–0. The Smoke House won, asserted the *Times,* because the players had reorganized the team and practiced more diligently.

After McKinney called off the scheduled game with the Tanks because of the "bitter feelings" between the teams, the Smoke House finished the season in an extemporaneous mishmash of games. He expected the Jackson Bearcats to replace the Tanks, but for some reason the Bearcats postponed the game. In their stead, he thought that the Columbus Maroons would come to Millbrook, but at the last minute the Maroons decided not to come. The Smoke House then rested on Sunday. The next Sunday, though they practiced faithfully for a third game against the Sunnybrooks, they were outplayed and "outsmarted" at Chillicothe and lost 28–0. Then they defeated the Jackson Bearcats 13–6 in a rescheduled game, the one that saw the three Tanks playing for the Bearcats in the fourth quarter. The Smoke House men savored the victory especially because the Tanks could not turn the tide against them. When the Boosters canceled a scheduled game, Haley scrambled around for another opponent and found one in a team from Williamsport, a village near Washington Court House. A small number of fans shivering in the cold at Millbrook watched the Smoke House win easily, 53–0, over the Williamsport club, which, said the *Times,* was no better than a junior high school team.[34] The Smoke House then closed the season in a farcical encounter that Haley hastily scheduled with the New Boston Strollers at Millbrook. A lightweight or junior squad, the Strollers had a good record against other lightweight teams, having beaten teams from Ironton and Ashland; they believed that they could defeat the bigger Smoke House men and thus lay claim to the "Independent Championship of Scioto County." The Smoke House eleven scored thirty-two points in the first half, then let up, winning 39–0 and then declaring themselves county champions. "Boy, what a distinction for a team to win," noted the *Register.*

The Smoke House players could take cold comfort from the putative championship. They completed the season with a record of five wins, three losses, and one tie, a slight improvement over 1921, but one posted against indifferent elevens from smaller communities around Portsmouth. They drew small crowds at Millbrook, five hundred or so, while the Tanks frequently played before fifteen hundred to two thousand fans. They permitted their schedule to deteriorate, notably in failing to meet the Tanks; certainly they would have been hard-pressed to defeat the Tanks, but the opportunity for a victory was worth the candle. No Smoke House players appealed to fans by virtue of physical or personal characteristics, and the team remained a colorless lot. The Smoke House men did not enlist any articulate spokesmen at the *Times* or *Sun* in their service, except perhaps when they were parties to a dispute with the Tanks. Their games received little press coverage and nothing retrospectively about the past season or prospects for 1923. Nor did they win over the business community as an ally identifying them with the progress of the community. The Smoke House eleven was a cipher in the city.

 At the close of the season in 1922, the Tanks had money in their treasury, probably a small amount, but enough, said Burke, to begin play in 1923. Something went awry, though, in the following months, leaving the team in a fiscal bind. A reporter for the *Irontonian* sounded the alarm bell in September, before practices were to begin, declaring that whether the "notorious" and "reputative" Tanks would take the field that fall was up to the citizenry of the community. Citing no specific figures, he said the question was "purely financial" and the citizens, merchants especially, had to give all possible encouragement to the Tanks to keep them playing. Composed of "fine gentlemen," a "tribe of the cleanest sports," the team had compiled a marvelous record and was one of the "greatest advertising assets" that the city had ever been "affronted [*sic*] with."[35]

No explanation appeared for why the Tanks, seemingly fiscally healthy at season's end in 1922, were now in straitened circumstances, but the reporter argued that scheduling seemed to be at the heart of a continuing financial problem. Lambert had arranged a good schedule in 1922, but cancellations, notably the Smoke House tilts, had forced him to accept games with weaker opponents. Thus the Tanks faced a dilemma: the better teams demanded excessively high guarantees to come to Beechwood, but lesser teams asking for smaller guarantees did not draw well. In fact, Lambert had attempted to induce "big state elevens" to come to Ironton in 1922, but the Tanks could not risk meeting their demands for guarantees. All-American, All-Conference, and All-State men playing for the big teams did not perform for nothing. Nor did the Tanks, who were players of the "same class." Indeed, teams in Columbus, Cincinnati, Dayton, and Huntington were even now making tempting offers to Tanks players—Brooks, for example. They were men of the "same caliber" as the All-Americans; had they played on a college team they "would no doubt have won great fame and made great names for themselves in rah, rah gridiron circles."[36] The fans would now have to pledge support for the Tanks or see good players departing and weaker elevens coming to Ironton. The scribe's words sounded the envy of the collegians' world from a community whose working-class families had few opportunities to send their sons and daughters to halls of ivy. It was town-and-gown rivalry played out at a far remove from college communities.

Only a few days after the reporter's story appeared, ten businessmen organized a committee to conduct a campaign to raise funds for the Tanks. They were prominent figures coming from a wide range of firms. A. J. Brumberg was the owner of a large clothing store, Tom Hudson and Walter L. Henry operated motor companies, A. C. Schubert ran a laundry and was vice-president of a loan company, A. L. Thuma was the superintendent of the local power company, and J. R. Paul was the sales manager for a cement company.

The committee soon reported success and turned over a "neat sum" to the Tanks. The *Irontonian* congratulated the businessmen for recognizing that the Tanks, having won "fame" on the gridiron and for their cleanliness, were a standing advertisement for the city. Burke also saw the Tanks as a wonderful advertisement. Increasingly in the decade, businessmen and journalists accepted as an article of faith that the Tanks promoted the interests of the community. No one ever offered more than glittering generalities about the material benefits derived from the Tanks; no one could identify revenue that they brought to the city. (Certainly downtown merchants, their stores closed on Sundays, did not sell their wares to out-of-town fans.) The campaign evidently successful, Davies announced that he would continue as coach. If he could not produce a winner, he declared, he would return the money to the committee. Thus the Tanks seemed to have passed through a crisis and could now prepare for play.

The Tanks quickly organized. They reelected Lambert manager and decided to practice every Tuesday and Thursday evening. The majority of players "wearing moleskins" in 1922 returned to the team, and a few new men, notably Terry Snowday, who had been an outstanding halfback at Centre, intended to be present at practices. Confident in their capabilities, the Tanks evinced an unbeatable spirit. They had "rollicking" practices, demonstrating that again they were the "man-killing" Tanks.[37]

Meanwhile, Lambert was working on a schedule that might test the Tanks' unbeatable spirit. He had looked for "big city" elevens in 1922 with little success but now was able to schedule games early in the season with Columbus teams and had "other big state teams in view." Ackroyd and others in Portsmouth were willing to bury the hatchet, and he was able to book two contests with the Smoke House. Rather condescendingly, Burke wished the Smoke House men well and said that the games could help Portsmouth build a good team. Besides, they could be profitable

Poor Old Portsmouth

for both teams. Lambert also scheduled two dates with the Boosters, who had the audacity to boast that they could beat the Tanks. Eventually in 1923, Lambert eliminated from the Tanks' schedule all the elevens from the small and midsize communities to the north of Ironton—Wellston, Jackson, Athens, and others. He did arrange one game with a team from the small community of Logan in West Virginia, supposedly a powerful squad. The Tanks opened play with an easy win in what amounted to a practice game over a local eleven sponsored by the Fraternal Order of Eagles. Their real season began against the Columbus Seagraves at Beechwood. The Seagraves seemed to be a formidable adversary. A leading semiprofessional team in Columbus, they had a battery of former high school, collegiate, and professional stars, including several erstwhile Panhandles, who expected to "scatter the remains of the Tanks over the field." The Tanks, their "wonderful" reputation at stake, were ready for the invasion of the big city team. Their practices were going well, and they could look to old stars for new strength. Only days before the game "Concrete" Poole, then playing at Lombard College in Illinois, and John Dempsey, a student at Knox College, wired Lambert that they would join the Tanks for the game; and Harry "Dutch" Crawford, an original Tank who had not come out for the team, caught the "fever" and suddenly appeared at practice. All the men playing for the Tanks would be wearing "classy" new uniforms of "excellent material," purchased, of course, from Brumberg's store.[38]

For the *Register,* the Tanks entered the game as knights of the community: "The Tanks have the support of the business interests of the city, providing Ironton with a wonderful bit of advertising, at a very small cost. They are a clean, gentlemanly group of footballers, who have never been known to engage in a game that was questionable, or to use rough tactics of any sort. They play football at all times, clean and out on the board for anybody to behold. Their great coach, T. Charlton Davies, is welding a potent machine."[39] The Tanks played the Seagraves before 2,147 fans who purchased tickets and an uncounted number of fence thieves. All saw in the Seagraves a team better on paper than on the field. Their offense "brilliant" and their defense "impregnable," the Tanks allowed the Seagraves no first downs and overwhelmed the visitors 18–0. Dempsey and Crawford were in the starting lineup, but Poole was not present because he played for Lombard against Notre Dame on Saturday previous to the Tanks game (Lombard lost).

The game barely ended before Lambert, exhilarated by the Tanks' showing, was calling teams in Columbus, Cincinnati, and Akron proposing games; he particularly wanted the L. B. Harrisons of the Greater Cincinnati Football Association, the

Home and Away

Wagner Pirates and West Side Athletic Club in Columbus, and the Akron Silents. Lambert had a game soon enough with the West Siders, canceling a game with the Washington Court House Independents in their favor. He had to pay for the game. Saying that local fans often complained that the Tanks laid a "rose strewn path" for themselves in scheduling weak opponents, Earle Norris, a fledgling reporter for the *Irontonian*, revealed that Lambert had secured the game with the West Side team only after offering it a "huge guarantee"—twice as much as ever paid before to any other eleven—and promising a large crowd.[40] Hearing the numbers at a long "persuasive" conference, the Columbus manager canceled a home game and said that his players would come to Ironton.

In view of the reports circulating in Ironton about the West Side club, Lambert had offered a guarantee that was appropriate and necessary. The club was the "cream" of Columbus, the team with the largest following in the city.[41] Masons from Ironton attending a Knights Templar meeting in Columbus returned with tales of the West Side's prowess. Playing for the team were "high class" men from several colleges and universities, including Notre Dame and Ohio State. Determined to make a good showing at Ironton, they practiced three hours a day. Attired in colorful orange and black uniforms, they presented an image of power.

Of course, the Tanks did not come into the game as sheep to be shorn. They had already played well against a Columbus team and were strengthened by Poole, the "big, jovial, hard-hitting" fullback who had returned from Lombard College, and "Big Boy" Harry Pope, the sturdy tackle who had played a game or so for the Smoke House in 1922 and had once rebuked Ironton for "flashing guns." Having offered the West Siders a large guarantee, the Tanks had to draw a large crowd. They believed that the game would draw well throughout the Tri-State. To create interest in the game, Lambert placed large display advertisements in the *Register* and *Irontonian*. He informed fans that the Tanks were erecting a new bleacher along a sideline; accommodating 750 people, it was the kind used by colleges, its surface protective of clothing. About two thousand fans came out to cheer on the Tanks. Before the game, Pope, a big man at 230 pounds, delighted them, walking ten feet on his hands along the sideline to demonstrate that he was in good physical condition and ready to play. Then they saw a "bitterly contested" game. The West Side scored early and, though the Tanks dominated play, held a lead of 6–0 until late in the fourth quarter when Davies threw a pass for a touchdown, and the successful conversion of the extra point gave the Tanks the victory 7–6.[42] The "splendid array" of collegiate stars were surprised at their defeat.

Almost inevitably, the game led to a controversy. On returning to Columbus, apparently some West Side players made complaints about the officiating that found their way into the *Ohio State Journal*. As the *Journal* reported it in a story appearing two days after the game, the West Side team incurred penalties of two hundred yards, the Tanks but thirty.[43] The players were suggesting, of course, that the officials had favored the Tanks in their calls. Ironton would have none of the story. The *Irontonian*, declaring that the West Side men had misinformed the *Journal*, pointed out that the Tanks, having badly beaten many teams in the Tri-State in recent years, did not look to referees for assistance. Departing Ironton, the West Side boys had been in good spirits and had praised the Tanks for their sportsmanship and "good will" but once in Columbus had been unable to accept the taste of defeat and thus had manufactured a falsehood.[44] At the *Register*, the editor and Burke contested the allegations. The editor asserted that the report in Columbus was a deliberate lie; he could not believe that a team as lucky to score as the West Side had been could have lied.[45] As Burke saw the affair, the West Side players, peeved at losing a game that they expected to take in a runaway victory, had attempted to keep the score out of the newspapers in Columbus and then had lied about the penalties. The Tanks, he argued, had drawn more yardage in penalties than had the West Side. For Burke, the Tanks' victory was almost a triumph of good over evil: the Tanks, indifferent to receiving payment for their play, played football for sheer pleasure, the West Side men for profit. Obviously smarting over their defeat, the West Side players were parties later in the season to a famous, or infamous, subterfuge perpetrated on the Tanks at Portsmouth.

The victory brought the Tanks undefeated into their next game against the Smoke House, a surrogated contest, as it were, for their unrealized dominion in 1922 when they could not count wins over the Portsmouth team that, aggrieved by the controversial game of 1921, refused to play them. The passage of time and the opportunity for a good gate before them, the teams reached an agreement to play twice in 1923.

 The Smoke House team facing the Tanks seemed to show promise. At reorganization in 1923, with Ackroyd returning as coach, ten veterans and eleven new men were candidates for the roster. Probably the outstanding new man to make the roster was Jake Pfau, a halfback who had played for Portsmouth High. Another rookie, Jack Creasy, a fullback destined for a dark fate, became captain of the squad. The Smoke House men practiced hard every evening under a new lighting system installed at a ball field on Sixteenth Street. They even scrimmaged one Sunday.

The Smoke House players began the season's play against Washington Court

House at Millbrook. Showing "fighting spirit and pep" before a "banner" crowd of fans paying fifty cents for admission, they defeated the Washington team 13–0, with two long drives resulting in touchdowns. Their next game, at Millbrook against the Seagraves eleven that had lost to the Tanks 18–0 only a week before, gave fans a basis for comparing their team with the Tanks. As had Tanks fans, Smoke House partisans read reports of a Seagraves team that had many collegiate and professional players on its roster. The Smoke House men, though practicing every evening, could not mount an offensive attack but managed to squeeze out a win on a safety, 2–0.

Thus the Smoke House and Tanks were unbeaten as they prepared for their game at Beechwood. Believing that they had a fast and strong eleven and practicing diligently, the Smoke House players thought that all was in "apple pie order" for a victory over the Tanks.[46] They brushed aside the comparative advantage of the Tanks in scores against the Seagraves, insisting that they had met a Seagraves eleven that had improved considerably since its loss to the Tanks. They divined in Portsmouth High's recent win over Ironton High, a team that Davies coached, a sign of their coming victory over the Ironton Tanks. But Davies, smarting over the loss, was steeling the Tanks for revenge. Smoke House fans shared their team's confidence, and more than five hundred journeyed to Ironton to cheer for their men. But they fell silent in the large crowd—at least 2,224 fans who purchased tickets—as the Tanks flattened the Smoke House 40–0. According to the *Irontonian,* the Smoke House men played like a boy scout eleven, like schoolchildren against the Yale varsity. They could take solace in their equal share of the gate, which gave them over $900.[47] For once, no disputes on or off the field attended the game.

The Tanks could not long savor their easy triumph. Now they had to go to Huntington to meet the Boosters, a team that might well contest their sovereignty in the valley. They had nearly beaten the Tanks in 1922 and were now undefeated in three games, including a victory over a strong Logan eleven. Recently, they had acquired two good new players, Homer Martin, a fullback from West Virginia University, and Terry Snowday, who had tried out for the Tanks earlier in the season. Norris believed that the Boosters were 40 percent stronger than they had been in 1922. The Tanks, however, would provide the Boosters with their first real test of the year in a game that might decide the championship of the Ohio Valley.[48]

The communities eagerly awaited the contest. Fans in Huntington were ever talking about the Boosters and their coach, Kemper Shelton. Around six hundred

Poor Old Portsmouth

fans from Ironton traveled to Huntington, the greater body by automobiles, a smaller group by traction and railroad cars and by bus. They were among a crowd of sixteen hundred at League Park, inclement weather cutting attendance. The Tanks won 7–0 in a bitterly fought clash. Davies's several sensational runs countered Snowday's outstanding defensive play.[49] Both Norris and Burke complained that the umpire, one Briggs, a hometown man, failed to call penalties against the Boosters as he should have. The Boosters might have fared better had Martin played; he missed a train at Elkins and did not get to Huntington. He would have an opportunity to redeem himself when the teams tangled in two weeks at Beechwood.

The Tanks could not spend all the intervening days preparing for the Boosters. First, they had to play the rugged Wildcats of Logan. Coaching the Wildcats, the "champions of the land where coal was king," was Art Hammond, the central ringer in the controversial Tanks–Smoke House game of 1921. Playing for them was Earle Shannon, another one of the ringers of 1921. The Logan men had recently lost to the Boosters by only a touchdown and were ironing out the weak points revealed in that game. Forewarned, the Tanks practiced hard for the contest. About three hundred fans from Logan came to Ironton via the Chesapeake and Ohio on the "Wildcat Special." Playing through a drenching rain that turned the field into mud, neither team could muster much offense. But the Tanks managed to score a touchdown and won 7–0.

The Tanks had now gone undefeated since their opening game of 1920, a stretch of thirty games, and had held their opponents scoreless in 1923. They were attracting attention throughout the state. Pete Stinchcomb, former teammate of Chic Harley at Ohio State and now the coach of the Columbus Tigers, a new entry into the NFL, wanted the Tanks to come to Columbus the following week for a game. The Tigers, nearly all former collegians, were holding their own in the league and undoubtedly would have tested the Tanks, but Lambert, having committed his team to a second game with the Boosters that might yield a good gate at Beechwood, turned down the proposal.[50] Stinchcomb was still interested in playing the Tanks and intended to scout them at Ironton the coming Sunday.

If Stinchcomb came to Beechwood, he saw a game shaped by the Boosters, fortified in spirit and flesh and intent on pulling down the mighty Tanks. In the days following his team's loss at Huntington, Coach Shelton added to his roster Art Hammond—certainly a "tramp athlete"—and others and intended to see that Martin did not miss his train again. Ridgley called the Boosters a new team, not the same "crude machine" that had faced the Tanks earlier.[51] Waggishly, Norris asserted that

Home and Away

the Boosters had procured players from every coal mine in West Virginia. Annoyed by what he perceived as boastful talk coming from Huntington, especially the language of the *Dispatch*, Norris depicted it as "yellow journalism," as a "paper victory" for the Boosters. Fans reading it, he said, had to believe that the Boosters, tearing the Tanks line into shreds, had already won an easy victory.[52] But when the Boosters took the real field, they would not be facing a high school line. Grim-visaged, the Tanks practiced, determined to demonstrate that they were not easy prey.

All expected a large crowd at Beechwood, perhaps as many as four thousand, to see the "greatest clash" of the season. A writer given to hyperbole described the impending battle in warlike terms: the "big scrap" occurred in Europe five years ago, and now fans could see another "big scrap."[53] The crowd, numbering around twenty-six hundred, with close to a thousand fans from Huntington and nearby communities along the Ohio River, fell short of predictions but was, nonetheless, one of the largest ever to gather at Beechwood. Obviously strengthened, the Boosters defeated the Tanks 12–6, turning back a Tanks late drive for a winning touchdown. Probably Martin did make the difference between the first and second games. He scored the Boosters' two touchdowns against a Tanks line that could not stop him. Hammond, too, played well for the Boosters. Though aware that the Boosters had loaded up, the Tanks and their fans had to swallow the loss as a bitter pill, indeed as hemlock. Several Tanks, Ridgley reported, shed "salty tears" at the end of the game, and Brooks cried as though his heart were breaking—of course, "Bill always cried." Fans and scribes in Ironton offered various explanations for the defeat: the Tanks were "terribly off color," were not "up to par," and fumbled too much.

Reportedly the Tanks were not discouraged going into their next game, one that could give Lambert leverage in scheduling clubs in the Cincinnati Football Association. For some time, he had unsuccessfully attempted to persuade teams in the league, especially one of the leading clubs, the L. B. Harrisons, to play the Tanks in Ironton or Cincinnati. Finally, he managed to schedule a game at Ironton with Saint Aloysius, a middling club in the league. Fans reading the *Irontonian* would have believed, though, that the Saints were one of the best teams in the state, one not to be "fooled with." A grapevine stretching to Cincinnati seemingly confirmed the accuracy of such language. In any case, the Tanks could commend themselves to the Harrisons and other teams in the association if they convincingly defeated Saint Aloysius before a good crowd. Norris called the game an "acid test" to determine where the Tanks might rank among the Cincinnati teams. The Tanks made short work of the Saints, using "straight football" to best them 31–0; a "lightweight" team, they were not what they were cracked up to be. The Saints manager believed that the Tanks had lived up to their reputation, praising them as a "powerful" team but tendering no opinion about their strength relative to association clubs.[54] Lambert was soon receiving inquiries from Columbus and Cincinnati teams about a Thanksgiving Day game, among them one from the Harrisons, and quickly he worked out terms for them to come to Ironton.

Before hosting the Harrisons, the Tanks had to take on the Smoke House again, this time at Millbrook. Their earlier victory suggested that they faced no great task. But they knew, too, that the rivalry with Portsmouth teams was ancient and not always honorable and that on two occasions at least the Smoke House men had proved to be nettlesome.

After their humiliating loss to the Tanks, the Smoke House men had played respectable ball, if judged by scores, but met fairly weak teams in winning three games and tying one. With only a small crowd on hand, they "never looked better" as they defeated a Lancaster eleven 64–0 a week following their loss at Ironton. Then, a game scheduled with Jackson canceled, they played the Chillicothe Athletic Club at Chillicothe. The game ended in a scoreless tie because, alleged the *Times,* home team fans came on to the field and impeded the "advance" of a Smoke House runner.[55] They played a "superior brand" of football in defeating Wellston at Millbrook 27–7, a Smoke House back running ninety-eight yards for a touchdown. At Millbrook they met Chillicothe for a second game, foiling a Chillicothe player's attempt at a sleeper play and winning 17–7. Evidently only the contest with Chillicothe, attended by a good-sized crowd, yielded a countable gate—about $300.

The Smoke House players could look forward to a good gate in their next game when the Tanks came to Millbrook—but also to a rugged encounter. Obviously they wished to avenge the earlier loss to the Tanks or, at the very least, make a better showing. If they used the lineup of the first game, certainly their prospects were not bright. Shored up by emotion and strenuous practices, neither of which could entirely cancel out the Tanks' physical advantages, they might avoid a trouncing. Of course, they might load up or even accept the stigma of canceling the game under some pretext—but at the cost of a lost gate. What they did was at once cowardly and deceitful and amusing and daring—all typical elements of semiprofessional football in the 1920s.

Clearly the Smoke House men attached great importance to the impending contest. Early in the week before the game, Ackroyd called them together for a special meeting to discuss the future of the team.[56] Discomfited by his warning that the team was deteriorating from the lack of practice but buoyed by his pep talk, all promised to attend all practices and declared, "We're going to beat the Tanks." Following one of their "long and hard" practices, they announced their intention to go beyond merely beating the Tanks: "The Tanks are going to be squashed, emptied, shot-full of holes and flattened."[57] The *Sun* and the *Times* seconded the players' optimistic pronouncements in roseate headlines over columns describing the Smoke House practices. Ackroyd, said the *Sun*, had created a powerful machine out of earlier chaos. Smoke House players, perhaps feeding on the sanguine talk around them, envisioned a win over the Tanks giving them a claim to the Tri-State championship. Ackroyd did not place his faith in victory entirely in practices and rhetoric. By all accounts, he was loading up for the Tanks. As the *Sun* reported on the day of the game, "It is conceded that new faces may be seen in today's lineup." No reporter revealed who the new men might be. Read later in light of what happened at Millbrook, such reports hinted, perhaps, at Smoke House skullduggery.

The heady language of the day heightened interest in the traditional rivalry. A fervor, said one reporter, equaling that of a Yale-Harvard game ensued. As many as a thousand Ironton fans intended to travel to the River City, leaving the streets of the city deserted. Hundreds in automobiles planned to leave in the early morning hours on Sunday to avoid the rush on the Ohio River road. Others expected to catch traction and railroad cars for the thirty-mile trip.

The crowd, estimated variously at three or four thousand, witnessed a curious spectacle, a bizarre episode in the sports history of the Ohio Valley. At 2:00 P.M. Ackroyd and, significantly, only a few of his men, cheered on by their fans, ran on to the field for warm-up drills.[58] The Tanks appeared soon, but, to the consternation of their followers, without Davies, Brooks, and Poole, who had gone to the Carnegie Tech–Notre Dame game at Pittsburgh on Saturday and had not yet arrived in Portsmouth. The Portsmouth "sportsmen waltzed up and down" the Ironton sidelines "hungry" for bets, but few Ironton fans, knowing that A. J. Layne, a local judge, had warned everyone not to bet on the game under the pain of arrest, would accept wagers.

At 2:15 a huge truck used for "moving household goods, bonded liquor, monkeys, and football players" drove up to the main gate, the driver demanding entrance. A lone sentry allowed it to pass through. No one could see its cargo. The truck backed under the goal posts at one end of the field. Then over the lowered tailgate, a group

Poor Old Portsmouth

of football players attired in Smoke House jerseys tumbled onto the ground. Almost immediately the crowd identified them as players of the Columbus West Side Athletic Club, the team the Tanks had defeated 7–6 in the game of penalties. For Ironton fans they were "cleverly and cunningly disguised as a wolf in a sheep's skin." As the Smoke House partisans cheered the West Side men, Irontonians felt a "sickening fear" and became all the queasier as they looked in vain for the missing Tanks.

Then, just as the game began, Davies, Brooks, and Poole rushed through the gate ready to play. The Tanks, contemptuous of the impostors, scored in the first half and went ahead 7–0 until the West Side scored in the third quarter to draw within a point, 7–6. Fans from Ashland, Huntington, Wheeling, New Boston, Columbus, Mud Sock, and, of course, Portsmouth, all communities wishing to see the famous Tanks fall, went wild with joy. But Davies soon turned shouts into silence, running seventy yards for a touchdown; later the Tanks crossed the goal line again, posting a final score of 21–6. The Smoke House players on the sidelines, said Norris, had "symptoms of dying" as the Tanks drove through the West Side team. He pictured them, too, as envious schoolboys: "On the sidelines rested the Portsmouth aggregation like a grammar school team witnessing the clash of two college elevens." Some made spectacles of themselves. Dewey Adams, the "famous" halfback, was a "sick" man; Ackroyd cried like a baby; and Jimmy Taylor, the quarterback, polluted the air with language scarcely fit for the Sabbath.[59] The Smoke House men suffered financial distress, too. From the paid admissions of a little more than two thousand, the Tanks received $800, the West Siders $600, the Smoke House players nothing, not a "franc."

Reaction to the scene at Millbrook varied among sportswriters. In a bare-boned column, the *Times* reporter, probably Pete Minego, simply stated that the West Side Athletic Club had "represented" Portsmouth and had lost 21–6 in a "quiet and orderly" game and that thus the Tanks could glory in a double victory, one over Portsmouth, one over Columbus.[60]

At Ironton, the response, of course, was different. The *Irontonian* was more amused than angry. Ironton had to give Portsmouth credit for a "delightful surprise party." The Floodwallers had been charming hosts who had learned a lesson, namely that when planning a "surprise party for the Tanks, get the Canton Bulldogs."[61] A reporter for the *Register* affected casualness in his description of the game, saying little about the Smoke House subterfuge. He did chide the West Side men for insisting on playing 15-minute quarters—sometimes teams played 12½-minute quarters— in the belief that they could wear down the "sandlotters" from Ironton. They deserved to leave the field of battle "chastened and humiliated."[62] Facetiously, Burke reported that the crowd thought that the West Side men were really the Columbus Tigers because they were in a cage in the truck.

The editor of the *Register* was more irritated than his reporters were. For him, the fault lay not only with the Smoke House team but also with all of Portsmouth. He noted that the Smoke House fans had, in effect, paid over $1,000 for the joy of a victory and then had to slink away from Millbrook after the Tanks downed the Columbus team. Smoke House players, he wrote, should resent the implication of their inferiority in the fielding of a foreign team in their name. Above all, Portsmouth had acted in a reprehensible way: "The pulling of such an unsportsmanlike stunt as hiring an entire team to take the place of their regular team, has been heard of but few times in the annals of sport. Our sympathy Portsmouth is yours."[63]

The varying responses to the episode said much about the state of semiprofessional football in the region and probably in the nation. It was a game awaiting definition of standards. Anything seemed to go in the name of winning. Appropriately, at almost that moment, Stagg was scorning such shenanigans as the essence of professional football. At bedrock, the Smoke House men—the manager, the coach, and the players—had behaved irresponsibly. In their pretense of girding up for a great game, they had deceived the whole community, not just fans. Unfortunately, fans and sportswriters in Portsmouth—and elsewhere—often viewed loading up as a harmless caper. They should have questioned the integrity of the Smoke House players—and perhaps their own—for their willingness to condone such conduct. But local pride was a powerful force not easily dislodged by reality.

Had the West Side won at Millbrook, surely the Tanks, their fans, and local sportswriters would have vented their anger against Portsmouth for many days. Probably they would have called for a cessation of competition with Portsmouth teams. A victory and their share of the gate in hand, the Tanks made no real issue of the Smoke House deception. In fact, they had the best of both worlds. They could complain, but mildly, about the trickery of Portsmouth or affect forbearance in not complaining and then rejoice in a triumph over scoundrels. In good conscience, they could not have railed against the Smoke House men. Through a good part of the season, they had on their roster one Jones, who played in a masked helmet to conceal his identity; he was, in fact, Ralph Alvis, who was then playing for West Virginia Wesleyan.

For the Smoke House men, the fiasco at Millbrook truly concluded their season. Neither they nor their fans and local sportswriters called for more games, not even a Thanksgiving Day encounter. The team disappeared almost completely from the sports pages of the *Times* and *Sun*, eclipsed by collegiate football, the coming of the basketball season, and plain indifference. At five wins, two losses, and a tie, the Smoke House players had compiled their best record in history. But their victories came against ordinary elevens, their losses to the great rival up the river. No important individuals or institutions in the community spoke on their behalf. As they had been at the close of the season in 1922, they were a cipher in the community in 1923.

 A few days after their win over the Smoke House, the Tanks met the Harrisons of Cincinnati on Thanksgiving Day at Beechwood. Norris was certain that in the offing there was "never such a Turkey day game." The Harrisons, with a lineup featuring collegiate stars, had defeated the powerful Potters and Christ Church in Cincinnati. As two of the leading teams in Ohio, the Tanks and the Harrisons would be fighting for the championship of southern Ohio. All over Ironton, "barbers, bankers, bootleggers, butchers" were asking friends, "Are you going to the Harrison-Tank game?" Despite a heavy rainfall, about twenty-five hundred fans were at Beechwood. Their Tanks came on to the field clad in the jerseys of the Ironton High team because their own jerseys were virtually the same color as those of the Harrisons.[64] The Tanks, their "sterling interference" cutting down the Harrisons and their defense denying them even one first down, won handily 20–0. Thus they won the championship of southern Ohio and were in position to claim the semi-professional championship of Ohio. Good hosts, the Tanks entertained the Harrisons at the Elks Club after the game, gaining, perhaps, a wider entry into the realm of Cincinnati football. In fact, soon the Harrisons were proposing that they and the Tanks meet twice in 1924.

Their Tanks apparently completing the season, Burke and his editor lauded them as ornaments of the community.[65] Burke saw them as leaders in their class. Big league teams could scour the nation for good players and pay them a hundred to a thousand dollars a game. In contrast, the Tanks worked at their daily chores, practiced an hour or so two or three times a week, and then turned out to give the "greatest town" the "greatest sport in the world." They did not assert that they could beat high-priced teams, but no "combination of local players" could halt their "forward march." They had become a big business in the city, had a substantial amount of money in their treasury ready for distribution to themselves, and had plans to make the next season even better. The community could ask no more of them, but they might ask more of the community.

Even as the Tanks had apparently concluded their season, Lambert was discussing terms for another game against the Boosters with their managers, Dug Freutel and

Home and Away

Roy Maners. By telegrams, telephones, and personal "pow wows," they negotiated questions on the split, the site, and a fourth game. Finally, they agreed to play at Ironton and to share the gate fifty-fifty.[66] Signifying the import of the game, they selected Hamilton and Eichenlaub, "high class" officials, to serve respectively as umpire and referee.

Through the few days preceding the game, sportswriters in both communities turned out column after column speculating on the game. All believed the contest would decide the championship of the Tri-State, and all predicted that one of the largest crowds in the history of Beechwood would be in attendance—that the Tanks might have to erect temporary bleachers to accommodate spectators. They gave their primary attention, though, to loading up, having heard rumors about new stars joining the teams. The "West Virginians," said a writer for the *Register*, "have just about assembled all the football brethren they could secure."[67] Maners, though, repeatedly insisted that the Boosters were not loading up. Similarly, Davies and Brooks were fending off stories about the Tanks "taking on new strength" and "loading to the gills." According to Burke, Ironton businessmen had offered Davies large sums to acquire new men, but he had refused to accept their money. Burke went on to argue that teams engaged in loading up could not rightfully claim victories for the community. If a community supported such a practice, it might as well call in an entire team from Chicago or Canton. Besides, a win obtained by loading up went to individuals, not to a team. Fortunately, he explained, the Tanks were willing to use only "home talent" from Ironton and Ashland.[68]

On Sunday morning of the "great" game, the *Irontonian* published profiles of the Tanks, twenty in all.[69] The *Irontonian* and the *Register* had often run stories briefly listing men on the Tanks roster, usually citing their collegiate experience, if any. But seldom did such lists provide any information on players besides their capabilities. The profiles or vignettes that the *Irontonian* set forth, a kind of inventory of the players' nicknames, their characteristic play, their education, full-time occupations, and their experience in football, suggested at once the significance of the game against the Boosters and the Tanks' increasingly close relationship with the community. The use of nicknames, perhaps more than any other element of personal definition, meant that players were integrated into the informal life of the community, that they did not stand apart from the give-and-take of everyday social intercourse.

Nearly all the Tanks bore homely appellations, some derived from given names or surnames, some from physical traits, some from style of play or behavior. A fan walking in downtown Ironton might say hello to "Bill," "Doc," "Concrete," "Dutch," "Ash," "Big Boy," "Poet," "Jack," "Diner," "Hans," "Kid," or "Hank." Eight had played football at a college or university, and twelve had played only in high school, eleven at Ironton High or at high schools in nearby communities. One had played football while in military service, two for the Lombards, one for the Irish Town Rags. They worked in factories and foundries in the city, as municipal employees, for the two railroads coming into the city, and as tradesmen.

The Tanks appeared for the battle a few hours after the article came out. A driving rain had turned the field at Beechwood into a "sea of yellow mud." The crowd ran close to two thousand, a good number for many games but far short of expectations. The fans "huddled together in the bleachers like wet chickens roosting in a tree top."[70] In the crowd, the feathers on their hats drooping, were many women. At least the Tanks fans could happily endure the rain. Their Tanks, seemingly oblivious to the weather, "outgeneraled, out classed, and out fought" the Boosters, inflicting a "humiliating" defeat on them, 26–0. A "splendid array of college stars" playing for the Boosters—for some reason Martin remained in Morgantown—could make only two first downs. Davies ran a punt for fifty yards for a touchdown. Had the teams played fifteen-minute quarters instead of the shorter ones, the margin might have been even greater.

Thus the Tanks gained revenge for the earlier defeat and captured, at least in print, the semiprofessional championship of the Ohio Valley and, argued a few writers, the championship of the state. Ridgley, though believing that Martin might have made a difference, described the Tanks as the greatest team in the history of the Ohio Valley.[71] The "splendid array" of Boosters players did not include any of the men named in the reports about loading up. At Portsmouth the *Times* attributed the Boosters' resounding defeat to the absence of several stars who had played in the second game; the Boosters had taken a "home" team to Ironton.[72] But the lineups for the Boosters for the two games, except for Martin, were substantially the same.

All was ending well for the Tanks. They had won ten games and lost one, and that one had been avenged. With real justification, except for defining the boundaries, they claimed two regional championships; with less reason, ignoring teams in northern Ohio, their partisans called them champions of the state. Ironton could be justly proud of them, declared the editor of the *Register*.[73] They found the community willing to support an inter-squad game to raise money for Nate Ball, who was vainly undergoing treatment in New Mexico for tuberculosis; evidently they collected several hundred dollars for him. The Chamber of Commerce gave them a testimonial dinner at the Marting Hotel at which an officer of the Chamber asserted that they were worth $100,000 annually to Ironton

Home and Away

in advertising.[74] Responding to the praise, Davies told the diners that the team would be even better in 1924. Best of all, with over $6,000 in the treasury, Lambert was able to give each player a check for $290 just before Christmas.[75] Thus they earned on average $26 dollars a game; at about that time, players for the metropolitan NFL were making far more, the Bears from $100 to $200 a game.[76]

Unlike the Smoke House, the Tanks had strengthened their position in the community in 1923, eliciting greater support from local businessman and enlisting the full-throated advocacy of the local press. Yet eventually they might pay a price for popularity. They were an independent, self-governing body ruling their own roost, but they had welcomed into their yard outside interests, which, calling them an advertising instrument for the community, might exercise increasing control over them. They had also widened the scope of their schedule in playing Columbus and Cincinnati elevens and wanted to go further afield in the state. Such expansive notions could be exhilarating but beyond their means, a Pandora's box of trouble.

5

He Must Choose

THE SEASONS OF 1924 AND 1925 saw continuity and marked change in the semiprofessional football of the Tri-State. Despite playing a schedule increasingly made up of big-city teams and a controversial change in their organization, the Tanks continued their winning ways. More than ever, they became the common property of the community, and yet their kinship with it nearly came asunder in 1925. And their very success threatened their independence and integrity. The Smoke House men unfortunately continued their downward course toward the demise of their team. At Ashland, a semiprofessional club drawing support from a treasury of iron began play in 1925, imposing change in the character of competition in the Ohio Valley.

At the opening of the season in 1924, the Tanks appeared ready for vaulting success. No financial crises loomed on the horizon. The community was eagerly awaiting kickoffs at Beechwood. Saying that the city was weary of baseball, Norris declared that "Ironton is strictly a football town and that is a fact."[1] He was skeptical about whether the Ironton High School Tigers, a losing team in 1923, could satisfy the fans' passion for football and viewed the Tanks as the team for the community, perhaps the best of its kind in the state. Several good recruits—Virgil Pope, Terry Snowday, Roger Snowday, Albert Zelt, and Walter Kurthalz, all but Pope residents of Ashland, intended to join the team. Old and new men alike would be suiting up in new jerseys, sweatshirts, and socks. Numbered and bright red, the jerseys were the "best obtainable"; the sweat shirts were gray with TANKS lettered on the back.

Returning to the Tanks as their captain and coach, Davies summoned candidates for the team to practices. He reaffirmed old rules of compulsory attendance and began working on a "diversified" offense.[2] Almost immediately he effected one cut among the candidates that won endorsement in the community. When Kenneth "Dum-Dum" Koerper, an outstanding halfback at Ironton high who was a senior there, came out for the team, Davies persuaded him to stay in high school and play for him there. Davies had to prepare the Tanks for stiff competition. Lambert was working on a schedule that could call on them to play several strong teams from Cincinnati, Columbus, Akron, and Louisville, as well as the Smoke House and the Boosters. He was continuing his schedule of 1923 designed to eliminate teams from the smaller communities to the north of Ironton and play in their stead big city teams. The small-town teams did not draw well, fans complained about soft touches in the schedule, and victories over a Columbus or Cincinnati team might give the Tanks greater repute in the state.

Lambert wished to enhance the prestige of his team by scheduling, and across the river in Ashland a sportswriter was seeking a share of it for his city. Just before the Tanks opened play, George Hatcher, a voluble columnist for the *Ashland Independent,* proposed (or announced) an appellate hijacking of the Tanks. According to Hatcher, at a meeting of the Tanks, the team had decided to use the name Ashland-Ironton Tanks. He offered apparent grounds for his report in noting that half of the squad attending the meeting were men from Ashland and that many Tanks fans at Beechwood were from Ashland.[3] Learning of the change, fans in Ashland, said Hatcher, were enthusiastic, their interest reaching a "boiling point." The Tanks immediately disavowed Hatcher's report. They acknowledged that the proposal had been aired at a recent meeting but insisted that they had not altered their name.[4] Hatcher might infer from their statement that they were conducting all business affairs under the name "Ironton Tanks" as informal recognition of Ashland's support of the team. And they threw a bone of sorts to Ashland when later they proclaimed their game against the Louisville Brecks to be "Ashland Day." Well into November Hatcher called the Tanks the Ashland-Ironton Tanks. Drumming up no

He Must Choose

support in Ashland or Ironton for the name, he ceased its use, referring to the Tanks simply as the Ironton Tanks.

The Tanks began play in a practice game with the Panthers, a "lightweight" team in the city. About five hundred fans watched them defeat the juniors, coming away from the game convinced that prospects were good for the Tanks. They opened their real season at Beechwood against the Jungle Imps in a continuation, in a sense, of their rivalry with the West Side team, many West Side players having come over to the Imps resolved to dissolve the "bitter dregs" of defeats at the Tanks' hands. Expecting a large crowd and hearing that many paying fans were complaining about "gate crashers," Lambert announced that the Tanks would take stern measures against people who used ladders and props to obtain an "overland route" to the game.[5] They intended to appoint special policemen to seize such offenders, who would have to appear in mayor's court the next day and pay a fine of $27.80. At the "shrill" note of the referee's whistle, fans would see, wrote a reporter, one of the most "spectacular" games ever played in Ohio. Reality was quite different.. A steady rain kept fence climbers at home and held the crowd down to about a thousand; the game was hardly exciting, and the Tanks easily beat the Imps 25–6.

Soon after the game, the Tanks met to decide cuts of candidates. It was a democratic yet closed process. The players had already selected a committee of six players, including Davies, who themselves theoretically could be cut, that recommended retention of eighteen men and Lambert as manager. The Tanks unanimously ratified the committee's men.

Their roster determined for the moment, the Tanks next met the one small-town eleven on their schedule, the Murray City Tigers. Murray City, the name belying its size, was a small town near Athens, its population about fifteen hundred in 1920. The community, Norris explained, was a typical mining town in the hills of Hocking County. The Tigers were largely former Ohio Conference "stars" living in Logan, Wellston, Nelsonville, and Athens who were working for mining companies. In 1923, seeking a game with them, Lambert had offered them a "sum of money that sounded and looked similar to the cost for the erection of the Russell-Ironton bridge but the miners were not in a money mood, as the mines had been running for some time without a strike being declared and consequently they refused the offer." But now they had signed a contract, which, though undisclosed, was for enough "gold to make King Midas look like a piker."[6]

As they did with nearly all of the Tanks' opponents coming to Beechwood, local sportswriters portrayed the Tigers as a strong team. They were close to the mark. Allegedly using players from Ohio State, Ohio University, and Washington and Lee—

Home and Away

and even Virgil Pope, who had momentarily left the Tanks—whose names did not appear on their eligibility list, the Tigers subjected the Tanks to a "gruesome struggle" before losing 7–0.[7]

The Tanks could look at their victory over the Tigers as satisfying only in their record of wins and losses, and their fans feared that it portended a defeat against the Louisville Brecks, who were coming next to Beechwood. One of the "big-city" elevens that Lambert was eager to schedule, the Brecks had entered the NFL in 1922 but had lost all six games that they played against league teams in two years. Though dropping out of the league in 1924, the Brecks, with a line averaging 190 pounds, seemed to be a rugged opponent. Genuinely fearing the Brecks, the Tanks welcomed Virgil Pope back to their ranks and looked around unsuccessfully for other men. A good crowd—twenty-seven hundred—was at once disappointed and pleased by the game. Their Tanks were great, but the "haughty and proud" Brecks proved to be a weak team, not getting even one first down and losing 31–0. Several "conscientious objectors" to the easy victory reported that the Tanks had not met the real Brecks—they were playing at Frankfort, Kentucky. Terry Snowday, who knew several Brecks, probably from his days at Centre, assured his teammates that they had played the "real" Brecks. But in its account of the game, the *Louisville Courier-Journal* named seven starters who did not make the trip to Ironton and remarked that their "absence" had handicapped the Brecks.[8]

Playing again at Beechwood, the Tanks met the Potters of Cincinnati, named after their sponsor, the Potter Shoe Company. The roster of the Potters, the champions of the Greater Cincinnati league, included nearly all the men who had played for Xavier University of Cincinnati in 1922, a team that had lost but one game that year. Writing to Lambert, Frank Lane, president of the Cincinnati league and prominent referee, said that fourteen Potters came from the Xavier squad. Among them were Herb Davis, Yabby Cushing, and Joe Linneman, all good backs, and "Pup" McWhorter, a giant tackle. After officiating the Tanks' game with the Brecks, Lane reiterated his warning: the Potters would prove a formidable foe. Evidently Cushing, the Potters' quarterback and coach, was certain of a victory for his eleven. He told an unidentified resident of Ironton that his teammates were eager to meet the Tanks —he had heard of their powers—and that they would give them the same drubbing that they had been administering to teams in Cincinnati.[9] Cushing's optimism or boasting did not alarm Tanks fans, who, attending a good Tanks practice, were confident of victory.

A "large delegation" of fans was coming from Cincinnati, along with contingents from Portsmouth, Ashland, Wellston, and elsewhere, and Ironton scribes anticipated seeing a capacity crowd at Beechwood. About thirty-five hundred attended the game, twenty-five hundred paying their way inside the fence, a thousand or so perching on treetops, ladders, and sheds outside the fence.[10] Fans "rode" a guard at the lower end of the park, and a scuffle broke out involving an armed youth. On the field, Lane and fellow officials maintained order. A "terrific battle" ensued between the "foremost" elevens of Ohio. The Tanks, scoring on two passes from Davies to Terry Snowday, won 14–0. The *Cincinnati Enquirer* reported the score but offered no comment on the game.

Continuing their run against urban teams, the Tanks, still at Beechwood, next played the Akron Silents or Mutes, one of the more unusual semiprofessional squads in Ohio. Organized in 1915 as a lightweight team, the Silents were deaf mutes working for the Goodyear Tire and Rubber Company. Many of them played at Gallaudet College, the school for the deaf in Washington, D.C.[11] Faring poorly in their early years but improving rapidly, the Silents claimed the semiprofessional championship of Ohio in 1918 but lost the championship of Akron to the Akron Pros, champions of the American Professional Football Association in 1920. From 1918 through 1922, they won forty-eight games and lost four. In 1921 they began to use a few speaking and hearing players, but their best player, a pile-driving runner, was a mute, Louis Seinenshon. He presented an unusual sight calling signals. With his back to the opposition and his teammates gathered in front of him in a huddle, he pointed to the plays printed on his pants. The Silents claimed the semiprofessional championship in 1922 but again lost the municipal title to the Pros. They played well in 1923 but once again fell to the Pros in the game deciding the championship of Akron.

Supposedly Lambert had tried for several years to book the Silents and finally did so in 1924—but at a price: he had to offer them a "heavy" guarantee, far more than he usually gave visitors. Lambert raised the price of tickets slightly to cover the increased expense. The *Irontonian* endorsed his decision, saying that "after all, the Tanks are not Manager Lambert's team, but belong to . . . Ironton and it is up to the fans to get the crowds out. . . . A very heavy guarantee is promised Akron and a large attendance is necessary to keep the Tanks above board on their receipts."[12] Whatever the guarantee, the Tanks deemed it worthwhile. They expected the game to draw well, and, according to Lambert and the *Irontonian,* the contest gave the Tanks the opportunity to win the semiprofessional championship of the state. That was a wild stretch of the imagination. Faltering, the Silents were in the middle of a losing season and would finish it with but three victories out of ten games. Managers, sportswriters, and other boosters were never at a loss in discovering championships to be won.

Home and Away

As the encounter neared, Lambert and the scribes whetted the interest of fans with incidental comments on preparations for play. The Silents would arrive on Saturday, accompanied by coaches, a trainer, and an umpire proficient in sign language. Coming to Beechwood was a crowd of over three thousand; about eighteen hundred bought tickets, and an estimated two thousand viewed the game from stepladders, treetops, and other vantage points. They saw a bitterly fought contest, one of the "brilliant" battles of the century. The teams fought like "savage tigers" through three scoreless quarters, and then the Tanks broke through in the fourth quarter, scoring three touchdowns for a 19–0 victory. Angered over some rough play, Terry Snowday shouted at the mutes in their "own language"—whatever that was. Ignoring the Silents' record and the fact that the season was at its midpoint, the *Irontonian* and *Register* ran headlines in their sports pages proclaiming the Tanks state champions.[13] But the *Akron Beacon-Journal* attached no such significance to the victory, summarizing the game in a sentence or two.[14]

Though cutting a wide swath through the big-city teams, the Tanks still had games against elevens in their backyard that could dim the luster of victories. The Boosters, losers of but one game, were waiting for them at League Park, eager for revenge for their loss in the final game of 1923 and believing that a win would give them a leg up on the Tri-State crown. As usual, there were rumors of the teams loading up, but neither eleven used new men. Tanks fans hoped the report that Homer Martin might not play would prove untrue, thus denying the Boosters an alibi when they lost. Before a crowd estimated at three thousand, fifteen hundred reportedly from Ironton, the Tanks, supposedly showing the effects of the battle with the Silents, defeated the Boosters 6–0. A pass from Davies to Terry Snowday accounted for the winning touchdown with three minutes to play.

One rival in the valley vanquished, the Tanks turned their attention again to the Smoke House. Controversies and surprises had attended nearly all the recent games between the two squads, and few observers would have dared contemplate anything else in the renewal of the rivalry.

The Smoke House men of 1924, nearly all from the squad of 1923, began their season's practice and play with virtually no fanfare. Opening their season against the Wellston Eagles at Wellston, the Smoke House, with Jake Pfau smashing into the heavier Eagles line, won 7–6. Their schedule a hand-me-down affair at the outset, the Smoke House men did not play for two weeks, meeting the Eagles again, this time at Millbrook. Their play apparently improved, for they defeated the Eagles 27–0. Their next game at Millbrook against the

Imps gave local fans an opportunity to assess their strength relative to the Tanks, who had already defeated the Imps 25–6. The Smoke House players expected to face a strong team with many stars, especially Moses Solomon, the Imps' coach and best running back—one of the fastest players in the state. They gave him top billing in a quarter-page advertisement for the game in the *Times*.[15] Solomon lived up to his reputation, running, passing, and punting the Imps to a victory 10–0. Another Columbus team, the Rochester Clothiers, then came to Millbrook. The Smoke House fared no better, a "revamped" lineup of some sort losing 23–6 to the "light but fast" Clothiers.

The outlook was not good for the Smoke House men when they met the Tanks early in November at Beechwood. They had lost two of four games, one to an eleven that the Tanks had already defeated easily, and, owing partly to injuries, were thrashing around in an attempt to shape a lineup capable of better play. The Tanks, showing their usual strength, were undefeated in seven games. Believing that the Smoke House was a mediocre team, they anticipated a fairly easy win. They knew, though, that the Smoke House managers and coach were making a "desperate" effort to strengthen their team.[16] Reportedly several men from Columbus teams, among them Solomon, and two or three players from the Boosters might appear in the Smoke House lineup. Though not complaining about the apparent loading up, the *Irontonian* advised the Smoke House not to drive a moving van onto the field with a new team. The several hundred Smoke House fans had no vans to rely on and little to cheer about. With Davies leading the way, the Tanks overwhelmed the Smoke House 44–0. At least two men in the starting lineup for the Smoke House had recently joined the team. One was Solomon, who passed well occasionally but not enough to score on the Tanks. The Smoke House men stopped the Tanks in the opening minutes but then faded, revealing a "woeful lack of stamina" and practice, said the *Times*. A disappointed Portsmouth crowd enjoyed a moment of comic relief when one of their number, M. M. Chilton, tried to cheer his "loudest," only to send his "store teeth" flying from his mouth; thereafter, he feared opening his mouth wide enough to sound a slight cheer.[17]

The Tanks, their regional rivals turned aside for the moment, looked to their most important game in years—a return contest with the Potters at Redland Field in Cincinnati. Beyond the nearby communities, they had not developed any continuing and visceral competition. Their games with the Columbus West Siders—in their own uniforms and Smoke House attire—had precipitated sharp exchanges among sportswriters, but no continuing competition

Home and Away

between the teams had ensued. Their rivalry with the Potters became another matter. For three years, they met the Cincinnati team in hotly contested games, each distinctive in its own way, and then played its successor for two years. Probably better than any other game, the second one in 1924 gave the rivalry viability. Obviously the Potters welcomed a return game at home as an opportunity to even the score with the Tanks. For the Tanks, a game played in Cincinnati before a large and presumably unfriendly crowd, their first foray into a large urban center, offered a chance to demonstrate their intrinsic worth, to prove that they were not just a small-town team living off sympathetic referees.

Before the Tanks could give their full attention to the Potters, they had to deal with a potentially divisive issue touching on the very nature of a small-town team attempting to compete in a wider world. The Tanks had come out of the game with the Smoke House with several players injured, including the peerless Davies and Snowday. At that point Solomon let Lambert know that he was willing to play for the Tanks—at $100 a game for their three remaining games of the season.[18] Lambert floated the proposal among the Tanks and several businessmen. A few players supported it, and three businessmen began soliciting others for money to pay Solomon. But then several players, among them Davies, objected to calling in Solomon. Fans were divided on the question. Some thought that it was unfair to pay Solomon more than the Tanks were then receiving; others saw nothing wrong in seeking adequate substitutes for injured players. At mid-week, the Tanks met to discuss the question. Speaking for the "great majority" of them, a "prominent" Tank wrote to the *Irontonian* setting forth their views, a statement of local pride. The players, he said, appreciated the generous support given them by fans, who, nonetheless, should accept Davies's decisions about needing new players. Preferential treatment of Solomon would damage the team's spirit. At the suggestion that the Tanks players contribute a portion of their pay to Solomon, he pointed out that their refusal to do so was hardly selfish, as some fans had intimated, considering that Solomon would receive more than they had in the entire season of 1923. If fans were eager to pay him a hundred dollars a game, should not Poole, Brooks, Davies, and Snowday receive the same amount? Besides, the Tanks would continue to win without outside help, and it would be better to win without Solomon than with him. Despite their injuries, they intended to defeat the Potters. The Tanks voted down the proposal to hire an "out-of-town" player and proceeded to engage in the "snappiest" practice of the year.[19]

Responding to the "prominent" player's arguments, a "100 Per Cent Booster" wrote to the *Register* arguing a less particularistic view but one that, if acted on, could threaten the independence and local character of the Tanks.[20] "Booster," though

He Must Choose

questioning whether the Tanks were as strong as they thought they were, conceded that they were an outstanding eleven whose morale could be damaged if they had to use out-of-town players. But they belonged to the community, which had supported them and now required assurance of continued success. They had become common property and should accept, if necessary to winning, the employment of outsiders. Moreover, the Tanks might find that more victories meant more money for them. It was in their own interest and that of the community to employ new men as necessary. They thus could remain a strong force for advertising the city.

Holding their ground, the Tanks entrained for Cincinnati on the Chesapeake and Ohio without Solomon. Lambert, attentive to the press, had as his guests on a special car Burke, Hatcher, and Earl Mittendorf of the *Irontonian*. About five hundred fans supposedly made the first run to Cincinnati for any community to a semi-professional football game there. The crowd of about thirty-three hundred, "excited" and "yelling," saw a "thrilling" contest. After a scoreless first half, Davies directed the Tanks to the only touchdown of the game, giving them the victory 7–3. All was right in the Tanks' world after the game: they had won a big game in a big city; they had played in the first semiprofessional game that Cincinnatians enjoyed to the limit; and the Potters had hosted them royally, giving them a sumptuous dinner at a downtown hotel after the game. Their record, moreover, remained unsullied at nine wins and no losses; their goal line had been crossed but once. They could easily afford to ignore injuries suffered during the fray.[21]

The Tanks then continued unbeaten, defeating a stubborn Covington Catholic Athletic Club 12–0 at Beechwood. They would face more of the good running and passing of the Covington captain, Virgil Perry, in another uniform. Now the Tanks had to fend off the Boosters in a Thanksgiving Day game at Beechwood. Having won all their games since their loss to the Tanks, the Boosters believed that a win would give them a claim to the Tri-State championship. They entered the game with several new players, among them Ken Houser, who had been playing with the Cleveland Bulldogs, NFL champions in their first year in the league. Ridgley believed that they had a better than even shot at beating the Tanks, but the *Irontonian* greatly exaggerated his optimism in saying that "according to friend Duke, who lives in the first house on the right of Alibi Street, there will not be enough of the Tanks left to tell the sad tale after Houser gets through with them." The Tanks could hardly have complained about the Boosters' loading up. Injuries hobbling Snowday and hampering one or two linemen, the Tanks called in Lingrell "Sonny" Winters, who had been playing for the Columbus Tigers, to shore up the backfield and Andy Nemecek, a burly tackle from Ohio State, to strengthen the line.

Home and Away

With a crowd of twenty-six hundred on hand, the Tanks mounted a "relentless" attack, holding the Boosters to one first down and defeating them 21–0. The *Irontonian* covered the game in detail in a front-page story comparing the Tanks with Leonidas and his warriors at Thermopylae.[22] Brooks and Pope "strutted" their stuff, and Winters was never better. But Houser was a disappointment. Ridgley had no doubt that: the Tanks were the better team. He singled out Brooks for praise, describing him as "250 pounds of bone, muscle and football brass."[23]

Once again the Tanks talked of their right to claim mythical titles in the Tri-State, southern Ohio, and the state. Any number of their fans in Ashland, though, were calling on them to meet the Middletown Armcos, then undefeated in their first season of play, to affirm a state championship. Lambert took no steps to do so. Instead, at their overtures, he was talking to the Cleveland Bulldogs, the champions of professional football in the nation and of the NFL, about a game in Ironton. Once the Tanks again defeated the Smoke House, to complete the season undefeated, he would continue negotiations with the Bulldogs.

The Smoke House men appeared to be no threat to the Tanks' perfect season. A few weeks earlier, the Tanks had decisively beaten them, and since then they had played no games and seemed to be moribund. Nonetheless, the Tanks and their fans were wary, knowing that the Smoke House might load up in a wholesale way. And indeed, on the eve of the game, the *Irontonian* reported the prospect of the Tanks facing an "imported" team using the Smoke House name.[24] Street talk had it that they had called in either the West Side eleven or the Columbus Wagner-Pirates. They had already secured the services of the Middletown Armcos, said one man. The rumor mill ground exceeding fine. Another report stated that the Tanks would meet a "galaxy" of stars, but did not say what team would "ride forth to the field in a closed moving van."[25] The *Sun* openly acknowledged that the Smoke House players had reinforced themselves but pointed out that the Tanks intended to use new players Winters and Nemecek. In a large advertisement in the *Sun*, the Smoke House listed two players from the Columbus Tigers of the NFL who would play for them.

The Tanks and the Smoke House met at Millbrook on a cold, dreary day, with snow covering the field. The crowd was not large, paid admissions numbering but 624. The field was wet and slippery with snow, and players could not run and cut as usual. Neither team could move the ball under such conditions, and the result was a scoreless tie devoid of any "exciting" plays. According to the *Times,* both teams were "slightly loaded," the Smoke House with Virgil Pope and Layne Tynes, the Tanks with Winters and Nemecek. At least six players in the starting lineup for the Smoke

House were not in it for the first game with the Tanks, but three had played previously for the team. Probably the outstanding "imported" player for Portsmouth was Tynes, a halfback from the University of Texas. Winters and Nemecek had played for the Tanks against the Boosters.[26]

Tanks fans did not attribute the tie to a strengthened Smoke House eleven. In their view, the Tanks had taken the game as a matter of course and had thus played in a "mediocre" way, discouraged by the deplorable playing conditions. Charles Collett, editor of the *Ironton News,* would write later that "the boys just didn't put out in an attempt to win." The *Times* saw the tie as a "shock" and a "moral victory" for the Smoke House against an aggregation of well-paid collegiate stars who looked like "ordinary" football players. Certainly the Tanks suffered a shock, the tie marring their otherwise perfect record. Never again would they come as close as they did in 1924 to an all-winning season. The game did little for the Tanks' treasury; out of their share of net receipts, the Tanks received slightly over $100.

The Cleveland Bulldogs continued to call on Lambert for a game, offering to play at Ironton for a "modest" share of the gate. Lambert and Guy Chamberlain, coach of the Bulldogs, nearly reached an agreement for a game, but the Tanks turned it down, saying that the weather could be inclement, that they had broken training, and that they could not "work up the spirit" for a game.[27] The Bulldogs then arranged a game with the Boosters at Huntington. Brooks, Poole, and Harry Pope joined the Boosters for the fray but could not spare them a trouncing, 28–0. By their rebuff of the Bulldogs, perhaps the Tanks and the community implied that they had no wish to enter the NFL, which was still struggling to gain a foothold in the national sporting scene.

Their season ended at eleven wins and a tie, the Tanks basked in the sunshine of praise and material rewards. The *Register* discerned in them uniqueness that set them apart from other professional teams: "They do not bind together like a professional team, but have a certain collegiate spirit . . . that makes them so powerful."[28] They would not be content, though, to stand on their record of 1924; they intended to be "bigger and better" in 1925, infused with fresh "young blood." They gloried in several banquets given in their honor. Ethel Murdock, their leading fan among women in the community, served them a special turkey dinner. And all received a payment of $350 for their play for the year—about $30 a game.

The Smoke House men, though savoring their surprising performance against the Tanks, were in shambles. They finished the season with an abbreviated schedule, their record at two wins, three losses, and one tie. Their managerial direction, if any existed, was hardly at work. They had become ghosts in the *Sun* and *Times,* shadows and sighs but with no substance in the sports pages. Yet there were people in Portsmouth—five hundred or so had gone to Ironton for a game—willing to be loyal to a semiprofessional team in the city. But it would have to do more than show up occasionally on the gridiron and win now and then to command support.

 As the Ironton Tanks worked their way to the snowy heights and the Portsmouth Smoke House languished, at Ashland semiprofessional football teams appeared sporadically, playing a year or so and then disappearing, seldom attracting much interest inside or outside the community. The All-Champions, the Playfair, the Tigers, and the Bulldogs all had come and gone, none with great success or strong support from the community.[29] Certainly, though, the residents of Ashland were interested in football; they gave solid support to the local high school team, the Tomcats.

Early in the 1924 season, Hatcher of the *Independent* had failed in a quixotic bid to transform the Tanks into an eleven for the city. But he did not wait long for a team to bear Ashland's name. That team, though, was not deeply rooted in the community. It was more nearly the product of industrial enterprise. In 1921 the American Rolling Mill Company purchased the Ashland Iron and Mining Company, which had been operating steelmaking facilities in the city.[30] Armco was a producer of specialty steels, its headquarters and principal mill at Middletown, Ohio. Installing a revolutionary continuous mill at the site, the company shortly had two thousand workers on its payroll, more than three thousand at the end of the decade.

When it came to Ashland, Armco, a pioneer in welfare capitalism, had a policy in place, "Armco Policies," for cooperating with employees in the organization of medical, social, educational, and recreational programs. Using the Employees Mutual Association as a conduit to workers, the company sponsored baseball, basketball, and football teams. At Middletown in 1924, the association created a football team, the Armco Blues, which did quite well that year. Pushed by Russell Smith, a football enthusiast from Canton and superintendent of the mill, the association in Ashland decided to organize a team for play in 1925. For the general athletic program, employees contributed seventy-five cents a month to the association, the company a dollar for each employee. Using persuasion to the point of coercion, foremen sold season tickets to workers for nine dollars, the cost to be deducted from their paychecks. At one point the selling of tickets became the subject of dispute. Nevertheless, the estimated budget for the football team eventually reached $50,000.[31]

R. T. Caldwell, a front office executive, and Smith, who became its manager, built the team. A hard-drinking man with a good command of four-letter words,

He Must Choose

Smith wanted the Armcos to become a "big-time" team. The Armco men had various ways, used separately or together, of creating a team. They could recruit players from the community and work force at the Ashland mill or from colleges and other semiprofessional teams in the region. They could offer prospective players employment with the company in blue- and white-collar positions. Obviously the Armcos possessed advantages in recruiting over other semiprofessional clubs.

For a moment they seemed to have a ready-made team at hand. Shorty Davies, evidently speaking for himself and several other Tanks who suddenly had become dissatisfied with their financial support in Ironton, came to them offering to move the Tanks to Ashland as the Armco Tanks.[32] Ashland was abuzz at the news, said Hatcher:

> Rumors were current in Ashland today that the famous Ironton Tanks football team will be known as "Ashland Armco Tanks" when the Big Red squad dons its gridiron togs for another campaign four weeks hence. It is said that the local Armco Association opened negotiations with "Shorty" Davies, who has captained the Tanks for many seasons, to purchase the entire club. The reports could not be confirmed this morning, however. John McNeal, Secretary and Treasurer of the Armco Association told the Independent this afternoon that he preferred not to make a statement, but promised that definite details of the matter will be announced within the next few days.[33]

The Armco men, the community soon learned, balked at the Tanks' price—$1,200 a game, the money to be divided equally among fifteen players. Davies accepted their offer to become the Armco coach at $115 a game, and at least three Tanks—Poole, Harry Pope, and Bill Wardaman—agreed to play in Ashland. But the greater part of the Tanks decided to remain in Ironton.

At the same time, the association announced that it would begin constructing a baseball and football park near the Armco mill on the west side of the city. Building the park depended on whether the association would organize a team for 1925 so contractors did not break ground until early September. The association modeled the park, to cost $25,000, after Redland Field and hired Mattie Schwab, the groundskeeper there, to lay out the fields.[34] All fans in the grandstand, seating about two thousand people, would have an "excellent" view. Outside the field would be six diamonds for "playground ball," a quarter-mile running track, and parking space for eight hundred automobiles. Besides using the park for employees, the association, obviously wishing to enhance its reputation in the community, intended to let the local high school teams use it.

Home and Away

 Davies called for a meeting of candidates for the Armco team just as work on the park began, and all seemed to augur well for what Hatcher called the "most forward step" taken in years in the athletic life of the community. But trouble brewed almost at the moment that Davies became the Armco coach. Davies, of course, was the center of the problem. An icon in Ironton until then, he immediately became the subject of debate there, with fans disputing two interrelated questions: out of loyalty to the community and the team, should he have accepted the Armco offer, and could he retain his position as athletic director and coach at Ironton High School while coaching a rival team of the Tanks in another community?

Fans split into two camps on the abstract question of loyalty, arguing their case heatedly on street corners, in poolrooms, and elsewhere. One, composed of a "host of friends," contended that Davies, who had been "voting for some time," was acting sensibly and honorably in going over to Ashland, the other that he should remain a Tank in Ironton regardless of financial considerations.[35] Davies argued that he was not indispensable to the Tanks and that he wished them well. Moreover, he had given "value received" to the Tanks, and now he could earn as much in one year with the Armcos as he had in five years of unstinting service to the Tanks. Not one other member of the Tanks, he insisted, would have turned the Armco berth down. His friends seconded his arguments and noted that local fans had not always given him and the Tanks "staunch" support. Shorty, they said, ought to make the most of his abilities. Besides, the "kickers" were men in the "gambling corps" who sustained the Tanks only when they won and put money in their dirty pockets and always knocked them when they lost.

Adversaries of Davies portrayed him as acting precipitously and having received as much from the community as he had given it. He ought to remain with the Tanks, they argued, out of loyalty to the community and his friends. More concretely, they raised what became the central issue. He had been given his post at the high school because of his ability as a football player. He had an "easy" position there, and taxpayers should not pay his salary—$2,000 a year—if he represented another city in sports. If he remained with the Tanks, receiving a divvy from their concession stand at Beechwood, he would earn as much as he could at Ashland. They hinted darkly that his position at the high school was in jeopardy. Had he acted fairly, he would have given Ironton an opportunity to meet or better, somehow, his offer from Armco. They contended, too, that "knockers" in Ashland had tried for some time to "bust up" the Tanks and were now using Davies to that end. Again in a veiled threat to strip him of his director's position, they called on Armco to "take care" of Davies for the entire year. In response, adherents of Davies asserted that the school would have to pay a successor as much or more than he had received. Was it right, they asked, to give an Ironton boy the gate in favor of an outsider—they already had some inkling who might take his position.

Davies did not hear empty talk when his detractors linked his employment as athletic director to his part-time berth as coach of the Armcos. The nexus was the vacated coach's position with the Tanks. Learning of Davies's resignation as their coach, the Tanks initiated a discussion about his position with Sonny Winters, the speedy halfback who had played several games with the Tanks in 1923 and 1924. Winters was then teaching in a school near Columbus and was playing for the Columbus Tigers. He was willing to come to Ironton as the Tanks' coach and as a player under certain conditions; he had to receive a share of the Tanks' gate or a specific salary for the season, and he had to have the position as athletic director at the high school. The Tanks were willing to satisfy his demands, and if Davies resigned the directorship, the Board of Education was willing to appoint Winters to that position. But Davies had refused to yield the post; thus the board had to find some way to "create" a vacancy in the position.

Coloring and complicating the impasse was the matter of the Tanks' standing in the community. As the season of 1925 approached, apparently some Tanks and fans were questioning whether Ironton really was able and willing to support the team. Rumors throughout the city had it that some veteran Tanks, apprehensive about the financial support that the community would give them, would not play for the Tanks in 1925. Davies's talk with the Armcos and his subsequent defection to them, along with that of the three players, manifested and heightened fans' and players' concern. Fans still felt anxiety even though most of the Tanks decided against going to Ashland and reports hinted that Lambert was looking for "new stars." Burke was certain, too, that the merchants of the city would not permit the Tanks, "the pride of Ironton," to pass out of existence; counseling his readers not to worry, he reminded them that the community had done more for the Tanks than any other city had for a semiprofessional team.[36] His certainty seemed warranted as a report appeared that the Merchants Retail Division of the Chamber of Commerce was contemplating a campaign to raise money for the Tanks.

Coming away from a meeting with Winters with a "favorable and lasting impression" and seeing him as the "best field leader" in Ohio and a remarkable triple threat man, the merchants were prepared to offer him all possible inducements to become

Home and Away

the Tanks' coach. Indeed, they would do all they could to advance "arrangements" to give him the post at the high school. Winters wished to settle in Ironton, and the fans, declared the merchants, would turn out 100 percent for him. And they resolved to conduct a campaign to raise $15,000 for the Tanks through the sale of fifteen hundred season tickets at $10 each. If the drive succeeded, they would guarantee each Tank $50 a game. Moreover, the Tanks could recruit "stars of prominence" and call for the best of "noble athletes" to fight for positions on the team.[37]

At a public meeting at the Elks Club, about two hundred players, merchants, and fans, acting as though they were at a tent revival, bore witness to their faith in the Tanks. Brooks and Lambert pledged that the Tanks would put forward their best effort in the coming season. Walter L. Henry, president of the Retail Merchants, promised that the merchants would continue to support the team and would labor long to raise funds for it. Fans fervently cheered for the Tanks "first, last, and always" but expressed concern over the vagueness of the meeting. They had heard no proposal for placing anyone in Davies's position as coach of the Tanks. Lambert, reelected manager at the meeting, answered that he had tendered the position to Winters and that he would accept it if the community would take care of him as it had Davies. But the vexatious problem remained. Davies had a contract and would not relinquish his position as director, and the board had to find a means to vacate him.

In the days just before and after the public meeting, his erstwhile partisans deserted Davies as they came to an "understanding" of the relationship between the directorship and the Tanks' coaching position, and momentum gathered to force him from his position. Buoyed by public opinion, the board voted unanimously to request Davies to resign. The members justified their vote on the grounds that there was "always an unwritten but recognized agreement on the part of the Board" that the Tanks' coach should be the athletic director at the high school. Thus the salary of the director would augment that of the Tanks' coach to the end of securing a "high class" football team for Ironton.[38]

On the day following the board's vote, Charles McCarthy, editor of the *Irontonian*, wrote the lead editorial, "He Must Choose," endorsing the decision. The board, he declared, was entirely within its rights in asking Davies to resign. It was no secret, and Davies knew it, that school administrators and civic leaders had created the position of athletic director for the man who led the Tanks. Davies had seen fit to leave the Tanks for financial reasons, but he could not expect to retain his position while he coached the eleven of a rival city, a team that would be playing the Tanks. It was "unthinkable and intolerable." His refusal to relinquish his post placed

He Must Choose

his community in a difficult position: "It is impossible for Ironton football fans to raise enough money to employ a man of Davies' caliber to lead the Tanks unless that man received remuneration from some other source, as Shorty received from his position. . . . He is blocking Ironton's chance to secure a new leader for the Tank team." McCarthy closed with conciliatory advice and a warning: Davies could resign and leave with the best wishes of his admirers or he could remain at the high school until the board found some way to "dispense with his service to the detriment of his reputation as an athlete. The choice is entirely his."[39]

At Ashland, Hatcher bitingly responded to McCarthy's editorial. He raised no questions, as he might have, about the legality of what the board wanted to do but argued, rather, that the superintendent and directors of Ironton High School were placing "semi-professional football and high school football in the same class." He had never known a high school to pay a "share of the salary requested by the coach of a professional team."[40]

Fans, merchants, journalists, and educators soon had their way. Only two days after the board requested his resignation, Davies handed it to the superintendent of the school system. He had finally understood, said a reporter for the *Irontonian*, that the position of athletic director had been "practically created" for the pilot of the Tanks. In the end, the fans and the public united in support of the board. They had demonstrated the importance of the Tanks to the community: "The Tanks are an institution. They are enthusiastically backed by the Ironton public and will be supported to the extent of the fans' ability."[41]

On the heels of Davies's resignation, Winters accepted the complementary positions in Ironton and issued a call to arms to the Tanks. Hatcher reiterated his earlier strictures against Ironton High School for being the first high school in the nation to pay professional athletes. High school football was not "run on a money basis"; the Ironton Board of Education did not pay high school boys to play football, yet had committed public funds for semiprofessional football.[42] McCarthy unwittingly gave some credence to Hatcher's allegation, repeating his argument that the athletic director's salary augmented his salary as coach of the Tanks, so that the board, by cooperating with the Tanks in selecting a candidate competent for both positions, made it possible for the Tanks to secure a "high class" coach.[43] Ashland had inveigled Davies into its camp to weaken the Tanks only to learn that Ironton had "plugged the break" with perhaps an even better player. Fortunately for Davies's financial future, Armco gave him a position, apparently a sinecure, in the Ashland mill. And he and Winters went about preparing their teams for the season's play.

Home and Away

Davies had to form a team in a few weeks. Along with Smith and officials of the association, he recruited players from nearby colleges and universities, high schools, and semiprofessional teams in the Tri-State, especially the Tanks and the Boosters. At the outset three Tanks had joined the Armcos, two of them residents of Ashland. At least four Boosters—"Bunk" McWilliams, C. G. "Gatling Gun" Gates, Tom Dandalet, and Leroy McNulty—were soon in the fold. Other men who had played for colleges and semiprofessional teams or both included Ashby Blevins, James "Red" Roberts, and "Dutch" Glass from Centre, Walter Kurtzhalz from Wilmington College, and Homer Martin from West Virginia University. Coming from Ironton High was "Dum Dum" Koerper. Not all these men were on the squad at the same time, some coming as others were leaving. The Armco people assembled a respectable roster in a short time, but whether their team could stand up against established elevens was another question. Observers in Ashland were confident that the Armcos would be one of the strongest teams in the Tri-State, indeed that they would be able to cope with some of the strongest independent teams in the nation.

Smith arranged a fairly strong schedule for the Armcos, only one patently weak team appearing on it. The Armcos, variously known as the Armcos, the Steelers, or the Yellowjackets, met five elevens from Columbus, the Boosters and Tanks twice, the Potters and Blues once. They played nine games at home. Six of their games were against the Boosters, Tanks, Potters, and Blues that, along with the Dayton Koors, constituted, in the view of one football historian, the Ohio Valley League.[44] Though competition among them was spirited and the strongest team each year named itself the champions of the Ohio Valley, they did not consider themselves to be members of a league. No one coordinated, much less directed, their scheduling. They agreed to no rules governing eligibility lists, use of collegiate players, and other matters. They played one another because they saw the prospects of good gates. Over time a formal league could have flourished, but few organizers of semiprofessional teams had sufficient resources or foresight for planning associative ventures beyond their own communities. The Armcos, an extension of a business entity, might have served as a force for organizing a league but never manifested real interest in doing so.

Clearly the Armcos did not begin their first season as a team of the community. Rather, they were dependent on the support and goodwill of a company recently arrived in the city, on the Employees Association, and on mill workers, who gave them entry to the larger population of Ashland. The five or six local sons on the team also could help tie the team to the community. Better yet, the Armcos could blur the distinction between company and community if they played exciting and winning football.

With few practices behind them, the Armcos opened their season late in September against the Columbus Rochester Clothiers. About two thousand spectators, surely curious about the new team and park, which was barely ready for play, crowded into the grandstand. Attired in orange and black uniforms, the Armcos, using a conventional single-wing attack, could not move the ball at crucial moments and lost 3–0. Then at Armco Park, with some new men in the lineup, they met the Ohio State Stoves of Columbus, reputedly a strong team, and easily defeated them 48–0.

Optimistic at their first victory, many Armcos looked forward to playing the Columbus West Side in their next game. Then they ran into the caprice of semi-professional football. A rumor began circulating in Ashland days before the game that at least four Armcos who had once played for the Boosters—Gates, McNulty, McWilliams, and Dandalet—intended to play for their old team on Sunday—not for the Armcos.[45] Ridgely, describing Huntington as the "home of clean athletes," gave credence to the rumor, stating that the men "POSITIVELY" would be in Boosters uniforms. Dismissing Ridgley's story as nonsense, Hatcher declared that the home of good athletes was "just awakening to the fact that they have no players" and was offering "all sorts of inducements" to lure the players back to Huntington.[46] At practices, McWilliams and company denied the reports, adding that they intended to remain with the Armcos for the entire season. Ridgley was one man short of being correct. McWilliams, Gates, and McNulty did not show up at Armco Park for the game against the West Siders and did not inform Davies that they would not play.

Shorn of three able players and outweighed fifteen to twenty pounds a man, the West Side backs "plowing" through their defensive line, the Armcos lost 21–0. Hatcher castigated the three men. Their word had seemed to make contracts with them unnecessary. But they had proved to be unfit to participate in any athletic contest. They were miscreants exemplifying a serious fault in professional football. With no rules to govern them, players jumped from one team to another and thus dishonored the game and betrayed fans. The men had promised to play for the Armcos and then had deserted them without a word, going to Huntington to play for the Boosters. The Armcos, Hatcher feared, might become a training center for the Boosters. He sarcastically noted that Ridgley surely did not have McWilliams, Gates, and McNulty in mind when he called Huntington the "home of great athletes."[47] Somehow patching things up with the Armcos, McWilliams returned to the team and played through the season of 1928.

In their opening games, the Armcos did not really touch the heart of the com-

Home and Away

munity, drawing neither praise nor reproach for their play. They had played teams not well known in Ashland and lost twice. To reach out to prospective fans, as a new team they had to win and develop a spirited rivalry with one or more teams, which probably could happen only if they met elevens from cities with geographical and historical ties to Ashland. Obviously the Ironton Tanks satisfied such requisites. For decades the cities had engaged in social and business intercourse, and since early in the twentieth century athletic teams from the high schools and adult amateur clubs from each city had been playing one another in baseball, football, and basketball. In their fourth game of the season, the Armcos began the competition with the Tanks that could give them a foothold in their city.

The Armcos bolstered their lineup for the game. Early in the week, Smith signed "Red" Roberts to a contract for the remainder of the season. Roberts, weighing 225 pounds, had played as an end, tackle, and fullback for Centre College and started for the squad that defeated Harvard in 1921 in the "upset of the century." That year Walter Camp placed him on his All-American team. Signing a contract, too, was Minos Gordy, an "immense" tackle who had also played for Centre against Harvard and had recently been with the Brecks. Rumor had it that the Armcos intended to sign two other "classy" players.

As the Armcos strengthened their roster, they were gathering support in the community. At a meeting of businessmen at the Hotel Ventura, Davies spoke about his team and introduced thirteen players, including the renowned Roberts. Several businessmen then gave short talks on the meaning of the Armcos for the community and pledged to support them. Benjamin Forgey, president and editor of the *Independent,* asserted that the Armcos provided the city with "advantages" in advertising, the "biggest and best thing" for the community in twenty-five years. For T. Lee Betterton, president of a coffee company, the team represented more than material success: "The people of Ashland appreciate what Armco has done for our city in the way of clean athletics. They also appreciate the class of men the association has brought here to furnish them with high-class football." Coming to the meeting from Armco headquarters in Middletown, Charles Hook, vice-president of Armco, sounded a similar theme as he linked football to character and courage. Saying that Armco employed men of such virtues, he went on to argue in a kind of non sequitur: "That is the reason we encourage athletics. I know of no sport that builds character more than football. But there is one thing that we stress among our players and that is, to play the game squarely. We expect Armco players to play to win, but to play the game cleanly—as far as it is possible." In that spirit, the Armcos would win Sunday regardless of the score. Hatcher, wanting more than a victory in spirit, warned the Tanks of the Armcos' power, writing in his daily column, "Look out, Tanks! The big locomotive is coming."[48]

The Tanks the Armcos were about to face were going through a season of success on the field and uncertainty off the field. Davies and three others had left the team. Though no one was sounding alarms about the team's treasury at the end of the season in 1924, a financial exigency was at hand as the 1925 season approached, probably precipitated by the Armcos' bidding for players. With Winters settled in his positions at the high school and with the Tanks, merchants, feeling more secure about the Tanks, had conducted an intensive campaign to raise $15,000 through the sale of fifteen hundred season tickets but had found, at best, only three hundred subscribers, enough for the Tanks to take the field again.[49]

Disappointed by the showing of their fans but hiding their feelings under a "screen of optimism," the Tanks prepared for the season's play. Winters drilled them hard, and he and Lambert looked for men to fill gaps created by the departure of players who had been with the team in 1924. Winters himself replaced Davies in the backfield. Kermit Frecka, a good running back who had played at West Virginian Wesleyan, took over for Terry Snowday, who had left football. To shore up the line weakened by Wardaman's defection, they signed Virgil Pope, the veteran from Wellston, and Olin Smith, who had been with the Cleveland Bulldogs in 1924 and was now the coach of the Catlettsburg high school team. Lambert was also working up a schedule for the Tanks that had them facing strong teams throughout the Ohio Valley and the state.

Fans in Ironton avidly followed the Tanks as they prepared for their opening game against the Paint Streeters of Chillicothe. More than a week before the game, about a thousand fans came out to watch the Tanks in a scrimmage. "Never before has the population been so worked up," said the *Register*, "that over a thousand of them would turn out to view the Big Red machine in a practice session, as they did on Saturday."[50] Fans gathered in front of Brumberg's store to look at the Tanks' new sweaters and sweatshirts on display. The jerseys were red "with stickum on front and rear to prevent tearing, for rib protection and for handling the ball in wet weather." Across the back of the white sweatshirts was the inscription "Ironton Tanks." The editor of the *Register* assured his readers that, though the Tanks had lost a great leader in Davies, Winters would "carry on in old ways" with a team that was as good as ever. Anticipating good crowds at Beechwood all season, Lambert persuaded the Board of Education to move the grandstand to the center of the sidelines and to erect bleachers on either side of it.

The Tanks opened the season with a flourish. They thrashed the Paint Streeters at Beechwood 29–0, Smith "hurling the interference around" and Winters displaying "outstanding" agility. Dominating play, they buried the Columbus Bobbs-Chevrolets 35–0, manhandling men who had once played for Ohio State and the Panhandles. The Tanks then turned to the Potters, with whom their rivalry was short but already intense. Having lost twice to the Tanks in 1924 and resolving to settle the score, the Potters added new men to their squad, including Virgil Perry. After a back was injured, the Tanks "fortified" themselves, signing Herb Stock, formerly a fullback with the Columbus Tigers. Entering the game, the Tanks also shored themselves up emotionally, adopting the French war cry at Verdun, "They Shall Not Pass." Before a crowd of three thousand at Beechwood, numbering hundreds from communities near Ironton, the Tanks vindicated their martial language, defeating the Potters 15–6 in a game "chock-full of real footballing." The Potters' coach had nothing but praise for the Tanks; they had, he said, faced the "strongest" players "available" in Cincinnati.[51]

Now the Tanks, undefeated in three games, and the Armcos, winners of one of three, met for the first time. Coming from two communities nearly touching each other, they were writing a new chapter in the pages of athletic rivalry. A good showing against the redoubtable Tanks would give the Armcos credibility in and outside of Ashland, whereas the Tanks stood to lose status if they did not win convincingly. But the teams might share a large gate.

The Tanks awaited the Armcos in Ironton, confident but hardly nonchalant, knowing that the Kentuckians had just added two outstanding linemen to their roster. The coaches put their teams through hard practices and blackboard drills. Fans "keyed up" for the "greatest game in the history" of the Ohio Valley—puffery was never in short supply before a game. Lambert expected a crowd of three to four thousand. He was not disappointed: paid attendance was 3,535, one of the largest in the history of Beechwood. The Armcos were stubborn at times, but the Tanks played a "fast and furious" game in defeating them 21–6. Ironton reporters exulted in the performance of the Tanks off the field. Before the game, an unidentified man, presumably a gambler, handed a sheet of paper to Winters with the Armcos' signals. Immediately, Winters destroyed it, saying that "we'll beat them fair or not at all."[52] The Tanks, displaying an "admirable spirit," wholeheartedly approved his decision.

He Must Choose

Before encountering the Tanks again, the Armcos played two games. They relished a victory, 13–0, over the West Side team at Armco Park as recompense for their earlier loss to the Columbus team, but it had no great emotional meaning for a community that had little interest in the losers. Fans could put more stock in the Armcos' coming game against a "natural" rival, the Middletown Armco Blues. Representing the Armco mills in Middletown, the Blues symbolized the authority and power, however beneficial, that controlled the lives of many people living, as it were, in a colonial outpost. The Blues appeared to be a powerful team. Undefeated in 1924 and into 1925, they had two good running backs in Howard Wykoff, the "Red Grange" of the Blues, and Jerry Mincher, who had played for Miami University.

Preparing for the game, the Armcos gave special attention to developing a defense against Wykoff. "Stop Wykoff" was the battle cry, reported Hatcher, who punctuated his daily columns with such expressions as "Let's take 'em gang, let's take 'em" and "Bring On Middletown." Underscoring the importance of the contest, the Blues traveled to Ashland on a special railroad car on Saturday evening. Hook came along to take part in the dedication ceremonies for Armco Park. A "colorful throng" of three thousand fans jammed their way into the park. There the Armcos stopped Wykoff and won 6–0 in a "hard fought" game. The newspapers of Middletown depreciated the Armcos' play, but the team and the community rejoiced in the victory over the "main office."[53] Now, though, the Armcos had to face the Tanks again.

After defeating the Armcos, the Tanks also had played two games, each against strong teams. First, they renewed their rivalry with the Boosters in a game evoking fire and determination. Coming into the game, the elevens were in a similar position. Each was undefeated, and each was playing under a new coach, for the Tanks, Winters, of course, for the Boosters, Jim "Red" Weaver, an All-American center who had played for Bo McMillan at Centre. Their records and reputations at stake, each team had resolved to win, to "smear" the other's clean slate. The Tanks sought victory to preserve their leading rank in semiprofessional football; the Boosters longed to beat the famous Ironton Tanks, one of the most celebrated "pro clubs in the United States," and replace them at the head of the pack.

As usual, rumors of loading up were rife. According to one widespread story, Weaver had persuaded "mysterious Mr. Wilson," an end, to join the Boosters.[54] Wilson did play and was, in fact, Gale Bullman, captain of the West Virginia Wesleyan squad in 1924. Winters expected to add two new players to the Tanks' roster but did not do so. Ridgley was more concerned about players already with the Tanks—Frecka a "wampus cat" and "good old, reliable Bill Brooks." Fans speculated at length on the tactics that the team might employ. On the morning of the game, more than five hundred Irontonians formed a motor caravan traveling to Huntington.

The fans at League Park saw a dramatic battle. "It was," said the *Register,* "a game to tell your grandchildren about." For three quarters, the teams were scoreless. Then in the fourth quarter, Winters, who had remained on the sidelines with a slight injury, entered the fray; he completed four consecutive passes, including one for a touchdown, and led the Tanks to the victory 12–0. Despite a decision deriving from plays requiring more finesse than power, the game had an elemental, brutal aspect: runners did not consider themselves down until the "ground came up and struck them violently in the face," and linemen "smashed" one another on every play. Weaver struck Frecka twice "in a manner" calling for penalties for unnecessary roughness. The officials ignored his tactics. A few days after the game, a reporter for the *Register* warned Weaver not to "resort to dirty tricks" against Frecka and other Tanks in the return game. Ironically, his complaints about rough play came only a week or so after a *Register* man had praised the Boosters and Tanks as "splendid fellows" who were "clean sports."[55]

Their victory reaffirmed the Tanks' dominance in the Ohio Valley. In meeting next the Wagner Pirates of Columbus, they had the opportunity to make their mark in Columbus, central Ohio, and the state. Their roster composed largely of men from Ohio State, the Pirates, champions of semiprofessional play in Columbus in 1924, were heading toward another title in 1925 when the Tanks met them and were already claiming the championship of Ohio.[56] They agreed to come to Ironton, said Norris, only after first demanding enough money to finance another European war but finally agreed to reasonable terms. They may have rued coming to the city. With Winters passing effectively and Frecka running well, the Tanks won 19–5. The Tanks then claimed the semiprofessional championship of Ohio. Implicitly, the *Columbus Dispatch* acknowledged the Tanks' primacy in the state, saying that in losing their first game of the season, the Columbus champions had been no match for the "strong" Tanks.[57]

Two weeks after they played at Beechwood, the Tanks, still undefeated, and the Armcos, victorious in their last two games, met at Armco Park. The Armcos, imaginatively stretching their record, viewed the encounter as a "turning point" for the semiprofessional championship of the "area." As usual, stories surfaced about the teams taking on new players. The most intriguing one was that the Armcos were talking to Jim Thorpe about signing a contract. Thorpe, the great Indian athlete, had played for the Canton Bulldogs and coached the Oorang Indians in the NFL but, at age thirty-seven, was in the twilight of his playing career. Hatcher wrote nothing on

Thorpe, but the *Register* and the *Irontonian* traced his rumored movements at Ashland: he was at the Armco plant for several days; he was ready to sign a contract with the Armcos; "badly off color," he could not wangle a contract from the Armcos.[58] Wherever he was, Thorpe did not appear in an Armco uniform. Of course, for many years managers had been planting such stories in newspapers to quicken interest in impending games.

Both teams were confident of victory. Coming out of a secret practice, several Armcos had boasted, "We're gonna' ride through the Tanks, like Sheridan did from Winchester." The Tanks, seeming to taunt the Armcos, said that they had "kid gloved" them in the first game but now would use all their power for a decisive win. A recent rainfall turned the sod into mud, and the teams slipped around on even terms until the second half, when the Tanks pushed across a touchdown and kicked a field goal to win 9–0. The Armcos made a respectable showing nonetheless and could realistically contemplate defeating the Tanks in 1926.

It seemed, though, all was not going well with the Armcos off the field. A few days before they were to meet the Columbus Bobbs at Armco Park, rumors that Davies had resigned swept through Ashland and beyond. They "flew thick and fast" with a little added at each telling; in one version the Employees Association forced him to resign, in another the players asked him to resign.[59] John McNeal, secretary-treasurer of the association, assured the *Independent* and *Irontonian* that he did not know the source of the stories and that there was "positively" nothing to them. The Armcos, he added, valued Davies and did not intend to let him go. Only hours after McNeal issued his statement, with Davies at the helm and returning a punt fifty yards on a rain-swept field to set up a touchdown, the Armcos defeated the Bobbs 6–0. Only a handful of fans braved the rain to see why the Armcos valued Davies. Later another explanation was forthcoming for the small crowd.

Neither the victory nor McNeal's words shut down the rumor mill, which continued to grind out stories about the Armcos. Hatcher wrote angrily of the "damnable rumors" swirling around the team.[60] Ashland, he insisted, could be proud of the Armcos, but the football committee of the association was facing "new worries" about the rumors denigrating the squad. Saying that he would set the record straight for the sake of one of the best semiprofessional teams in the nation, he recounted the rumors: the Armcos had not practiced for two weeks before the game against the Tanks and had not tried to beat them; the Armcos had not scheduled a game the Sunday that they played the Bobbs; the association had asked Davies to resign as coach.

He asked Campbell Allen, chairman of football committee, to comment on the rumors. Allen vehemently scotched them. The team, he said, had not practiced "as much as it should [have] because of weather and the condition of the field." A coach should not order a team to practice when practice was of no value. The players had given their "heart and soul" in their play against the Tanks. He accused Ironton sportswriters of deliberately airing the errant story of no game in Ashland as a means of drawing more fans to the Tanks-Boosters game at Beechwood. And he saw the false story of Davies's resignation originating in Ironton because people there did not "think" much of Davies's playing for Ashland. Hearing Allen, Hatcher asserted that the Armco "crowd" had faith in the team despite discouraging factors and that semiprofessional football was at Ashland to stay.

Davies and Armcos then set out to prove their worth to the community. They believed that a win over their next opponent, the Potters, would bolster their prestige, especially measured against the Boosters, who had recently lost to the Potters by a touchdown. Led by Perry, the Potters overwhelmed the Armcos 20–0. Probably to the chagrin of the Armcos, the *Enquirer* portrayed them as "soft pickings."[61] Undoubtedly, as the roster proved the next year, Armco people departed Cincinnati believing that Perry would be a worthy addition to their team.

The Armcos then met the Boosters at Ashland. The game promised to be a showcase for a clash between redheaded men and former teammates from the Centre eleven that had beaten Harvard in 1921, "Red" Weaver of the Boosters and "Red" Roberts of the Armcos. The crowd, expected to be "large," apparently was quite ordinary. Probably football fans in Ashland had greater interest that weekend in the Tomcats of Ashland High School, who had completed an undefeated season and claimed the mythical championship of Kentucky. Despite piling up a substantial advantage in first downs, the Armcos could not score on a muddy field; the game ended in a scoreless tie. At Huntington the following Sunday, again the Armcos failed to score, losing 7–0 in their final game of the season.

The Armcos could look back on a season that started reasonably well and then deteriorated; in their final six games, they reached the end zone only twice. They posted a record of fours wins, six losses, and a tie. Clearly their high point was the victory over their counterparts in Middletown. For a new team organizing just at the outset of a season and playing the better semiprofessional teams in southern Ohio, the Armcos had acquitted themselves well. The Employees Association was ready to foot their bills, and for the moment they were not dependent on the community for support. But eventually, if they wished to become more than a plaything for the association and the company, to become a team of the community, they had to win games. They could not count on thousands of fans to come to Armco Park like the indefatigable Walter Mayo, who, rain or shine, was at every game, standing on the sidelines chewing apple-flavored gum.

With their second victory over the Armcos, their seventh of the season, the Tanks remained undefeated; they had yet to play some strong teams but surely had visions of an all-winning record. They were attracting attention in Cincinnati and Columbus, and from Canton, the shrine of professional football in Ohio, the Bulldogs had agreed to come to Ironton for a game. Irontonians felt pride in believing that their city was a fount of achievement in football. But the Tanks also were becoming the subject of a controversy in Columbus reaching into other parts of the state that did not reflect wholly well on them.

It began in an incidental way in the *Ohio State Journal*. In his account of a Bobbs loss to the Potters, 7–0, a reporter remarked that the Columbus team had held the Cincinnatians to their lowest score of the year. Then Floyd Paul, an auditor in Columbus, wrote to Clyde Tuttle, sports editor of the *Journal* who wrote a daily column, "Tuttle's Tales," pointing out that the Tanks had yielded but six points to the Potters in a victory earlier in the season.[62] Paul went on to state, incorrectly, that the Tanks had not lost a game in six years and to declare that they could beat any other team in the state, including the Columbus Tigers of the NFL. There followed a series of letters to Tuttle arguing the question of whether visiting teams could receive a fair deal from officials at Ironton. William Dutcher, a salesman in Columbus who followed semiprofessional football in Ohio, insisted that they could not. Jerry Cochran, manager of the Columbus Tigers, agreed with him and complained that he could not get reasonable terms from the Tanks for a game with his team. Defending the Tanks were R. E. Neal of Steubenville, Carl Smith, manager of the Wagner Pirates, and W. J. Bingham of Columbus, who said visiting teams at Ironton received a fair shake. Bingham was an especially able advocate. After reading accounts of the Tanks' games, he had concluded that they had lost as "much ground in penalties" as they had gained. Joe Carr, president of the NFL, also entered the debate; Cochran, he said, was simply "riled up" because the Tanks passed over the Tigers for stronger teams. No matter where the truth lay, a cloud had passed over the Tanks leaving a residue of skepticism about the nature of their wins.

Though undefeated, the Tanks could not yet claim outright the Tri-State championship. Their principal challengers to the title, the Boosters, were coming to town.

Home and Away

They had met but two Tri-State elevens, the Tanks and the Smoke House, losing and winning; a victory over the Tanks at Beechwood would give them a leg up on the championship. The game created no little interest. Ridgley saw in it the idealization of football. Professional football in the Tri-State, he wrote, was in good hands, in those of "rah rah" boys playing as hard as ever. They knew that reputation alone would not carry them through a tough game. Tanks and Boosters in their dressing rooms were as serious as warriors going into battle. Players berated one another for not playing well. Brooks was grim and might go into his "sob act"—then his adversaries had better "LOOK OUT." Moreover, the semiprofessional game was democratic. The many men working on Saturdays could attend the Boosters' and Tanks' games on Sundays—and not be "annoyed" by cheerleaders.[63]

The game provided an opportunity for women in Ironton to idolize the Tanks. Wishing to show their esteem for the players, a group of "fanettes," mostly wives of businessmen, began a drive to raise funds for the purchase of blankets and hooded coats for them. They gathered at the gate on the day of the game and solicited contributions. Several businessmen made donations of $25. The solicitation had "comforting" results, said a punster for the *Register*, raising $247 for the purchase of gray blankets with the words "Ironton Tanks" lettered on them in red and white.

Intent on winning, the Boosters and Tanks attempted to load up. The Boosters signed several men who had played for West Virginia University, and the Tanks took on two men who had been playing for the Columbus Tigers, the eleven whose manager recently lambasted them. The Tanks resorted to various means to drum up even more interest in the game. For the first time in weeks, they had a daytime practice, thus giving fans a better opportunity to see them at work. Stock and Virgil Pope prepared an "elaborate" program for the game and walked from store to store asking merchants to buy advertising in it. Following the high school game between Ironton and Jackson, the Tanks "trotted" onto the field in their red jerseys, a "regular horde of real football men" who gave the appearance of a "Bolshevik or I. W. W. [Industrial Workers of the World] parade, judging from the flaming red one of the jerseys."[64]

The game hardly reached the intensity of preparations for it. A driving rain and gale held paid admissions to less than two thousand. It was, one writer quipped, "a great day for ducks." Ridgley said that the field was no place for the Ladies Aid Society. Neither team could move the ball in the mud, water, and wind, and the game ended in a scoreless tie. The Tanks blocked six Boosters punts, none kicked on fourth down, and recovered but one. Having broken the Tanks' string of victories, the Boosters left the field with a sense of triumph, and Weaver, believing that his

He Must Choose

team was superior to the Tanks, wanted to play them a third time. But it was the last time in the decade that the two teams met. The Boosters did not resume play in 1926, evidently because of financial problems.

Widening their regional competition, the Tanks then met a team from Dayton for the first time. The Koors, sponsored by Carl Koors, co-owner of a cafe in downtown Dayton, were not the premier paid eleven of the city. They played in the shadow of the Dayton Triangles, a charter member of the NFL, but the Triangles were no great shakes, having won but three games in the league from 1923 through 1925. The Koors came to Ironton with a few Triangles, Al Mahrt, Everett DeWeese, and Norb Sacksteder, a good running back. Fans saw "thrilling" and "sensational" plays. It was "one of the most stirring contests of the season," said the *Dayton Herald*.[65] With the game tied 7–7 late in the fourth quarter, Sacksteder intercepted a pass at the Koors' two-yard line and returned the ball eighty-eight yards before a Tank pulled him down. It was so dark that fans could see nothing but striped shirts "tearing" down the field. The Tanks proclaimed the Koors the "best" team to face them all year. Acknowledging by inference the Tanks' prowess, the *Dayton Journal* reveled in the praise. Seeing the tie as a blot on the Tanks' record and the prospect of a good gate, Lambert hastily arranged another game with the Koors at Beechwood for mid- December.

On Thanksgiving Day, soon after their tie with the Koors, the Tanks met the Canton Bulldogs, a member of the NFL, at Beechwood. It was their first contest with any team from the "big league." Sports scribes and fans in Ironton swelled with pride. The Tanks had tendered the largest guarantee in their history, an undisclosed figure, to the Bulldogs, and the Bulldogs were to receive the lion's share of the gate. Altogether, estimated one sportswriter, the Tanks would expend $4,000 on the game.[66]

But the cost would be worth every penny, every hour worked preparing for the game. The Bulldogs, declared the *Register* in breaking news of scheduling of the contest, would come to Ironton as one of the "greatest" teams in professional football. The Canton Bulldogs had been undefeated champions of the NFL in 1922 and 1923, but the Bulldogs coming to Ironton in 1925 had little kinship with the title holders. In 1924 the Canton owner, his payroll rising, moved his franchise to the larger market of Cleveland, taking along nearly all of the players and the name "Bulldogs." There they won another title in 1924. Then in 1925 a new team in Canton, using the old canine tag, entered the league with a substantially new roster. But several old Bulldogs were on the new team, including the legendary tackle Wilbur "Fats" Henry, who had refused to move to Cleveland. And such first-rate players as Harry Robb, the quarterback, and Pete Calac, a good running back who had played with Jim Thorpe at Carlisle, were on the roster. The new Bulldogs, in fact, had a better record in the league in 1925 than the Bulldogs to the north. The Tanks meeting the Bulldogs were not completely of the old lineage either; Lambert had acquired four men from the Columbus Tigers who had played for that team the previous Sunday in a 6–0 loss to the Bulldogs and two men from the Boosters and Armcos.

The Tanks saw the game as a test of their ability to stage a "big" event and intended to put their best foot forward. Lambert expected the crowd to number as high as six thousand. The Armcos, Boosters, and Smoke House were idle so he expected many fans to come to Beechwood from Ashland, Huntington, and Portsmouth, as well as from smaller communities such as Wellston, Jackson, Catlettsburg, and Chillicothe. He took special measures for controlling the crowd. Securing public assistance for what legally was a private entity, he instructed the police force of the city—all members were on duty—to clear the field along the sidelines of everyone but players, managers, and newsmen.[67] Though unable to obtain Lane, he hired three men from outside of Ironton to officiate the game.

The game was disappointing for the Tanks. A driving rain turned the field into a dismal swamp, with grass and mud mixed into an outdoor pottage. Police had no great crowd to control. About eighteen hundred fans were in the stands, surely splotching red ink on the Tanks' ledger. Umbrellas nearly formed a single cover over the grandstand and bleachers. Before the game, Tanks fans presented a "handsomely engraved" white gold watch to Winters, who was unable to blush because of the "mud massage" on his face. Though Henry did not play, the Bulldogs dominated the line of scrimmage, even as Brooks hurled his 250 pounds of "iron bound muscle" against them. Despite losing 12–0, the Tanks went down "fighting" and took heart at hearing praise from the Bulldogs, who said that they were as strong as any other team that they had met in the NFL and that they should enter the league. Tanks fans believed that the game had put the team "on the map." But the leading newspaper in Canton, the *Repository,* giving no coverage to the game, did not locate Ironton on any map.

Words of praise, though, could not erase the Tanks' unprecedented string of three games without a victory and could not protect the team against a coming battle with the rugged Potters in Cincinnati. The Potters had lost but four games in two years, three of them to the Tanks, and had set their minds and hearts to winning the game and vengeance. The editor of the *Register* used the game as an opportunity to publish a "Sunday Editorial" on the importance of the Tanks to the community and the reciprocal responsibilities of the citizenry. Playing in Cincinnati, the Tanks, already having brought "notice, fame and wide recognition" to Ironton, were now giving it more publicity.[68] For their part, Irontonians had to take action to build a covered grandstand at Beechwood and to install a team room and sanitary facilities for the Tanks.

Before a crowd of six thousand, the largest ever to attend a semiprofessional game at Redland Field, the Tanks and Potters waged a fierce battle. The Potters, led by Perry, a "team in himself," offered a persistent challenge to the Tanks, but with Brooks tossing Potters backs for losses and Winters slashing through the line, the Tanks were "too good" and eventually prevailed 9–0. For Burke, in winning the Tanks proved that they ranked with the best teams in the NFL. The victory underscored the Bulldogs' suggestion that the Tanks enter the NFL. It was not entirely a foolish notion. At the time, four or five clubs in small cities (but larger than Ironton) were in the league, and the Tanks certainly could have stood up to them in play and other teams in the league. Whether the community could have borne the additional costs of membership—travel expenses and an enlarged payroll—was quite another matter. The crowds at Beechwood in 1925, averaging about twenty-nine hundred, were considerably smaller than those that the metropolitan NFL clubs drew. Good crowds in New York and Chicago typically ran anywhere from ten to fifteen thousand, but attendance in smaller cities like Green Bay and Pottsville often numbered three to five thousand.[69] In any case, no one in the Tanks organization or in the community proposed entry into the league.

The Tanks closed their season at Beechwood in a return game with the Koors. Local sportswriters attempted to lure fans to the park by their descriptions of the first game, a "real classic," and their expectations for the second. The Tanks, led by Winters, who displayed "brilliant" broken field running, took sweet revenge on the visitors, winning 24–6. The *Register* called the win for the Tanks the "greatest ever experienced" in their history.[70] Given the Koors' standing as an ordinary semiprofessional team and other Tanks victories, the claim was errant nonsense.

Their season at an end, the Tanks could count nine wins, one loss, and two ties; their victories over the teams tying them more than balanced the account. Their record came out of a schedule composed of the best teams in the Tri-State and southern and central Ohio, nearly all from larger cities than Ironton. In good heart, the Tanks again feasted at Ethel Murdock's home. Lambert also gave them a banquet at his home. Frank Lane, a guest, gave a brief talk, saying that the Tanks needed a larger grandstand at Beechwood to accommodate the growing crowds coming out for their games.[71]

Local fans were already talking in a like manner, and men at the post of the American Legion were calling for an increase in the seating capacity at Beechwood. They believed that the Tanks were worth a quarter-million dollars in advertising and that merchants ought to take up the project. Such ventures were the stuff out of which the Tanks were becoming public property and by which they could lose much of their autonomy.

 At Portsmouth, as the Tanks faced unsettling change early in their season and went on to play well and as the Armcos were organizing their team, the Smoke House men seemed to be moving to a good season. They had ended the season of 1924 dispossessed, in shambles, with no ties to the community, no effective managerial direction. Now they had a new coach, Moses Solomon, the speedy halfback who had played for them in a few games in 1924. He had two full teams engaged in stiff workouts for several hours every weekday evening and was developing new plays for them. Harry Doerr, one of the founders of the team, was now the manager and was out looking for new players and fitfully building a schedule. Viewing the team in practice, a reporter for the *Times* called it one of the "best" in years; a sportswriter for the *Sun* agreed and called on fans to support the team.

The Smoke House also had elicited a measure of help from the city. Municipal authorities recently had begun developing an athletic complex on the east side of the city called Labold Field, one already far superior to Millbrook. They were erecting bleachers to accommodate three thousand spectators for football games and had other projects in mind. Doerr wanted his team to play there, and the city granted his request. The team might also look forward to use of a stadium there. Three civic clubs—the Elks, Rotary, and Kiwanis—were planning to conduct a campaign to raise $125,000 to build tennis courts, a clubhouse, and a stadium seating eight thousand people.[72]

At the beginning of play, the Smoke House men seemed to justify the journalists' reports. Meeting a "strong" Wellston club, with Solomon making some long runs, they won 30–0. Then the season turned to dross. Going to Huntington, the Smoke House lost to the Boosters 34–0. Worse than the loss, Solomon broke his collarbone and was out for the season. Scheduled next to play Murray City, the Smoke House met instead a squad of Sabbatarians. The local ministerial association, riding the crest of a tent revival in the city, called on the trustees of Labold Field, public appointees, to ban all athletic contests there on Sundays. Acceding to the request (or demand), the trustees denied use of the field to the Smoke House.[73] Doerr had to cancel the game with Murray City and faced the prospect of forfeiting $300 guaranteed to the visitors. The Smoke House players considered playing out the season

He Must Choose

on the road but, discouraged by the loss of Solomon, disbanded the team. A few weeks later, the trustees rescinded their decision, but it came too late for the Smoke House players to reassemble.

So ended the Smoke House. No one in Portsmouth mourned the passing of the team. Smoke House men had played for seven years, mostly the biblical lean years, winning few important games and never defeating their arch rival, the Tanks. They never held the heart of Portsmouth, emotionally or materially, never came near to becoming a team of the town. The community had to await the coming of new venture in football for that to happen.

6

It Isn't Whether You Win or Lose, It's How You Play the Game

THE MIDDLE YEARS of the decade saw the Tanks and Armcos engaging in a battle for supremacy in semiprofessional football in the Ohio Valley, with two teams from Portsmouth, first the Presidents and then the Shoe-Steels, gathering, or attempting to gather, strength to become parties to the contest. Each team came to play from different settings. The Tanks, almost venerable, were increasingly becoming common property of the community or at least of the business community and thus occasionally found themselves embroiled in controversy threatening their autonomy. At Ashland, the Armcos, creation of a powerful steel company and its employees, were living in an antiseptic atmosphere largely free of controversy—but also of vitality. The Portsmouth teams were looking to small business concerns and individuals for vigorous direction that might summon up support from the entire community. More than ever, all the teams were going beyond the corporate boundaries of their communities in the search for collegiate players to give them victories.

After the collapse of their team in 1925, the Smoke House players did not seek or receive backing for reconstituting it. They had won only nominal support from fans, and attendance at Millbrook seldom exceeded a thousand for games except when the Tanks came to town. Though old Smoke House players were still in the community, many ready to play, no institutional entity seemed ready in the summer of 1926 to organize a semiprofessional team for Portsmouth. But the city, more than twice as large as Ironton and Ashland, had known the game for seven years and still might be willing to embrace the right kind of team. Then, almost at the equinox, the community learned that an eleven might be playing in the city.

Jack Walter, manager of the Scioto Motor Company, issued a call to football players in Portsmouth, especially former high school and Smoke House players, to a meeting at the company's showroom and to try out for a new team.[1] Walter was acting on behalf of Roscoe Funderberg, president of the motor company, which was a dealership for the Studebaker firm; his team derived its name from a popular Studebaker model, the President. Never revealing how much financial support he was willing to commit to the team, clearly Funderberg was prepared to bear all costs of uniforms and equipment, travel, services of game officials, and use of Labold. Probably players shared in net gate receipts. Walter became the manager of the team; Rhoades Van Nostrand, who had played for Portsmouth High, took the coach's position. Later, Dan Fries, once the coach of the Smoke House and now at Portsmouth High, became the line coach. Walter announced that he planned to book the "cream of middleweight" teams in the area. Evidently he had in mind the smaller, junior versions of the Tanks and Armcos, but he ended up with a squad of many former Smoke House players who expected to compete against traditional teams.

Walter called for the meeting and tryouts on short notice. He had already scheduled a game at Labold with the Ironton Panthers, the Tanks' junior team. The men who engaged in the "hard practices" every evening in the several days before the game were largely of the Smoke House lineage. Among them were old-line players Dewey Adams, Harold "Heckie" DeVoss, Jake Shields, Clarence Englebrecht and Jake Pfau.[2] The roster was fairly representative of the occupational structure in the city—steelworkers and shoe workers employed in factories, skilled tradesmen including a baker and a draftsman, a municipal fireman, and a professional man, an attorney.

To attract a good crowd for the first game, Walter arranged for it to be one of two contests, the other a baseball game. Men paid seventy-five cents, women fifty cents for admission.[3] The Presidents, weighing on average 170 pounds, did not play well despite winning 7–0. The reporter for the *Times* found their play disappointing; they did not operate like a "well-oiled machine" and obviously needed much more practice. But he saw the possibilities for a good team.

Perhaps taking the reporter's comments to heart, the Presidents agreed to enter into "intensive" practices in preparation for meeting the "fast" Tilton 33s, a team from Xenia, one of the "best" in the Miami Valley. As they practiced, they discovered that they had a rival in the city, the Portsmouth Merchants. Their origins and players were not described in the *Sun* and *Times,* but their name implied that they were sponsored by merchants in the city. None of the Merchants had played for the Smoke House, but their manager, Gus Putzek, was the first manager of the Smoke House eleven. Pat Shoemaker was their coach. The rivalry between the fledgling teams became more than a matter of competing for fans when they contended for use of Labold Field.

At the outset, no conflict occurred. In their second Sunday of play, the Presidents journeyed to Xenia to meet the Tiltons; the Merchants played their first game at Labold against the Panthers. The Presidents won 6–0, owing in part to the defensive play of "Dixie" Walker, an end who had once played for the Frankford Yellow Jackets and who had come to Portsmouth to work on construction of a bridge.[4] The next day Funderberg hosted a victory dinner for his Presidents, giving them a short "pep" talk and declaring that the team was "working up" to a game against the Tanks. The Merchants, in the meantime, had played the Panthers to a tie, with no celebratory dinner afterward. On the following Sunday, the Presidents were at Labold playing the Tiltons again. A crowd of about five hundred saw them defeat the visitors a second time, 20–7. The Merchants journeyed to Wellston and played to a scoreless tie with the local team.

Perhaps inevitably, the teams came into conflict over use of Labold. It was the only facility in the city suited for a game; the bleachers accommodated about three thousand people. Both teams practiced at times at Mound or York park, and the Merchants played one game at York but neither had stands for spectators. The managers were scheduling games virtually week by week. Each eleven preferred to play at home so as to receive a larger share of the gate and avoid the inconvenience of travel. At some point both teams would want to use Labold and thus force the Board of Trustees controlling use of the municipal field to deny it to one of them. Worse yet, both would assume that they had use of the field on the same day.

For their fourth Sunday of play, Walter announced that the Presidents were meeting the Wagner Pirates at Labold, but the Merchants said that they had scheduled a game there with the Jackson Bearcats. No record indicated which team had reserved the date for its game. But the Presidents, their roster numbering many well-known former Smoke House men, proposing to schedule the "famous" Tanks, and already commanding more interest in the community and space in the *Sun* and *Times* than the Merchants, had the inside track. Responding to the Presidents' status, the board awarded them use of Labold. Whether or not because of the loss of Labold, the Merchants or the Bearcats canceled their game, the Merchants arranging to meet a team from Russell at Russell.

The board, though, did not give the Presidents use of Labold on Sundays for the remainder of the season, proposing instead a curious way of dealing with the problem.[5] The teams should merge and the coaches would divide it into two teams, one to play at home carrying out contracts already signed by either the Merchants or Presidents, the other playing out-of-town games already scheduled. The "picked" teams might vary from week to week, depending on the opponent they were to play so that each would have a chance to win. Thus Portsmouth might field a team capable of beating the Tanks, another to defeat a lesser team at Chillicothe, Jackson, or Washington Court House. Out of the merged team, the trustees argued, eventually a strong squad of young men would emerge.

The proposal was aborting almost at the moment the trustees offered it, the newspapers reporting that nearly the entire membership of each team would vote against it.[6] Probably the bitterness of the dispute and the prospective loss of identity and constant alteration of lineups contributed to the opposition. Both teams rejected the proposal but agreed to another, simpler solution. They would play each other in two Sundays for preference in use of Labold. For some reason, perhaps existing commitments, the Presidents had the better of the bargain. If they won, they could use the field any Sunday they wanted for the remainder of the season; if the Merchants won, they would receive four dates, all to be fixed later. For the decisive game, the teams would share equally in the gate. They would not have to exchange eligibility lists, seemingly an invitation to loading up. Later, though, they agreed to use their regular lineups and posted $100 as a guarantee that they would appear for the game.

For all the importance of the game with the Merchants, the Presidents had to fasten their attention on their coming contest with the Pirates. A victory over the Wagner Pirates, an eleven of declining standing in semiprofessional circles but still apparently no easy prey, would enhance the Presidents' status within and outside the city. The Tanks would then be more willing to give them a game, another means of improving their reputation. Indicating their perception of the Presidents and the popular view of them, especially relative to the Merchants, the *Times* and *Sun* ran six long stories on the approaching Presidents-Pirates game and only two three- or four-line references to the Merchants-Russell game.[7]

The Presidents were facing the "heavyweight" champions of Columbus, a team that had given the Tanks a battle in 1925. But the Presidents, said sportswriters, had an "invincible" line. On the eve of the game, Funderberg placed a third-page display advertisement in the *Sun* calling his team the "pride of Portsmouth."[8] "Gents'" tickets were one dollar, ladies' seventy-five cents. With a crowd of fifteen hundred on hand, the largest thus far of their season, the Presidents, playing "good football," defeated the Pirates 12–0. The *Sun* gave scant coverage, the *Times* none, to the Merchants' 6–3 victory the same day over Russell.

The Presidents soon earned dividends from their win. Earlier Walter had made overtures to the Tanks about playing home-and-home games, but the Ironton men had rebuffed them, apparently believing that the Presidents would not draw well. Now Sonny Winters called to say that the Tanks were willing to negotiate terms for a game. The *Sun* attributed the Tanks' reversal directly to the Presidents' victory over the Pirates.[9] Winters insisted, though, that he had never doubted the Presidents' strength but acknowledged that many fans in Ironton did. Several Presidents men questioned their team's ability to compete with the Tanks until Dan Fries said that he believed that if the Presidents adhered to training rules and practiced daily, they could beat the Tanks. Many of the Portsmouth men had played against the Tanks, and young men, "new blood," had joined them. Meanwhile, he said, the Tanks were growing older and were ready for a trimming.

The Presidents could not, however, turn their recent win and optimism into good terms when Lambert and Walter met in negotiations. Lambert would not accede to Walter's demand for a guarantee of $700 for coming to Ironton for the game, paring it down to $400, about half of what the Tanks had been offering some teams.[10] The managers then fixed the date of the game for mid-November. In demanding $700s, Walter, complained the *Ironton Tribune,* successor to the *Register* as the city's evening newspaper, had sought to "dictate" terms to the Tanks; "Mussolini," said its reporter, "had nothing on this Bunch."

As Walter negotiated, the Presidents and the Merchants prepared for the battle. The Merchants practiced diligently, as did the Presidents under electric lights at Mound Park. Apparently neither team loaded up. The Presidents did not see the game as a "grudge match," saying that it was "just another football game." Both teams had their fans, interest in the game was great, and the crowd, said the *Sun,* might reach "record proportions." But it was "disappointingly small," diminished perhaps because several hundred people viewed the game from their automobiles outside the fence. On a damp field the Presidents won 12–0. The Merchants played more games thereafter, but always against minor teams from Ashland, Jackson, Chillicothe, and elsewhere. They were now a cockboat sailing in the wake of a man-of-war, their crowds small, the papers reporting their games in a perfunctory manner. They did not reorganize in 1927.

Their local rival vanquished, the Presidents would meet the scourge of the Ohio Valley with a perfect record if they could defeat the Chillicothe Merchants at Labold in their next game. Believing that the Merchants would not be "easy" and looking forward to their game with the Tanks, they signed two new players, an end from Purdue and a tackle from West Virginia University. Reportedly, Chillicothe had signed on six new recruits, all "stars" from central Ohio. Again on a wet field, the Presidents won 12–0, a small crowd watching them slip and slide. The ejection of Adams for rough play in the fourth quarter enlivened the game, particularly because all but eleven of the Presidents were already in the showers. But the Presidents held on with the ten men. Thus they took six wins and no losses into their game against the Tanks.

Only two weeks before the Presidents met the Tanks, the Armcos had played the Big Red at Ashland. The Armcos came into the game undefeated in four games, their goal line uncrossed, a good showing for a team in only the second year of play. They had access, of course, to ample resources and received effective managerial direction. At the opening of Armcos' play in 1925, after a late-summer decision to organize the team, the officials of the Employees Association, notably John McNeal and Campbell Allen, had not had time to plan carefully for the coming season. They were ready in 1926. As the season approached, with Russell Smith guiding them, they had moved toward building a schedule, procuring new players, and mustering support in the community.

They had already resolved a problem regarding the coach's position. Clearly Davies was not comfortable in his berth and resigned midway through the summer. He accepted a position as a coach at South Point High School and then returned to the Tanks. Remembering the "dashing" play of Virgil Perry against the Armcos as a Potter, Allen and Smith offered him the vacated position and employment at the Armco mill. The Potters had proffered him attractive terms to continue playing for them, but he believed that prospects were brighter at Ashland. He had hardly settled in the city when the association people asked him to attend the Knute Rockne grid school in Indiana.

Perry returned to Ashland after three weeks at Rockne's school convinced that he had been at the feet of a master. Now he understood, he exclaimed, why Notre Dame was always a winner, why Notre Dame and the Four Horsemen were undefeated in 1924. In his six years as a player and coach in collegiate and professional football, he had never learned as much "inside football" as he had from Rockne in three weeks. Rockne knew football and how to instruct players and coaches in its play. Perry was the only professional coach there, and Rockne, knowing that instructions for high school and college coaches was not useful for professional men, spent many hours after regular classes teaching him how to manage paid players. Perry also admired Rockne for his vigor and efficiency; the great coach always conducted his lectures and "field work" on schedule.[11]

Almost within hours after his return, Perry ordered candidates for the team to report to practice. Rockne-like, he drew up his plans for practice carefully and adhered to them meticulously. His prescription for winning was practice and more practice. He expected about fifty men to report at the initial session, and he intended to give all a fair trial. Through the first two weeks, he spent much of his time with newcomers, looking for unknown strength before starting intensive practice, and then cut the roster to twenty. Once practice began—three times a week starting at five in the evening and lasting two to three hours—he pushed players through exercises to get them in the "pink of condition" but also patiently explained and demonstrated techniques of blocking and tackling. Observing a practice, Hatcher remarked that he had never seen players work as hard as the Armcos. To promote sales of season tickets, Perry invited the public to attend a "strenuous" practice.[12]

During the summer, Perry, Smith, and Allen had recruited many of the men who had endured the practices. Scouring the cities, towns, and colleges in Ohio, West Virginia, and Kentucky, they looked for the "best that could be had," men who would make the Armcos a "powerful team."[13] They offered prospects $50 a game and white-collar positions at the Armco plant for the season or assistance in finding other employment at Ashland. Louis Ware, a halfback from Transylvania who joined the team in 1927, estimated that one-third to one-half of the players were employees at Armco.[14] Several men worked in the public schools as coaches. Perry was always on the lookout, too, for players already working at Armco, saying that "there looms a wealth of good material in the plant outside of the experienced men who have been imported." Perry wanted his players to be in "town throughout the week"; he did not want men coming to Ashland on the weekend to play for him.

The recruiters effected a wholesale change in the Armcos' roster. Of the twenty-five men who played for the team at one time or another in 1926, only five had been on the roster in 1925.[15] All but five had played for collegiate teams—five at Miami University, three at Ohio State, two at West Virginia University, two at Marshall, two at Centre, and the remainder at such schools as Lafayette, Wilmington, and William and Mary. As pictured in the *Independent,* they brought a wealth of talent and experience to the Armcos. One man was a "powerful wing man," another was a "stalking young fullback," still another was "fast and elusive," and yet another was "big and rugged." Interesting and promising was Johnny "Stu" Stuart, a halfback who had played with Chic Harley at Ohio State and the St. Louis Cardinals as a pitcher; he signed a contract with the Armcos after a squabble with the Cardinals finally resulted in his release from them. The Armcos could not, though, persuade Red Weaver of the Boosters to join them. Red Roberts left the team, unwilling to sign for another season's play even after he had agreed to do so. If the Armcos could not win every game with the men they signed, it would be because, said Hatcher, "luck ruled otherwise."[16]

As the association men were recruiting players for a "most powerful team," they were constructing a schedule worthy of it. As Allen remarked, they wanted "none but the best teams . . . brought here."[17] Perry agreed, saying that he would not permit the Armcos to play "set-ups," that the fans deserved to see good teams. They largely avoided the improvised scheduling characteristic of other semiprofessional teams of the day (of course, collegiate teams then did not develop schedules far in advance of a season's play). By the opening of the season, the schedule was nearly in place. It was a fan's schedule. The Armcos would play their first six games at home before going on the road for three of their last four games. They faced strong teams, the Potters and Tanks five times, the Triangles, the Bobbs, the Columbus Tigers, and the Blues once.

In 1925, owing in part to the constraints of time, the association and Davies did not make a concerted effort to tie their team to the community. A so-called pep meeting had had few results, and Davies had not gone out to civic clubs with messages about the team. But early in 1926, Allen, Smith, and Perry went to businessmen and civic clubs to enlist their support for the Armcos. At a pep meeting held at the Armco plant before the season began, Armco men and business and professional men joined in pledging their support for the team and assistance for a campaign to sell season tickets.[18] Perry spoke to them, his words full of promise: "When we beat the Ironton Tanks on October 24, our success will have been assured. I have played against the Tanks for three years and I know what it takes to beat them, and I believe that I have the team." Smith tied Perry's talk to the impending sales campaign, predicting victories and financial success for the team. Hatcher called it one of the "most enthusiastic hot weather 'pep' meetings" ever held in Ashland. In a lead editorial, the editor of the *Independent* declared that if the young men carrying the Armco banner could create such an atmosphere, "sports lovers" in the community should unite and buy tickets and let the players know of the "irresistible mass desire to win in the stands and along the sidelines."[19] Addressing a meeting of the Lions Club, Perry attempted to link his team to the community, portraying the Armcos as men who might become solid citizens of the city. His ambition was, he said, to lead a "football team that citizens of Ashland will be proud to claim . . . with every player working hard and boosting Ashland—a team that will practice and make this city his home." And he intended to have his men ready to defeat the Tanks.

Sanguine talk did not translate into successful sales of season tickets. The manager of the drive called on volunteers to sell two thousand tickets—$8 each for all home games—one thousand in the city, one thousand in the Armco plant.[20] They plastered the Armco works with "brilliant" posters touting the prospects of the team and placed window stickers on automobiles around the city bearing the words "Boost Ashland Armco Football." The manager of sales in the city reported that fans in Ashland were elated over the outlook for the Armcos and that sales would exceed one thousand there. Sales at the plant also seemed to be going well. Only a few days after the campaign began, Allen expected soon to reach the goal of two thousand tickets sold. But a few days later,, an estimate had it that only one thousand tickets had been sold. No report on final sales figures ever appeared in the *Independent,* telling evidence that the campaign had fallen short of its goal. Apparently the Armcos had far to go in selling their football to the residents of Ashland.

Nonetheless, with sounds of optimism ringing in their ears, fans in Ashland could believe or hope that the Armcos would sweep all before them. They did so early on. They opened play defeating the Koors 6–0 before three thousand fans enduring "chilling winds." Then they met the Bobbs-Chevrolets, reportedly strengthened by the addition of "new stars."[21] Playing under a torrid sun, the Armcos won handily 30–0; their defense permitted the Bobbs no first downs, and the offense, with Perry the spearhead, rolled over old and new stars. They expected a stern test playing the Potters in their third game. But with their defense again impenetrable, the Armcos won 13–0 in a "keenly contested" game. In their fourth game, the Armcos faced their kin, the Armco Blues. Accompanied by two hundred fans, the Blues arrived in Ashland on Saturday night, welcomed by a parade of automobiles and two bands bearing placards reading "Beat Middletown." Only hours later, the Armcos did beat Middletown, 20–0. A sportswriter for the *Middletown News-Signal* thought that the

Blues could take honor in losing because the "Ashland people have spared no expense in securing some of the best college stars available."[22]

Undoubtedly, the Armcos and their fans took pride in the four consecutive wins over opponents held scoreless, but the prize that they longed for was victory over the Tanks. The Tanks remained the icons of success and power in semiprofessional football in the valley, undefeated in five games, scoring 150 points and holding their opponents scoreless. A team that could beat them, especially one in its infancy, would gain visibility outside the community, glory inside. And so when the Armcos met the Tanks at Ashland midway through the season, David had an opportunity to slay Goliath in all his strength.

The Tanks thus far were playing through a highly successful season although material and organizational conditions were changing their face in the community. In the closing months of the season in 1925, various individuals and clubs, concerned that large crowds would tax the capacity of Beechwood, began to talk about construction of a larger and covered grandstand at the park. The *Tribune* had called on citizens to support such a venture, and the American Legion had urged businessmen to lead the way. Then early in the new year, the Legion invited men from the Lions and Rotary Clubs, the Chamber of Commerce, and the Board of Education, which owned Beechwood and adjacent land, and the general public to a meeting to discuss proposals for a "covered stadium."[23]

Two vague proposals resulted that soon "faded out." Then in April, in a seemingly tangled arrangement, a committee composed of the "various committees appointed by the clubs and societies to consider the Beechwood stadium project," created yet another committee, a "permanent committee" to develop and implement plans for construction of a stadium. The thirty-two members of the new body included many of the leading citizens of Ironton. Among them were six merchants, four industrialists, four bankers, two journalists, three physicians, a lawyer, a building contractor, and a salesman. Two clerks and a stenographer, probably taking on clerical duties, were also on the committee.[24]

To finance construction of a covered grandstand seating about thirty-one hundred persons and costing over $30,000, the committee, known as the Ironton Stadium Association or the Beechwood Stadium Association, issued three hundred shares of stock, each with a par value of $100 and yielding an annual return in interest of 7 percent. The shares of stock were really bonds. The association asked the board for a twenty-year lease on the property and all revenue derived from concessions, advertising at the park, and reserved and box seats; the board would receive income from the sale of general admission tickets.[25] At retirement of the stock, the association would turn the facility over to the board. The board accepted the proposal, and the association began its work.

Selling the stock was no problem. Many members of the association and other individuals and organizations had already pledged to purchase shares. Newton Johnson, a prominent banker, and Homer Edwards, secretary of a savings and loan association, bought fifty, the American Legion fifty, the Capper Motor Sales ten. Burke, Brooks, and Lambert also took a few shares.[26] A reconstituted association soon had cash in hand and began awarding contracts to general and sub-contractors. Receiving the general contract was G. P. Mahl and Son. Construction moved ahead rapidly and was not impeded when the association, finding costs higher than estimates, had to raise an additional $4,000 by selling more stock. Midway through October, when the Tanks met the Cleveland Indians, the new stadium was ready for a football game. By that time, subscribers had paid their pledges, fans had bought many reserved seats, and the association had a debt of only $3,500.[27]

Yet no one clearly defined the obligations of the Tanks, if any. Obviously they had to make continuing use of the facility and win there to draw good crowds to create income for the association. More than that, members of the association, elites in the city, had transformed the Tanks, who simply wanted to play football, into an instrument for modernizing the city.[28] Accordingly, the association could expect to exercise some voice in the Tanks' affairs—in scheduling, for instance. In fact, if not by a formal document, the "Stadium Corporation controlled the Tanks."[29] To protect their interests, the members vested direction of the Tanks' routine affairs in Lambert and Winters and a players' committee responsible for selecting the roster. Acting under the authority of the association, Lambert and Winters signed players to contracts calling for them to receive $50 a game. For the first time in their history, the Tanks had their salaries contractually fixed. No document defined the powers or responsibilities of the association, but apparently the members believed that attendance at the new stadium would yield the revenue necessary to meet expenses. Their conceptualization of the Tanks and the loose arrangements for governing them inevitably led to confusion and controversy.

Early in the season, after the Tanks had played two games, the players' committee became deadlocked over the last two players to be retained and the last two to be released. Lambert finally cast the deciding vote. Andrews, Frecka, and Poole then challenged the right of Winters and Lambert to vote on the question; Smith and Brooks, the other two members of the committee, supported Winters and Lambert.

It Isn't Whether You Win or Lose

The three dissidents then threatened to quit the team and organize their own team under the name Tanks. The association met hurriedly and voted not to lease Beechwood to any other team than the one led by Winters. Poole and Andrews and three or four other "mutineers" refused to sign contracts, declaring that they were "holdouts." Lambert warned them that he had other men waiting in the wings to take their places. Fans reportedly stood solidly behind Winters and Lambert. The *Tribune* scolded the men, saying that $50 a game was a "handsome salary" and that few young men could earn that much a week in other occupations.[30] Besides, if they refused to sign, soon they would be out of the "Big Parade." Teams in the NFL and in the new American Football League were reducing their squads, giving independent elevens everywhere the pick of many good players at reasonable salaries. Then the association decided to abandon the "system that had caused trouble" and "created grievances," delegating all authority to sign and release players to the coach and business manager. The businessmen in the association completely supported Winters and Lambert, and regarded complaints about their selection of players as "petty foments." Chastised, the holdouts signed their contracts and set about playing football.

The Tanks appeared to be a good team as they entered play in 1926. Shorty Davies had returned to the fold, and perennials like Brooks were ready to play. Of the seventeen men who played in nearly every game, fourteen had some experience as collegiate players, three at Ohio State, one at Purdue, one at West Virginia University, five at small Ohio colleges, the remainder at other midwestern schools. They had to prove their mettle playing teams in a schedule seemingly more difficult than that of 1925. Among their opponents would be the Armcos, Potters, and Blues and three big city teams, the Cleveland Indians, the Akron Mutes, and the Kansas City Cowboys of the NFL.

The Tanks began the season on a remarkable run, winning their first five games, all at home, without surrendering a point and scoring at least twenty-three points in each game. Looking "bigger, better and faster than ever before," they defeated the Columbus All-Stars 27–0 in their first game. Next they met the "fast" and "furious" Blues and won 27–0. Then they swept the Wagner Pirates off the "football map" 34–0—a neat lacing, said the *Columbus Dispatch*.[31] Their "formidable line" controlling play, the Tanks next subdued the Koors 23–0. But the Tanks felt some trepidation as they prepared to meet their next opponent, the Cleveland Indians, which had many "classy collegians" on their roster. They faced the Indians in front of a crowd of over three thousand attending the first game played at the recently completed stadium, a monument in wood, cement, and steel, said a sportswriter, to the fans' loyalty to and enthusiasm for the Tanks. The Indians were no match for the

Tanks, falling 47–0. At the game's end, they declared that the Tanks were the "smoothest working team we ever saw."[32]

Now the Tanks, undefeated and unscored on in five games, had to play their first game outside of Beechwood, going to Armco Park to meet the Armcos, who were also undefeated and unscored on in four games. The winner could take great satisfaction in a victory over a natural rival, resulting, perhaps, in mythical championships. Through the days approaching the game, the *Independent* and *Tribune* turned out numerous speculative and predictive columns on the size of the crowd, the tactics of the teams, and the degree of loading up. The *Tribune* saw the game as the "greatest professional" contest in the annals of sports in the Ohio Valley. Gamblers and garden-variety fans were wagering in the neighborhood of $20,000 on the outcome of the game, the odds on the Tanks two to one. Armco officials deplored the betting and warned fans that gambling was illegal in Kentucky (pari-mutuel betting was legal).

Because neither manager loaded up, the game might measure the usual strength of the teams. Unfortunately, neither eleven could really display its wares. A drizzling rain before the game and a heavy downpour during the first half turned the chalk-lined turf into a roily sea of mud, an "oozy, slippery, gooey, sticky mess."[33] The *Register* called the game a "cross-channel" swim, a "loud duck-quaking contest." The Tanks wanted to call the game off, but the Armcos, believing that they had a better chance than the Tanks to win in the mud, refused. Of course, they could not easily turn away five thousand fans in the stands braving the rain. The game saw frequent fumbles and a continuous exchange of punts—thirty-seven altogether—conservative tactics such as professional teams often employed. Safety men seldom tried to catch punts, with the result that neither team received the break it was looking for. Midway through the second half the Tanks broke the stalemate slightly but decisively: Olin Smith blocked a punt, the Armcos recovered the ball in the end zone, but the Tanks scored a safety. Winters then punted time and again, the Tanks holding on to win 2–0. Despite the conditions, Ridgley thought that the game was thrilling. The few Tanks fans who left the park early and those who did not attend could see a film of the game a week later at the Marting theater.

Their record still perfect, the Tanks returned to Beechwood to host the Akron Silents. The *Tribune* portrayed the Silents as the semiprofessional champions of Akron, as 40 percent stronger than in 1925, and, with their deceptive use of hand signals, as a "colorful" team. They were, in fact, in eclipse in the semiprofessional football of Akron and had little going for them except the desire to avenge their defeat at the Tanks' hands in 1925. The Tanks had no problem in downing the Mutes

It Isn't Whether You Win or Lose

27–0. Lambert had recently said that he was "about to pull his hair" in his effort to book good teams for the Tanks. He scheduled reputedly strong elevens, and then the Tanks would "promptly step out and trounce the invaders."[34] Again he could pull his hair.

Near at hand, though, the Tanks might find a worthy foe. The Presidents were coming to town undefeated in six games, having allowed their opponents but one touchdown. Early in the season, newly organized and depending on many former Smoke House players, they did not appear to be a strong team, and Lambert had been reluctant to schedule them and did so only when they accepted terms favorable to the Tanks. Now their record and tradition seemed to give the game an exciting dimension. At Portsmouth fans were beginning to follow the Presidents with considerable interest, as many as a hundred people gathering to watch them practice. The players, "fighting mad" at the jibes of Tanks fans, were optimistic and called on their townsmen to "turn out" for the game.[35] It was at once a matter of honor and the gate. By the terms of the contract, which called for the crowd to reach fifteen hundred before the Presidents received a split of the gate, the Tanks "literally forced" the Presidents to guarantee a good crowd; if Portsmouth did not send a large contingent to Ironton, the Presidents would receive little reward for their play. Lambert sent 250 tickets for reserved seats to the Presidents, and within hours fans had purchased over 200. Soon newspapers in both communities were reporting that, if the weather was good, a thousand fans would be descending on Beechwood from Portsmouth.

On the morning of the game, the *Sun* reported fans heading for Ironton in a procession of assorted vehicles: "In smooth-riding limousines, in clattering flivers, some by traction cars and some even by trucks, Portsmouth's grid fandom will trek toward Ironton's Beechwood Stadium."[36] A squad of Portsmouth backs, their identities secret, intended to travel by a "big" limousine. The remainder of the team was coming on a newly painted bus, the "Rambler," and in three automobiles. At Ironton all the players would go into seclusion at the Marting Hotel to await battle.

Though their fans believed at first that the Tanks would easily win, the Tanks were taking the game seriously, practicing diligently and developing new plays. Scribes in Ironton saw the Presidents as a threat. Fans, hearing reports out of Portsmouth about the Presidents' resolution, were coming to realize, said Burke, that the Presidents were not a "what's-the-use-it's-another-pushover." For the first time in years, except for the story of the secreted Presidents in the limousine, there were no reports that the teams were loading up.

The Presidents did give the Tanks a fight. Before a crowd of twenty-five hundred, including the large delegation from Portsmouth, the Tanks scored early in the game but could not mount much of an attack thereafter. The Presidents could not score, however, and lost 9–0. The *Tribune*, praising the Presidents for their "fight," declared that the Tanks had won a "glorious" victory over a tough opponent. Minego of the *Times* thought that the Presidents had done themselves "proud," and the *Sun* basked in the *Tribune*'s unwonted praise, noting that not often did a losing team receive compliments from the rival's newspaper.[37] The Presidents did well at the gate, too, receiving $800. For once at a Portsmouth-Ironton game, no untoward incidents occurred.

The Tanks now had run their string of victories and whitewashes to eight and expected to beat their next opponent, the Columbus Tigers, hoping to hold them scoreless. A member of the NFL, the Tigers had not won a league game in 1925 and were going through another dismal season, their last in the circuit. In the expediency typical of the day in scheduling, Jerry Cochran, the Tigers' manager, begged off the game, explaining that his "boys" had suffered numerous injuries recently in games against the Buffalo Rangers and Kansas City Cowboys. Lambert, knowing that the Tigers could not be a good draw, was not concerned and arranged a game with the Kokomo American Legion team at Beechwood. The Legionnaires came to Ironton as champions of semiprofessional football in Indiana and a roster reportedly composed of "stars" from several Indiana colleges, one Notre Dame, but the Tanks bested them 15–0.

Their great record intact, the Tanks could envision completing a historic season. But they had hurdles in front of them. They would meet the Armcos and Kansas City Cowboys of the NFL at Beechwood on consecutive weekends. Then they would go to Cincinnati to meet the Potters and return to Beechwood to play the Presidents again.

After losing to the Tanks late in October, the Armcos played reasonably well, winning two games, both against weak teams. Their offense running with "machine-like precision," they defeated the Columbus Tigers at Armco Park 20–0. The next week the Oorang Indians came to Ashland. Their colorful aspect was more interesting than the game. Organized in 1922 by Jim Thorpe and other Indians, many from Haskell Institute, and sponsored by Walter Lingo, who operated the Oorang Kennel at LaRue, Ohio, the Indians took their name from a breed of Airedale.[38] They played in the NFL in 1922 and 1923, but not well, winning but three games. Thorpe, a player-coach, left the team after the 1923 season, and the Indians dropped out of the league that year. Their remnants playing as an

It Isn't Whether You Win or Lose

independent team, they remained objects of curiosity, more nearly a circus or carnival than a football squad. The *Independent* rattled off their names—Chief Fox, Running Dear, Baptiste Thunder Tomahawk, and so on. Arriving at Ashland on Saturday, they stayed overnight at the Meade Hotel, where curious fans talked to them. Before the game, Chief Long Time Sleep entertained the crowd with an Indian war dance. His fellow Indians danced poorly on the field, losing 45–0. Hatcher called their performance the "poorest exhibition" of football he had ever seen. Perhaps they once had made a creditable showing on the gridiron but not now, he said.[39]

A week later, the Armcos had the opportunity to even the score with the Tanks. All observers expected a huge crowd to gather at Beechwood; the *Tribune* even predicted that ten thousand fans might be crammed into the park. Both teams strengthened themselves. The Tanks added two linemen to their roster, Myles Evans from Ohio Wesleyan and Joe Mulbarger, a hulk of a tackle who had played for many semiprofessional teams in Ohio; the Armcos acquired Boni Petcoff, a 230-pound tackle who had captained the Ohio State team in 1924 and had played on several semiprofessional teams in central Ohio. (Petcoff, who later became a physician, was the subject of great amusement among his teammates when in one game they could not understand him because he had given his dentures to his girlfriend.)

A snowstorm struck the Ohio Valley so instead of skidding in the mud as they had in the first game, the teams skated on a frozen turf in front of a crowd of four thousand. The Armcos, Hatcher believed, "outclassed" the Tanks, recording seven first downs and holding them to none, and reaching their four-yard line as the game ended. But in the second quarter, Olin Smith, already a bête noire for the Armcos for having blocked a kick in the first game that led to the Tanks' victory, pounced on an Armco fumble and ran it sixty-five yards for the touchdown that held up for another Tanks win, 7–0. The gate, $5,204, was a record for the Tanks at Beechwood.[40]

The Armcos attempted to break their scoring drought in their last scheduled game against the Triangles, the winners of but one game in the NFL that year. Nonetheless, Hatcher, calling the Triangles a "strong" team, argued that the game might yet involve the question of whether the Armcos and Tanks should meet for a third time; if the Armcos, already winners over one NFL team, the Tigers, made a good showing against the Triangles, the victor would emerge with a "national rating." Hatcher was exhibiting a marvelous stretch of imagination. If any reason attached to his logic, it vanished at Armco Park. The Armcos limited the Triangles to a field goal but lost 3–0. Hatcher said nothing about a third game with the Tanks— but perhaps because Smith had just arranged a postseason game with the Potters at Redland Field.

129

Home and Away

On the eve of the game, the Armcos heard company officials and others praise them at a banquet at the Ventura Hotel. S. R. Rectanus, general manager of the Ashland mill, congratulated Perry and his men for their "fine spirit" and "sportsmanship." Smith offered a similar commendation. Speaking for the Employees Association, J. C. Miller declared that the season was a success despite the losses to the Tanks and a slight deficit incurred by the association. James Anderson, the coach of the Ashland High team, which was claiming the mythical championship of Kentucky, also had laudatory words for the Armcos. He had, he admitted, always considered professional football a "most brutal game" the "most brutal team" usually emerging the winner. After seeing the Armcos play, he could say that he had "never seen" better examples of sportsmanship. Perry responded to the encomium with plaudits for the association—it was a great pleasure to work for it—and for his team; all the players had demonstrated their sportsmanship and had proved that "it isn't whether you win or lose, it's how you play the game." Surely the banquet was a love feast.[41]

Hours later, the Armcos and Potters met again at Redland Field. The Armcos seemed to justify the praise accorded them for their sportsmanship. With only two penalties called, the "tussle" was the "cleanest" ever played at Redland Field, said an *Enquirer* reporter.[42] But the Armcos could not turn clean play into field goals or touchdowns and once again played a scoreless tie with the Potters, their fourth consecutive game without a score. Thus the Armcos finished the season with a record of six wins, three losses, and a tie. That mark was respectable, but, considering their good start and their failure to score in their last four games, it was a disappointment to players and fans alike. The Armcos did close the season, though, seemingly on firm ground in the community. Attendance had been reasonably good, suggesting that their support reached beyond the Armco plant. The *Independent* continued to be a full-throated advocate for them, and businessmen in the community seemed willing, if called on, to give them sustenance of some sort. But no one praised the Armcos for "advertising" the community. And unlike the Tanks, they were far from becoming a "team of the town" capable of evoking emotional fervor from the community.

Their record unblemished in ten games after defeating the Armcos a second time, the Tanks faced a rugged eleven in the Kansas City Cowboys on Thanksgiving Day at Beechwood. In their third year in the NFL, the Cowboys were on their way to their first winning season, finishing fourth in the circuit. They came to Ironton by odd circumstances. Originally, Lambert expected

It Isn't Whether You Win or Lose

the Cleveland Panthers to meet the Tanks. A member of the American League that C. C. ("Cash and Carry") Pyle, the promoter who had signed Red Grange to his controversial contract, had created literally to force the owners of the NFL to admit his New York Yankees into their league, the Panthers had gone into receivership early in November, their only assets thirty-three muddy uniforms.[43] The league was also about to fall. Learning of the Panthers' apparent demise, Lambert managed to arrange in their stead the Kansas City Cowboys of the NFL, a team that played most of its games on the road. He had to guarantee them $1,500.[44]

The Tanks knew little about the Cowboys but heard rumors that their regulars would not be coming to Ironton. Saying that he expected the Tanks to go all out to beat his team, the Cowboys' manager denied the story, adding that he would give $2,000 to anyone who could prove otherwise. A *Tribune* reporter, more or less verifying the manager's statement, saw one of the Cowboys' stars, Pete Bloodgood, practicing his kicking at Labold two days before the game. Whether or not they were the regulars, the Cowboys staying at the Marting Hotel were "all splendid chaps." One fan recalled them as a spectacle in Ironton: "They all wore 10-gallon hats and cowboy boots. They were really a colorful sight on the streets of Ironton."[45] Even if they lacked some regulars, they were still nearly too much for the Tanks. Outweighed by a "massive avoirdupois," the Tanks could hardly penetrate the Cowboys' line, running for only nineteen yards and punting fourteen times; but they managed to hold off the Cowboys in a scoreless tie. For the first time in the season, the Tanks did not walk off the field as winners.

The Tanks were still undefeated and unscored on when they went to Cincinnati the next weekend to meet the Potters at Redland Field. A thousand or more Tanks fans journeyed to Cincinnati by special Norfolk and Western excursion cars, anticipating that their team would resume its winning ways and thus claim the championship of Ohio and Kentucky.[46] They were a small part of the crowd of about eight thousand, the largest ever to see the Tanks until they played the Akron Awnings in Akron in 1928. To the surprise and delight of the home fans, the Potters, probably "strengthened" recently, pushed the Tanks around and won 28–0. Burke lamented the Tanks' lost offense. Later he labeled a report that all the Tanks were drunk during the game "baloney." One commentator thought that the Tanks were weary from playing three games in eight days. Certainly they had to feel anguish. They lost their first game of the season and saw their goal line crossed for the first time. They would long remember the unhappy day in Cincinnati.

Their confidence shaken and their season sullied—but hardly a shambles—the Tanks prepared to meet the Presidents again at Beechwood in the last game of the year for both teams. The Presidents had been in a rather unsettled state since their loss to the Tanks early in November, their schedule in chaos, their place in the community seemingly threatened, their play indifferent. They were playing out a schedule virtually improvised week by week. Walter had been considering games with the Jackson Bearcats and with teams in McArthur and Wellston and other small towns near Portsmouth. Some fans suggested that the Presidents were looking for "soft spots" for their schedule. To allay such talk, Walter was looking for stronger elevens in Ohio and found the Bobbs willing to come to Portsmouth.

Perhaps Walter was responding, too, to an unusual proposal floating around the city. Pyle had come to Portsmouth early in November proposing that businessmen there assume ownership of the Cleveland Panthers and move the team to their city.[47] In collapse, the Panthers were looking for new management and would be willing, said Pyle, to come to Portsmouth for the remainder of the season. They could defeat all opposition, and their games with the Tanks and Armcos would draw well. The "enterprising" businessmen of Portsmouth would be passing up a good bet for advertising their city if they failed to take over the Panthers. Tantalizing the enterprising men, Pyle noted that Huntington would furnish a good home for the Panthers. For a moment the Presidents may have been looking over their shoulder at the Panthers, fearing that the Cleveland team might displace them. They could take heart, though, in reading an editorial in the *Times* complimenting them for their play against the Tanks and lauding them as a "real team," as "boys" who were better than "we knew."[48] Perhaps the editorial defused the threat, if there was one, posed by the Panthers, because the businessmen failed to act on Pyle's proposal.

The Presidents prepared for the Bobbs team as though their survival were at stake. They practiced rigorously and developed new plays for a "fast passing attack." Minego warned the Presidents and their fans that the Bobbs had fleet halfbacks who could mount a "wild running" attack. Nonetheless, the Presidents won the proverbially "hard fought" game 12–0 over the "worthy foe." Minego employed the same ceremonious language preceding the Presidents' following game against the Cincinnati Friars in Portsmouth. The Presidents practiced vigorously in preparation for the "cream" of semiprofessional football in Cincinnati. They won easily, 31–0. Neither the Bobbs nor the Friars drew more than five or six hundred fans to Labold.

The games with the Bobbs and Friars were symptomatic of a problem facing the Presidents and the Tanks and Armcos. In the days preceding any game, no matter the opponent, managers and sportswriters ritualistically portrayed it as a powerful eleven. Undoubtedly, fans discounted much of such talk and did not hurry to purchase tickets when teams of unknown strength, except in sports columns, came to

It Isn't Whether You Win or Lose

Labold or Beechwood. Consequently, a team might depend on two or three games with traditionally good elevens to balance its books. Apparently such was the case when the Presidents met the Armco Blues at Labold the Sunday following their victory over the Friars.

Scheduling the Blues on short notice, Walter told fans that he had used "gobs" of money to induce a "good" team to come to Portsmouth.[49] Now there had to be at least fifteen hundred spectators or the Presidents—the manager, the coach, and the players alike—would have to dig into their own pockets to cover expenses. More than that, he saw the size of the crowd as a measure of whether the Presidents could schedule strong teams in 1927. He placed a display advertisement in the *Sun* urging fans to see the Presidents "get ready for the Tanks." As they described the probable tactics of the teams, the sportswriters for the *Sun* and *Times* joined in his call for a large crowd. And the largest crowd of the year, eighteen hundred, came to Labold, perhaps evidence of community support for the Presidents. But the crowd could not help them on the field. The Blues completely contained the Presidents' offense and won 6–0 in a "bang-up" game. Their win, said the *Middletown Journal,* was a "glorious victory" over the heavier Presidents, the "beef trust."[50]

Walter had arranged the Presidents' coming game with the Tanks only after torturous negotiations with Lambert. Saying that the Tanks and the Stadium Association were in a bind because attendance at recent games had slipped and that the covered grandstand at Beechwood provided a hedge against bad weather, Lambert would not yield on the site of the game, prevailing in his insistence that the teams meet again in Ironton. He did accede to more "liberal" financial terms for the Presidents—a larger guarantee and evidently 50 percent of the gate—than they had received in the first game. Walter's men wavered for a moment, complaining that the Tanks had promised to come to Portsmouth for the second game, but they agreed to go to Ironton, believing that the game there might draw a record crowd.[51]

As the teams practiced, unlike before the first game, sportswriters in the communities exchanged charges and countercharges about loading up. What they said implied something, accurately or not, about the nature of their teams. Fans in Portsmouth reportedly opposed the practice, and the Presidents, asserted a *Sun* reporter, did not intend to take on new men.[52] But reports surfaced that they had acquired Red Weaver, who had been with the Cleveland Panthers, and two "speedy" halfbacks from the east, Leonard de Lat and David Charlesworth. Responding to allegations in the *Tribune* about the loading up, the *Times* openly acknowledged that the Presidents had signed Weaver, De Lat, and Charlesworth—but then went on to argue that the Presidents were as much a "home grown" team as the Tanks. The

Presidents had "brought" only four recruits to their roster, three other players had come to the city of their own accord, and all the remaining men on the roster were longtime residents of Portsmouth. In contrast, "very few" Tanks were from Ironton; many had come to the city only because of their "football ability."[53]

At least in Portsmouth, signs pointed to a large crowd coming to Beechwood. Ticket sales were "brisk," three hundred sold in a day or so. Estimates of the number of fans going to Ironton ran from five hundred to fifteen hundred.[54] Interest in the Presidents seemed to gather speed as the days passed. Boosters arranged a parade for the team on Saturday night; the American Legion drum corps led it, followed by the Rambler, automobiles carrying the players, and "ardent" fans walking in the rear. Sunday morning saw fans traveling to Ironton by automobiles, buses, and railroad and traction cars. The Portsmouth Public Service Company, operator of the traction line, attempted to drum up business, advertising the sale of round-trip tickets at a dollar each. All the players journeyed to Ironton by two buses provided by the Cannon Ball Transportation Company.

Predictions of the size of the crowd were far off the mark. Eight hundred fans from Portsmouth came to Beechwood, well short of expectations. Altogether, the crowd numbered about two thousand, sorely disappointing the Tanks and the association people, who were looking for as many as five thousand. Presidents fans were disappointed in the game, the Tanks brushing their men aside 33–0. The Presidents had De Lat and Charlesworth in the lineup, and Jerry Mincher besides, but Weaver did not appear for them. The new men, far from helping the Presidents, more likely cluttered up their offense, having had little or no practice with them. Thus the Presidents closed play with eight wins and three losses, the Tanks at eleven wins, a loss, and a tie.

The Presidents returned home to lick their wounds and to attend a banquet at the Hurth Hotel to celebrate a successful season.[55] Funderberg hosted the dinner and invited about twenty businessmen to attend. The players heard Walter praise them for their play and talk of a proposal for their team to enter an Ohio Valley league in 1927. He intended to recruit new talent, college stars who would move to Portsmouth to join a nucleus of local players to form a team giving the city a "flying start" in the league. He did not provide specific details on the proposed league—on what teams or cities would constitute it, what kind of scheduling membership would entail, and so on. Ironically, after Walter spoke, Jake Pfau rose and spoke of a team more local in origin. Obviously smarting over the loss to the Tanks, he called on Ironton to organize an "All-Ironton" eleven to play an "All-Portsmouth" eleven— teams composed solely of actual residents of the communities. He sent a challenge

It Isn't Whether You Win or Lose

to Lambert to play later in the month, but nothing came of it. Hearing of Walter's comments, Burke smugly approved them: "So the boys down on Chillicothe street can get together, raise a pot, and go after some real athletes, getting them to locate in the city. This is the plan followed by the Tanks, Ashland Armcos and other teams and ought to be successful."[56]

About ten days later, the players and the community learned more about the proposed league. At a meeting of the Ironton Stadium Association, stockholders appointed three men—L. B. Andrews, Frank Wieteki, and George Mahl—to a committee to take the initiative in organizing the Ohio Valley League.[57] The men expected to invite Ashland, Portsmouth, and Huntington and perhaps Chillicothe and Charleston to join Ironton as members of the league. The projectors pointed to attendance at Ironton-Ashland, Ironton-Portsmouth, and Ironton-Huntington games as evidence that such a league could thrive. They conferred with Johnny Stuart at Huntington and elicited his agreement to organize a team for the city, and they intended soon to call a meeting of men in the river cities to begin planning for the league. The proposal had merit. Such a league would go a long way toward solving the chronic problems of scheduling for the teams in the cities and heighten rivalry among them. A round-robin of home-and-home games would give each team six games with historical or natural rivals. Unfortunately, for some reason never explained in the sports columns, the meeting did not take place, and the league died aborning, the prospective members continuing to "gang their own gait."

Nonetheless, the Presidents seemed to be ready to become a viable team for Portsmouth. They had posted a good record, though not against all first-rate teams, but building that sort of schedule was difficult for any semiprofessional team of the day. They had brought big-city elevens to Labold from Cincinnati and Columbus and given fans a glimpse of the snowy heights of success. Though the largest crowd at Labold—eighteen hundred—hardly equaled what the Tanks often drew at Beechwood, apparently they had turned out a profit. At a meeting of the players at season's end, Walter read a financial report and announced the distribution of dividends to them from the revenues. At the same meeting, the players appointed a committee to arrange a team dance and to organize a basketball team and baseball team for play in and around Portsmouth. Though small ventures, they could give the Presidents a broadened presence in the community and invite wider support.

At Ironton the Tanks were closing the door on bittersweet notes. Their season had been remarkable until the Potters defeated them in Cincinnati. They had begun playing before large crowds in a new grandstand but had seen attendance gradually slacken, except for the Armco game, as the season wore on. The season's receipts

135

Home and Away

were over $30,000. Each player received $637 for his season's play. Unfortunately, the association incurred an operating deficit of $3,000.[58] To help erase the deficit, the Tanks ran a campaign to sell books of twelve tickets at $1.25 each to so-called guarantors for a benefit game to be played on the day after New Year's between a squad led by Winters and one led by Davies. Only about two hundred fans showed up at Labold, but because guarantors had already purchased tickets, the small turnout did not affect the campaign. Burke said that the books had been "cleared" for the season but did not cite substantiating figures.[59] The field was in bad condition, with deep ruts and frozen chunks of dirt preventing "regular formations" and conventional tackling. On the first play of the game, the Winters eleven scored a safety. Thereafter all was passing and punting and no scoring. Yet spectators and players alike seemed to enjoy the spectacle—men slipping and sliding on the ground. It was an appropriate, a seriocomic way for the year to end and begin.

7

Knock the Tanks and You Knock Ironton

THE TANKS OF 1926 had a remarkable season, scored on in but one game, their only loss. The next year, however, they suffered, from additional loss of independence, from financial problems, and from slippage on the field. Across the river in Ashland, the Armcos were gathering strength and, though not sweeping the Tanks aside, made a legitimate claim to primacy in the Ohio Valley. At Portsmouth new winds were blowing. There a new manager and a legendary player began to dress the old ragamuffin football in more attractive vestments.

Very early in 1927 the Ironton Stadium Association, obviously reacting to the financial problems that had brought about a benefit football game, announced a new policy governing the Tanks. Heretofore, there had been no clearly defined relationship between the association and the Tanks. Now, by fiat, the directors asserted authority over the team.[1] They appointed a committee of three directors, L. B. Andrews, an attorney, chairing it, to manage the Tanks. They argued that they had to protect the people, mostly directors, who had subscribed to the stock for building the grandstand at Beechwood; the association had

137

to see that the Tanks, the principal source of income for retiring the debt, operated on a "strictly business basis." The affairs of the team had been "too haphazard"; too often the community did not know until the advent of a season whether the Tanks would play; dissension over the roster was a continuing prospect. To ensure Ironton that a "first class" team free of cliques would represent it, the committee would manage the "financial end" of the team and select a manager to handle the "playing end" of its games.

Only a day or so after the directors announced the new policy, the football committee selected the manager for the Tanks, Bill Brooks, because of his "long association" with the Tanks and his "general ability."[2] He would be responsible for booking games, arranging transportation for the team, and conducting other business. Along with the committee, he also would select a coach and captain of the team, who would handle personnel, conduct workouts, and weed out candidates for the team. They and the manager would share the task of recruiting new players. The committee was also taking steps to organize a proposed Ohio Valley League. Burke was certain that with the league in place, the manager would find his duties in scheduling reduced to looking for a few outside teams to play.

Brooks and the committee soon ran into a thicket in their choice of a coach. Initially, they considered reappointing Sonny Winters to the position, but then suddenly and surprisingly, the Board of Education appointed Davies football coach at Ironton High, the position that all "understood" belonged to the coach of the Tanks.[3] Thus the door was open to Davies to return to the Tanks as their mentor. According to the *Tribune,* Winters had not reapplied for his high school post. At the same time, the football committee was in a deadlock in choosing between Winters and Davies as the Tanks' coach.

Many residents complained to the board that it had acted prematurely in appointing Davies to his old position, noting that ordinarily it did not offer contracts to teachers for another two or three months. Now Davies had an undue advantage over Winters in vying for the Tanks position. At a parents-teachers meeting, parents expressed their dissatisfaction with the board's action and declared that the coach of the high school team, his time at a premium, should not serve as the Tanks' coach. The *Tribune* joined in the dispute. Charles McCarthy, formerly editor of the *Irontonian* but now editor of the *Tribune,* editorially condemned the board, saying that it had acted in haste and without consulting the community.[4] McCarthy denied finding fault with Davies but complained of the covert process by which the board had named him coach. What pressure had come to bear on the board he did not know, but the whole affair had left a bad taste in the community. At the committee's

Knock the Tanks and You Knock Ironton

decision to appoint Davies coach of the Tanks, he called for a "divorcement" of the athletic program at the high school from the "professionalism" of the Tanks, arguing that it was not conducive to progress of the high school team for its coach also to coach a professional team.[5] Without explaining the causative force at work, he said that fans would flock to high school games. Until the Stadium Association liquidated its debt, however, he was willing to see Davies continue in both positions.

Davies became coach again just as men from the semiprofessional teams in Ironton, Ashland, Huntington, and Portsmouth met in Ironton to discuss organization of the proposed Ohio Valley league.[6] They looked primarily at the issue of salaries for players. The Portsmouth representative wanted limits at a low figure, evidently below what was current, but the Ironton man said that the minimum would have to remain at about $50 a game. They reached no agreement on that or any other issue. Burke, who was present, thought that Portsmouth merchants ought to be able and willing to raise $5,000 as a "starter" fund for their team. After all, "Sportsmen" in the smaller city of Ironton had collected several thousand dollars each year to erase deficits or to begin the season on the right foot. He reported that players in Portsmouth were looking for a "star" to come to the city and take charge of their team. Portsmouth, he was certain, could field a team capable of competing against the strong teams in Ashland, Huntington, and Ironton. He was less certain a few weeks later, when he learned that warring factions in Portsmouth were talking about entering teams into the league.[7] He counseled them to join forces and find a businessman to initiate a campaign to raise $5,000 to import eight or ten good players to the city. They could shape a team serving as a good "advertisement" for the city. Ashland, Huntington, and Ironton were all looking around for good players, and Portsmouth should join the hunt, too. Together, the cities could turn the spotlight of professional football on the new league. Burke alluded to the league in several columns in the ensuing weeks, but no one took any more steps to organize it.

Whether or not the Tanks played in a new league, Davies intended to coach a strong team. He had ambitious plans, said Burke. Late in the winter, he went on a scouting trip for new players through West Virginia and Pennsylvania but returned to Ironton empty-handed.[8] Throughout the spring and summer, he and Brooks lined up several men for tryouts and took on three men from West Virginia Wesleyan, Paul Kemerer, Dana Longh, and John Moore. In July Davies went to South Bend to take Rockne's course for coaches and returned optimistic about the Tanks' coming season. At the opening of practices in September, though, he was still casting about for players. That was not an easy task, because several central and northern Ohio cities, organizing teams for a proposed new league, were beating the bushes for players.[9] The *Ohio State Journal* had proposed the organization of the Midwestern Football League that would affiliate with the NFL; supposedly the Ashland Armcos, the Cleveland Panthers, the Massillon Maroons, the Dayton Koors, the Canton Bulldogs, and teams from Akron, Youngstown, and Columbus would enter the league. In fact, after three Ohio clubs left the NFL following the season of 1926, Jerry Cochran, manager of the Columbus Tigers, had called a meeting of representatives from Ironton, Ashland, Cincinnati, Portsmouth, Akron, Canton, Columbus, Dayton, Massillon, Cleveland, Youngstown, and Louisville and proposed the organization of the new league, but it was too late in the year for them to act on his proposal, and nothing came of it.

On the eve of the first game, Davies had cut the roster to twenty-two and after that reduced it to seventeen. Altogether, at one time or another, thirty-three men tried out for the team. Of the seventeen players who appeared in at least half of the Tanks' games in 1927, eight had been on the roster in 1926. The other nine were not entirely new to the Tanks, at least two having played for them in one or more seasons before 1926. No fewer than fourteen had played collegiate football.[10]

As the opening game approached, the Stadium Association initiated a campaign to sell season tickets, a book of ten at $16.50 for box seats, $14 for general admission seats. Twenty high school girls, selected by the principal, undertook a special sales drive; those selling the greatest number would receive cash prizes. Fans could purchase tickets from the girls or at two downtown business firms. Such an arrangement clearly bespoke strong ties between the Tanks and the community. To attract more fans, the association announced that it was installing additional toilets and concession stands. With Brooks still seeking games for the Tanks, they began their season at Beechwood against the Bobbs-Chevrolets. Despite the girls' efforts, the crowd numbered less than a thousand. Though winning 7–0, the Tanks played a lackluster game. Then, against the Armco Blues at Beechwood, again before a slim crowd, the Tanks played indifferently in a scoreless tie.

Attendance flat and facing a deficit of $1,500 after but two games, the Stadium Association took a step precipitating a crisis that threatened the Tanks' existence. At a meeting after the Armco game, the directors decided that the association could not continue the "original plan" calling for payment of salaries to players regardless of expenses. Since the players had not signed contracts, the directors reasoned, rather speciously, that the association had "escaped debts" to them; the first two games, in their view, were merely trial workouts. Instead of paying the players salaries, the association would relinquish control of the team and let the Tanks split net receipts evenly. The directors intended also to offer the Tanks ownership of the grand-

Downtown Ashland, c. 1926 *Courtesy of Arnold Hanners Photographic Collection, Boyd County Public Library, Ashland*

Downtown Ironton, c. 1930 *Courtesy of Briggs Lawrence County Public Library*

The Selby Shoe Company, Portsmouth, c. 1925. Of the several shoe factories in Portsmouth, the Selby factory was the largest. *Courtesy of Portsmouth Public Library*

Tanks, 1922: "Shorty" Davies, back row, far left; Bill Brooks, front row, far left
Courtesy of Lawrence County Historical Society

Bill Brooks, c. 1922 *Courtesy of Lawrence County Historical Society*

Armco Park grandstand, c. 1925 *Courtesy of Arnold Hanners Photographic Collection, Boyd County Public Library, Ashland*

Tanks, 1925 *Courtesy of* Ironton Tribune

Beechwood Grandstand, 1926 *Courtesy of* Ironton Tribune

Virgil Perry, Armcos coach, 1927 Armco Bulletin *14 (September–October 1927)*

Armcos, c. 1927 *Courtesy of Arnold Hanners Photographic Collection, Boyd County Public Library, Ashland*

Armcos game at Armco Park, c. 1927 *Courtesy of Arnold Hanners Photographic Collection, Boyd County Public Library, Ashland*

Portsmouth Shoe-Steels and Coach Jim Thorpe, 1927 (mural on Portsmouth floodwall)
Photograph by Marilou Becker

Tanks, c. 1928 *Courtesy of* Ironton Tribune

Tanks fans at Redland Field (Tanks vs. Guards, 1928)
Courtesy of Lawrence County Historical Society

Carl Brumbaugh, a Spartan in 1929, Chicago Bears quarterback in 1930
Phil Brumbaugh Collection

Earl "Greasy" Neale, Tanks coach, 1930.
A childhood friend, whom Neale called
"Dirty," gave him the nickname "Greasy."
Reproduced from Coffin Corner 18 (1996)

Tanks defeating Bears at Redland Field, 1930 *Courtesy of* Ironton Tribune

Glenn Presnell, c. 1930 *Reproduced from C. Robert Barnett,* The Spartans and the Tanks

Earl "Dutch" Clark, Spartans back, 1931–32 *Reproduced from C. Robert Barnett,* The Spartans and the Tanks

Ox Emerson

Grover "Ox" Emerson, Spartans lineman, 1931–33. Emerson received his nickname because he missed a blocking assignment; the quarterback said to him, "You are a big dumb ox."
Reproduced from Coffin Corner 19 (1997)

George "Potsy" Clark, Spartans coach, 1931–33. When Clark was about six years old, a veterinarian in his hometown of Carthage, Illinois, gave him the nickname "Potsy"; the inelegant name stayed with him. *Reproduced from* Coffin Corner, n.d.

Potsy Clark

Spartans tryouts, 1932 *Photograph by Charles Clevenger*

Spartans, 1932, at Ebbets Field, Brooklyn *Courtesy of Scioto Ribber Company*

Spartans-Packers ticket, 1932 *Courtesy of Scioto Ribber Company*

Spartans vs. Packers, 1932 (mural on Portsmouth floodwall) *Courtesy of 1994 Portsmouth Murals, Inc.; photograph by Tom Rogowski*

George Halas, Chicago Bears coach, 1932
Courtesy of Pro Football Hall of Fame

Playoff game, Spartans vs. Bears, Chicago Stadium, 1932 *Courtesy of Pro Football Hall of Fame*

Harold "Red" Grange—"Sincerely to 'My good pal' Carl [Brumbaugh]" *Phil Brumbaugh Collection*

Spartans ready to board bus for trip to Chicago *Courtesy of John Carpenter*

Knock the Tanks and You Knock Ironton

stand for $300 a game, the fee to cover payments for insurance, the watchman's salary, and interest to stockholders of the association. Word leaked out almost immediately that the players believed ownership of the grandstand would be burdensome and that they would resort to use of "home-grown entertainment" to cut operating expenses. Though not willing to accept the directors' interpretation of the first two games as "trial workouts," they reportedly were ready to accept the proposal that they share in net receipts in lieu of salaries. They expected to appeal to the community for renewed support. The directors appointed a special committee to meet with the players and review all proposals.[11]

Anticipating the Tanks' plea for support, E. N. Meck, general manager of the Selby Shoe Company, addressed the Rotarians on the day of the directors' meeting, speaking for a holy cause, his rhetoric Babbitry at its florid best. The response of the community to the Tanks' crisis would signify, he asserted, the difference between the ordinary and the great individual, the "dormant, dead city and the progressive, alive, up and doing community," and the nation falling into oblivion and the nation in "advance of the world." Too often in the life of an individual, city, or nation, warned Meck, people did not understand what was important until it was too late. The names Washington and Lincoln signified "loyalty and patriotism"; they were men who never shirked their duty. Like the nation, men had to grow physically, and thus athletes were important to the city, models for its citizenry. "What more glorious example of the athletic prowess and coordinate effort," Meck asked, "has any city than Ironton in the achievement of the TANKS since their inception in the year 1920?" What other city could boast fifty-nine wins, with only eight losses and four ties, 1,256 points to 101 in seven years? "What a wonderful record." He chastised those who would belittle an institution "far greater than Ironton" or who would sit passively while others belittled it. The Tanks could not hope to win without support, and honor and glory belonged to men who would "stick and carry" as Ironton was being weighed in the balance. Meck called, finally, for the citizenry to rise as one in dedication to the Tanks: "Let us as one march out to the stadium next Sunday and every Sunday thereafter, rain or shine, and show these boys that we are with them. Let us as one, destroy the knockers as men without honor in their own homes. Let it be not said that the Ironton TANKS were not beaten by Armco or Portsmouth but by the traitors within their own town. You are IRONTON. Knock the TANKS and you knock Ironton; knock Ironton and you disparage yourselves for 'YOU ARE IRONTON.'"[12] The Rotarians listened, applauded and went home.

The players, meeting hours after Meck's exhortation, reportedly evinced a fighting spirit, believing that their team would survive.[13] They decided, for the moment, to

Home and Away

accept the association's proposal that they share in net receipts from games. Evidently seeing himself as a cause of the financial problem, Brooks resigned as the Tanks' manager, saying that he could not meet his responsibilities for scheduling and other matters and continue to play—and he preferred to play. The players then selected a committee to assist Davies until the team had a new manager. McCarthy of the *Tribune* was less optimistic about the Tanks' prospects than the players. The Stadium Association had "turned the team back on itself," and he was skeptical about whether the "boys" could get through the season sharing the gate. He feared that they were mired in a "hopeless muddle."[14]

The players and the association continued to discuss terms of separation as the next game approached. Coming to Beechwood were the Birmingham Boosters of Toledo, reputedly a "fast and heavy outfit." Brooks had scheduled the contest in August, offering the Boosters a guarantee of $750. Burke saw the game as an opportunity for fans to give the Tanks a "new lease on life," a means for them to go forward.[15] Now was the time to "forget arguments and bickering of the past and rally to the support of the team that has done more to advertise Ironton than the city could have ever done for itself." A day or so before the game, the Tanks came to a tentative agreement with the association for use of Beechwood. They would bear all operating expenses at the stadium and would receive all revenue from the sale of general admission tickets at $1.10 giving ticket holders access only to the bleachers. For twenty-five cents more, they could sit in the grandstand; the association would receive all revenue derived from such sales until it had taken in $270, any amount beyond that going to the Tanks. It would retain ownership of the grandstand. Speaking for the association, Meck revealed that a "representative" group of boosters were ready to assist the Tanks financially. A collection among stockholders and boosters would raise $1,600 to be used, the Tanks understood, to pay them for their first two games and to acquire additional players. The players were willing to use their share to induce Winters, who was playing for the Ashland Armcos, to return to Ironton.

The Tanks then met the Boosters, their "spirit revived" and their flesh strengthened with the addition of three players, one of whom was Paul "Flop" Gorrill, an end who had played at Ohio State. Winters, though, would not rejoin the Tanks. Old and new players had no problems with the Boosters, methodically grinding out a victory, 25–7. The reporter for the *Toledo Blade* called the Tanks' line a "stonewall" and said that the Tanks' back easily went through and around the Boosters' line.[16] If attendance was good, the *Tribune* took no note of it; in view of the Tanks' subsequent decision, probably it was disappointing.

Only a few days later, the Tanks announced that they had canceled their next

Knock the Tanks and You Knock Ironton

game with the Shelby Blues and disbanded for the year. Their decision came out of the failure of the association to pay them for the first two games. According to the Tanks, the association, in violation of the recent agreement, had refused to turn over $450 taken from the gate of those games.[17] And they had not received any part of the $1,600 that Meck had pledged to them. They also complained that the association had no right to compel them to play ten games at Beechwood. Declaring that the association would make no concessions on these issues, the players gathered their togs and left Beechwood. But the directors denied the charge of intransigence. They were willing, they said, to consider compromises on both issues, and they expected local boosters soon to meet their pledge to contribute $1,600 to the Tanks. For the moment, though, neither the players nor the directors were discussing the vexatious questions with one another.

The community was divided, too, in assessing blame for the apparent demise of the Tanks. Many fans believed that the association men started the trouble by taking over the Tanks and "throwing them over" after the opening games lost money. Others found fault with the players for going off "half-cocked"—for not meeting long enough with the directors to iron out their differences. Fans saw varying prospects for the Tanks. Some were certain that, somehow, the team would continue to play and reach even greater heights, but a group of "interested" parties wanted to reorganize the squad, letting it begin with lowered expectations and move gradually to old levels of achievement—whatever they were. A fan writing to the *Tribune* called for a public meeting to deal with the issues separating the players and directors, but for the moment all was at a standstill.

The players and the directors did not require a public meeting to come to an agreement. They met only a few days after the Tanks announced their disbandment and negotiated several compromises.[18] The Tanks would pay the association $125 a game for use of Beechwood. They had to play at least seven games at the park. After the seventh game, they would receive $1,600 for the first two games; a citizens' group would raise the money by a popular subscription. Soon the players signed the agreement, resumed practices, and elected Nick McMahon, the theater entrepreneur and former Tank, as their manager.

Notwithstanding the apparent rescue of the Tanks, McCarthy argued that their heyday was over and that football fans ought to give their primary allegiance to the local high school team, the Tigers. The future, he said, held "little in store" for the Tanks. The community had gloried in their record, but now they were falling prey to internal dissension and financial realities Now a "highly paid team," the Tanks had become too costly for Ironton. If cities such as Cleveland, Cincinnati, Dayton,

Columbus, and Akron could not support a professional team with a weekly payroll of $1,000, how could Ironton do so? The hundreds of fans from Huntington, Ashland, and other communities who had once come to Ironton were now patronizing the Armcos. The Tanks could not retrieve that loss. And now it was the "joyful duty" of the *Tribune* to call the fans' attention to the high school team, a "game and cocky bunch" of boys, amateurs, battling teams from Columbus, Dayton, and other big cities. They deserved the support that high school teams in Portsmouth and Huntington were receiving—twelve thousand fans had recently attended a Huntington game. The Tanks might be saved, however, if they lowered their aspirations. Fans would not come out in large numbers to see elevens from Columbus or Toledo that had little chance of winning, but they would support the Tanks and other good valley teams playing one another.[19] The Tanks were the linchpin among them. No one publicly gathered at McCarthy's standard.

After missing one week of play, the Tanks met the Shelby Blues, who, coached by Pete Stinchcomb, numbered on their roster players from Ohio State and Michigan State, as well as from small colleges in northern Ohio. The game did not create much interest in Ironton. The crowd at Beechwood was considerably less than two thousand. Though finding the Blues no "pushover," the Tanks defeated them 14–0 and could have scored more, said Burke.

Undefeated in four games, only a tie marring their record, the Tanks had not yet faced one of their "natural" rivals. But waiting for them at Armco Park were the Ashland Armcos, with an identical record of three wins and a tie. Set back a week because of the schism in Ironton, the game could go a long way in settling claims to mythical championships and in shoring up or damaging the pride of players, fans, and communities.

 In contrast with the Tanks, the Armcos were going through a placid season despite substantive changes in their roster. Their operation, an extension of the Armco company, an efficient producer of steel, was far tidier than that of the Tanks. They did, however, have problems on the field. In 1926, after winning five of their first six games, the Armcos did not score a point in their last four games, losing two and tying two. To strengthen the offense, Virgil Perry reordered his roster for the coming season. Reportedly, he received applications from many "high-class" players because the Employees Association paid players promptly each month and was willing to pay selected players more than $50 a game. Ashland, complained Collett of the *News,* was one of the neighboring cities spending money like a drunken sailor for players.[20]

Knock the Tanks and You Knock Ironton

Perry did not begin to consider applicants until after he returned to Ashland in August from a coaching school conducted by Glenn "Pop" Warner, the famed pioneer of the single-wing and double-wing formations.[21] Believing that he had to shape his backfield to "fit" Warner's system, he moved himself from the quarterback's position to his "natural" position as a halfback and brought in Sonny Winters to play quarterback. He bolstered his line with the addition of three men, including Red Roberts, who had played several games for the Armcos in 1925. A teammate believed that Roberts received $225 a game on his return to the Armcos.[22] Perry's roster, as it took shape two and three games into the schedule, was a mixture of recruits and veterans. Of the fourteen men who played in more than half of the Armcos' games in 1927, eight had been in the lineup at one point in 1926; six had not been on the roster that year.

As Perry recruited players and ran practices, Russell Smith was building a schedule. He found the task daunting. After booking the Tanks for two games, he complained that he could not easily secure other strong teams.[23] Athletic directors at colleges, he contended, could readily build schedules satisfying alumni and students who wanted their teams to roll up big scores against weak opponents, but he had to book elevens that patrons of professional football believed would provide good competition. With some pulling and tugging, he had a fairly firm schedule in hand as the season opened, and apparently it held up well. The Armcos had eleven games in front of them, eight at home—Smith was able to offer solid guarantees—and six against four teams that they had met in 1926. Altogether, Smith arranged a reasonably attractive and difficult schedule.

Despite problems in scheduling, the Armcos had little interest, but more than the Tanks had, in joining the midwestern league proposed by Cochran a few weeks before the season began. Cochran envisioned a league in parity with the NFL, the members to be the Cleveland Panthers, the Canton Bulldogs, the Massillon Maroons, the Dayton Koors, the Ashland Armcos, and teams from Akron, Youngstown, and Columbus. Perry attended the one meeting of the representatives of the other clubs but did not commit the Armcos to enter the league. Officials of the Employees Association were wary. They noted that other leagues had failed—probably they had in mind the American League—and argued that Ashland was not large enough to support a team in the proposed league. They feared that thus the association might fall into bankruptcy. A few days after Perry returned from Columbus, they decided not to enter the league, explaining that the Armcos' schedule was too far along for revision but that they would reconsider the question for 1928.[24] At Ashland a hard business attitude governed football affairs, and dreams were never grandiose.

Home and Away

If the directors of the association were realistic and businesslike in their view of the new league and in eschewing overambitious goals for their team, they could also argue, as did Brady Black, a new sportswriter for the *Independent,* that the Armcos were about as good as a semiprofessional team needed to be to sustain the integrity of the sport in Ashland. The association, he reported, had no wish to field a professional eleven. It was not simply because Ashland was not large enough to compete with cities like Columbus or Akron. The directors of the association could keep football in Ashland on a "higher plane" if they limited the team to young men who made their living in a "regular employment" and played football as a sideline on the weekends. The Tanks had been successful with such a view of the sport. Fans there or in Ashland would not have become interested in the Tanks or Armcos if the stars had been "tramps," professional players moving from community to community. Members of the Armco squad, said Brady, were solid citizens engaged in useful vocations, some in nearby cities, many in Ashland. Petcoff was a physician in Columbus, Joe Work ran a printing business in Cincinnati, and Stuart owned a sporting goods store in Huntington. Tynes managed a collection agency in Ashland, Roberts a restaurant in the city. At least seven players were Armco employees. They were all as "clean and sportsmanlike a group" as could be found on any collegiate team.[25] Ironically, even as Brady asserted that fans would not have supported the Tanks had they been "tramp" athletes, the Tanks were increasingly moving to the use of itinerant players. Though a majority of the Tanks had full-time occupations in Ironton as public school teachers, railroad workers, and municipal employees, as many as five men in 1927—the three players from West Virginia Wesleyan, for instance—came to Ironton on the weekends to play for $50 a game.

The Armcos' first foe of the season was the Koors, still playing second fiddle in Dayton to the Triangles, chronically one of the weakest clubs in the NFL. The Koors "pranced" on the field wearing uniforms with a "weird" combination of red and white hues so each player looked like two men. But the Armcos, as expected, wore them down for the victory, 22–6. Then the Armcos made the Cleveland Panthers, who had survived the dissolution of the American League and liens, look like a "bunch of school boys," defeating them 30–0. Black saw their following game against the Blues as an index of their standing among teams in the Ohio Valley, notably the Tanks, whom the Blues had played to a scoreless tie at Ironton a week earlier. The Armcos won 16–6, enduring the Blues' rough play and squirting of tobacco juice into their eyes. They then played to a scoreless tie with the Dayton Triangles, a doormat of the NFL yet receiving a "tremendous" guarantee from Smith. The crowd of thirty-five hundred gave the Armcos but a small profit.

Knock the Tanks and You Knock Ironton

Before each of the early games, Brady wrote extensively depicting the Armcos' foes as powerful. He spoke of Abe Stuber of the Blues as a great runner and passer, of Earl Britton, who had run interference for Grange at Illinois, as a member of the Triangles' "sensational" backfield. At the same time, he always lavished praise on the Armcos as a "great" and "spirited" eleven. Black, of course, was acting as a publicist for the Armcos. He was one of a company of sportswriters at Ashland, Ironton, and Portsmouth—Burke, Minego, Hatcher, and others—whose columns were standing advertisements for the local team's next game. The writers were local versions of the "Gee Whizzers" in national circles, the sportswriters who gloried in the exploits of the Ruths and Dempseys of the day.[26] Typically, the local men described coming opponents as collegiate stars capable of prodigious feats. They were, of course, attempting to persuade fans to patronize the Armcos, Tanks, or Presidents. Burke was one of the stockholders in the Ironton Stadium Association, and Hatcher had close ties to the Employees Association. They could not go wrong in exaggerating the strength of a foe. If the local eleven lost, the writer had been on the mark; if it won, he and his readers could savor the victory. Readers, though, might discount what they read about the strength of an opponent.

The columnists were at work as the Armcos and Tanks, each undefeated, prepared to meet at Armco Park. Their rivalry, after only two years, had reached an intense level. It was similar, said Black, to that between Harvard and Yale, between Army and Navy.[27] Black saw the game as "historic battle," McCarthy as the "Battle of the Ages," Burke as a "titanic struggle." Partisans of each team alleged that the other was loading up. Fans of the Tanks were certain that Marty Karow, a former star back at Ohio State, would be playing for the Armcos. Perry insisted that the rumor was "all bunk" and that he was satisfied with his lineup. Rooters for the Armcos expected to see at least three new men in the Tanks' lineup, one of them Wallace "Doc" Elliott, a fullback from Purdue who had played for the Canton Bulldogs. If the Tanks' bankroll could stand it, Black noted sarcastically, several "other transient celebrities may wear the Red."[28] Like a Baltimore and Ohio timetable, the Tanks' lineup was subject to change without notice. One story had the Tanks using six ringers. The Tanks did not bother to contradict the reports of loading up, even acknowledging the prospective use of Elliott.

A large crowd was expected at Armco Park for the game; advance sales of reserved seats exceeded two thousand. Knowing that a large delegation of red-hot Tanks fans would be at Armco, McCarthy counseled them against "unseemly display or words." Sunday saw good weather and nearly five thousand fans at Armco Park. As Perry had assured fans, the Armcos did not use any new men. As Armco

147

fans said that they would, the Tanks had at least three new men in their lineup; besides Elliott, Paul Hogan, a halfback from Washington and Jefferson, and Martin Herman, a tackle from Detroit University, became Tanks, remaining with the team for the remainder of the season. They could not win the day for the Tanks, though; the game ended in a scoreless tie. But their fans believed the Tanks would have won had not an official impeded a run by Davies. Ridgley thought that the teams were "evenly matched as straws in a new broom."

Playing to a tie and their records identical, neither the Tanks nor the Armcos had a clear claim to dominance of semiprofessional football on the banks of the Ohio. And nudging them for a position in the run for rank was a new team in Portsmouth managed and coached by assertive men determined to win football games.

At the close of the season in 1926, all seemed in order for the Presidents to continue play in 1927. Apparently Roscoe Funderberg had been able to meet their expenses out of revenue from gate receipts and expected to enter his team in a new league. With a year's experience behind him, Walter might be able to give the Presidents better management, especially in building a schedule. The *Sun* and *Times* were giving the team more coverage and support, and the players seemed interested in going into the community as members of the Presidents. Reportedly Portsmouth was inviting players to come to the city to take "good" positions at steel plants and elsewhere.[29]

At summer's end in 1927, though, there was no new league for the Presidents to enter, players had not gone into the community to promote the team, and Funderberg had taken no steps to reorganize the team. But standing in the wings was twenty-five-year-old Jacques "Jack" Creasy, the director of public services for Portsmouth and sometime football player for the Smoke House. He resolved to organize a team and eventually received material support from the Selby Shoe Company and the Whitaker-Glessner steel mill.[30] Late in August, he purchased the Presidents' equipment from Funderberg and called on all men interested in forming a "representative grid squad" for Portsmouth to attend a special meeting. He announced, too, that he was making "every effort" to sign Jim Thorpe as a player-coach. Already he had introduced Thorpe around town to many prominent persons, and Thorpe had said that he liked the city. At another meeting a few days later, the prospective players urged Creasy to go to Marion, Ohio, where Thorpe was living, and sign him to a contract. Creasy said that he would go soon and offer Thorpe "one of the largest guarantees" ever made to a player to come to Portsmouth. He did not reveal the source of income permitting him to make an offer, but a new team could not count on the gate

Knock the Tanks and You Knock Ironton

from its opening games or season to yield it. Almost certainly, he had persuaded executives at the shoe company and steel mill and perhaps other businesses to take care of Thorpe. In any case, Creasy expected Thorpe to sign a contract and come to the city and place Portsmouth "back on the football map."[31]

In the meantime, serving as coach as well as manager, Creasy was a whirling dervish of activity, initiating practices, distributing tickets to civic clubs and players to sell for the first game of the season against the Columbus Clothiers, and conducting a contest to select a name for the team. He was able to forgo the trip to Marion because Thorpe, on his way to Beckley, West Virginia, stopped in Portsmouth to discuss the position with him, promising that his answer would be forthcoming.[32] Much to the jubilance of the players and Creasy, the great athlete soon sent a telegram to the manager accepting the berth. He would "complete his baseball engagement [at Marion] . . . Sunday, change his spiked shoes for his grid cleats and report here [Portsmouth] not later than next Tuesday." Thorpe was nearly forty years old and had lost the decisive edge of his speed and power. A nomad, he brought with him the experience of playing with eight different clubs in the NFL, mostly with the Canton Bulldogs, most recently in 1926. He also brought a problem with the bottle. Though Creasy seemingly believed that Thorpe was still a good player, clearly he saw him as an icon in American sport, a "great drawing card." Creasy, said a reporter for the *Sun*, had effected a "bold stroke."[33]

In mid-September Thorpe was in Portsmouth ready to take charge of the team, now named the Shoe-Steels. He sounded a resolute note on meeting reporters: "I mean business and Portsmouth is going to have a real eleven this fall." He was confident and enthusiastic and thought he had "good material" on hand, but he would not predict what the team would do on the field. Certainly Thorpe put his players through intensive workouts, and surely the community seemed interested in what he was doing. With a crowd of over five hundred men, women, and children looking on as the sun beat down on the field, he kept the players so busy in conditioning drills for three hours that they looked as though they had played two games. Soon he had the offense drilling with the "speed and precision" of the Rockettes. Thorpe himself ran in a scrimmage, declaring afterward that he would enter the game against the Clothiers in "tip-top shape." Hours before the game, hedging on the outcome, he knew that if "my players play football and don't go up in a balloon we'll win the game."[34]

Thorpe entered the first game with the roster pared to twenty-two men. Of these, twelve, nearly all residents of Portsmouth—among them Tiny Englebrecht, Adams, Shields, and Pfau—had played for the Presidents in 1926.[35] The roster changed substantially over the course of the season. At one time or another, thirty-eight men were on the roster, twenty-six of whom had never played for any Portsmouth team. In 1926 only three men had collegiate experience; in 1927 sixteen men, nearly all from outside of the city, had played for such schools as Ohio State, Miami, Indiana University, and Marshall. Only two or three players in 1926 had once been with semiprofessional or professional teams other than the Smoke House or Presidents; at the very least, fifteen in 1927 had played for the Canton Bulldogs, the Columbus Tigers, the Triangles, and other clubs. Clearly the character of semiprofessional football in Portsmouth was changing—from homegrown men playing for the love of the game and community to "imported" men playing for the love of the game, repute— and money. Creasy was moving his team and fans to professional football. Creasy and Thorpe imparted to the community a sense of intensity, a determination to win heretofore unknown in Portsmouth. As Thorpe worked the Shoe-Steels, Creasy was canvassing the city in an effort to sell tickets for the first game and mounting advertising "pasteboards" by the hundreds at the Smoke House and other business places.

Thorpe was probably a drawing card, for the crowd at the opening game was one of the largest ever to attend a semiprofessional game in Portsmouth, around twenty-five hundred. The Clothiers were an ordinary eleven, and the Shoe-Steels won 13–0 in a game devoid of "sensational" plays. Because of an infected foot, Thorpe did not play but, disobeying his physician's order, roamed the sidelines. Then the Steels met four more run-of-the-mill teams, all at Labold. They lost to the Bobbs 12–0 and defeated the Springfield Bulldogs 6–0, the Logan Wildcats 8–6, and a team from Martins Ferry 26–7. Nagging injuries bothered Thorpe, and he played but occasionally. His best performance came against the Bulldogs. The *Springfield News* said that he "starred" in the game, and, according to *Times,* he "hit the line so hard" that five men tackling him had to be taken from the game.[36]

Creasy, believing that the string of victories, though over ordinary teams at best, gave the Steels greater credibility in scheduling, sought out elevens of more prestige. He tasted the fruit of success, he thought, in arranging a game at Redland Field with the Cincinnati Home Guards, the successor to the Potters. But the Guards may have given the Steels a game primarily because their coach's name was still a household word in football circles. Fathers wanted their sons to say that they had seen the great Jim Thorpe play.[37] The Guards offered Creasy a date at 37 percent of the gate, supposedly the highest ever given a visiting team but still lower than visiting teams received elsewhere. Seeing an opportunity for glory and gold, Creasy and Thorpe

Knock the Tanks and You Knock Ironton

went to work. Creasy "reinforced" the Steels for the game, signing two new players. One of them, Russell Hathway, a big guard who had played for the Pottsville Maroons and Buffalo Bisons in the NFL, became an important figure in the rise of professional football in Portsmouth. Thorpe sent the Steels through "stiff workouts," gave players "tongue lashings," and developed new plays and formations.[38]

With interest in the game growing, the Norfolk and Western decided to run an excursion train to Cincinnati to accommodate "several hundred" fans. The reporter of the *Enquirer* believed that the crowd, five to seven thousand, was the largest ever to attend a semiprofessional football game in Cincinnati.[39] Certainly at the time it was among the largest; attendance at such games there usually ran three and four thousand. Whatever their number, the fans saw a "spectacular battle." For the Steels, Freddy Shipp, the quarterback, played a "great game," and Thorpe threw a pass for a touchdown. But the Guards, loading up a "little," won 19–12. Nonetheless, the Steels had played a "glorious" game, and their fans, seeing the crowd go "wild" over them, left Cincinnati bursting with pride. Like fans who had remained in Cincinnati, they thought that at long last the community had a "real" team, one that had put the city "on the map."

Fans felt pride that their team had played in the "big city" and played well. But the Shoe-Steels had to do more to take a special place in the history of football in Portsmouth. They had to vanquish the great bugbear of semiprofessional teams in the city: the "famous" Tanks from the "ancient and hereditary enemy," the city of Ironton. Since 1919, when the Tanks began play, no Portsmouth team had defeated them. The Tanks had met the Smoke House and Presidents twelve times, winning eight and tying four. Before the Steels could seek a measure of redemption for the community, long the butt of derisive ridicule in Ironton for its failure in semiprofessional football, Creasy had to schedule a game with the Tanks. That took no little pain—the Tanks could be imperious.

After Creasy and Nick McMahon had once agreed to home-and-home games, the first to be played at Portsmouth, McMahon demanded that the Shoe-Steels come to Ironton first, arguing that since the Armcos would be out of town, the crowd would be larger there than at Portsmouth. Their teams scrounging around for money, the managers would not yield on the question. McMahon declared that "both games were off unless the Shoe-Steels agreed to come to Ironton for the first game."[40] McMahon, observed the *Sun,* was like a child who said, "We won't play in your backyard, but come over and slide down our cellar door." But Creasy, saying that he had made a commitment to local fans to play first at Portsmouth, was adamant. He

Home and Away

"raved and stormed," accusing the Tanks of sheer greed—of contempt for the spirit of the sport.[41] His Tanks were struggling financially and did not wish to forgo a profitable gate, so McMahon consented to come to Portsmouth for the first game.

Knowing the history of losses, Thorpe and Creasy set their sights on a victory. Thorpe conducted hard practices, leaving no "stone unturned" in perfecting the Steels' blocking and tackling. Especially, he wanted more speed to maintain a "fierce" offensive attack. Hearing Thorpe, Creasy recruited reinforcements, Walter Jean (Gean, Le Jean) and Winston "Speedy" Charles. Jean, a guard, had played for the Packers and Maroons; Charles was a halfback who had been with the Ashland Armcos in 1926. With these new men, said the *Times,* the Steels could give the Tanks "what Paddy gave the drum."[42] The Tanks did not "sit patiently" while Thorpe and Creasy prepared for the "battle of battles." They had defeated the once powerful Akron Indians, , now in decline and out of the NFL, 27–0. They were also practicing hard. About thirty-five hundred fans, a thousand from Ironton, saw the Tanks wear out the Steels 18–0. Thorpe played a steady game, as did Jean, but to no avail. Rubbing salt in wounds, the *Tribune* asserted that Ironton was weary of winning and might move the Tanks to Portsmouth.

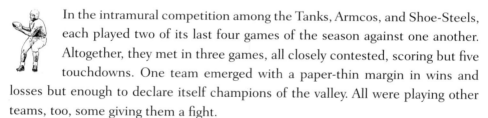

In the intramural competition among the Tanks, Armcos, and Shoe-Steels, each played two of its last four games of the season against one another. Altogether, they met in three games, all closely contested, scoring but five touchdowns. One team emerged with a paper-thin margin in wins and losses but enough to declare itself champions of the valley. All were playing other teams, too, some giving them a fight.

The Tanks and Armcos met in the first of the games, their second encounter, just after the Tanks defeated the Steels. Since the Tanks and Armcos had tied at Armco Park, the Armcos had played two games. First they met the Canton Bulldogs at Ashland. Though the celebrated Bulldogs of old in name only, the Canton men were not a pushover; the Armcos edged them 7–0, an official's decision in the fourth quarter costing the Bulldogs a touchdown. Still undefeated, the Armcos then journeyed to Middletown to meet the Blues. The Blues had lost but one game, that to the Armcos, and, using the "family purse," had strengthened their lineup with the addition of Al "Pup" Graham, the outstanding guard who had played with the Triangles earlier in the season against the Armcos. About five hundred Armco fans took an excursion train to Middletown. Blues fans, too, looked forward to the game and the big parade preceding it on Saturday. On Sunday the Blues turned the tables on

Knock the Tanks and You Knock Ironton

their kinsmen, winning 16–9. Stuber ran ninety-two yards with an intercepted pass, and Graham spent much of the afternoon in the Armcos' backfield.

The sheen of the season glimmering in their first loss, the Armcos still had an opportunity for distinction in their next game, to become the first Armco eleven to defeat the Tanks. Undefeated and tied twice, the Tanks had yielded but one touchdown in seven games and would be playing before a partisan crowd at Beechwood. Increasing their advantage, they added as many as five players to their roster.[43] The Armcos added no one. Advance sales of tickets were good in both communities. According to the *Tribune,* the "greatest crowd" in the history of Tanks football attended the game, a "battle of the giants."[44] The Armcos led 7–0 going into the fourth quarter, and then Frecka ran forty-four yards for a touchdown and kicked the extra point to give the Tanks another tie with the Armcos. The game, said Ridgley, was as good as one could find between the Atlantic and Pacific Oceans.

Black, though also seeing a "good game," said that it had left a bad taste in his mouth.[45] Attendance at Ironton, even at a record of thirty-five hundred, was less than the forty-seven hundred at the first game in Ashland. He attributed the decline, in part, to the "orgy" of defensive play characterizing semiprofessional football and to the Tanks' loading up, an admission of inferiority. Thus the Tanks had removed the element of "sport" from the game. If the teams met for a third time, as the Tanks wished, they should agree to eligibility rules restricting the use of new players. Calling Black's column "amateurish," McCarthy remonstrated.[46] The Ashland writer had forgotten that the Tanks' foes often loaded up. Once the Huntington Boosters had imported half of their squad to play the Tanks, and on one occasion the Armcos had loaded up with Perry. Could Ashland or any other city, he asked, number half of its team as local sons, as could Ironton? Besides, did the Armcos want to play a pushover?

Still undefeated but tied three times, the Tanks now met the Steels in a return game two weeks after defeating them at Labold. In the intervening week, the Steels had beaten the Hocking Valley club of Columbus, an ordinary team, 13–7, on a touchdown late in the game. In view of their earlier loss to the Tanks, their showing against the Hocking Valley club, and their appearance before a hostile crowd, the Steels seemed to be on a fool's errand coming to Ironton. But Thorpe attributed the loss to the Tanks to "bonehead plays," and Steels fans could take "high hope" out of rumors circulating in Portsmouth and Ironton that Creasy had reinforcements: George Kinderdine and Chal Joseph of the Triangles—their team had an open date —and Emil Mayer from Catholic University, all linemen. The *Sun* and the *Times* said that it was "common knowledge on Chillicothe Street" that Kinderdine, Joseph, and Mayer would be in uniform for the Steels. Creasy was "sawing wood" and would not comment on the rumors. Fans in Portsmouth saw the prospect of "victory at last" over the Tanks. As usual, both teams went through rigorous practices preparing for the game. Because of rain, the Steels worked out two afternoons in the hall of a dancing academy. Thorpe, despite a bad knee and a recent "sickness," expected to play. A "vast" throng of Steels fans, a thousand or more, traveled to Beechwood, becoming part of a crowd of thirty-eight hundred.[47]

The Portsmouth fans were not disappointed in their team. A "raving, rampaging" Steels eleven, Kinderdine, Joseph, and Mayer "curing" the weakness in the line, raised an impenetrable defense and won 7–0. Thorpe weighed in with some "deadly tackling." Fans from Portsmouth gloried in the "thrilling victory." For them the crack of the pistol ending the game was a happy funeral note sounding over the Tanks. Their victory gave the Steels immortality in the common memory and seemingly assured them of continuing to play the next year and beyond. Fans of the Tanks were dumbfounded. McCarthy, though offering no alibis, suggested that had the Tanks sought out new players, they might have won.[48]

With the tie against the Armcos and the loss to the Steels and their next game coming against the strong Armco Blues, the Tanks faced an unusual and unpleasant prospect. Never had they lost two games in a season, and never had they played three consecutive games without a win. Now what the record said could not happen might come to pass. Clearly the Blues, their lineup composed of former collegians, were capable of giving the Tanks a battle, and recently they had handed the Ashland Armcos their first defeat. They were making claims to the championship of southern Ohio and wished to strengthen their case with a victory over the Tanks. The Tanks' offense had been deteriorating; they had scored only one touchdown in the past two games. Thus the Blues came to Ironton believing that the Tanks were vulnerable. And they were. On Thanksgiving Day, a small crowd saw the "hard tackling" Blues dominate play to win 8–0. Three days later, the Tanks closed their season, going to Logan to meet the Wildcats in a game that McMahon arranged at the last minute because of the "liberal financial offer" of the Wildcats. The Wildcats used several collegiate players whose season had just ended, but the Tanks held them and their teammates off and won 14–0.

Their season ended, the Tanks could hardly take pride in their record—six wins, two losses, and three ties. For the first time in their history, they lost two games in a season. They won barely half of their games. Their offense creaking, they failed to score in four contests. Though no one fixed blame on Davies, specific players, or ele-

Knock the Tanks and You Knock Ironton

ments in the offense, the backfield, anchored by Davies and Frecka, was aging and had not received the infusion of new players that the line had. Some observers felt that dissension among the players had contributed to ineffectual play. If the Tanks sponsored dances or if fans gave them banquets at season's end, reporters did not mention them.

Early in the season, McCarthy had urged Tanks fans to give their allegiance to the high school team; now at season's end, arguing that the Tanks were a public institution and seeing them in slippage, he devoted three lengthy editorials to assessing their problems and proposing solutions. He called for immediate action to improve the team for next year.[49] The Tanks had to acquire new men to shore up their offense; Benny Friedman and Bennie Oosterbaan, stars from the University of Michigan, were available, for example, and the Tanks should make offers to them. They should also rid themselves of men who were troublemakers and were of little value. The Stadium Association had to let the public know its view on financing the team and come to a written agreement with the Tanks on their management. In a second editorial, McCarthy called for action to get the Tanks' house in order.[50] He feared that the "secret diplomacy" entwined in the appointment of Davies as coach early in the year was at work again. Fans were demanding that the team be reorganized, but unfortunately the players were about to assume control of the Tanks' affairs. A coterie of players had nearly annihilated the team in 1927, and that would happen again unless an "external" business manager gave the club firm direction. He clarified his argument in a third editorial. Without identifying who had made the decisions on players, he complained that new players had joined the team for a game or so and received far more money than local men had, and alleged that several players who were not really capable would be retained if a manager did not step in to take over selection of men based on their abilities.[51] Otherwise, the quarreling that was commonplace in 1927 would continue. He noted in closing that Creasy of the Steels was a model for the kind of direction needed for the Tanks.

Late in December, at a meeting of the association, the stockholders made decisions that indirectly addressed the problem of selecting players. They reappointed McMahon as manager and named him a director, and passed a resolution barring the association from "participation" in the management of the Tanks.[52] They intended to give McMahon greater freedom and authority in the selection of players —to free him from interference from the association and players. According to Glenn Presnell, who was the Tanks' coach in 1928 and 1929, he and McMahon alone recruited and released players.[53]

If the Tanks did not enjoy their usual success on the field, they did at least do reasonably well on the ledger. Near Christmas, they divided the money in their treasury, $7,980, into fourteen full shares of $570. Included was $1,300 contributed by merchants earlier in the year—the guarantee had been $1,600.[54] The players received payment for their play in the first two games of the season, the subject at dispute earlier in the season. Several players received stipends for one or two games.

 Meanwhile, the Steels and Armcos were on course for a game to conclude the season's play. After the Steels defeated the Tanks, Creasy called Smith and started "agitation" for the contest, and they soon came to terms. Before meeting the Armcos, the Steels improved their record and reputation in a return game with the Bobbs. They had lost to the Bobbs in the second game of the season but now were a different team. Kinderdine and Joseph were again available. A fine running back, Walter "Sneeze" Aichu, sometimes called the "Jap star" but in fact of mixed Pacific blood, had also joined them. The Bobbs, too, added half a dozen men, their names secret. But they could not deflect the Steels. A "rollicking" crowd on hand at Labold, the Steels thrashed the Bobbs 32–0.

The Armcos also came into the game on a successful note. After their second tie with the Tanks, they met the Canton Bulldogs for a return game at Armco Park. Smith believed that because that game was so close, a second game would draw well in Ashland. The crowd numbered about the same as for the first game, and again the Armcos won narrowly, 6–0. The Armcos then met the Kokomo American Legion Indians at home. Using a passing attack to good advantage, the Armcos defeated the Indians 14–0.

Now the Steels and Armcos would meet in their last game of the year, one that would give the winner a claim to various crowns. By an imaginative manipulation of comparative scores, Creasy and Smith argued that the game would decide the championship of the Ohio Valley.[55] Clearly if the Armcos won, they could make a reasonable claim to the Ohio Valley title. The victorious team could also call itself the champion of the Tri-State. Both teams, having won preceding games, were confident of victory. The Steels bolstered confidence through loading up. With Jake Pfau perhaps sidelined with an injury, Creasy looked for a replacement and more from the Green Bay Packers, who had just completed its season. He induced four backs—Joe "Red" Dunn, Eddie Kotal, Rex Enright, and Pid Purdy—to join the Armcos.[56] But Purdy and Enright were injured in an automobile accident on the way to Portsmouth and could not play. The Armcos, said Black, had a policy against loading up, and few reports surfaced about recruits coming on to their roster. Perry turned down a request from the "fastest" Tank, Kermit Frecka, to join the Armcos

Knock the Tanks and You Knock Ironton

for the game. But he did take on one Haynes, a "giant" tackle from the Kokomo Indians, to replace an injured lineman.

The Steels suffered an unusual loss only days before the game when Thorpe announced that he would not be playing or coaching against the Armcos.[57] His contract, he explained, called for him to coach ten games, no more. He quarreled bitterly with Creasy over that or some other issue. Creasy offered him a raise, but he refused it, sulking over a problem that he would not publicly disclose. He did say that if he could find a suitable place in Portsmouth for his dogs, he would stay for the game. Whatever the problem, the contract or the dogs, he departed. Fans did not chastise him, but they could not have been happy with him. Jean, a veteran of professional wars, assumed his post at Creasy's request.

According to sportswriters in Ashland and Portsmouth, fans in both communities had their blood up over the coming "battle of the ages." The Selby company and the Glessner mill were pushing employees to buy tickets and form a crowd of three thousand that would make the Armco fans look "like a scrimmage." At a "big booster" meeting at the Armco plant, a hundred fans gathered, several exhorting the audience as though they were speaking at an "old-fashioned testimonial." Before learning that Thorpe would not be present, Black urged parents to take their children to Armco Park to see the "husky redskin," the greatest "living athlete" in the nation.[58] "Old Father Time" was stalking Thorpe—Black mistakenly had him forty-five years old—but he was still better than most younger players. At the news that Thorpe would not be at the game, Black complimented the Steels for disclosing the fact. Reporters, wishful thinkers, expected as many as seven thousand fans to attend the game.

For a change, weather conditions on the day of the game were good. About thirty-two hundred fans were at Armco Park, thousands below the reporters' expectations. They witnessed a spectacle of sorts. As past champions of the valley, Tanks players had seats of honor along the sideline. As Black described the Shoe-Steels, they wore, collectively, a Jacob's coat of many colors, clad "in uniforms that varied all the way from the Green Jerseys of the Green Bay Packers and the Blue and White of the Dayton Triangles to the Blue of the Middletown Armcos and common white shirts."[59] The game was bitterly fought, the "greatest game ever," the teams showing more "fight and teamwork than at Ohio State." With seven minutes to play and leading 6–0, the Steels had victory in their grasp. Then Johnny Stuart of the Armcos ran a punt back for fifty-four yards, eluding Joseph and others, to the Steels' two-yard line. The Armcos scored in two plays, and Louis Ware drop-kicked the extra point for the 7–6 victory. Decades later, Ware still vividly recalled Stuart's run as the most exciting one he saw in his football career.[60] The *Times* man called the run a "freak

Home and Away

play," the ball having bounced the "wrong way" into Stuart's hands. He praised all the players, as did Black, who thought that the Steels had played "nobly." Roberts came out of the game in awe of Aichu: "Damn, if I ain't seen everythin', a man who can run three directions at the same time!"[61] Though Portsmouth players and fans were "keenly disappointed," they had caught sight of the mountain—of a championship —and could realistically envision seeing it in its full ascent.

The Steels had a record of seven wins and four losses and still might improve it in a few days. Creasy had challenged the Tanks to yet another game. But for some reason, he could not effect an agreement with the Tanks. A visionary of sorts, he was also talking about a postseason round-robin series among the Tanks, Armcos, and Steels; that, too, came to nothing. The Steels, who had been waiting to learn the outcome of his challenge to the Tanks, packed their grips and "faded away" to their homes. Creasy was optimistic about the future of the Steels. A committee of fans was already planning for the next season, and no financial crisis loomed on the horizon. He had signed four players for 1928, and Jean had agreed to continue as the Steels' coach. Nearly all the men in uniform against the Armcos were willing to return, but he could not sign them yet because of an NFL rule—many had played with a league club in 1927—holding them under contract with their teams until late in the summer. Creasy intimated that he would be looking for other players throughout the year. Practices would begin September 1, and he expected to have the entire team assembled by that time and would not add players to the roster, with a few exceptions, as the season progressed. He had the best of intentions and awaited the days and months to turn them into reality.

The outlook was also good for the Armcos. With the best record in their brief history—seven wins, a loss, and three ties—they claimed the championship of the Ohio Valley and the Tri-State. They had yet to defeat the Tanks, but that great victory seemed inevitable if they continued to improve. Their season-ending banquet seemed to presage a golden future as a team of the community. About a hundred boosters gathered at the Ventura Hotel.[62] Various company dignitaries spoke. Perry said that he had, at the outset of the season, great faith in the sixteen men he had picked for the team. And they had vindicated his judgment. The Employees Association presented gold cigarette lighters to thirteen players and fountain pens to the men who did not smoke. Armco people were always efficient. The association gave Perry a leather briefcase and a large cup for scoring more points—forty-eight—than any other player. One booster wanted to award a silver football to the most valuable lineman, but he found no agreement on the subject and finally dedicated it to the entire line.

8

Turn the Town Upside Down with a Really Good Football Team

Through the biennium of 1928 and 1929, the semiprofessional teams of Portsmouth, Ironton, and Ashland experienced dramatic changes, two becoming essentially professional clubs and one crashing on economic shoals. Two communities participated in the changing fortunes of their teams and one detached itself. The competition among the three clubs was intense, even fierce, with one team becoming increasingly dominant, the Tanks at last no longer the juggernaut rolling over opponents.

At season's end for the Shoe-Steels in 1927, Creasy seemed on his way to building a team that had some standing in the community. His team had defeated the Tanks, had enlisted some support from local newspapers and business interests, and had, apparently, solid players returning in 1928. But he would never again see "football played along the river shore." In July 1928, he was stricken with appendicitis, complicated by endocarditis, and then developed pneumonia and died at the age of twenty-six.[1] Mourned by "townsmen of a stiller town," he left a legacy of mounting interest in Portsmouth in professional football.

Home and Away

For the first time in the life of the community, a body of prominent citizens rose to give emotional and material support to a team. Midway through August, H. Coleman Grimes, editor of the *Times,* and Howard Graf, an executive of the First National Bank, acting on behalf of "football enthusiasts" who wished to organize a team, issued a call to businessmen to attend a meeting at the Hurth Hotel. They expected or hoped to form a "football board" to direct affairs of the club in a "business-like manner."[2] Unlike the management of previous teams in the city, the manager would not have complete charge of operations but would come under the "direct ruling" of the board. Somehow, that arrangement would ensure "clean athletics" and make Portsmouth one of the best football towns in the state.

Walter Jean, understanding that he would coach the new team, wrote to Grimes saying that he was ready for a "great" season. He knew that the people of Portsmouth, having supported the Shoe-Steels when they did not play well early in 1927, had proved their desire for a professional team; they were a "large and loyal population" who would "support the very best team."[3] He sent Grimes a list of eighteen men who should compose the team. He was certain that these men, nearly all collegians, could compete with the best players in the land. Of the eighteen, ten had played for the Steels in 1927; seven of them did appear in the new team's lineup at one time or another in 1928—but only three for more than four games. Only two were longtime residents of Portsmouth.

A reporter for the *Times* gave Jean's words an expansive interpretation, writing that, eighteen of the best players in the nation had "tentatively signed" contracts. The reporter also had the coach saying that if the fans were willing to support a mediocre team as they had in 1927, he "would turn the town upside down with a really good football team." Fans were in the streets declaring that they wanted a good football team and that they were ready to give it their full support.[4]

Very soon about fifty businessmen, along with "some" fans, met at the Hurth Hotel to create an entity to manage a team. They agreed to organize a temporary stock company for financing a club "similar to the Shoe-Steels" and elected William Gableman, a prominent businessman, as president, Dr. George Brown as vice president, along with two other officers and seven directors.[5] In a few days, they expected to elect officers and directors to a permanent organization. For the first time in Portsmouth, a football board would exercise complete control of a professional football team that would become "self-supporting." Graf, the treasurer, reported on anticipated expenses and circulated forms to everyone for subscription to stock of the association. In short order, he had enough subscriptions to assure the start of the season. The directors decided to ask Jean, who already was recruiting players, to come to Portsmouth at

Turn the Town Upside Down

once and "line-up" players to begin practice in a few weeks. They believed that the men who had played for the Steels in the final game of 1927 were ready to return. With the new men Jean was recruiting, they would constitute, all believed, a "great" team. Tentatively arranged, the schedule called for the club to play at least ten games, including four with the Tanks and the Armcos.

As fans awaited the coach's arrival in the city, they measured him in heroic dimensions, 240 pounds on a six-foot frame. They saw him as one of the most "colorful" men ever to play in Portsmouth. He was intelligent, a "forceful speaker," a "college-bred athlete and gentleman."[6] He had played guard for the Packers in 1925 and 1926. He had command of several languages and in "business life" was a chemist (a pharmacist). Ever confident, he expected to lead the greatest team that had ever represented the city in football. Besides his duties as a coach and player, he was responsible for recruiting players and planning the schedule; in short, he was also acting as a manager. He would spare no expense, he asserted, in getting the best teams possible to come to Labold.

Jean arrived in Portsmouth a day or so after the meeting of the businessmen. Almost immediately, the officers and directors met with him and formulated plans for the coming season. They decided not to organize a permanent body until they had received subscriptions to all the stock to be issued.[7] They authorized Jean to sign players and to arrange the schedule as he saw fit. He was certain that he could have thirty "colorful" men signed to contracts on a few days' notice. Of course, the team would carry only eighteen players. Even though Jean was reaching out for men, they would find that they had to conform to a "strict" set of rules stipulated in contracts drawn in conformance with those in use in the NFL. All men had to attend practices five days each week and had to live in the city during the season. As in the NFL, players whose performance was not satisfactory were subject to release on six days' notice. Jean expected to sign men who had been with NFL clubs and thus were familiar with the rules.

Jean went on the road into the Midwest in his search for players. At Green Bay, he expected Curly Lambeau, coach and manager of the Packers, to "farm" out some "high class" players to his team.[8] Of course, he knew Lambeau, and Lambeau, who had struggled to build a small-city team, was willing, said a *Times* man, to assist another such team. At Lambeau's recommendation, he acquired Keith Molesworth, a "wonderful" running back who had played for Monmouth College, and Ray Hollisey, a burly guard from Wisconsin Normal. He persuaded Hathaway, Aichu, Joseph, and Mayer, all players for the Steels in their closing games, to sign contracts. He also took on two local men who had played for the Presidents and Shoe-Steels, Jake Pfau

161

Home and Away

and Heckie DeVoss. Jean signed all the men as professional players taking up a full-time occupation at a fixed salary, though what they received no one revealed publicly. If they remained long enough in the city, as did Molesworth, they saw their occupation listed in the city directory as "football player." Rather rapidly Jean and the football board were creating a professional football team.

The directors, too, were busy. They appointed a special committee to organize a campaign to solicit more funds for the team and to sell season tickets—nine dollars a ticket, probably for seven games. They announced a contest to select a name for the team, the prize a season ticket. They ordered uniforms. Apparently at their urging, businessmen and "interested" citizens persuaded municipal officials to place on the ballot a bond issue to raise $80,000 for the construction of a stadium at Labold. A stadium, the projectors argued, would induce a minor league baseball team and a "first class" football team to come to the city.[9] Such teams would provide "advertising value" for the city.

Soon the Portsmouth team seemed almost ready for the season. Jean was putting his players through rigorous practices in preparation for their opening game against the Columbus Bobbs. The schedule was taking shape, the temporary association was about to give way to a permanent body, and fans were buying tickets. And from a list of one hundred proposed names, the special committee selected "Spartans."[10] Submitted by Bret Hurth, the fourteen-year-old son of the owner of the Hurth Hotel, the name was complementary to the nickname of the Portsmouth high school team, the Trojans. Clearly it suggested valor, "fight" with a capital "F." And it did not allude to any specific business firm in the community, a requisite because many companies were supporting the club.

Midway in September, just before the Spartans played their first game, the temporary management governing them transformed itself into a permanent body, the Portsmouth Football Association. Brown became its president, Gableman the vice president, Grimes the secretary, and Graf the treasurer.[11] Elected to the Board of Directors were George Ahrends, Dr. Frank Coburn, Earl Cunningham, Harry Doerr, Edward Leach, Joseph Horchow, and Dr. T. G. McCormick. All prominent men in the community, they gave the Spartans the imprimatur of repute that the old semi-professional teams had not enjoyed. Increasingly taking on the aspect of a business organization in sports, the association opened a downtown office to conduct business after 6:00 P.M. every weekday. It also employed a window decorator to create a display of Spartan objects—jerseys and helmets—at the First National Bank.

All seemed to be going well for the Spartans as they opened play at Labold against the Bobbs. Despite a torrid sun, a good crowd—about two thousand—came for the first game. The game program was dedicated to Creasy, and the American Legion Drum and Bugle Corps presented a fanfare. The Spartans came on to the field attired in black jerseys with a one-inch gray stripe around the waist and snow-white numerals on the back, black stockings encircled by two narrow gray stripes, and solid blue pants. Linemen donned blue helmets bearing one-inch gray stripes, the backfield white helmets. Flashing a good running and passing attack, the Spartans then downed a stubborn Bobbs eleven, 20–12.

The men in Portsmouth had expected to assemble players for a stable roster. But the directors and the coach, apparently able to draw on funds on short notice, thirsting for victories, and noting the availability of players released from NFL clubs, could not remain committed to such a goal. Through the second to the last game of the season, they added new players, at least sixteen, some for a few games as "reserves," some for the remainder of the season. Among other NFL clubs, they had played for the Packers, the Yankees, and the Triangles. George "Hobby" Kinderdine and Al Graham of the Triangles were in an odd lot in the shuffling. They played for the Spartans against the Bobbs, then for the Triangles through all their games, and finally for the Spartans in their final two games.

Jean himself became a part of the change in the roster owing to his behavior in the Spartans' second game of the season against the Springfield Bulldogs. In what was virtually a practice session at Labold—about twelve hundred fans were in attendance —the Spartans overwhelmed the visitors 54–7. The sportswriter for the *Times* reported no untoward incidents in the game, but two days later, the directors released Jean, offering no reason at first for their sudden decision.[12] Molesworth assumed duties as coach of the backfield, Hathaway of the line. Graf became the manager. A few days later, the directors explained that Jean had displayed "ungentlemanly conduct" at the game; he "did not select with care the language he used in replying to a remark from a fan in the stands."[13] Because his contract had no release clause, Jean threatened to initiate a civil suit to collect his full season's salary as coach. The directors, insisting that he had not met requirements that the board had laid down at the start of the season, would not yield. Jean did not sue and soon was playing for the Cincinnati Guards.

Directed by two coaches, the Spartans went on to play twelve more games, seven of them against the two Armco teams and the Tanks, the real core of their schedule. They first met the Middletown Armco Blues. The Blues had been regularly playing the Tanks and the Ashland Armcos since 1926, winning two, losing three, and tying one; if the Spartans aspired to parity with their Tri-State rivals, they had to fare well against this common foe. Using several new players, they turned back the Blues 13–0,

Molesworth providing the thrill of the day with an eighty-yard return of a punt for a touchdown. The *Times* sounded an alarm after the game, noting that the attendance of eighteen hundred, though six hundred more than at the Bulldogs game, left the Spartans well below the three thousand needed to break even.[14] Moreover, some business firms had not met their pledges for contributions to the Spartans. In their next game, the Spartans played "mediocre" football in beating the Mendel Tailors 31–6. Again, the crowd, apparently less than two thousand, was disappointing.

Undefeated in four games, the Spartans now had to go on the road for the first time, to Ashland to meet the Armcos, unbeaten in three games. The Spartans would have their mettle tested on the field and would also learn whether they could draw a good crowd.

Until the mid- and late 1920s, the Tanks and the Portsmouth teams usually played through a season, then temporarily disbanded, with only the players responsible for their reorganization as a new season approached. In the meantime, sportswriters and fans compartmentalized sports by seasons, and football disappeared almost completely from print and everyday talk. Ordinarily but not certainly, late in the summer, a manager called on players to meet for a reorganizational meeting or for the first practice. But with the appearance of a stadium association in Ironton and the football association in Portsmouth and the bureaucratization of football in the communities, some degree of continuity obtained. In this respect, they were catching up with Ashland, where the Employees Association provided continuing oversight of the Armcos. They had, though, a different view of football. At Ashland, the association, which sponsored other athletic teams and educational and cultural activities, did not single out football for special attention, and the larger community did not identify Armco football as a carrier of civic pride, a secular religion, "advertising" the community, as fans and businessmen in Ironton saw the Tanks and as businessmen in Portsmouth were coming to regard the Spartans. Paid football in Ashland was not as important as in the cities across the river.

In the summer of 1928, fans could reasonably assume that the Employees Association intended to field a team in the fall. Late in July Perry left the city for a three-week course at Pop Warner's coaching school in Duluth.[15] Black was apprehensive about the players who would be available to Perry; several from the squad of 1927, so rumors said, had indicated that they might not return to the Armcos. As many as five, in fact, did not report for the Armcos' opening practices, instead entering various professions and business ventures. Among those missing were Petcoff and Ware.

Turn the Town Upside Down

But in Bunk McWilliams and Red Roberts, Perry had the nucleus of a good line, and nearly all of his backfield returned. He was himself the key runner.

On his return from Warner's school, Perry declared his intention to abandon football of "line plunging" and "brute strength." He had learned in the middle of the season of 1927, he explained, that such tactics were not popular with Armco fans. Instead, he would rely on a wide-open attack requiring "fast action" and "spin plays." To that end, he had decided to use the formations that he had learned from Howard Jones at Warner's school. Jones, head coach at the University of Southern California, had his eleven come out of the huddle into a preliminary formation, a T, for example, and then shift into a single-wing formation and run from it with but the slightest hesitation.[16] Rockne had pioneered the technique using the Notre Dame box. Perry argued, correctly, that to understand and develop the timing and coordination necessitated by the Jones's offense, players had to spend unlimited time in practice. Since all the Armcos lived in or near Ashland, he expected them to be at lengthy practices every evening. He planned to draw up contracts giving him the authority to fine them $5 to $25 for missing a practice.

At one time or another, Perry had about twenty-seven men at his preseason practices learning the intricacies of Jones's system. Nine or ten were recruits, veterans and rookies, who had played at such schools as the Universities of Tennessee and Pittsburgh, Vanderbilt, Washington, Texas A&M, and Marshall. Two excellent players joined the team soon after the season's play began: Pooley Hubert, who, playing for the University of Alabama, had thrown a long touchdown pass to Johnny Mack Brown in the Rose Bowl game of 1925, and Jules Archoska, an end who had played for Syracuse. Ware and Petcoff returned on weekends to play several games; Perry apparently was willing to exempt them from the practices necessary to learn Jones's offense. Of the eleven men who appeared in at least half of the Armcos' games in 1927, seven played in at least seven of their eleven games in 1928. Altogether, the Armcos seemed to be as good as the previous year's squad. And if they became adept at Jones's "fast action," perhaps they would become a memorable team for the community.

Measured by advance sales of season tickets, certainly many fans expected to see the Armcos playing good wide-open football. Well before the opening game, sales reached 1,800, far surpassing the total number for 1927, 1,382.[17] The number, though, may have overstated the community's interest in the Armcos. In 1927 employees at the Armco plant, about half of the men working there, accounted for all sales of season tickets, and in 1928 again they were the purchasers of all the tickets.[18] But they may not have been purchasing them of their own free will. Rumors were circulating that foremen at the plant were forcing workers to buy tickets and that workers believed that they had to buy them. Years later, an Armco player recalled that the atmosphere at the plant was conducive to such coercion.[19] Supposedly, many employees were reselling their tickets—bootlegging them—uptown. Worse yet, some workers made a partial payment for the tickets, resold them, and never paid the association in full. Smith moved quickly against the wrongdoers. He admonished foremen not to use coercion to sell tickets and told workers that they were under no obligation to buy them—he wanted only true backers to buy them. He had notices posted in all departments informing employees who expected to realize "no good" from the tickets or to resell them that they could obtain refunds from the association. The association, moreover, would make it embarrassing for persons who scalped or bought scalped tickets because it intended to conduct a rigid investigation of circumstances of sales. Officials would be on the lookout for persons dealing in tickets not yet paid for.[20] The association was taking on a formidable task in an era when bootlegging in alcohol was almost normal behavior.

The schedule for the Armcos and their fans, though not fully in place before the opening game, did represent more planning than usual. For the first time, managers of the Armcos, Tanks, and Spartans met to discuss dates and terms for games among their teams.[21] Rather easily arranging home-and-home games with natural rivals, the Tanks, Spartans, and Blues, Smith avoided some of the improvisation in scheduling of earlier years when managers were freebooters searching for easy prey. He also arranged two games with the Guards of Cincinnati and brought to Ashland the Columbus Tigers, the Triangles, the Canton Rogers Jewelers, and the Logan Wildcats. Though not a big league schedule, it was about as good as could be developed among the independent teams of Ohio and the Ohio Valley.

Perry and his Armcos, professing their abandonment of "trench warfare," had the first test of their wide-open offense in the season's opener against the Logan Wildcats. Though defeating the Wildcats 13–0, the Armcos showed little of their wide-open play. Despite the large advance sale of season tickets, the crowd numbered only about two thousand. Officials of the association, keeping their word, refused to admit many persons, saying that they were attempting to use tickets of association members who had not paid for them in full.

Playing for the Armcos against the Guards in their second game was Hubert, who had missed the encounter with the Wildcats. Perry expected him to provide the blocking needed in the Armcos' "intricate" offense. Arriving in Ashland too late for practices, he prepared for the game only by reading diagrams and did little to help the Armcos in their narrow 6–0 victory.[22] Facing their counterparts, the Blues, in their next game, the Armcos exacted revenge for their loss to them in 1926, winning 13–0. Their advantage in pounds, not in their wide-open attack, gave the Armcos the victory.[23]

Each undefeated, the Armcos and Spartans would now meet for the first time. The Spartans had scored 118 points in four games, and the Armcos had not given up a point in three games. Each had beaten the Blues 13–0. Thus, asserted the *Sun,* the game would be a "football classic," the "opening battle" for the Tri-State championship, said the *Times,* the first important "setto" for the title, noted the *Independent.* According to Black, fans in the three Tri-State cities were taking the series among their teams as seriously as alumni of Yale, Harvard, and Princeton viewed their three-cornered competition. He commented at length on the development of semiprofessional football in the region, saying that with the rise of the Armcos and Spartans, it had reached a "high plane." Particularly supportive of the sport, he believed, were the contracts that the teams had begun using. Now, for any game, a team could use only players who had been with it in one previous game. Such a restriction reduced the use of "tramp athletes" and discouraged gambling elements constituting the "greatest menace" to the integrity of semiprofessional football.

The contractual rule came into play in the week before the Spartans-Armcos clash. Earlier Bob "Chic" Dazell had joined the Spartans. He had been in the lineup against the Blues but had suffered a fractured ankle playing against the Mendel Tailors. The Spartans wanted to replace him but, if they abided by the contractual agreement, could not do so; the Armcos, displaying "true sportsmanship," then consented to a replacement, Dwight Fyock, from the University of Pittsburgh.[24] Evidently without specific permission from the Armcos, the Spartans also signed another man to a contract.

If the Armcos' willingness to waive the contractual rule created any goodwill, some of it dissipated at and after the game. Before about four thousand fans, the Armcos downed the Spartans 13–0 in a "colorful" contest, Perry's long run on one drive proving decisive. Dick Young, a new sportswriter for the *Times,* insisted that the Spartans had outplayed the Armcos, their advantage fifteen to ten in first downs; and Spartans' fans attributed their team's loss to "bad breaks" and an official's "rotten decision" on a interference call. A columnist from the *Ironton News* agreed, saying that the official had become a "twelfth man" for the Armcos. Black would have none of the "alibis" and explained in detail the rules governing interference.[25]

In his column, Young reported that fifteen "scraps" had occurred among fans in the stands. Men often took flasks with them into the stands, but gambling, rather than drinking, probably was at the bottom of the problem. According to Black, "dyed-in-the-wool" fans had "wagered everything from their shirts to their toothbrushes yesterday and kept the Armco cops busier than the" one-armed paper hanger with the hives" and had resorted to fists to resolve their disputes. In a moment of comic relief, Black reported that when a tackler had knocked Molesworth out-of-bounds in the fourth quarter, the halfback had fallen on Roscoe Bruenfield, the Armcos' "colored" trainer, and given him his biggest scare since he had nearly piloted a Hudson automobile off a hill in West Virginia the previous summer.

 The Armcos and the Spartans were just beginning their play in Tri-State competition. Each had to meet the redoubtable Tanks in the next two weeks, the Spartans first playing them at Labold, the Armcos then hosting them at Armco Park. The Tanks of 1928 were hardly the team of 1927. Assessing the record of 1927, the directors of the Stadium Association resolved to cast a wide net to strengthen the Tanks. They wanted to recruit more collegians from outside the Ohio Valley and secure employment for them in and around Ironton. Using Walter Camp's *Annual Football Guide* as a mailing list, McMahon sent letters to numerous all-conference selections inviting them to become candidates for the Tanks team and offering to assist them in finding full-time employment during the season and off-season, especially as teachers and coaches in the public schools.[26]

Altogether, about twenty-five collegians responded to McMahon's letters. Coaches, other players, and interested parties recommended ten or twelve more men to him.[27] Frank Thomas, William Alexander, and Don Faurot, respectively head coaches at the University of Chattanooga, Georgia Tech, and Northeast Missouri State Teachers College, each recommended two or three players. A sportswriter for the *Chicago News,* Frank Haggerty, wrote to McMahon on behalf of a halfback at Lombard College; Edward Bland, a player at Bradley Institute, urged him to write to three of his teammates. Nearly all the players writing to McMahon expressed interest in teaching and coaching positions, and all wanted to learn more about salaries, especially stipends for games. Would they receive, they asked, $50 or $75 for each game that they played or an annual salary based on the number of games on the Tanks' schedule? Several offered their own proposals for employment in Ironton. One was willing to teach boxing to boys at the Elks Hall; another one, interested in a career in journalism, said that he would come to Ironton if McMahon could get him on the staff of a local newspaper.

Other than two men from Carnegie Tech and four from the University of Nebraska, no one from "big-time" schools wrote to McMahon. He received inquiries from such small schools as Bradley, Mercer, and DePauw. Two or three men were

Turn the Town Upside Down

completing careers at such small schools as Bradley, Northeast Missouri, and Mercer. But he struck gold in the players from Nebraska. In March Glenn Presnell, a tailback there, wrote of his interest in the Tanks and noted that two or three teammates were also interested.[28] At spring break, he, Bill Bronson, a quarterback, and Lloyd Grow, a center, drove to Ironton to meet with McMahon and the directors. Presnell, standing 5 feet, 10 inches, and weighing 193 pounds, seemed a real prospect. He had started for Nebraska for three years and in 1927 made the All-American team selected by the *New York Sun*. Captivated by him and knowing that the Tanks would be taking on many young players, the directors offered Presnell a contract as player-coach at $150 a game and guaranteed him a position teaching science at Ironton High.[29] For the moment, they tendered no contracts to Presnell's companions. Presnell accepted their offer. More than fifty years later, he recalled the factors leading to his decision:

> You have to understand there was no college draft then and you could play for whoever made the best offer. I had an offer from the New York Giants for about $150 or $175 a game. But that was just for three months. I also had an offer to coach and teach at one of the best high schools in Nebraska for $1,600 per year, which was pretty good. The Tanks offered me a job teaching at Ironton High School at $1,600 for nine months. That really appealed to me because I had my degree in physical education and science and knew I wanted to be a teacher in the future.
>
> In Ironton, everything seemed kind of crowded together by the hills, particularly after being in the plains around Nebraska. But the people were very friendly and welcomed me with open arms.
>
> I knew almost at once that this was where I wanted to play football and teach.[30]

As it turned out, as a player and citizen, Presnell gave the community as much as he received. Five decades later, Harold Rolph, who became a Tank in 1929, voiced a similar sentiment about the place of the Tanks in the community: "None of them were tramp athletes. Well, maybe one or two, but I think five or six of them married Ironton girls and lived here year round. They really added to the community. If you were a Tank, you were invited to the finest homes in Ironton for dinners and parties. Ironton was a football town and the townspeople liked to associate with the players."[31] At the time, Burke portrayed the recruits in similar language, saying that the fans were making them "town boys."

Returning to Nebraska, the three players "upset" their automobile but escaped serious injuries. Presnell kept in constant touch with McMahon, acting as an inter-

Home and Away

mediary in negotiating terms with Grow and Bronson and with Evard Lee, an end, who had not gone to Ironton. Eventually all three signed contracts. McMahon found employment for Grow as a sales clerk in a men's clothing store and a position for Lee as a teacher at Ironton High. Besides the Nebraskans, McMahon signed several other collegians, notably Farrar "Phony" Smith and Charlton "Little Bit" Pierce from Mercer and Jake Fort of Peru Normal in Nebraska. He also acquired several veterans who had played for other semiprofessional teams and the Tanks in the past. Davies, though losing his edge, remained on the roster. But the emotional, the "Faithful" warhorse Bill Brooks was missing. Always in shape, he had saved many a game for the Tanks.[32] Eventually, the Tanks' roster, numbering twenty, had only four men who had been with the team in 1927.

As recruits and veterans came to Ironton and reported for practices, fans speculated on the team they would constitute. McCarthy commented in a lead editorial that the Tanks would be good but would lose some games.[33] After all, Ashland and Portsmouth were developing "splendid" elevens. The fans could only ask the Tanks to make an honest effort and to play in a sportsmanlike manner. Besides, if they won all the time, fans would become nonchalant and attendance would fall. Burke was more optimistic than his editor. He believed that the Tanks had the material to make their greatest team in history.[34] He spoke of Presnell as a "powerful erect young man," of Lee as "rangy and fast," of Fort as a "marvelous runner."

All seemed to be going well as practices began. The players were enthusiastic about Presnell and giving their all. A newly formed boosters' club held a public reception for the players at the Elks Hall. Confident that McMahon was leading the team in the right direction, the football committee of the association continued him as manager for another year. C. E. Vidt, a member of the committee, was out asking businessmen, apparently with some success, to purchase more stock in the association. At the same time, McMahon was working on a schedule, which saw the Tanks playing six games on the road, more than ever before. Noting that the Tanks were the "best drawing card" in the state, he reported that he had negotiated a guarantee in a "handsome amount" for two games in Akron against the Akron Awnings and had received good terms for a game in Cincinnati against the Guards.

As the opening game approached, against the Bobbs, players, fans, and newsmen all foresaw a successful season. McCarthy was more sanguine than he had been earlier. Pointing to the "great college stars with the Tanks," he rated the team as "better than ever" and one that would give "honor, sportsmanship, decency and fair play to the game."[35] All was "hotsytotsy," said Burke, who, continuing his original optimism, asserted that in the Tanks the Bobbs would face a new mode in "grace and . . . body

Turn the Town Upside Down

lines," a team of "greater horsepower and . . . considerably faster" than their predecessors. On the day of the first game, he saw the squad becoming one of the greatest teams ever to appear at Beechwood.[36]

The Tanks opened the season justifying expectations and predictions. Meeting the Bobbs at Beechwood on "Glenn Presnell Day," as the Stadium Association designated it, the Tanks routed them 52–0 before a relatively small crowd of fifteen hundred. Next they played the Cleveland Panthers at home and dispatched them 47–0. A reporter for the *Cleveland Plain Dealer* lauded them for their "wide-open" play, and Burke called them a "smart football team."[37]

A "handsome" guarantee awaiting them, the Tanks traveled to Akron to meet the Awnings, then emerging as the premier eleven of the city. Knowing that the Awnings might prove a tough adversary for the favored Tanks, Tanks fans rallied in support of their team. About eight hundred "motored" to Buchtel Field in Akron, joining a large crowd of nearly nine thousand.[38] More than three thousand fans gathered at the *Tribune* office to hear a radio broadcast of the game—not merely a wire report— the first game ever broadcast in the city. They listened to a play-by-play account of an intensely fought game ending in a tie. Probably Presnell's fumble at the Awnings' eight-yard line cost the Tanks a victory.

Burke had little to say about the game, but James Schlemmer of the *Akron Beacon-Journal,* standing in awe of the Tanks, exulted in the Awnings' play:

> The fans went into alternate spasms of fear and rejoicing in the Awning achievement. [It] was the most colossal epoch-making affair of this season or last.
>
> No more gigantic team; no more talented eleven; no more superbly groomed outfit ever trod upon the stadium turf than the big red from Ironton.
>
> No Awning team—yes, no Akron team ever rose to greater fighting pitch nor called upon so many other traits than new physical and mental skill to prevent defeat. It was a genuine Awning victory to keep from being beaten by these Tanks . . . in suppressing these Goliath-like Tanks.[39]

The Tanks, even if chagrined at the tie, must have been surprised to learn that the Awnings had defeated them.

Still unbeaten and unscored on, the Tanks met their first Tri-State opponent, the Spartans, at Labold in mid-October. Surprisingly, little controversy attended the teams' preparations for another "battle of the ages." Indeed, all seemed to be sweetness and light. Because injuries hobbled many players on both squads, the managers agreed to waive the use of eligibility lists and to permit the signing of new players.

Among others, the Spartans added the "Jap Wizard ball carrier," Sneeze Aichu, to their roster; he had been with them in the opening game of the season but then had left the team. The Tanks found three new players, two linemen and a halfback. The crowd, five thousand, was the largest in the history of Labold Field. Reporters had predicted a high-scoring game, but the contest ended in a scoreless tie. Nonetheless, fans and reporters thought that the game was interesting. Young called it the "most hard fought game ever played in the valley." It was better than the Ohio State–Michigan clash, said fans who had seen that contest the preceding day.

The bloom gone from the rose in the wake of consecutive scoreless ties, the Tanks now had to go to Ashland to meet the Armcos. After defeating the Spartans, the Armcos, too, had seen their record tarnished. Despite their lowly rank in the NFL—they did not win a game in 1928—the Triangles came to Ashland and, riddling the Armco defense with a "sparkling overhead attack," won 10–7. Dismayed by the defeat, the Armcos saw their game with the Tanks as an opportunity to ease pain and avenge injuries of old against a foe they had never beaten. Perry, resorting to measures that might give his Armcos an advantage, spirited them out of town to an undisclosed location for the week's practice, believing that isolation from the community would somehow give them an acute consciousness of their task—crushing the Tanks. "Dread secrecy," wrote Black, "hung over where the Orange and Black Steelmakers were going today when they left Ashland. Not even the players knew where they were headed. Mystery shrouded them."[40] Later, reporters learned that the Armcos had gone to Mount Sterling, Kentucky, and had scrimmaged a high school team there.

Nearly five thousand fans came to Armco Park for what Burke called the "greatest football menu ever dished up to the public." As usual, the game was a low-scoring affair. At the very outset, the Tanks' offense suffered a blow, Presnell sustaining an injury that sidelined him for the remainder of the game. Perhaps seclusion served the Armcos well. They controlled play through much of the contest and, blocking the Tanks' attempt at an extra point late in the game, won 7–6. At last, after three years, the Armcos had beaten the Tanks. The world turned upside down, McCarthy felt constrained to comment editorially about the game. Though admitting that alibis were futile, he noted that the loss of Presnell had hampered the Tanks' offense. But he had no complaints. The game had been "splendidly officiated," was clean and hard-fought, and was an "exhibition of fine sportsmanship." He had a warning, though, for Perry: "There is another day coming."[41] He could console himself, too, with his own counsel: the Tanks needed to lose occasionally so that fans would not lose interest in them.

On the verge of going four consecutive games without a victory, the Tanks next journeyed to Cincinnati to meet the Guards. The Guards had lost but one game, that to the Ashland Armcos, and had defeated the Spartans 13--0 a week before playing the Tanks. Without defining the nature of the championship at stake, the Guards called the contest a "title game." About five hundred fans took Norfolk and Western cars to Redland Field, where they attempted to cheer the Tanks in the face of seventy-five hundred Guards fans. Penalties and disputes marred play, and officials ejected Jimmy Tays, captain of the Guards, for fighting. Scoring a touchdown in the fourth quarter, Davies gave the Tanks a "glorious victory," 7–0.[42]

The Spartans now came to Ironton. Since their scoreless tie with the Tanks, they had played two games. First, they had met the Guards at Redland Field. To bolster their line for the game, Graf acquired Harold "Tubby" Griffin, who, at 245 pounds, played guard and center; he remained with the Spartans for several years and became an important figure in their rise to prominence. Cold weather hindered play, which was "ragged." The Guards, using a questionable shift and mounting a "slashing" offense, won 13–0. Returning to Labold, "rejuvenated" despite the loss, the Spartans played like a "well-oiled" machine in beating the Logan Wildcats 35–0 before a small crowd.

The second game between the Tanks and Spartans was, in many respects, a replica of the first. Sportswriters, employing their usual rhetoric, looked for the "battle of battles" and more. Fans coming to Beechwood from Portsmouth and nearby small communities, the crowd was again large, numbering about four thousand. Again the fans saw no scoring; the Tanks were unable to turn their advantage in yardage gained into touchdowns or field goals. Again, a spectator, a woman, compared the game with an Ohio State–Michigan game. Almost as the gun sounded ending the game, sportswriters and fans were calling for a third game, believing that it could settle the question of which team was better and perhaps decide the championship of the Ohio Valley. Graf and McMahon, seeing the prospect of a good gate, agreed to a date in December, the game to be played at Beechwood because the covered grandstand afforded spectators some protection against inclement weather.

The second scoreless tie, marking five consecutive games for the Tanks with but one win and two touchdowns, occasioned some restlessness among fans eager to count victories week by week, not every two or three weeks. Inevitably, they found fault with Presnell, once a golden boy, writing anonymous letters to him, McMahon, the players, and the directors of the association counseling them on how to win. Learning of the letters, McCarthy called their authors cowards who misunderstood and misrepresented Presnell's problems. The Tanks, he asserted, were at their strongest in years, but so were the Portsmouth and Ashland teams. Presnell was a "great student" of the game but probably had never seen a professional eleven until he came to Ironton. Yet his team was holding other professional teams scoreless and had a winning record. The community had never seen a player equal to him. If fans had complaints, they should take them directly to McMahon, not by anonymous letters to him or anyone else.[43]

Presnell and the Tanks soon gave the fans something to cheer about, or at least less to complain about. They met the Armco Blues at Middletown. The Blues, employing "dazzling" passes, gave the Tanks a battle, but "breaks," said a Middletown reporter, denied them touchdowns. Eventually, the Tanks prevailed 13–0, as Presnell and Lee ran for touchdowns. Another Middletown scribe left the game declaring that he understood why Presnell had been "honored" as an All-American.[44]

With the Ashland Armcos next coming to Beechwood, Presnell would need his All-American abilities to lead the Tanks to a victory. The game gave the Tanks their last chance, perhaps, to deny the Armcos a clear claim to championships of the Ohio Valley and the Tri-State. Coming into the game, the Armcos had won eight games, one over the Tanks and one over the Spartans, and had lost but one, that to the Triangles; the Tanks had lost only one but had two ties, and the Spartans had two losses and two ties. In Tri-State competition, with two victories and no losses, the Armcos seemingly had an insurmountable lead over the Tanks and Spartans, each having lost one game and tied two.

After their signal victory over the Tanks in mid-season, the Armcos played three games before meeting the Tanks again. They first met the Canton Bulldogs. The Armcos expected the Bulldogs to offer them a stern test— or at least Black told fans that the Bulldogs were a rugged eleven. He portrayed them as the team that had succeeded the original Bulldogs when they left for Cleveland in 1924. The new Bulldogs in Canton had disbanded in 1927, several of the players joining another new Canton team, the Rogers Jewelers, which generally played second-level semiprofessional teams. When on the road the team called itself the Bulldogs for promotional purposes.[45] Few fans in Ashland knew of the tattered history of the Bulldogs, and Black, if he knew it, did not tell his readers.

The Armcos had relatively little trouble with the Bulldogs, winning 13–0. Many fans in the crowd, numbering about two thousand, were confused about the Bulldogs. Why, they asked, did they wear jerseys with the letters "Rogers Jewelers"? Black cleared up the question. They were indeed the Bulldogs; they were wearing the jerseys as an "advertising stunt." The man for the *Repository* offered a slightly different and more forthright explanation, saying that the Jewelers were the successors to the Bulldogs.[46] Such was the elastic world of semiprofessional football and some reporters who covered it.

Their record now six wins and a loss, the Armcos next met the Blues in Middletown, their first game on the road. The Blues, a very ordinary eleven, had lost to the Armcos earlier in the season. But since then, their coach, Abe Stuber, had strengthened them with several new players, and the squad was eager to do battle with the Armcos. Building on the natural interest in the game, the Employees Association in Middletown and Armco management drummed up support for it. They organized a "big parade" downtown on Saturday evening, with automobiles carrying players and festooned with banners led by the local American Legion Drum and Bugle Corps. A fireworks display followed the parade.[47] The community was "all steamed up," was "worked up." Fans in Ashland, at least workers in the mill, also had their blood up for the game. As many as five hundred, four hundred from the mill, a hundred "from town," took a special excursion train to Middletown. An estimated fifteen hundred fans came from Ashland and that the crowd, one of the largest in the athletic history of the city, numbered about six thousand.[48] The Armcos, outweighing the Blues, dominated line play and passed well to win 14–0. After the game, local Armco officials gave a dinner for the teams and invited guests, and the president of the company, George Verity, gave a short address.

Returning to Ashland, the Armcos easily subdued the Columbus Tigers 26–0 and moved into the final, crucial stretch of their season. They had to face three rugged opponents, the Tanks, the Spartans, and the Guards, all on the road. They had defeated each team, but by narrow margins, and would have to do so again to continue their standing as the leading eleven in the valley.

First came the Tanks. Neither team loading up or preparing unusual tactics, some of the tension and controversy usually attending games between the teams was not evident. But both camps expressed concern about the behavior of fans, evidently fearing that in a large crowd at a game of great importance, someone had to kick over the traces. McCarthy predicted that thousands of fans "and their ladies" would be in the grandstand, and they did not want to suffer the annoyance of a few men parading around the aisles "howling for attention and notice."[49] He called on the mayor and police chief to send enough patrolmen to Beechwood to control such men. "Pitch 'em out," he said. In another editorial, he singled out men in their cups: "If any man is found drinking or behaving in a boisterous manner, he should be ejected immediately." Black warned "flask toters" to watch out, to leave their "cut-glass at home" because the "Feds" would be in the stands in plain clothes.[50] In the

Home and Away

crowd, held to about three thousand by a bitter cold snap and a snowstorm, several men, perhaps drinking too much, did come to blows and involuntarily left the grandstand.

They missed a closely contested contest. Neither team could mount much of an offense on the snow-swept field. But Presnell, his broken-field running leaving Armco defenders sprawled on the field, accounted for more yardage than all Armco runners. In the third quarter, he completed a pass of twenty yards to Lee and then kicked a field goal that held up for the Tanks' victory 3–0. A few days after the game, McCarthy delivered a paean of praise for Presnell in an editorial. He was the equal of any three Armco men, he was never downed by one man as he "evaded, ducked, twisted, and straight-armed his way along," he was the "highest class grid hero ever to show his wares in the Ohio Valley," he was a "general, a leader."[51] Those who had found fault with him were unthinking men who probably had lost a few dollars on a game.

As a result of their loss to the Tanks, the Armcos saw their record in wins and losses, seven and two, fall below the Tanks' five wins and one loss; the Armcos still held the advantage in Tri-State competition at two wins and a loss, but the Tanks were closing the gap with a record of one win, a loss, and two ties. On Thanksgiving Day, the Armcos had an opportunity to regain their former advantage when they played the Spartans at Labold while the Tanks traveled to Akron to meet the Awnings again.

They faced a difficult task. Since tying the Tanks three weeks earlier, the Spartans had won two games at Labold, defeating the Athletic Club of Wabash, Indiana, 60–0, and the Columbus Tigers, 13–0. Though victories of no consequence, they gave the Spartans greater confidence and, so one scribe noted, improved timing of their offensive play. The Spartans, seeking revenge for their earlier loss to the Armcos, had acquired new men while the Armcos had stood pat even though several linemen had incurred hobbling injuries. The teams met in a drizzling rain that held the crowd well below the five thousand predicted by sportswriters. Their advantages apparently telling, the Spartans crushed the Armcos 19–0. Besides the loss, Perry suffered a broken jaw. Black conceded that the Spartans had won a "clear-cut" victory. No longer, chortled the *Times,* would Portsmouth be the butt of upriver fans.[52]

With their second consecutive loss, the Armcos' season turned sour. Winning at Akron, the Tanks had improved their record, and both the Tanks and Spartans had drawn abreast of the Armcos in Tri-State play. Unless they tied in their third game, one of them would pass the Armcos. The Armcos could earn a modicum of redemption, though, if they could defeat the Guards at Cincinnati in their final game. But they entered the game with players still hobbled, and the Guards were in "good condition." "Displaying their best form of the season," as the *Enquirer* put it, and playing before a large partisan crowd, the Guards overran the Armcos 20–0.[53] Somehow, the Armcos managed more first downs than the Guards. But they could take little solace in first downs and their final record of eight wins and four losses. Their vaunted new style of offense had scored no points in the last three games.

On the evening following the game, the Employees Association gave the players a banquet at the Hotel Gibson in Cincinnati. It was akin to a wake. Though all the speakers attempted to put a good face on the season, all seemed to call attention to the season-ending losses. Even as he praised the Armcos for their spirit, Frank Lane, intending also to laud the association, asked rhetorically whether any other organization would have feted a team after it had lost three straight games. H. E. Miller, speaking for the association, offered honeyed words of support while also noting the skein of losses. Representing workers in the mill, Jim Shea spoke in the same vein. Perry darkened the mood, too, announcing that he was resigning as coach but would remain with the team as a player. After declaring the season a success, the record of eight and four an "inspiration," Russell Smith, the toastmaster, reported that the association had lost money on the operation of the team.[54] The players must have been happy to beat a retreat from the Gibson.

While the Armcos were finishing the season disastrously, the Tanks and Spartans, neither having lost a game since late in October, were playing well through the second half of their schedule on their way to a third encounter with each other to close the season. Each went on the road preceding the game, the Tanks returning to Akron to play the Awnings and the Spartans going to Middletown to meet the Blues.

The Tanks especially anticipated a hard game. Earlier the Awnings had tied them and were eager to prove their mettle again. Schlemmer of the *Beacon-Journal* said that the championship of the state was at stake, and nearly nine thousand fans came to Buchtel Field to root for the Awnings. With Presnell running a punt back for forty-five yards and completing a pass for twenty-five and their defense suffocating the Awnings, the Tanks won 19–0. About eight hundred fans in Ironton at the Elks Hall heard of Presnell's heroic play firsthand. There M. A. Cloran, using a megaphone, relayed a play-by-play description of the game to them from Burke, who was walking the sideline and talking by telephone to Cloran through a trunk line. "The Tanks," admitted Schlemmer, "were simply too good, too powerful, too fortunate in making and taking advantage of breaks." Besides winning, the Tanks made a "nice

Home and Away

sum" out of the gate; "McMahon stuffed about thirty-three hundred into his keester."[55] At Middletown the Spartans played indifferently against the Blues. Their offense did little, but Molesworth gave them the victory 7–0 when he returned a punt sixty-five yards for a touchdown in the second quarter.

The teams returned to their communities to prepare for their Armageddon on the gridiron. They spent "extra hours" in practice and devised new plays and new formations. Fans and sportswriters thought the Tank's victory over the Awnings had decided the semiprofessional championship of the state. But reviewing the Tanks' domination of Portsmouth elevens in the past, Young and Minego declared that with "highly paid athletes" now representing the city, as they had for Ironton for many year, Portsmouth might challenge the Tanks and supplant them as the elect in the valley. At last, "history [was] history"; what mattered was the next game.

Certainly the next game seemed to create great interest among fans. Sales of tickets in Ironton were brisk, and early on fans in Portsmouth had bought over a thousand and were asking for more. Barring rain or snow, McMahon looked for a crowd of five thousand or more to occupy every inch of Beechwood. The weather was satisfactory, but McMahon and others misread the level of interest in the game. Young, apparently gaining access to the box office count, reported attendance at 3,422.[56] The teams taking the field in front of the crowd, whatever it was, were essentially the same as in the second game. Again defensive play dominated, resulting in a "battle of punts"; the Tanks punted fifteen times, the Spartans eight. Though gaining more yardage from scrimmage than the Tanks—145 to 104—the Spartans came up short. Presnell ran for one touchdown and caught a pass for another, giving the Tanks the victory 14–0. The Spartans, gloated Burke, got "what the little boy shot at"—nothing.

Though Graf looked around for another game for the Spartans, their long season was now at an end. Their loss at Beechwood left them with a record of nine wins, three losses, and two ties. They could point to the ties with the Tanks and the victory over the Armcos as evidence that they were a credible team for the community. Obviously they were looking for support in small talk, in the streets, and in the bleachers and grandstand at Labold. And they did reasonably well. Attendance at their games was better than that at the Shoe-Steels' games in 1927. In 1927, for the five home games for which sportswriters provided estimates on the size of crowds, attendance averaged 1,660; in 1928, for the six home games for which reporters cited numbers, the average attendance was nearly 2,400. On the road the Shoe-Steels' games averaged 3,400, for the Spartans 4,300.

Turn the Town Upside Down

The Portsmouth Football Association did not publicly disclose revenue and operating expenses, and sportswriters offered the community no more than hints or opinions on the Spartans' financial status. Quite early in the season, the directors did state that they were "satisfied" with attendance but needed larger crowds to cover their expenses.[57] Midway through the season, the *Times,* editorially praising the high school team and the Spartans for their "splendid" play, noted that the professional team was "self-supporting." But Young, writing as the season moved into the final month, had doubts about whether the people of Portsmouth would support a professional eleven able to compete with the Tanks and Armcos; thus far, he complained, only "mediocre" crowds had come out to Labold to see the Spartans. As the season wound down, Minego also seemed to find fans wanting in their support. Merchants, he recalled, had given liberally of their time and money at the beginning of the season to create a team capable of "advertising" the community. The Spartans had built a reputation enabling them to schedule well-known teams, but now they required the support of the townspeople.[58]

As the season ended, apparently the association faced no straitened circumstances threatening the existence of its team. Early in December the directors called on businessmen to meet with them to discuss plans for 1929, saying that they wanted to take steps to underwrite the club immediately as a means of signing Molesworth and Hathaway and other players to contracts in the near future.[59] At another meeting a few days later, a "representative" number of businessmen and industrial leaders pledged their support for the coming season.[60] The directors decided to form a ticket committee to begin selling season tickets for 1929, expecting to use the revenue to sign players before they left Portsmouth. Directors, businessmen, players, and other townspeople soon gathered at the Elks Club for a banquet, some announcing, some listening, to plans for 1929. They learned that the ticket sale would start soon, the committee hoping to sell fifteen hundred tickets at $10 each, and that Hathaway had signed a contract. Gableman outlined plans for another ballot to raise money for the construction of a new stadium. All applauded at the announcement that Molesworth had just married a young woman from Russell—perhaps all but Griffin, who had regarded her as his "steady."

The banquets over, the players began making decisions about their lives. Five men signed contracts for 1929 or said that they intended to do so.[61] Others kept their counsel. Ten or eleven left Portsmouth to return to their occupations in other communities, and six or seven remained in the city in full-time employment. What they did was a microcosm of the life of backs and linemen playing for small-city franchises in leagues or for independent teams. The old Triangles commuting to Portsmouth

Home and Away

from Dayton during the season simply continued living in their residences and working in their full-time occupations. Other players took up old and new positions and occupations: one as a deputy sheriff in Wisconsin, another as a proprietor of a chemical firm in Ohio, one as a laborer in a steel mill in Pennsylvania, another as a basketball coach at a college in Wisconsin, yet another as a plumber in Akron, and one as a ranger in the forestry service in Pennsylvania. The men remaining in Portsmouth had blue- and white-collar employment in the steel mills, shoe factories, and other concerns in the city. Six or seven of them sustained the visibility of the Spartans during the off-season when they organized a basketball team, the Baseman's Selects, that competed against other "fast" teams in the Tri-State.

With the victory over the Spartans, the Tanks claimed supremacy again in the Tri-State and the Ohio Valley. McMahon, wishing to add to their laurels and earnings, cast about for another game to play, attempting to induce the Awnings to come to Ironton. But many of the Tanks were hesitant about extending play, and the Awnings balked at tentative dates. So he closed the door on the season. Except in some minor respects, the Tanks could review their season as a success. They had begun and concluded play successfully but had gone through a distressing run of five games when their offense stalled. They had bested one of the best elevens in Ohio but had lost and tied two games against regional rivals. They could take pride in losing but one game and claiming at least two mythical championships. Though their record of seven wins, a loss, and three ties was good, for the second straight year they had won fewer than eight games. In four consecutive seasons before 1927, they had won nine or more games. But as editors and sportswriters were quick to note, their decline in wins and losses was not a measure of their deterioration in play but of the improvement of the elevens they were playing.

If the players had any lingering doubts about their record, they could take satisfaction in knowing that the fans in Ironton had ceased grousing about them, in fact were praising them. McCarthy congratulated the Tanks for their play and saw in them a "wonderful nucleus" for a good season in 1929. He had high praise for Presnell, a "born leader," a "clean-minded, clean-living" example for the youth of the community; he was already an "institution" in Ironton, and the Tanks management had to keep him in the city.[62]

Surely the Stadium Association was not displeased with the Tanks. They had played before good crowds at home and on the road. At three games—at Cincinnati and Akron—the crowd numbered nearly nine thousand, until then a record for the Tanks. At home, the numbers, though not setting records, were respectable, reach-

180

ing four thousand for a Spartans game. According to one report, the association ended the season in the black by $1,400. The Tanks incurred net losses in four games, ranging from $454 to $1,116; they realized net profits in six games, from $218 to $1,172.58. As the season ended, the directors thus were able to declare a dividend of 6 percent on shares of stock.[63] All seemed to be going well for the famous Tanks of Ironton, Ohio.

9

Portsmouth Is Football Crazy

THE MEN PLAYING AS Spartans, Tanks, and Armcos in 1928 and 1929 were professional players. No longer hometown boys, they did not derive their livelihood entirely from their play, but their off-season and full-time employment, whether as teachers or in a shoe factory or steel mill, stemmed from their athletic calling. Earlier in the decade, playing as a Tank or for the Smoke House, a local man, fully employed in or near the community, decided to play football for a town team, hoping to enjoy himself and to receive a few dollars for his efforts.

As the teams became professional, they were hardly more stable than the old town teams. More than ever before, they were dependent on fans and businessmen to pay their way. The Tanks, after 1928, had to look to a community with limited resources to maintain their position among increasingly larger competitors. At Portsmouth, the community had to sustain a professional team that, requiring more expansive competition, called on it for increasing levels of support. But the Armcos at Ashland, never really a team of the town, had limited aspirations and a well-defined source of support that did not permit pride and sentiment to dictate expansive ventures.

Portsmouth Is Football Crazy

As had been the case in Ironton in 1927, when the Stadium Association had broken with old seasonal rhythm and ritual in taking up affairs of football in the winter, spring, and summer, the Portsmouth Football Association in 1929 did not let the calendar determine planning for the coming season's play. Early in April, the association held an organizational meeting. The members returned George Brown to the presidency but chose a new vice president, Adolph Glockner, who would play an increasingly important role in its affairs.[1] They also created an executive committee to handle ongoing business and especially to work with the new coach, Harold Griffin, Russ Hathaway, for some reason, having decided to relinquish the position. They also turned over the managerial duties to Griffin.

No directors publicly voiced an ambition to take the Spartans into the upper reaches of professional football, but the directors and fans knew that small-city franchises still existed in the NFL and that the league might admit others. In the summer, the directors did discuss a proposal for organizing an Ohio professional league that would include the Spartans.[2] Advanced by promoters in Chillicothe and Canton, it called for nine clubs—the Canton Bulldogs, the Massillon Maroons, the Chillicothe Eagles, the Guards, the two Armcos, the Cleveland Panthers, the Tanks, and the Spartans—to form the Buckeye League. Griffin endorsed the proposal, saying that such a league would facilitate scheduling and enhance competition among the teams. His directors were willing to pursue the question, but for reasons not clearly divulged, several clubs, among them the Ashland Armcos, would not move ahead with planning. And the proposal, like others before it, disappeared from view.

Undoubtedly, a factor in any move by the Spartans beyond an independent status was Labold Field. The rickety grandstand and bleachers there, cramped to the last inch, might accommodate five thousand fans, good enough for regional competition but inadequate for play beyond that level. For some time, sports fans and promoters had been calling for construction of a stadium seating ten thousand people and the building of recreational facilities—tennis courts, a track, and so on. In 1928 the voters had rejected a bond issue calling for the expenditure of $80,000 for such purposes. Other proposals followed for construction of a smaller facility, but nothing happened. Recreational and football enthusiasts, though, continued to discuss the subject, and the issue eventually would become a decisive factor in the Spartans' destiny.

In the meantime, the association was gathering momentum for the season's play. Late in June, at its call a hundred boosters gathered at the Masonic Temple to hear preliminary plans for a campaign to sell season tickets.[3] A few days later, the directors

Home and Away

announced details of the campaign, noting that all the business and industrial interests of the city supported it. It would last for six days in July, the goal to sell two thousand tickets. A ticket listed at $11 would sell for $10; the buyers could put $2 down and pay the remainder to any one of the five banks in the city. A select committee would canvass downtown merchants, another special committee would solicit employees at industrial plants, and members of the association would buttonhole the man in the street, who could also buy tickets at retail establishments. To hasten these sales, the directors declared that no season tickets would be available after the campaign ended. They tied the drive to their expectations of the Spartans. They intended, they asserted, to sign only players of "character" who would be a credit to the community, an "all-star" array vastly superior to any other squad playing in the valley in 1928. Despite all the noise of selling, the association did not widely reveal the results of the campaign. Evidently, it did raise enough money to move into the season meeting its obligations.

At the boosters' meeting Griffin also appeared, announcing progress on the signing of players of "character." He and the directors had been "scouring" the South and Midwest for players and would continue to do so well into August. They were recruiting players under good conditions. Opportunities in the NFL for players, veterans or rookies, were not as widespread as they had been a few years earlier. Midway in the decade, as many as twenty-two clubs were in the league, in part foils intended to block the expansion of the American Football League; by 1927, with the collapse of the American League and readjustments in the NFL, the number fell to twelve, in 1928 to ten. Three of the Ohio franchises, the Akron Indians, the Canton Bulldogs, and the Columbus Tigers, disappeared forever. Recruiters thus might find the hunting more rewarding. Players might come to Portsmouth out of the associative network operating in football. Griffin was well known at the University of Iowa and might turn his friendships there to good account. Supposedly Curly Lambeau was urging men who did not make the Packers to look at the Spartans. And the directors were able to open doors to off-season employment in Portsmouth for players; in the summer of 1929 at least five were working in the Portsmouth works of the Wheeling Steel Company.

Certainly Griffin was able to find good pickings early in his quest for backs. In June he signed three outstanding collegians, Chuck Bennett, Roy Witt, and Roy Lumpkin. Bennett, a halfback, had just completed his senior year at Indiana University; he was one of the players working at the Wheeling Steel Mill that summer. Captain of an outstanding team at the University of Tennessee in 1928, Witt was an excellent punter and passer. The great prize was Lumpkin. A Texan, "Father" Lumpkin

Portsmouth Is Football Crazy

attended Georgia Tech and had been outstanding in its national championship team of 1928. Standing six feet, two inches, weighing 210 pounds, he gained repute as thundering fullback running and blocking. Picaresque, outgoing, good-natured, the subject of numerous amusing anecdotes, he almost instantly became a popular figure in the community. Off-season he often appeared on local wrestling and boxing cards. Forty years after he played his last game for the Spartans, surviving fans still smiled as they recalled his antics off and on the field. He signed a contract late in June, worked for a while as a lifeguard at a local swimming pool, and then returned south to take care of some business.[4] Fans in Portsmouth feared that he would not return. Learning of their apprehension, Burke at Ironton, already nettled by the Spartans' aggressive search for players—they "overlooked none"—parodied them in doggerel in "Horatio Lumpkin":

> Oh Lumpkin, Father Lumpkin
> > To whom the Spartans pray,
> We had you for a moment,
> > Oh, why could you not stay?
>
> You lifted up our spirit,
> > Made Peerless grid fans gay,
> But now that you have left us
> > We'll paint the Floodwall grey.[5]

But Lumpkin did return. Recognizing him on the street, fans greeted him with "wild acclaim." One report had it that coaches at Georgia Tech attempted to persuade him to play out his remaining season of eligibility, but he refused their blandishments and a loud wail then emanated from Atlanta.[6]

Later in the summer, Griffin signed Carl Brumbaugh, another good running back. Brumbaugh, a native of Ohio but known as the "Florida Kid," had played three years for the University of Florida and in 1928 was the second leading scorer in the nation.[7] The "fastest and shiftiest member" of the Spartans, a "pack of bone and muscle" at 168 pounds, he was with them for only one year and then went to the Bears, becoming the quarterback of the T that Ralph Jones rehabilitated for George Halas in 1930. Obviously using his ties to the University of Iowa, Griffin signed three men who had played for the Hawkeyes, Paul Armil, a quarterback, and Ernie Jessen and Vincent Schleusner, two tackles. But Jessen, owing to his wife's illness, did not appear until well after the season began, and Schleusner, learning that he had one more year of eligibility at Iowa, did not come until 1930. Griffin landed an outstanding tackle from the University of Indians in Clare Randolph, who had been an

Home and Away

All-American in 1928. He also signed Kermit Frecka, who had played for the Tanks for several years but who had been living in Portsmouth all the while.

Griffin and the association did not look entirely to new blood to build the Spartans of 1929. Of the thirty-five to forty men who were with the team at one time or another in 1929—from the beginning of practices to the end of the season—at least ten had been on the roster in 1928. As practices opened early in September, Griffin was coaching an assemblage of players who might well become an outstanding team. Young, though, was engaging in hyperbole when he asserted that the Spartans had gathered together the "greatest array of stars in the country," that they had a score or more of the greatest players in the nation. He was a little closer to the mark in describing the Spartans as the "idols of many a college gathered into one of the greatest teams the Ohio Valley has ever known."[8]

Learning almost daily of new players arriving or expected to arrive at the railroad station and of the teams scheduled to appear at Labold, the "downtown coaching staff" was "buzzing" about the Spartans, and knots of men at popular hangouts were recounting tales of past seasons and discussing prospects for the coming season. "Portsmouth is football crazy," said Young.[9] Perhaps they saw permanence in their craze at the news that the football association was filing incorporation papers with the state of Ohio to become the Portsmouth Football Corporation.

The coming of collegiate stars did not assure a great team. Men had to practice and prove themselves capable of cohesive play. And they had to prove themselves against a much more difficult schedule than any other Portsmouth eleven had heretofore faced. Opening the season, their schedule fairly well in place, they were to meet the Packers at Green Bay. They had three dates for games with the Tanks, two with each of the Armco teams, two with the Guards, and one with the Awnings. Seemingly, they had relatively soft touches in the Chillicothe Eagles and the Mendel Tailors. Altogether, the Spartans ended up playing fifteen games, nine at home, six away, five of the road games coming in a row.

Griffin opened practice early in September amid exuberance. Hundreds of enthusiastic fans—the "Floodwall gang"—lined the floodwall along York Park to view the players sweating and straining. After about ten days of practice, Griffin pared the squad down to about twenty men to travel to Green Bay to play the Packers. Before they departed, the new football corporation gave them a dinner party resembling a pep meeting for a college team.[10] No collegiate yells or bonfires accompanied the party, but several directors, acting as cheerleaders, delivered inspirational talks. As the players boarded a railroad car at about midnight, a group of "true-blue fans" gave them a rousing cheer. Their freight included white helmets and new "flashy white" jerseys bearing large orange numerals, replacements for the black jerseys of previous years.

At Green Bay, the Spartans met a team that, bolstered by Lambeau's recent acquisition of three outstanding players, Johnny Blood, Cal Hubbard, and Mike Michalske, would go undefeated in league play. Though facing a nonleague opponent, the Packers regarded the game as one that would test their reputation and strength. Before a crowd of five thousand, the Spartans contained the Packers' offense fairly well, yielding only two touchdowns, but they could not muster any offense and lost 14–0. Young attributed the loss to the Packers' use of substitutes, an "avalanche" of fresh men, and the Spartans' poor passing. A reporter for the *Green Bay Gazette,* showering praise on the Packers, noted that the Spartans had bright prospects. They had played a "great game" and were "always dangerous." Bennett was "outstanding" and Lumpkin was "good on line plunging."[11]

The Spartans had played one of the leading professional elevens in the nation, after only ten days or so of practice. Nonetheless, fans and players alike found the loss disappointing, hardly an auspicious start for a squad packed with collegiate "stars." Returning to Portsmouth, the Spartans prepared for their opening home game against the Chillicothe Eagles, a team led by Bryon Eby, a fine back from Ohio State. Also playing for the Eagles were at least three former Spartans. The Spartan people looked for a large crowd at Labold, perhaps the largest ever to see an opening game in Portsmouth. Inviting players from the Portsmouth high school team and three other high schools in the area to the game, the Spartans' management enlarged the crowd slightly and enhanced the team's public image.[12] A good crowd, about twenty-five hundred, saw the Spartans win 7–0 in a game devoid of offense and exciting plays. Numerous penalties and arguments among the players dragged out the play. When Griffin became "too anxious" and ran up and down the sidelines berating the officials, they ejected him. Fans censored him, and the next day he called the Times to offer a public apology for his behavior.

His team's drab victory over the Eagles offering little promise for a good season and large crowds at Labold, Griffen, disappointed in his interior ground game, resolved to use his "flashy backs" in "open football"—in end runs and passing. He also acquired two new tackles, reputedly "All Southern Men." Whether because of a strengthened lineup, altered offensive tactics, or weaker opponents, the Spartans easily won their next two games. At Labold, they defeated the Middletown Armcos, an aging team making increasing use of players released from NFL teams, 32–0. Coming next to Labold were the Detroit Tigers, touted as a strong eleven that in recent years had defeated at least two NFL teams. The Tigers at Labold were not the

Tigers of yore. Passing and running from scrimmage for long gains, blocking punts, intercepting passes, and recovering fumbles, the Spartans turned the Tigers into harmless pussycats, defeating them 79–0.

Now the Spartans prepared for their first game with any visceral content—a contest with the Tanks at Labold. At the same time, the directors of the new corporation were running into problems that would test the viability of their venture into professional football. They had promised players signing contracts employment in Portsmouth business and industrial firms, but at least three men had been waiting empty-handed for a month after joining the Spartans.[13] Evidently for that reason, the directors abruptly released four men, two of whom went over to the Blues. They were dealing, too, with the question of their identity in the community. When they announced the decision to transform the association into a corporation, a rumor began to float through the community that "outsiders" were taking control of the Spartans. Going out of his way to spike the story, Brown noted that all the directors had been directors in the association. They were all residents of Portsmouth or Scioto County, he declared, and exercised exclusive control of the Spartans.[14] And he pointed out that for their services, they received but one dollar a year.

Of more serious import was the question that the directors raised about the responsibility of the fans—of the community—to the Spartans. Using the *Times* and the *Sun* as a pulpit, Coleman Grimes, a director and president of the Portsmouth Publishing Company, which owned both newspapers, had his sportswriters sermonizing readers. The directors of the football corporation, they wrote, had dug into their own pockets to wipe out a deficit in 1928 and had spared no expense in 1929 to assemble the "greatest galaxy of gridiron stars ever known in the Ohio Valley."[15] But attendance at Labold had not yet reached three thousand, and the corporation had lost a thousand dollars at each of the first two games. Fans at Tanks games at Labold might tax facilities, but they could not compensate for small crowds at other games. If the fans did not come out in good numbers for all the Spartans' games at Labold, there might be no teams playing the Spartans there. The directors barely veiled their message when they revealed that the Atlantic City Americans had invited the Spartans to play them in New Jersey, assuring them that a crowd of at least ten thousand would be in attendance.

The Tanks coming to Labold to tax its facilities were largely the creation of Nick McMahon. At the conclusion of the season in 1928, Tanks fans and players saw bright prospects for 1929. The Tanks had finished the season in a flourish, winning five of their last six games and tying one, all against strong opponents, and apparently nearly all the players were willing to return to the team. McMahon, of course, did not want to stand pat with veterans, some of whom might not show in Ironton despite their winterly assurances, and was shopping around through the summer for a few new players at pivotal positions.

Surely he did add strength to the Tanks' line. Early on he signed on Jim Welsh of Colgate, all of 265 pounds, to play tackle, and Dick Powell, a big end who had been with the Awnings in 1928. From Haskell, the Indian school, he signed Tiny Roebuck, a tackle weighing 245 pounds, Locally, he found Harold Rolph, who had played tackle for Xavier in Cincinnati. In Pooley Hubert, the erstwhile Armco, he acquired early in the season a back capable of passing and punting. Combing the "Texas Circuit," he brought to Ironton Pat Kneiff, a halfback from Southern Methodist. The recruits in the backfield partially offset the loss of Frecka to the Spartans. Though as many as twenty-four recruits were with the Tanks at one time or another through the season, only three—Kneiff, Powell, and Welsh—became starters. Of the ten men who had played in 1928, eight appeared in at least half of the games in 1929. The two who did not—one was Presnell—suffered disabling injuries early in the season.

McMahon probably built a roster that midway through the decade would have dominated semiprofessional football in the Ohio Valley. But now the Spartans and Armcos were also acquiring new men and were ready to challenge the Tanks. From Portsmouth came a stream of reports that the Spartans were signing new players. The Spartans, noted Burke, had a score of the greatest players in the nation; he thought that they were out to "control" all the best collegiate players, to "overlook" none. Their sweeping hand, though, did not frighten the Tanks. "Hell almighty!" exclaimed Dick Alvis, "they can only play eleven of them no matter how many they get!" Notwithstanding the bravado of heroes, Burke was not unhappy at learning the news—premature as it turned out—that Lumpkin was leaving the Spartans. The Armcos were also beating the bushes for good players, and frequent reports came across the river about their recruits from Ohio State and Notre Dame.

As McMahon recruited, he was working up the Tanks' schedule. By mid-August, earlier than usual, he thought that he had it largely in place. Calling for five home and seven road games, it offered Tanks fans some new fare. For the first time in their history, the Tanks expected to play a Chicago team, the Cardinals, and to meet a team named the Canton Bulldogs twice. They would travel to Akron twice to take on the Awnings and once to Cincinnati to play the Guards. Anticipating good crowds, he had the Tanks meeting the Spartans three times, twice at Portsmouth. They would engage the Armcos in a home-and-home series. He was able to arrange the games with the Armcos only after a dispute with Russell Smith, who prevailed in his demand

Home and Away

that the visiting team receive a guarantee of a thousand dollars and only the revenue from its sale of tickets, a provision seemingly benefiting the Kentuckians. Their weakest opponent appeared to be the Mendel Tailors, whom they would meet in the opening game of the season. McMahon's schedule was a fair representation of the games that the Tanks actually played.

Fans and journalists alike looked forward to a good season as the Tanks opened their season against the Mendel Tailors. Having followed them in practices, Burke believed that they looked like "champions," their line a "Wall of China." On the morning of the game, McCarthy rejoiced in the tradition of the day: "Today is to Ironton what Derby Day is to Kentucky." Football was bigger and better than ever, he said.[16] Despite tradition, apparently only about fifteen hundred fans came to Beechwood. Momentarily, the Tailors held the Tanks off, but then the Tanks ran off six touchdowns, Presnell scoring three in the fourth quarter, and won 39–0.

The Tanks then won two more games, their scores at polarity. Their advantage in weight 3,819 pounds to 3,078, noted Burke, they wore down the Chillicothe Eagles, a team composed largely of former Ohio State players, for a win, 6–0.[17] Then resorting to some improvisation—shenanigans one could have called it—McMahon canceled a game with the Canton Bulldogs because they had played poorly in a loss to the Armcos the previous week and scheduled in their stead the Birmingham Boosters of Toledo. Coming to Ironton with an "array of stars," the Boosters, thought Burke, were a "rather conceited group of foot-ballers," believing as they did that they could beat the state champions—the Tanks. He ridiculed them for their Slavic names—Gozdowski, Sakovck, and so on: "They are in town, honey, as the old pancake flour advertisements say. And you can tell your Aunt Jemima if they're as hard to lick on the gridiron as it is to pronounce their Christian names then the Big Red is in for a pretty afternoon." The Boosters, belying their reputation, were easy for the Tanks to "lick." With Presnell leading the attack, the Tanks demolished the Boosters 78–0. Outweighed and outgeneraled, the Boosters hardly furnished a scrimmage for the Tanks.[18]

Thus the Tanks journeyed to Labold undefeated in three games to face the Spartans, winners of three games, their only loss to the powerful Packers. For both elevens and their fans, the game was crucial. The Spartans, only in their second year of play, hoped the game would initiate their movement to dominance in the football of the Ohio Valley, and the Tanks sought reaffirmation of their hegemony. For Young in the "battle of the ages," the squads would place in array "the finest collection of football stars ever assembled in the Buckeye state." At

Ironton, Burke described the Spartans and Tanks as "two of the greatest teams in the Ohio Valley."

The players, their coaches, and the managers, like the sportswriters, saw the impending clash as a monumental battle. Presnell drilled the Tanks intensively at each practice, and McMahon hurried to sign Hubert to a contract. Griffin conducted secret practices to shield his Spartans from Ironton scouts. Father Lumpkin, Young reported, was "wearing headgear and socks, which means that he is getting in trim for a tough contest." Bennett and Molesworth were straining at the bit, and Brumbaugh was "aching" to crack the Tanks' line. And Randolph was eager for the fray to begin. Powell of the Tanks was talking about teaching the Spartans a lesson in hard knocks. "Boy, oh boy," exclaimed Young, "what a scrap that will be." Assessing the relative strengths of the teams, scribes agreed that the Tanks had a superior defense, a "formidable," a "beefy," almost "impregnable" line and better punting; the Spartans had the edge in their ground and passing attack.[19]

The Spartans' officials faced an unprecedented demand for tickets. Civic duty seemed to require residents of Portsmouth to be at Labold to support the Spartans against the Tanks.[20] At Ironton, all able-bodied residents were "evacuating" their homes and businesses and journeying to the floodwall city. Reportedly, football fans in Dayton, Cincinnati, Columbus, Huntington, and many smaller communities were scrambling for tickets. By midweek before the game, the Spartans had sold three thousand reserved seats and were calling on various parties in Columbus, Cincinnati, Springfield, Huntington, and elsewhere for assistance in locating bleachers for use at Labold. Paid admissions eventually reached fifty-four hundred, and about eight hundred spectators came into Labold on passes of various sorts, truly a record crowd for professional football in the Tri-State.

As it should have been, the "battle of the ages" was close and tense. The Spartans dominated offensive play, their 205 yards from scrimmage more than doubling the Tanks' 71, but they could not score, offside penalties often halting their attack. Unable to move the ball, the Tanks did score. In the third quarter, they recovered Bennett's fumble, and then Welsh place-kicked a field goal from the Spartans' twenty-five-yard line. The Tanks made the score hold up and won 3–0. For years fans referred to the field goal as the "$10,000 field goal" because bettors on the Tanks reportedly picked up $10,000 on their wagers. One story had it that the "cleaning made on that one kick" caused the panic on Wall Street. Among those who lost money was Lumpkin, who wagered "every saw[buck]" on the game.[21]

Perhaps the intense athletic rivalry between Portsmouth and Ironton, made acute by the circumstances of 1929, led to what Young called the "roughest" game ever

Home and Away

played at Labold. As he saw the play, the Tanks resorted to "leg-twisting," slugging, and kneeing to remove the Spartans' stars. He alleged that one Tank, whose name he would not reveal, came into the game intoxicated. But Collett of the *Ironton News* blamed the Spartans and officials for the roughness. Many Spartans, he explained, were new to professional football in the Ohio Valley and, assuming that they had wide latitude in their play, started their rough tactics on the first snap of the ball.[22] The officials had not reproved or ejected them as they should have. On one play, the Spartans picked up Kneiff, carried him ten yards, and "slammed him down—it was the worst play we ever saw." The Tanks retaliated in kind. The combatants suffered many injuries. Five Spartans bore the scars of battle—a broken leg and twisted legs and knees. At least three Tanks incurred injuries that took them out of the game. Altogether, four men were treated at a local hospital. Probably Presnell was the victim of the most violent play of the day. Lumpkin hit him as him as he was returning a punt at full speed, tearing three ribs from his sternum. Tradition long had it that Lumpkin had vowed to "knock Presnell out of the game." Yet Presnell, who had a vivid memory of the game more than sixty years later, discounted the story and indeed did not recall that play was particularly rough.[23]

After the game, the roughness moved beyond the gridiron. Believing that the officials had cost their team a victory, some Spartans fans vented their wrath against them. Several fans rushed the umpire, Ray Eichenlaub, and handled him roughly. Harry Kaylor struck him on the jaw. The police arrested Kaylor, released him, and arrested him again when he and his friends "planned a sortie" into a restaurant where Ironton fans were dining. One of the fans milling around Russell Finsterwald, the head linesmen, hit him in the face. A group of "town boys" rushed Jim Durfee, the referee, but did not harm him. Young condemned the boys, noting, though, that Durfee, walking with a limp, had been unable to follow the ball during the game. When two Ironton fans hit a Portsmouth man, a crowd gathered around them offering bodily harm. The local fire chief intervened and escorted them to a nearby house; the crowd followed and threatened to enter the house to "get" them. They escaped by slipping out the back door. The mayor of Portsmouth, though disgusted by the officials' work on the field, denounced the Portsmouth troublemakers.[24]

Surveying the wreckage of the game, Collett and Young feared that the future of professional football in the Ohio Valley was at stake.[25] They agreed that rough play and rowdyism could kill the "classic competition" among teams from Ironton, Portsmouth, and Ashland. They shared, too, the view that fans from both Ironton and Portsmouth were responsible for the disorder attending the game and called on leaders of the communities to "stamp out unsportsmanlike debauchery." But they also saw the solution in officials who would control play and eject players for rough tactics. Affecting great disdain for misbehavior of fans and players at Labold, Black at Ashland wrote of a "battle of busted beaks and beezers," a "disgusting spectacle," one that his community would not countenance.[26] The sportswriters' words, though not moving governmental leaders or directors of football associations to corrective measures, struck a responsive chord among a few readers and other writers.

Having defeated the Spartans, reputedly a strong team, the Tanks were at their customary position at the head of football in the Ohio Valley. But within the week, they had to face a strong contender seeking to supplant them. Across the river the Armcos, already a traditional rival only four years after their organization, had been preparing to untrack the Tanks. They were coming to Beechwood determined to correct their play at the end of the 1928 season and with a new coach and several new luminaries in the line and backfield.

Before the season opened in 1929, the Armcos had come to a decision that seemed to commit them to a continuing battle with the Tanks and Spartans. Early in July, the Employees Association, confirming rumors, announced that NFL owners had offered the Armcos a franchise in the league. Supposedly the association would take the franchise held by the Kansas City Cowboys, thus eliminating the costly long rail jumps.[27] If the owners did, in fact, tender such a proposal, they did so informally. They did not note it in the minutes recording business at their annual meeting in 1929. In any event, according to Black, the association was seriously considering the proposal, looking at it from two views. As a member of the league, the Armcos would build a roster of great athletes—at increased expense—and leading professional teams would come to the city, but eventually the Armcos probably would have to terminate their "keen" series with the Tanks and Spartans. The association had to weigh a derivative question too: who would be more popular among Armco employees, the Armcos in the NFL, with the inherent advantages of competition in a league, or the Armcos as an independent team playing "high class" clubs in the neighborhood rivalry that had grown in the recent past?

In short order, the association decided that the Armcos would remain an independent team.[28] The decision turned, at the periphery, on whether the Armcos could secure favorable terms from the Tanks and Spartans on the share of the gate for their games. But essentially the association grounded its conclusion on a larger issue, the role of the Armcos in the company and community. For the association, the Armcos did not exist to entertain or to advertise the community, as Irontonians sometimes viewed the Tanks. Noted for its paternalistic policies, the Armco company subsidized the association as an instrument to create and sustain a stable and productive work force. Certainly the company did reach out to the entire community but usually in a much more direct, encompassing way—for example, in providing recreational facilities for the public, in supporting a hospital, a public nursing bureau, or a library.[29] And the company did not regard a football team as a plaything. Only a week or so after reaching its decision not to join the NFL, the association reaffirmed it position, turning away from discussions and vague proposals concerning the organization of an Ohio Valley league and a Buckeye league.[30]

Nonetheless, the association sought to field a strong team in 1929. Earlier it had selected a new coach, Paul Davis, who had played at South Dakota State and reputedly was an effective manager of men. With Russell Smith vigorously recruiting, the Armcos looked like a good team as play was about to begin. Black thought they could be called a "great" team. Certainly they looked different from the squad of 1928. At least nineteen men who were on the roster at one time or another in 1929 had not been with the team the previous year; eight men who had been on the roster in 1928 returned in 1929. Among the recruits were several who had made their mark as collegiate players and who would play well for the Armcos.[31] Ralph Drennon was an All-Southern guard from Georgia Tech, and Leo Raskowski had been an All-American tackle at Ohio State. Joining them on the line was a good end, Joe Kresky, who had played at the University of Wisconsin. Loren "Tiny" Lewis, an All-Western Conference man at Northwestern, became a starting fullback, and Johnny Niemic, an excellent back from Notre Dame, ran beside him. But no one could rely on his collegiate reputation to play. Saying that he intended to carry twenty-two men on the roster, Davis made it clear that second-stringers could readily trade places with first-stringers if they showed more "stuff" in a game or in one of the scrimmages that he conducted in each of the five daily practices during the week. It was an unusual approach. Ordinarily, once the season began, only sixteen or seventeen men were on a roster, thus precluding scrimmages.

As Smith drew up the schedule before the season began, aside from the valley elevens, it was quite different from that of 1928. The Armcos had contracts with the Blues and Spartans for home-and-home games and expected to play the Tanks twice. Excepting one, all the others were to be home games. They expected to meet two NFL teams, the Cardinals and the Buffalo Bisons, and a former member of the league, the Duluth Eskimos, as well as the Chillicothe Eagles, the Cleveland Panthers, and the Massillon Maroons. Outside the games with the valley teams, the

Portsmouth Is Football Crazy

schedule became a shambles, the Armcos playing only three of the six games with elevens originally on their slate.

The Eskimos begged off the opening game, supposedly because of injuries to many of their players, so Smith managed to schedule a game with the Fort Wayne Pyramids, reputedly a strong team with Notre Dame men on their roster. All the Armcos played in a rout of the Pyramids, 79–0, the Irish of no avail. Then Smith engaged in an exercise that was nothing if not opportunistic or devious. Pointing to the questionable backing and strength of the Massillon Maroons, he canceled their coming game at Ashland. In fact, he saw in their replacement, the Canton Bulldogs, another version of the legendary Bulldogs, a better draw because they had just won over the Chicago Cardinals. His Armcos easily defeated the "Bow-Wows" 22–0. A reporter for the *Repository* called them a powerful eleven."[32] Next, in a game measuring them against the Spartans and Tanks, the Armcos beat the Chillicothe Eagles 14–6. The Spartans having bested the Eagles 7–0 and the Tanks edging them 6–0, the Armcos might count themselves one point better than the Spartans, two better than the Tanks—small and meaningless margins. Then meeting the Blues in a game seemingly missing its usual fervor, the Armcos won 34–0, their fourth win in a row.

Undefeated, the Armcos next had to cross the river to face the Tanks, also unbeaten in four games. Rank and reputation rested on the outcome of the game. The Tanks, still recovering from the battle of bruises and broken bones, had to play without Presnell, but many Steelmen were apprehensive, fearing that the Tanks had them "jinxed" at Beechwood. In both communities, fans counted the days and then the hours before the kickoff. Well before that, the Tanks sold out all seats and were offering tickets only for standing room. On Saturday evening in Ironton, the Lions Club sponsored a pep rally and gave away noisemakers; the high school band led a parade from the downtown business district to the Elks Hall, where the president of the Lions, F. O. Ross, introduced the Tanks and urged all in the crowd to be loyal to the athletes who were giving the city good clean football. The next morning, just hours before the game, McCarthy lectured Tanks fans on their conduct at Beechwood. They should, he insisted, treat the hundreds of Armco fans with respect and in the spirit of good sportsmanship.[33] The Tanks took pride in playing their customary clean game and wanted to be equally proud of their fans. If the Tanks lost, all fans should take defeat gracefully.

A few hours later, a record crowd, estimated at six thousand, gathered at Beechwood and behaved admirably. On the field, the Tanks and Armcos fought tooth and nail. The Tanks had a clear advantage in yards gained from scrimmage nine to six and in yardage gained from scrimmage, but their only score was a safety resulting from a blocked punt. Late in the fourth quarter, Lewis scored a touchdown following Niemic's long runback of a punt, giving his teammates the lead and the victory 7–2. Burke was certain that he would have reported a victory had Presnell played. Still, he said, the Tanks had performed "nobly" in a thrilling game. Neither he nor McCarthy took immediate note of the noble play of Elliott, who threw a punch at the referee and was ejected from the game. Later Elliott apologized to the referee.

Returning to Ashland undefeated, the Armcos had the opportunity to stand astride the Tanks and Spartans in the Tri-State and all the other elevens in the Ohio Valley. They would now play the Spartans, a loser to the Tanks only two weeks earlier. After their loss to the Tanks, a physical and emotional reverse, the Spartans looked for a measure of balm when they journeyed to Redland Field to face the Guards. Only hours before the game, because of injuries incurred during the Tanks game, Griffin acquired three new men. About five hundred fans followed the Spartans to Cincinnati by rail to become part of a crowd of over four thousand. They saw their Spartans dominate play after the first quarter, though scoring but one touchdown, which the Guards matched with a score stemming from a poor punt. The game ended in a tie at 6–6.

The Spartans now had posted three wins, two losses, and a tie, hardly a record worthy of a "galaxy" of outstanding collegians or one giving their fans a sense of pride. Neither the coach nor sportswriters publicly offered an explanation for the Spartans' failure to score more points and win. The offense had done little in the first two games, then picked up against two opponents—one of very dubious strength—and fallen flat in the next two games. Before the Guards game, Griffin had sought to shore up his eleven with new men. Though solid players, they scarcely accounted for the Spartans' remarkable run through the remainder of the season.

It began against the Armcos at Ashland. As usual, the approach of the game gave sportswriters in both communities the opportunity to write about "powerful" linemen and "speedy" backs who would engage in a "rugged" contest, one testing their will and strength. The game was also a test of whether fans in Portsmouth would support their team at the gate. Griffin and Smith, as had McMahon and Smith, had entered into an agreement on sharing the gate that directly measured that support. Instead of splitting receipts by a percentage—say 60 percent for the home team, 40 for the visiting eleven—each team would receive all the revenue from the sale of tickets in its community. The visiting team had no guarantee. The Spartans needed to sell eighteen hundred tickets in Portsmouth to break even—to cover the expenses of going to Ashland. Sales lagged early in the week and finally numbered about two

Portsmouth Is Football Crazy

thousand.[34] Apparently the Spartans met the expenses—but with little to spare. Surely the Armcos did much better. Altogether, the crowd was about sixty-five hundred, three thousand fans jamming into the regular stands on the west side of Armco Park, 1,800 occupying new bleachers erected on the east side and 1,400 standing around the field. According to Young, the many fans attired in New York and Parisian coats and frocks presented the aspect of a fashion show. So important did the Armcos deem the game that they hired an extra official to observe line play.

Armco fans had to be disappointed in the game. Favored by about eight points because supposedly they had a better line, the Armcos, "bewildered" by the Spartans' speed and "deceptive attack," fell 19–0. Lumpkin ripped their line apart, Armil accounted for seventy-nine yards rushing, and Bennett ran sixty-five yards for a touchdown. Creating a fictional fan, "The Lady in the Grandstand," Young had her saying, on learning that Bennett had soft-boiled eggs and tea for breakfast, "Let's send to China for all the tea and set the hens laying if that makes 'em run 65 yards."[35] Several times the Armcos moved into Spartan territory and then faltered; on one occasion Randolph tackled Lewis one yard short of the goal line.

The Spartans' victory came at the cost of injuries to several players, notably Molesworth and Brumbaugh, Brumbaugh's curtailing his play for the remainder of the season. Counting the injuries, Griffin suffered an emotional wound, a "heavy heart." Some Armcos had more than a heavy heart. After the game, several went to Bunk McWilliams's home to drown their defeat in liberal portions of Carter County corn squeezings. Lewis, still fuming over his failure to score from the one-yard line, turned on Raskowski and demanded, "How come you stood there picking your nose and let Randolph get through?"[36] Then he proceeded to throw the big tackle through a window.

The Spartans could relish their victory but briefly, knowing that, with injuries seemingly vitiating their strength, they had next to face the Tanks in Ironton. The Tanks then were in an unusual passage. After beating the Spartans without the benefit of a touchdown, they could manage only a safety in losing to the Armcos. Presnell's loss was obviously damaging to their offense. Then they became the center of a political debate. Three candidates for election to the Lawrence County Board of Education, all attacking William Paul, the superintendent, accused the current board of preferential treatment in employing Tanks as teachers in the interest of the Stadium Association—of turning the school system into a hiring hall for the association.[37] The directors and the board members vehemently denied the accusation. In no case, they argued, had a Tank taken a teaching position at the expense of a local candidate or displaced a teacher in the system. The number of Tanks teaching in

Home and Away

the county was small, and those who were teaching had their degrees and were fully qualified to teach. They dismissed the complaints as carping, as mere "politics."

Surely, though, employment in the schools was important to the Tanks. Harold Rolph, a Tank who taught at Ironton High, remembered close connections among the Tanks, the schools, and the community: "It was common knowledge that if you played for the Tanks you could get a job teaching in Lawrence County. The school system had about 12 or 13 high schools and a Tank coached or taught at almost every one. It really worked well, because all of the players who were given teaching jobs had degrees from good schools. More than that, they were real gentlemen and fit right into community life."[38] Collett pictured the ties between the Tanks and the schools as something more than an informal process at work. The directors of the association, he said, were eager to pay off their debt quickly but knew that they had to field a team of good players that would draw large crowds to Beechwood. But they also knew that they could not bid for players commanding substantial weekly salaries, especially in a region where two other clubs were competing for them. Without the resources to meet a payroll that could run over $2,000 a week, they devised a plan to solve their problem: "The combination of Tom Hudson, Nick McMahon, Wm. C. Paul and others, sold an idea to the county school boards to employ coaches recommended by the Tanks. In this way, the Tank management brought college stars to town, assured them of work in the schools, with extra pay on Sundays to play professional football. It worked. The schools got high class men at salaries they could afford to pay, and the Tanks got the best which otherwise would cost them more than the team could afford."[39] McMahon often dangled the prospect of teaching in the public schools in front of men interested in playing for the Tanks, and he was able to deliver some positions. In 1928 and 1929 at least seven Tanks were teaching, and usually coaching, in Pedro, Proctorville, Coal Grove, and South Point in the county and in Ironton. Of course, around the nation football players often secured employment as teachers and coaches in schools. Apparently voters in Lawrence County had no great concern over the appearance of Tanks in the classroom. They returned two of the incumbents to the county board. The one challenger whom they seemed to elect lost his race in a recount of the votes.

Distracted momentarily by the controversy, the Tanks had to fasten their attention on their coming game at Akron with the Awnings, still one of the stronger teams in northeastern Ohio. The Awnings, seeing the Tanks as the leading team in southern Ohio, said that the game might decide the championship of the state.[40] Traveling in a "large bus," the Tanks arrived in Akron on Saturday and the next day, their reputation preceding them, found a huge crowd, about twelve thousand, awaiting

Portsmouth Is Football Crazy

them at League Park. They met in the Awnings a "wild aggressive" team whose charge, asserted the *Beacon-Journal*, forced the Tanks to fumble eight times.[41] Again the Tanks could muster little offense, their only touchdown coming after they recovered an Awnings fumble at the eight-yard line. Their defense held up, and they left Akron with a victory, 7–5. Saying more about the repute of the Tanks than their play, the Awnings saw the score as a moral victory.

Now the Tanks and Spartans would meet again. Interest in the game ran high, perhaps higher than usual, in both communities. The Tanks had lost but one game despite their moribund offense, and the Spartans were seeking revenge for one of their two losses; the winner would have the edge in the race for Tri-State and valley championships. As the Spartans began practice, Lumpkin went to Atlanta to visit a brother who had become ill; he intended to return soon but could not say when, leaving his teammates on tenterhooks. Fans hung on to reports on the condition of injured players: Presnell was in pain and could not start; Roebuck, another Tank, had injured one of his "hoofs"; Brumbaugh and Chal Joseph could not play for the Spartans, but Molesworth might be ready. When Lumpkin returned to Portsmouth three days before the game, saying that "I'd rather score a touchdown against the Tanks than fly," the Spartans and their fans rejoiced.

Fans in Portsmouth clamored for tickets, purchasing eleven hundred in forty-five minutes and altogether at least two thousand, perhaps twenty-five hundred. McMahon bought bleachers seating six hundred people and arranged to move fourteen hundred bleacher seats from Labold, using twelve vans to transport them to Beechwood. At the game, over seven thousand fans were sitting in the stadium and the temporary stands and standing near the field. Sitting together in a show of goodwill were about sixty members of the Portsmouth Lions Club, seventy from the Ironton club; the friendly Lions had agreed to attend the game as a body, the club from the losing community to treat the other to dinner.

The great crowd saw the Spartans and Tanks begin play on a muddy field, neither a decided favorite. But the Spartans controlled play from the opening to the closing minutes of the game. With Bennett scoring three touchdowns, the Spartans displayed "flashy" running and passing in a "driving attack" that resulted in a "stinging," a "staggering" defeat for the Tanks, 20–0. Only the Potters, with a victory of 28–0 in 1928, had ever beaten the Tanks by a larger margin. Despite or because of the one-sided nature of play, the fans, in contrast with their conduct at the first game, were orderly. And the players refrained from rough or "dirty" play. According to Burke and McCarthy, the Tanks were good-natured losers, the Spartans gracious winners.

Home and Away

At Portsmouth sportswriters and fans could not help but revel in the Spartans' decisive "shattering of an old jinx." A reporter for the *Sun* had the Spartans throwing sand in the Tanks' face. Lynn Wittenburg, a new sportswriter for the *Times*, turned out several columns on individual players and their performances and the repartee along the sidelines and in the crowd. For him, in one fell swoop, the Spartans had wiped out a string of Tanks victories, gaining revenge fortyfold, a bountiful feast after years of penury. Exuberant, he wrote some celebratory doggerel, using "Casey at the Bat" as his point of departure:

> Casey, the mighty of Mudville struck out,
> The Tanks, the chesty, of Cannonville passed out.
> And in the passing they went out with their boots on,
> But that was about all they had on.
>
> Is there a fan with soul so dead
>   Who never to himself hath said,
> This is the game, the game for me,
>   Lumpkin and Bennett and touchdowns three?
> Up in Ironton on their own door step,
>   paying off big that old, old debt,
> With a team of stars that shine as gold
>   That got revenge, yes forty-fold.[42]

Besides glory and redemption, surely the Spartans took a healthy profit from the game. With a visitor's share of the gate at 40 percent, they would have received at least $3,000 of the gross revenue of $9,000.[43]

The Spartans, Tanks, and Armcos were all about halfway through their schedules. In their direct competition, the Spartans had the advantage, winning two and losing one; the Armcos were close behind at a win and a loss; and the Tanks were still in the race at a victory and two losses. All played one another once more, and thus each had the opportunity to conclude the season leading the pack.

The Armcos and Tanks played the first of the remaining games among the three teams. Having met the Tanks and Spartans hand-running, the Armcos needed respite and found it in the Kokomo American Legion and Cleveland Panthers before meeting the Tanks again. Shaken from their pedestal by the Spartans, the Armcos were ready to believe boilerplate about the "strong" legionnaires. But they demolished the Kokomos 32–0, Paul "Horsemeat" Taylor and Bunk McWilliams moving into the

Portsmouth Is Football Crazy

backfield in a moment of zaniness. Then they hardly broke sweat in defeating the Cleveland Panthers 48–0. Fans knew that the Panthers were no great shakes, and a small crowd came to Armco Park.

Meanwhile, after losing to the Spartans, the Tanks played one game before coming to Armco Park. They went into that game against the Guards at Redland Field having scored but twelve points in their last four games, losing two of them. Tanks fans, accustomed to victory after victory, expressed disappointment as their team faltered but were not yet pointing fingers at players or Coach Presnell, whose injury had probably cost his team a touchdown or so. Nor did the players offer explanations or excuses for their record, saying instead that they had resolved to defeat the Guards. McMahon, scurrying around in his search for men to stay the team's descent, enlisted four new men in the Tanks' cause, one Sonny Winters. Still the Tanks could not change course. They could not mount an offense at Redland, and the Guards won 5–0 on a field goal and safety.

Coming to Armco Park, for the first time in their history the Tanks had lost three games in a season. Over their last five games, they had scored but one touchdown. And in playing the Armcos they faced the prospect of losing to one team twice in a season, an unprecedented failure for a Tanks eleven. Thus McMahon was again "scouring the wilds of America" for players who might stanch the Tanks' bleeding. Firing and hiring players as he had since the loss to the Spartans, he was creating, said Black, a "mystery" team. "Who," asked Black, "will Armco play Sunday?" McMahon did indeed acquire three new men for the game.[44] Smith of the Armcos countered, signing Howard Kriss to a contract just before the game; Kriss, a back who had been playing for the Panthers, proved to be an excellent runner against the Tanks.

Counting the crowd at Ashland, Smith had to regret the agreement with the Tanks on sharing the gate—each team was to take all the revenue from sales of tickets in its community. At Ironton, attendance had been over six thousand; on a rainy day at Ashland, the crowd numbered about thirty-five hundred. The muddy field, inhibiting a running game, dictated offensive strategy. With the ball deep in its own territory, a team might punt early in a series of downs rather than risk fumbling and await a break for a scoring opportunity. On every series inside their own half of the field, the Armcos punted on first down, altogether twenty-two times; the Tanks often punted on second and third down, twenty times. Pinned down near their own goal line in the third quarter, the Tanks punted short into their own territory. Then Lewis passed to Kriss, who made a "dazzling" run of twenty-one yards for a touchdown. Neither team could move the ball thereafter, and the Armcos left the field with the victory, 7–0.

Home and Away

Thus the Tanks had lost three straight games without scoring a point, an unexampled skein of failure for them. And yet, even as they prepared to play the Spartans again in Portsmouth, Burke contended that since the teams had split two games, the contest would decide which one could claim the state championship. The outlook for the Tanks was not good. Since defeating the Tanks, the Spartans had played and won two games in impressive fashion, one against the Awnings, the other against the Blues. At Akron, before a crowd of seventy-two hundred, they defeated the Awnings on a muddy field, 15–6, Bennett's seventy-seven-yard run for a touchdown the decisive score. A sportswriter for the *Beacon-Journal,* probably Schlemmer, declared that "no team in modern football history ever presented as a smooth-working, hard-running backfield in Akron as Portsmouth did yesterday."[45] He lavished praise on Lumpkin for doing the work of two men in running interference. Then going to Middletown, they met a Blues club with George Kinderdine and Al Graham, sometime players for the Spartans in 1928, in the lineup, but they easily dispatched the Blues, 22–0.

Fans and sportswriters now began to raise questions about where the Spartans ranked among the professional teams of the state and nation. Were they simply a good team on a hot streak that had to end when they met the Tanks or Armcos? Or were they a new kind of team in the valley, a professional team that would have to look elsewhere for worthwhile competition and that would acquit itself well against any other professional team in the nation? The answer could come as the Spartans ran a gauntlet of tough foes—the Tanks, Guards, and Armcos—over a span of eight days.

First came the Tanks. Smarting from their humiliating loss to the Spartans a few weeks earlier and their three consecutive defeats, the Tanks arrived at Labold with a vision of vindicating their proud history. Fans in Ironton, used to long streaks of victories, were beginning to grumble. Burke counseled patience, reminding them that wins, though sweet, were not inevitable. But along with the fans, he still believed that the Tanks could close the season on a successful note. By a victory over the Spartans, the Tanks would earn the intrinsic satisfaction of diminishing the stain of the earlier loss, and by winning two of the three games against the Spartans, they could also claim the state championship—a dubious argument. Fans and sports columnists in Ironton thought that victory was hardly out of the question. They heard that Presnell was ready to return to the lineup and that McMahon had acquired three new linemen and two new "ball toters."[46] Fans in Portsmouth listened to rumors that the Tanks were loading up. McMahon, they learned, was scouring the country for players, traveling until "he [was] footsore to find some flashy backs and strong linemen" to stop the Spartans. Attuned for years to such reports, they

Portsmouth Is Football Crazy

discounted other stories saying that the Tanks would not change their roster. No matter who wore the Tanks' uniforms, Spartans fans were confident of a second victory over their old nemesis. As one observer noted, they were "drinking deep of the sweet intoxicant of revenge." Seeing a win on the horizon, Grimes, editor of the *Times* and a member of the board of the football corporation, was ready to claim the state championship. A second straight victory over the Tanks would be a landmark, he thought, in the long rivalry between Portsmouth and Ironton reaching back to the decades "before his daddy and grand-daddy before him played ball," when combat was sometimes bloody, sometimes friendly.[47] Some fans took encouragement in discerning, somehow, what they believed to be Ironton's loss of interest in the Tanks.

Measured by attendance, the interest of fans in both communities in this game was less than in the earlier contests. The crowd numbered thirty-five hundred, a good turnout for other games but three thousand fewer than had attended the first game at Portsmouth. The seventy Ironton Lions who roared at Beechwood dwindled to twenty at Labold. Tanks fans who elected to remain home spared themselves an unpleasant sight. The Spartans, reaching a "state of perfection" in a "merciless attack," gave the Tanks the most "terrible shellacking" in their "long and glorious history," yielding but eighteen yards to them in yardage from scrimmage and outscoring them 38–0. All the Spartans played well, said Burke, but he could not accord one Tank a laudatory word. Presnell did not play. If the Tanks came to Labold "overloaded" with "additional" players costing $1,200, as the *Times* asserted, they failed to stay the Spartans. In fact, four new men did play for the Tanks but none of any great repute or ability. The Tanks were even wanting in equipment. All the Spartans wore "mud-cleated shoes while there was not a pair of long spikes in the Tank lineup."[48] One fact seemed obvious at the game's end: the old mudsill had become the new mountain, the old mountain the mudsill.

Though sportswriters in Ironton and Portsmouth had portrayed the game as one settling claims to the state championship, columnists in Portsmouth now looked to the Spartans' coming contest with the Guards at Labold as truly decisive.[49] They noted that the Guards had recently defeated the Tanks and had held the Spartans to a tie early in the season. They wished, of course, to see a good crowd at Labold. But the "great clash," played on Thanksgiving Day, drew only about twenty-five hundred fans, few from Cincinnati. The few had little to cheer about. Dominating play, the Spartans won 25–0 and for the second straight week could claim the championship of Ohio.

As Portsmouth scribes understood their world of football, the Spartans could add

Home and Away

three more titles to their laurels if they defeated the Armcos a second time. The Spartans then had a record of nine wins, two losses, and a tie; the Armcos were at eight wins, a loss, and a tie. In Tri-State competition, the Spartans were at three wins and a loss, the Armcos at two wins and a loss. The winner would have the edge in the contest for the Tri-State and valley titles. Declaring that the Armcos were the best team in Kentucky, the *Sun* insisted that by a victory the Spartans could also proclaim themselves champions of the state.[50]

If comparative scores meant anything, the Armcos could not be optimistic about beating the Spartans. Only a week after the Spartans had easily defeated the Blues 22–0, the Armcos went to Middletown to play the Blues. They had beaten the Blues handily earlier in the season and were decided favorites to win again. But they could not score in a intense defensive game that ended in a scoreless tie. As was customary, after the game players of both teams and officials from both mills gathered at the Manchester Hotel for dinner. The coaches and Charles Hook addressed the guests, and all enjoyed an evening of "good fellowship."

Good fellowship was not what the Armcos and Spartans had in mind going into their game. The players on each team were determined to "smash out" a victory. They met on a cold Sunday at Labold before a good crowd of over four thousand, playing on a field hard as concrete. The Spartans, finding "hocus-pocus" plays of no use, turned to brute power to grind out a win, 19–0, inflicting injuries on several Armcos. No one now disputed their dominance in the Ohio Valley and the Tri-State, but no one laid claim to a title in Kentucky for them. Disappointed and concerned about mounting injuries to the Armcos, Smith canceled their game with the Chicago Cardinals and closed their season.

Even as the Spartans were sealing their titles, they, their coach, and the directors of the corporation were looking for new worlds to conquer. Feeding their expansive spirit was personal and civic pride. Along with fans in the street, they could read sports columns in the *Sun* and *Times* comparing the Spartans favorably with the best collegiate and professional teams in the nation.[51] The directors, asserting that the Spartans had "outclassed" all opponents in the region, were talking about seeking a franchise in the NFL. As a wedge for entering the league, in November they tentatively scheduled a game with the Chicago Cardinals to be played at Labold in mid-December. Then, seeing a game with the Packers, undefeated and champions of the NFL, as a better draw and as one that would enhance the Spartans' repute, they entered into negotiations with Lambeau for his team to come to Labold in place of the Cardinals.

From the start, the arrangements for the game were tentative, indeed inchoate.

Portsmouth Is Football Crazy

The Spartans had to guarantee the Packers $4,500 and raise another $2,500 to pay their own players.[52] To meet the guarantee, the directors called on one hundred persons to pledge $50 each within one week, which would be returned if sales of tickets covered the expenditure of $7,000. If the "red-blooded" Portsmouth fans bought all the available tickets, the Spartans would realize $9,400, more than enough to cover expenses of the game and to reduce the corporation's deficit for the year. The game would be more than an exhibition, said the *Sun*; it would determine the professional championship of the nation. If the directors could not arrange the game, they expected to send the Spartans against the St. Louis Blues for the national championship of independent professional teams.

Within a few days, nearly fifty persons pledged to pay $50, and in another day the one hundred pledges seemed assured. Then the Packers raised an obstacle. Scheduling a barnstorming tour, they intended to play the Memphis Tigers in Tennessee on the same day that the Spartans planned to host them. Would the Spartans shift their proposed game back a week? All the Spartan players but one agreed to remain in the city for the game.

The problem of a date seemingly solved and ticket sales proceeding well, Joe Carr, president of the NFL, raised another roadblock. Saying that by-laws of the league prohibited teams from playing elevens whose collegiate players had not graduated and that Lumpkin had not graduated from Georgia Tech, he would not permit the Packers to go to Portsmouth.[53] Directors of the Portsmouth corporation and personal friends of Carr appealed to him to reverse his decision, but to no avail. Griffin hurried to Columbus to confer with Carr, offering to substitute Tiny Lewis for Lumpkin; Carr would not relent, adding that the Packers would be foolish to risk their undefeated record against the Spartans.[54] At one point, Lambeau, insisting that Carr had no authority over the Packers once the season ended, declared that he would defy him and post a bond guaranteeing the Packers' appearance in Portsmouth.[55] But he decided to accept Carr's order and called off the game, perhaps more out of fear of losing to the Spartans than fear of the president. Lambeau was singing a different tune in Green Bay. There fans heard little of Carr's stand, and Lambeau told them that he canceled the game because his players were "anxious to wind up the season."[56] In any case, Portsmouth fans would long remember and resent Lambeau for his failure to keep his word; in their view the Packers could not be national champions until they met and beat the Spartans. They took great delight in the Packers' loss to the Memphis Tigers later in December; it was proof, they argued, that Carr knew that the Spartans would defeat the Packers.

As the directors and Griffin were attempting to arrange the game with the Packers,

Home and Away

Spartan players were continuing to play. Following the game against the Armcos, they met the Chillicothe Eagles for a second time in 1929. The Eagles had been operating in the red and welcomed the game as an opportunity to cut their losses—and to defeat the lofty Spartans; the Spartan directors looked to the game for a good gate—they needed a crowd of at least two thousand to wipe out their deficit of $400.[57] They mounted, with some success, a vigorous campaign to sell tickets; rumors of the Eagles loading up may have advanced sales. Spartan fans also found the game interesting because of the special circumstances surrounding it; otherwise it would not have attracted their attention. A few days before the contest, the Spartans released four players, including Brumbaugh, whose gimpy knee had limited his play in recent weeks. Immediately, the Eagles offered contracts to all four to play against their former teammates. Only Brumbaugh accepted a contract, the others saying that they wished to avoid any allegations that they would provide information to the Eagles on the Spartans' plays and formation. A fairly good crowd, about twenty-five hundred, was at Labold, many curious about Brumbaugh and his role in the game. If Brumbaugh gave any information to the Eagles, it was not useful. The Spartans easily won 30–7, all the while fans jeering Brumbaugh, who, nonetheless, made a few good runs.

The Spartans attracted the crowd that they said they needed to wipe out their deficit, but apparently they were still at the margin.[58] The directors cast about for one more game, explaining that they needed a crowd of two thousand to break even for the season and that they had promised fans fifteen games. They found an opponent in the Mendel Tailors, a very ordinary team. The Spartans ripped the Tailors apart 44–0, evidently before a small crowd. The directors faced a "slight" operating deficit but wiped it out by issuing notes of credit.

So the Spartans had finally brought a glorious season to an end, their record standing at twelve wins, two losses, and a tie. Portsmouth fans had waited many years to root for a real team, and now they could cheer in full-throated enthusiasm. Even the players, conscious of their place in the history of football in the community, were sad-eyed as they left Labold. Throughout the season, the Spartans brought to the community a new brand of professional football, one portending even more unusual changes. Increasingly, too, they became tied to everyday life of the fans through the course of face-to-face relations. For men playing for the Smoke House or the Presidents, such relations were natural and innate; most were natives or longtime residents of the city, relatives, neighbors, friends, and fellow workers of hundreds of other people in the community. To a large extent the Spartans of 1928 and to an even larger extent the Spartans of 1929 came into the city as strangers with no ties to residents.

Portsmouth Is Football Crazy

Usually residing there for but a season, they seemed to be transients who would not participate in everyday life but who eventually forged ties with the community. Living arrangements provided the principal nexus between players and residents. Nearly all the Spartans were young single men. Many of them became boarders, singly or in pairs, with families or in rooming houses; a few lived in apartments. By all accounts, the boarders and their hosts enjoyed cordial relationships. Years later, one Spartan recalled that the players "enjoyed" the fans and vice versa.[59] Fans invited players to their homes for dinners and various social events, and they met one another at restaurants, pool halls, and other public places. Lumpkin was especially popular in the community, a prankster, a "good-hearted" man. Usually, he remained in Portsmouth after a season's play, engaging in amusing antics as a boxer and wrestler on local cards.

In somewhat more formal ways, the Spartans were becoming household words. Civic clubs gave them increasing recognition as solid citizens, especially as they won more games. The Lions Club hosted them twice at luncheons during the season of 1929, and the Rotarians "honored" them at a dinner when the season closed. Several players attended noon meetings of these clubs and gave short speeches. The Spartans sustained a favorable presence in the community. Seven or eight, as in 1928, organized basketball teams at the end of the season that played other quintets in the vicinity. At their second annual banquet, the players expressed their appreciation to fans for their support. They also sponsored a dance at the season's end at Baesman's Dancing Academy, a huge success with five hundred couples in attendance.

As a corporate entity, the Spartans were playing a role in the movement toward construction of a new stadium at Labold. For several years, civic organizations, the Lions, the Kiwanis, and other clubs, had been calling for development of the field into a recreational park with a swimming pool, tennis courts, and a baseball diamond, as well as a football stadium. In 1928 they had unsuccessfully sought to raise $80,000 for such facilities through a subscription drive, and early in 1929 they had asked the municipal council to place on the ballot a proposal to raise the money through the issuance of bonds. The council put the question to the voters in the fall, saying that the facility would be a memorial to veterans.[60] Ostensibly, the park would serve the entire community; but clearly the spokesmen for it and the recreational board saw the stadium as the centerpiece, a showcase for the Spartans enabling them to go on to higher reaches in professional football. Of the $80,000, the board allocated the lions' share, $70,000, for the construction of a stadium seating 13,500 people. Sitting on the board and casting a vote for the ballot was Grimes, also a member of the Spartans' board of directors. Shortly before the election, the football corporation purchased a large display advertisement in the *Times* calling for support of the proposal, noting that Ashland and Ironton had erected new stadia for their teams. The proposal won a majority vote, 3,687 for it, 3,631 against, but because the law required approval by 55 percent of votes cast, the issue failed.[61]

Then the municipal council took a step demonstrating that football was the way of the world for it. Cutting all facilities from the project except the stadium but trimming its cost, the council authorized the use of private capital for construction. By its resolution, the city would lease a part of Labold for twenty years to the highest bidder willing to construct a steel and concrete stadium costing at least $30,000 and seating at least four thousand spectators.[62] The leasee would receive a share of the proceeds derived from the sale of tickets to athletic events held at the stadium. Not until midway through 1930 would the council take bids. Though envisioning a project of lesser magnitude than originally proposed, the council opened the door, as it turned out, to the construction of a stadium tailored to the Spartans' expansive goals.

At season's end the goals became clearer as the Spartan directors prepared for another year's play, giving the community ample evidence that their team would take the field again and might move to a new level of competition. Midway through the season of 1929, Ridgley was calling for the organization of a professional league in the Ohio Valley composed of teams from Ashland, Ironton, Huntington, and Portsmouth.[63] The proposal had merit for developing regularity of scheduling among natural rivals. But their attention fixed on a larger, more immediate prospect, the Spartans gave it scant attention. Shortly after the council adopted the resolution to accept bids for construction of a stadium, Spartan officials let the community know, more or less by the grapevine, of their intention to seek entry for their team into the NFL within a few years. They had already opened the door by scheduling games with the Packers and Cardinals. Their celerity in signing players in November and early in December, long before independent teams ordinarily built rosters, also implied that they were moving in a new direction. They also signaled their movement to stability and expansion when in December they signed Griffin to a three-year contract as coach of the Spartans. At their direction, he began writing letters to graduating collegiate stars throughout the nation—as many as five hundred, he said —providing them with information about the Spartans and asking them about their availability for 1930. Almost simultaneously, they announced at a reorganizational meeting of the corporation that they had instructed Griffin to file an application for the Spartans to join the NFL. The NFL owners, sounding as though they had already been considering the Spartans for membership in the league, declared that all the Spartans, having completed a year of probation, were eligible for play in their league. Griffin could go to the owners' meeting at Dayton in January, application in hand, anticipating a favorable reception.

Coming out of their second loss to the Spartans, the Tanks were tattered and torn, having lost four games in a row without scoring a point. Yet they could salvage a piece of respectability in the record, if not in repute, if they could win their last game of the season at Akron against the Awnings. Then their record would stand at six wins and five losses; a loss would reverse the numbers. The difference would be minimal, but for American sports fans the difference between success and failure, winning and losing. Desperate, McMahon recruited five new men, releasing six at the same time; again they were journeymen, not players who could turn a sow's ear into a silk purse. Presnell, though, was finally ready to play and might give the Tanks precious yards and first downs. The Awnings, though, were athirst for revenge against the team that had handed them their only loss in 1928 and had beaten them earlier in the season. At Akron, with few of their fans on hand, again the Tanks were moribund on offense, their only score a field goal. In the fourth quarter, Ralph Stanford of the Awnings intercepted a pass and ran it back fifty-four yards for a touchdown, giving his team the victory 7–3. The Awnings were so delirious that they "smooched" Stanford.

And so the Tanks' season ended in yet another failure of the offense, yet another defeat. Measured by the historical record, the team had played through a disastrous season, made more galling by their opening the season with four consecutive wins. In the following seven games, the Tanks could win but one, finishing with a record of five wins and six losses; through their last eight games, they scored only fifteen points, one touchdown. Never had a Tanks eleven performed so abysmally. Fans, curiously, did not e search intensively for an explanation for the Tanks' failure, certainly not blaming specific players, the coach, or the manager as the ones responsible for losses. Many attributed the Tanks' slide to injuries, notably Presnell's.

At the season's end, the football committee discussed the Tanks' play and the means to rehabilitate the team. Committee members did not, reported Burke, intend to take up a "housecleaning" at the top, finding no fault with Presnell or McMahon.[64] But they did believe that they had to give the team an infusion of younger players. They reappointed McMahon to the manager's position, charging him to recruit "bigger and better players." Burke tied his explanation for the dismal season to the committee's view, alleging that the Tanks had been "burdened by some veteran professionals who took the easiest way out of games and the disease spread." The veterans—he did not identify them—had, he believed, demoralized the squad, making teamwork impossible.

Decades later, Presnell, his memory good, recalled nothing of the sort and offered less subjective explanations for his team's decline.[65] Laid up in bed for days with his injury, he was unable to give the Tanks the direction they needed. Of greater importance, he thought, was the depth of the roster. Often, with but sixteen or seventeen men in uniform, many of them with nagging injuries, he was short-handed in maneuvering players and saw the team wear down toward the end of games. Especially in the second half of the season, McMahon's addition of new men proved counterproductive. They would come to Ironton on a Saturday before a game, never having practiced with the team. Presnell would meet with them at the Elks Club and diagram plays on paper for them. Before the last game at Akron, he sat in a hotel room with five new players diagramming plays. Under such circumstances, players could not develop the required timing for execution of plays. One loss almost opened the door to a succeeding loss as McMahon signed new players for each game. No one plumbing the causes of defeat noted, as they had before the season began, that the Tanks were playing substantially improved teams, the Spartans and Armcos, in seven games.

The Tanks also suffered losses on the ledger in 1929. At the annual meeting of the stockholders of the Stadium Association, held in December, the attendants heard that they were facing a deficit of $1,800. Thus they agreed that the directors should not make any stock payments, believing that then "everything would be fine."[66] To wipe out the deficit, one stockholder proposed the sale of the stadium, originally to be given to the school, to the school board for $10,000. Earlier the directors had suggested $20,000,—but the stockholders backed off on learning that the board owned the land on which the stadium had been built. As a matter of policy, the stockholders directed the Tanks management to recruit more full-time players and to rely less on men coming into town on the weekends. Despite the defeats, the deficit, and the stock market crash, no one proposed that the Tanks be disbanded. But no one feted them with banquets.

Off the field, too, the Tanks lost some repute. For many years, sportswriters, businessmen, and fans generally had viewed the players, whether they came to the city from out of town or were hometown men, as "clean-cut," solid citizens who were a credit to the community. The "imported" players, as Harold Rolph had noted, usually were not "tramp" athletes, and enough of them became permanent residents of Ironton to give the Tanks the coloration of stability. They married Ironton women,

Portsmouth Is Football Crazy

became a part of everyday life, and entered businesses and professions. Yet all were Adam's children and could kick over the traces. And stories were afloat in Ironton in 1929 that, though involving only several players, dulled the image of the Tanks a degree. Dick Powell and Tiny Roebuck, after taking too much home brew, removed a privy from its foundations and deposited it in the middle of busy street, tying up traffic down a couple of blocks. Residents of Ironton knew that several players were patronizing the establishment of Mae Davis in the red-light district on Buckhorn Street. Roebuck had too much tomato brandy there one night and ran amok, sending scantily clad painted ladies in search of open windows to escape.[67] Davis, who was married at one time to a Tank, Dick Alvis, hit him with a bottle of home brew and silenced him.

At Ashland, the Armcos appeared to be on stabler ground than the Tanks at season's end. Despite concluding play with a tie and the painful loss to the Spartans and losing claims to championships, the Armcos could boast a good record at eight wins, two losses, and a tie and faced no calls for their rehabilitation. They disappeared, as usual, from the sports pages of the *Independent*. The Employees Association issued no public statements about plans for 1930, and fans turned their attention to other sports, expecting to see the Armcos meeting the Tanks, Spartans, and other foes at Armco Park in the fall of 1930. Noting the placidity with which the community viewed the Armcos, an observer might have questioned whether the team had yet found a real place in the life of the city.

10
Portsmouth Is in the Big League

THE YEAR 1930 was remarkable for the change in the fortunes of the Armcos, Spartans, and Tanks. Suddenly, the Armcos were no longer on the field contesting the dominion of the Tanks and Spartans in the Tri-State and Ohio Valley. The Spartans, not surprisingly, were in the NFL, their rivalry with the Tanks still viable, even heightened, because their new status made them an inviting target for a David with a sling and smooth stones. The Tanks, replaced by the Spartans as the leading eleven in the valley, were taking steps to regain their old glory. All the while, their communities viewed the changing scene in varying ways—with indifference, enthusiasm, and sorrow.

At the season's end in 1929, the Employees Association at Armco gave no indication that the Armcos might not continue to play in 1930, but neither did it make public statements about planning for the coming season. Perhaps officials of the association and the company were biding their time as they measured industrial activity after the stock market crash in October of 1929.

Portsmouth Is in the Big League

Generally Armco weathered the Great Depression reasonably well, but it did see a decline in orders for its steel in the spring of 1930.

Then early in July, without rumors forewarning workers in the mill or residents in Ashland, the association announced that at the recommendation of its athletic council, it was cutting the Armco football team from the employees' recreational program.[1] Slack operations in the steel industry and in the local mill, explained the officials, accounted for the decision. Because an unspecified number of mill workers had been laid off and current employees were working fewer hours, sales of season tickets, they reasoned, had to fall off. The Armcos depended on their support from the Armco organization, not on public patronage as did the Tanks and Spartans. The team was not a "paying proposition" and rather than field a mediocre eleven with players commanding smaller weekly salaries, they preferred to dissolve it and, depending on economic conditions, reorganize it another year, perhaps in 1931. In the meantime, they urged Armco workers to support the high school Tomcats and the Tanks. Workers could thus assist the Tanks in sustaining their "high class" program.

The announcement elicited hardly a whimper of complaint from workers in the mill or residents in the community. Black lamely wrote only that the fall looked like a "dim affair" without the Armco-Tanks series. The association continued the employees' basketball program and other recreational activities. At Ironton, the *Tribune* lamented the decision, pointing out that the Tanks had to give up two games yielding good gates and easing the problem of scheduling.[2]

Clearly the Armcos never reached the heart of Ashland as the Tanks touched that of Ironton. The creation of a steel company, they did not originate out of the community. They never passed into emotional ownership by the community, never became a source of pride for it as the Tanks did for Ironton. Moreover, the football fans of Ashland—and there were many—gave their loyalty primarily to the local high school team, the Tomcats. That was easy to do. From 1925 through 1929, the Tomcats lost only one game and were claimants to three state titles and a national championship. It was not unusual for them to draw crowds of seven and eight thousand to their big games.

Midway through December 1929, the directors of the Portsmouth Football Corporation had announced their intention to seek a franchise in the NFL, and early in January they submitted the application to club owners meeting in Dayton.[3] Explaining the decision, Grimes asserted that the Spartans could not cover expenses playing teams from Middletown, Columbus, and other communities in southern Ohio. They could beat them, and badly, but not draw well. To attract larger crowds, they had to play strong teams that could be found only in the NFL. If admitted to the NFL, the Spartans, he said, would continue to play the Tanks and Armcos for a while. The directors were confident that the NFL owners would admit the Spartans because of their good record, but Wittenburg of the *Times* feared that Carr would throw the application in the wastebasket as he had the Spartans' proposal to play the Packers at the close of the recent season.

Wittenburg need not have worried. The NFL owners admitted nearly any club able to pay the membership fee, $2,500. They had little concern about the financial stability of a franchise or the size of its market. Pell-mell, individuals or associated individuals from small, medium, and large cities—Racine, Kenosha, Rochester, and New York, for example—sought and received franchises throughout the 1920s. Often they operated their teams with revenue from other ventures or bankrolled them out of their personal income.[4] Inevitably, their financial status shaky, clubs were constantly withdrawing from the league. From 1923 through 1926, teams in the circuit numbered from twenty to twenty-two; through the same years at least twenty-two new teams came into the league as twenty-five were departing. A great shakedown after the season of 1926 left twelve teams in play in 1927, the number falling to ten in 1928 and rising again to twelve in 1929. The apparent stability masked the fact that clubs were still coming and going through a revolving door; the three years saw six teams entering the league, eight exiting.

Certainly the NFL men felt predisposed to approve the Spartans' application. Even as they received it, they met in an executive session, discussing among other subjects the state of professional football in the league and beyond in 1929; they agreed that "several individual [independent] teams of outstanding importance were developed in various sections of the country, [such] as Portsmouth and Ironton, Ohio, Ashland Ky., and Memphis, Tenn."[5] And they knew that the Spartans were working toward the construction of a new stadium in Portsmouth. After reviewing the application, the owners were nearly ready to admit the Spartans to the league. So said Griffin, who had talked to Tim Mara of the Giants by telephone. Mara supported them, as did Dr. Webber Kelly of the Packers and George Halas of the Bears, and other owners were likely to accept their recommendations for approval of entrance. Though acknowledging that Portsmouth would be the smallest city ever to receive a franchise (Pottsville and Green Bay were, in fact, smaller), they saw the city as a linchpin connecting western and eastern clubs of the league. A western team could play another western team on a Wednesday night, travel to Portsmouth

Portsmouth Is in the Big League

for a Sunday game, and then proceed to an eastern city for a Wednesday game. An eastern team could reverse directions on the route.

If the NFL owners saw geography speaking for Portsmouth, neither they nor the Spartans let population become a doubting voice in their plans, as they might well have. Aside from the Packers, the Spartans would become the only nonmetropolitan franchise in the league. Their market in raw population would compare favorably only with the Packers'. In an eleven-county area encircling Portsmouth the population was about 430,000 in 1930; in nine counties around Green Bay, the population was about 376,000. Eventually seating about ten thousand spectators, the stadium that the Spartans expected to play in would be among the three smallest in the league cities; even if fans regularly occupied all seats, the franchise might not survive against the larger cities.

For the moment, though, the Spartans faced a more immediate problem. Before the owners would formally approve their admission, the directors had to deposit $2,500 in the NFL treasury to guarantee the "faithful performance" of the club's operation. They did not have the sum at hand. They sent a distress signal to the community, calling on fans to contribute the necessary money within two days to meet the deadline. The *Sun* urged "boosters of postgraduate football" in the city—fans and businessmen—to turn their pockets inside out.[6] Without a franchise in the NFL, the Spartans could not meet worthy competition beyond the Tanks and Armcos and thus would not field a team. It would then follow that no one would construct a new stadium— "no franchise, no team, no stadium." At a hastily called public meeting, ten businessmen agreed to contribute the $2,500, receiving promissory notes bearing 7 percent interest to be paid in ninety days. The directors sent the money to the NFL office in Columbus, and at their annual meeting in June, the owners approved the Spartans' application.

While the directors sought membership in the league, municipal authorities in Portsmouth were working on the related question of a new stadium. Originally, the city council had enacted legislation authorizing the lease of Labold for twenty years to the highest bidder willing to construct a stadium meeting certain requirements. If the Spartans entered the NFL, probably the lease would become more valuable and bidders more numerous. To protect the city's interest, the council approved a new ordinance in March restricting renewal of the lease to ten years, permitting the city to purchase the stadium at any time, and requiring the successful bidder to start construction within six months after the city's acceptance of a bid.[7]

The city began to receive bids in April and early in May accepted one submitted by the Universal Stadium Corporation. Named specifically for its mission, the corporation was the creation of Harry Snyder, a prominent and longtime building contractor in the city. In his bid of $50 annually for the lease of Labold, he proposed to construct a stadium far larger and costlier than the council had originally required. Instead of accommodating four thousand spectators, it would seat eight to ten thousand; instead of costing as little as $30,000, it would run as high as $100,000. He had to depend on income from rental of the stadium to retire the debt that he would incur in building it. Soon becoming a director on the Spartans' board, certainly he hoped that the team would draw well at the stadium and pay well for its use. He wasted little time in breaking ground. In July municipal and school dignitaries and ordinary citizens gathered at the field, listened to speeches about dreams coming true, and watched the mayor turn the first shovel full of dirt. Though all were exuberant, few expected the stadium to be ready for use by the fall.

As municipal administrators looked over paperwork for the stadium and construction workers dug footers and poured cement for it, the Spartans were preparing for play in 1930. Unlike in the years when the semiprofessional teams of the city shut down activities as the season ended, the Spartans of 1929 continued operations, at least in a limited way, after the players stored their togs in December. The directors had reorganized the corporation, selecting several new board members and appointing Harry Doerr as general manager of the team. At the same time, Griffin already had signed as many as fourteen players from the roster of 1929 to return in 1930 and was writing to collegiate players all over the nation urging them to become Spartans. By March he had applications from twenty of the "best known" players in the country. Early in May, he was negotiating terms with nine or ten "stars" from the Midwest and Far West, including Earl "Dutch" Clark, a stellar halfback at Colorado College, and Willis Glassgow, an All-American back at the University of Iowa in 1929. He signed Glassgow but not Clark, who had one more year of eligibility at Colorado. In June he persuaded Fred Roberts, a guard from the University of Iowa who had made an All-American team in 1929, to join the Spartans. Midway through June he had twenty-five men in the Spartans' fold and was still looking for stars. When in July officials of the Armco Employees Association announced their decision not to field a team in 1930, Griffin immediately offered a contract to Tiny Lewis. McMahon also wanted his signature, but Lewis decided to go with the Spartans, explaining that "Portsmouth is in the big league and has a good team, and I hope to play regularly on it."[8] Late in July Griffin could count thirty-four players on the roster. Thirteen had played for the Spartans in 1929; nearly all the remaining twenty-one had never played professional football. The thirty-four came from

Portsmouth Is in the Big League

twenty-four colleges and universities—Notre Dame, the Universities of Nebraska, Iowa, North Dakota, and Georgia, Ohio State University, and others. The *Times* thought that Griffin had assembled the "best team" in the nation.

Along with Doerr, Griffin was working on the schedule. The team now a member of an established league, they could avoid much of the extemporaneity marking scheduling of independent elevens. At the same time, though, evidently they had to take a back seat as the established clubs controlled the patterns of dates and travel. Announced late in July, much earlier than usual but with a few tentative dates, the schedule called for the Spartans to play eighteen games, eight at home, ten on the road. Fifteen games were with league teams. Later Grimes asserted, correctly, that the Spartans were the first team in the NFL to meet all other league clubs. The Tanks were still on the schedule, tentatively for three games, two in Ironton.

The Spartans were manifesting optimism and a sense of status and continuity as the season approached. They mounted a campaign in the summer for the sale of season tickets with Dudley Harris, a big tackle, managing it as a full-time employee.[9] Fans could purchase tickets at $12 each, paying $1 down and the remainder in installments. Stockholders, sanguine about their team's capability and little concerned about worsening economic conditions in the nation, transformed their nonprofit corporation into one for profit and authorized the issuance of 250 shares of stock at $100 a share.[10] In consonance with their club's new place in football, they changed the name of the Portsmouth Football Corporation to the Portsmouth National Football League Corporation.

The summer wearing on as the Spartans readied their roster and schedule, the stadium where they would play was going up. Coleman Grimes went to Labold late in August a few days before the Spartans began practice and reported to readers of the *Times* what he saw and what he expected to see there.[11] Carpenters, he wrote, were erecting twenty tiers of temporary wooden stands for use in the first game, building them in such a way that they would be used later as forms for concrete. They were also piling up bleachers. Workers had poured cement for box seats and footers. Under the stadium would be rest rooms, dressing rooms, showers, lockers, a rub-down room, and a concession booth. A "commodious" press box would cap the stadium. Leveled, underlaid with tile, and seeded, the field was taking on the aspect of a verdant pasture. Modern electricity would serve the fans: they could hear running accounts of games on an intricate address system and see games at night on a field flooded by a lighting system of the "latest design." Fence thieves would be disappointed, finding an eight-foot wooden fence encircling the field barring their entrance to it. Fans could enter the stadium on a dry cinder path. Outside

Home and Away

the stadium fans would have plenty of free parking. The facility would be, Grimes concluded, a model for communities throughout the state. Later, his civic pride welling up, Wittenburg counted the stadium and field as yet another monument of progress for the community, which recently had seen the construction of a new floodwall, courthouse, and railroad depot.

Their "football blood up," fans awaited the coming of "stars" to the city and gathered at their "favorite meeting places" to discuss the outlook for the season. Hundreds hurried to the opening practices at Labold. They saw Griffin, with about forty men on hand, some trying out without contracts, running the first session under a "merciless sun," the backs passing and punting, the linemen "butting, shoving and blocking each other." A few days after practices began, a large crowd surrounded and threatened to engulf the field as the Spartans engaged in their first scrimmage, a "tag" game played without tackling. Standing among the fans was Wittenburg. As he pictured the Spartans, they were on paper and in their embryonic stage, in their speed and weight a "worldbeater." One could become dizzy, he asserted, looking at the collection of stars; if they could coordinate their play, some NFL teams were in for a lesson in football.[12]

Griffin had to use practices to prepare the team for play, and since he eventually had to use a roster of twenty-two, he had to pare players early. Because the margin between two players at one position was often narrow, he or any coach could make a wrong decision, but usually not one decisively affecting a team. His first cut lived long in the common memory as a mistake. After only a few practices, he released Molesworth, who had played for the Spartans for the past two years. Supposedly all in the community knew that Griffin was angry with the back for stealing and marrying his girl. Almost immediately Molesworth signed with the Tanks and a year later began the first of his six years with the Bears. Griffin's other cuts presumably were more rational. The team that he shaped was a mixture of the old and new. About half of the roster had been with the Spartans in 1929, the other half was recent recruits; of the players who started the first game in 1930, six were holdovers, five new men.

The players surviving the cuts wore new uniforms. Abandoning the old blue and white colors, Spartan officials arrayed the team in all purple uniforms, with white numerals on the backs of the jerseys and white wings on the forehead of the helmets. Their choice of color did not derive solely from aesthetic considerations. Supposedly, the all-purple uniforms would not show dirt and mud as clearly as the old uniforms had. And the material used in them, the same as that found covering airplane wings, would be twice as durable as any other fabric.

Portsmouth Is in the Big League

The Spartans had not quite two weeks to prepare for their season's opener against a league opponent, the Newark Tornadoes. Griffin thus worked the players through long, rigorous sessions. At the stadium, men labored at a feverish pitch on the stadium seats, on a "gigantic" scoreboard at the north end of the field, on a steel fence between the bleachers and the field, and more. The Postal Telegraph Company was laying a wire to the press box. Municipal and Spartan officials were planning "special exercises" for the game. The mayor, Robert Bryan, and the city manager, C. A. Harrell, intended to make short dedication speeches to the fans over the "addressograph." At the invitation of the Spartans, Joe Carr would occupy a special box with the mayor and manager. Municipal police were busy planning procedures to move automobiles rapidly in and out of the grounds.

As Wittenburg saw it, the Spartans faced a tough opponent in the "famous" men of Newark. Though their league record was ordinary at three wins, four losses, and four ties in 1929, their line was highly trained and their backfield, all from Holy Cross, was strong. He pictured interesting implications in the game: it pitted eastern and western clubs in the "post graduate loop" against each other and the "college breds" of the West against the "intellectuals" from the East.[13]

The scene at the new stadium on the day of the game was worthy of a Brueghel's brush.[14] More than four thousand fans were in the stadium and bleachers despite a heavy rainfall that had left puddles of water on seats and turned the field into a watery sponge. Hundreds of people climbed into trees and on housetops and the floodwall for a distant view of the game. Eluding patrolmen, boys scrambled over the fence around the field. The "twobit" crowd, the "kids," spilled out of their special bleachers into an area called the "bullpen." Dedication ceremonies did not go off well. Bryan and Harrell gave their addresses over a loudspeaker that was not functioning, and the crowd ignored them. A "radio company" worked feverishly to substitute electrical megaphones until the loudspeaker was operating in the second half. As planned, Carr was sitting in a box on the fifty-yard line; he shook hands with the captains of the teams, and the game began.

The game had some farcical aspects. At the opening kickoff, the irrepressible Lumpkin tossed his helmet aside and played the entire game without it. Rooting around on a wet field, both teams soon looked like what the cat dragged in. Believing that his men had loafed in the first half, Griffin blasted the players at halftime and lectured them on defending against a man in motion. They played a better game in the second half and came away with a victory 13–6. Bennett scored both touchdowns, men in the crowd showering the sky with their straw hats as he crossed the goal line.

Home and Away

At Ironton fans were curious and interested in what the Spartans were doing—and perhaps envious, too, of a city that now had a team in the NFL. In the days before the game, the *Tribune* provided several accounts of the Spartans' preparations for their first game in the league. The Tanks not playing, numerous Irontonians attended the game, and Burke was there covering it for the *Tribune*. Greasy Neale, the new Tanks coach, and McMahon also were there. Many fans returned to Ironton skeptical about the Spartans, believing they were not invincible and that the Tanks would give them a real battle. Generally, the Irontonians praised the new facility at Labold. Burke noted that one could enter and leave the stadium without touching mud and that, though uncovered like those at Beechwood, the stadium seats were "roomy" and comfortable. He found the running account of the game blaring out on the loudspeaker rather monotonous. Their deep purple jerseys, pants, and stockings reminded him of "brownie" suits that one might see at a grade school program.

Their first victory in the league in hand, the Spartans awaited a historic game, a Wednesday night game ten days hence against the Brooklyn Dodgers. In the meantime, the players, the coach, and the manager turned to various activities increasingly defining theirs as a full-fledged professional franchise. Griffin had the team practicing two to three hours every day but Sunday, a regimen never followed by the semiprofessional elevens in the city in the 1920s. He insisted that players be in condition, fining three of them $100 each and placing them on probation (but suspending the fine) for breaking training rules. He also called on his men to "play clean football." Releasing six or seven men, at least three of whom joined the Tanks, he pared the roster down to twenty-two.

As a way to draw fans to the new stadium, just before their game with the Dodgers the Spartans released details on the financial aspects of their operation. The roster cut to twenty-two, their payroll, said Griffin, would run $60,000 for the year.[15] Travel by rail, food, accommodations, and equipment would raise the annual expenditure to $85,000. Someone among the Spartans pored over rail schedules and maps to calculate their mileage on road trips. Their longest journey, a single-game trip to Minneapolis, would be 1,654 miles. On a journey through the East when they would play in four cities over sixteen days, the Spartans would travel 1,994 miles. They would go 1,212 miles on a two-game trip to Chicago and Green Bay lasting nine days. A journey to Memphis, taking four days, would add another 1,202 miles to their log. A trip to Chicago for one game would account for 812 miles. Altogether, the Spartans would travel nearly 7,000 miles for thirty-eight days through twelve states; the fare by Pullman for players and other personnel would run about $11,000. Staying in mid-level hotels would cost several thousand dollars. Each player received

Portsmouth Is in the Big League

$2.50 a day for meals. A player's outfit—two pairs of shoes (one for practices, one for games), pants, jerseys, shoulder pads, socks, and headgear—cost $55 dollars, or about $1,400 for the entire team. The Spartans expected to use six official footballs costing $9.35 every week. In the dressing room each week players used five gallons of rubbing alcohol, one quart of iodine, and five hundred yards of bandages and tape. For each game, the corporation expended $3,000 to place the team on the field, an average of $137 a player. Readers of such figures could have measured the value of professional football in the city against their ability or inclination to support it.

The Spartans had little trouble mustering interest in their night game against the Dodgers, one of the first night games played by league teams. For several weeks, workers had been erecting poles along the field at Labold and mounting lamps on them. Fans were curious about the lighting effect and, with police directing the congested traffic, swarmed around Labold two nights before the game to see a test of the system. Unfortunately, six of the two-thousand-watt lamps burned out immediately. People wishing to see all the lamps ablaze had to return the next night or for the game.

The novelty of night play the center of attention, Griffin sought to drum up some interest in the Dodgers. A new team, their owner having acquired the Triangles' franchise, the Dodgers did not appear to be a strong eleven. But Griffin, who had scouted them in their opening game against the Bears, insisted that they were far better than he had expected. Touting them as worthy foes and boosting the Spartans as a superb team were Vaughan A. Talbott, secretary of the Chamber of Commerce in Portsmouth, and his son Vaughan H. Talbott. The senior Talbott traveled to Wellston, Jackson, Ashland, Catlettsburg, Huntington, and Gallipolis calling on businessmen to come to Labold for the big game.[16] His son went on a similar mission to Manchester, Maysville, Georgetown, Hillsboro, Greenfield, and Wilmington. The Talbotts asserted that the Spartans, though bearing a specific place name, were the common property of all communities in southern Ohio and along the Ohio River.

The game itself, though, was almost secondary to its ceremonial aspects, the novelty of play at night and the vitality of the crowd. Labold became, for the night, a shrine of civic religion and a symbol of progress for the community. Indeed, at the very moment that the lamps "dispelled the gloom" of the night, churches in the city dutifully pealed their bells. Around sixty-five hundred fans, as many as a thousand from the outlying communities that the Talbotts had visited, sat in the stadium and bleachers. The night was unseasonably warm so men were uncoated, the women in their summer finery. All emitted a tremendous roar at the illumination of the field, and all were "shouting and raving" throughout the game. Bugs in infinite numbers

Home and Away

soon were flying around the lamps. In the "bullpen" boys kept up an incessant roar. Presumably more dignified were thirty-one "prominent" businessmen from out of town who attended the game as guests of the Spartans. Attempting to prevent people from seeing the game for nothing and perhaps effecting an increase in paid attendance, the Spartans stretched a canvas on top of the wooden fence at the north end of the field to block the view of spectators standing on William Street and strung barbed wire all along the top of the fence to stop climbers. But even eight special policemen patrolling along the fence could not stay boys and young adults from scrambling over it, the effort, said Wittenburg, akin to "trying to halt the tide of the sea."[17]

Fans saw and heard ceremonies of various sorts. The Portsmouth High School band, attired in dark jackets and white trousers, played the national anthem before the game began as both teams lined up on the forty-yard line; the captains and coaches "huddled" at the fifty-yard line. At halftime, after the high school band played and paraded, the senior Talbott introduced presidents of chambers of commerce from surrounding communities. He also presented Roy Gillen, state senator from Wellston, to the fans; because Gillen was blind, the junior Talbott served as his play-by-play announcer. Announcing the game for all fans was T. J. Henderson, who had been the football and basketball announcer for Ohio State for several years.

The conditions of play seemed satisfactory. In a front-page story, John MacMillan of the *Times*, a new reporter, declared that the lamps lit the field as though it were in daylight, so well, in fact, that no shadows appeared. Spectators could easily follow plays. To improve visibility of the ball, the Spartans coated it with white lacquer that filled its seams and grainy surface and made it difficult to pass. Game officials wiped it with resin to reduce its slipperiness. According to Wittenburg, the white "ghost ball" looked like a huge ostrich egg, but as it picked up dirt, it took on the appearance of "spotted hen fruit." Many football people, said MacMillan, had been skeptical about a night game, but all the fans "stamped it unequivocally" a success. Visitors from all over the Tri-State had been awestruck by the spectacle. Shorty Davies pronounced the game a wonder, and other "distinguished" visitors were unstinting in their praise. "Night football," the *Times* was certain, had "come to stay, at least in Portsmouth."[18]

Giving their attention primarily to the crowd, the ceremonies, and conditions of play, Wittenburg and MacMillan devoted little space in their columns to the game itself. About all a reader could learn from them was that the Spartans won 12–0, that Bennett was a "mud horse," and that Glasgow was "spectacular." But fans knew enough to be euphoric. Their Spartans had won a game played under innovative circumstances giving their community enhanced repute. Fans and visitors alike were lionizing Griffin for his handling of the team and praising Snyder for his "public spiritedness" in seeing to the construction of the stadium.

Following the game, because the lacquered football was as "smooth as glass," Griffin bought twenty-four new balls and left them unwhitened. He also had a problem with uniforms. Observers of the game thought that the uniforms, virtually all purple, needed more contrasting colors. Besides, after only two games, the jerseys were tearing easily. The Spartan management ordered new uniforms, purple jerseys with black stripes on the front and white numerals on the back, black pants made of an airplane cloth with a purple knit insert on the back. Socks and headgear would remain the same.

The Spartans were off to a good start in league play in winning their first two games, albeit the Tornadoes and Dodgers were not strong teams. But the victories, sweet in suggesting that the Spartans could successfully compete in the NFL, could turn to dross. Following their game with the Dodgers, the Spartans had to meet the Tanks in Ironton. A loss to an independent team would damage the Spartans' record and reputation. They had little to gain except a good gate in playing the Tanks, but earlier the directors had assured fans that the Spartans would continue to schedule the team from the city of "ancient" rivalry. Moreover, the Spartans did not want to be accused of ducking out of a game for fear of losing it. And having beaten the Tanks handily in two games in 1929, they were not encumbered with the old belief that the Irontonians were demigods on the gridiron.

The Tanks awaiting the Spartans at Beechwood were going through a year marked by quickening change. As the directors of the Stadium Association had directed him, early in 1930 McMahon was looking for "bigger and better players" for the Tanks. By May he had recruited a bevy of first-line collegians, among them "Dynamite" Joe Gembis, Clair Sloan, and Carl Pignatelli, all from large midwestern universities—the Universities of Michigan, Iowa, and Nebraska.[19] That summer he continued his search and found more men willing to come to Ironton.

At the close of the season in 1929, the members of the football committee, saying that they were satisfied with the Tanks' leadership, had reappointed McMahon as manager but had not returned Presnell to the coach's position. There was some talk among them about returning Shorty Davies to the post. Presnell was not entirely comfortable in the position and did not object to stepping aside and remaining as a player. Deciding to depart from the customary practice of selecting an active player as the mentor, always a means of saving money, the members defined the position as that of a full-time coach.

Conducting only a cursory search, if one at all, they offered the berth to thirty-nine-year-old Earle "Greasy" Neale, a well-known football coach and baseball player. He had played baseball for the Cincinnati Reds and Philadelphia Phillies for eight years and had served as head football coach at West Virginia Wesleyan, Washington and Jefferson, and the University of Virginia.[20] He was the pioneer in the development of the naked reverse or "dance play." When the Tanks approached him about their coaching position, he was the manager of a minor league baseball team in Clarksburg, West Virginia. He agreed to come to Ironton with the understanding that he would remain at Clarksburg until the baseball season ended early in September. His contract with the Tanks called for him to devote all his "attention and time" to the team until the end of the season.

Neale and the community were optimistic about the outlook for the Tanks. When shown the Tanks' roster, he said that "you have here a real bunch of players and I'm confident I can give you a real team." With some reason, Tanks' officials asserted that they had "stepped ahead" of others in acquiring Neale. Burke rejoiced at the news, writing, "It looks like Tank year. AND HOW!" Early on Presnell found Neale to be an astute football man, recalling that "he had one of the finest football minds that I have ever seen. We did things in 1930 with the Tanks, things like looping and angle charges, that are still being done today and are considered new ideas."[21]

While waiting for Neale to arrive in Ironton, McMahon attempted to arrange a schedule for the Tanks. It was a scavenger hunt, but it yielded strong opponents, new and old: the Tanks would meet the Spartans three times, the Awnings twice, two good NFL clubs, a tough Southern independent eleven, and the Chillicothe Eagles. They would play but one "soft" team.

Late in the summer as practices began, McMahon continued to sign candidates for the team. Dick Powell, the rugged end who had played in 1929, signed a contract only after "much bickering." John "Popeye" Wager, a lineman, who later became a star for the Spartans, joined the team soon after practices began. Denny Meyers, a guard from the University of Iowa, also came to Ironton; later he would become the head coach at Boston College. Among players coming over from the Spartans at their release were Molesworth and Koester Christensen, an end from Michigan State. At the opening game, the "overhauled" Tanks had become substantially a new team; of the eleven men in the starting lineup, only two had been on the roster in 1929.[22]

Portsmouth Is in the Big League

Because his Clarksburg baseball nine was playing an important series, Neale did not come to Ironton to direct practices until mid-September. Once on the scene, Neale stamped him imprint on the Tanks. His training rules were minimal but rigid. All players had to be "under covers by midnight," and anyone caught drinking would be fined or suspended. Believing that "practice made perfect," Neale organized practices carefully. He began sessions promptly at 5:00 P.M. every weekday and drilled his men rigorously. Taking note of the practices, McCarthy told his readers that the new coach was driving the team at top speed and that the players were responding in fine fashion.[23]

With the Tanks' opening game against the Spartans approaching at Beechwood, the community eagerly waited to see what Neale had brought. At restaurants, in their clubs and churches, on streetcars, fans discussed the Tanks' chances against the new NFL club, many seeing in the game an opportunity for Ironton to remind Portsmouth that their city was still the sovereign of football in the valley. Little Johnny Ashme, a printer's devil who idolized Dick Powell and wanted to see him battle Lumpkin, was certain that the Tanks would reassert their superiority over the Spartans.[24] About a hundred Irontonians, as well as the players, journeyed at midweek to see the Spartans play the Dodgers and returned optimistic about what the Tanks would show against them. McCarthy was nearly as confident of victory, believing the Tanks to be a "rejuvenated" team under Neale, who was a master tactician and as tricky as a "sack full of monkeys." He promised loyalty for himself and the community to the Tanks if they played hard, lost graciously, and won generously.

Knowing that the Tanks could be a formidable foe—that they and their coach had seen the Spartans in two games—Griffin set his men to "stiff" practices using new plays and formations. The Tanks also were going through hard workouts but, having not yet opened play, had no need to prepare new offensive tactics. On the eve of the game, the Tanks were confident that they could defeat the Spartans. Ironton fans were even making "threats" about what their team would do to the Spartans. But bettors had the Tanks as underdogs, the odds two to one on the Spartans. As usual, reporters predicted that a record-breaking crowd would attend the game, with as many as two to three thousand fans coming from Portsmouth. They would see the greatest collection of collegiate stars ever to appear under southern Ohio skies—stars from the Big Ten, the Southern Conference, the Missouri Valley Conference, and other circuits.[25]

The crowd was indeed large, about sixty-five hundred, but not as large as that attending the Tanks-Spartans game at Beechwood in 1929. Defensive play dominated through the first three quarters, with neither team able to score. Finally the Tanks scored early in the fourth quarter but missed the extra point. The Spartans quickly responded with a touchdown but missed the extra point, too. The Tanks, though, were offside, and according to the current rules, the offensive team automatically received the extra point when the defensive team committed an infraction on an attempt for an extra point. Ironton fans could hardly believe their eyes when they read the scoreboard showing the Spartans ahead 7–6; the score still stood at the game's end.

The Tanks came off well in all accounts of the game. MacMillan of the *Times*, saying that the Spartans had been disappointing, declared that "All Glory Goes to Ironton." For Burke, the Spartans were like the British band at Yorktown, ready to play "The World Turned Upside Down." Taking the same view as the reporters, McCarthy effusively praised Neale as having surpassed any other professional coach in his ability to organize and instruct young football players; he had created a "marvelous" machine out of players with only about two weeks of practice. Griffin offered no alibis, remarking that his players had made a "miserable" showing but adding that all teams had good and bad days.

McCarthy was riding a wave of euphoria cresting over football players and football fans in the community. Encouraged by their good showing, the Tanks enthusiastically prepared for their coming game at Beechwood against the Chillicothe Eagles. They knew, though, that the Eagles, with a good line manned by former Ohio State players, would not fall easily. Less realistic was a group of fans and businessmen apparently acting under the auspices of the Stadium Association. They wildly asserted that the Tanks had proved themselves equal to any other professional team in the nation. They organized a "Boost the Tanks Drive" intended to send thousands of Irontonians to Beechwood for the game with the Eagles.[26] A score or more of business firms, financial institutions, and civic clubs—a tire shop, two pharmacies, a restaurant, a hardware store, a savings and loan company, the Lions club, and others—bought a full-page display advertisement in the *Tribune* calling on the community to "Back the Tanks." The Tanks had given "All They Had for Ironton," and now the citizenry should repay them in kind—or at least attend the game against the Eagles. "No National League Team," the boosters boasted, "Can Show Us Better Football Than the Tanks. . . . Let's All Be There."

For all the optimism and boosterism, which, after all, could not suffuse the entire community, the crowd at the game was not unusually large—twenty-five hundred or so. The game hardly measured up to the rhetoric of excitement preceding it. Though quadrupling the Eagles' yardage from scrimmage, 179 to 40, the Tanks did not reel off any long plays or run up many points, grinding out two touchdowns for the victory, 14–0. The mundane win seemingly dimmed the glow of the boosters, and the community heard much less spread-eagle talk about the Tanks for the moment.

The Tanks then traveled to Akron to meet the Awnings, their first road game of the season. Fans there were eager to see the "famous Tanks" and their new coach, knowing that for Ironton "football is their bread and butter and Coach Earle Neale is retained to see to it that the Tanks remain one of the nation's best teams."[27] They were also eager to boo Dick Powell, who had once played for the Awnings. They saw little scoring. Gembis kicked a field goal in the last quarter for a Tanks win, 3–0.

Returning to Ironton, a second victory on their record, the Tanks had to prepare to meet the Spartans in Portsmouth. They had played well in losing to the Spartans in the first game but had followed it with ordinary play in two subsequent wins. They could read in Griffin's comments after the first game a warning that they might face a much different team now, one determined to prove that it was better than the narrow victory had suggested.

Before meeting the Tanks again, the Spartans played three games in two weeks, all against league opponents, one on the road. Following their victory over the Tanks, they met their first old-line league eleven when the Chicago Cardinals came to Labold the next Sunday. The Cardinals' owner, David "Doc" Jones, had purchased the Cardinals after they had played through a disastrous season in 1928 and then had hired Ernie Nevers as a player-coach. Nevers, a great running back, led the Cardinals to an improved record in 1929. Fans in Portsmouth were eager to see him play, along with Clare Randolph, a Cardinal center who had been with the Spartans in 1928, and Fred "Duke" Slater, a big lineman, one of the few blacks in the NFL.

Both teams set their sights on a victory. Griffin, dissatisfied with the Spartans' offense in the Tanks' game because it was not sufficiently deceptive in passing, installed Pop Warner's "C" formation, a variation of the double wing, and drilled the team for hours perfecting it.[28] The Cardinals arrived in Portsmouth on Saturday and immediately held a secret practice. A good crowd, about sixty-five hundred, saw two "alert, stubborn hard-charging" teams in action. For all their practicing, the game ended in a scoreless tie. The Spartans had an edge in yardage from scrimmage and reached the Cardinals' two-yard line in the first quarter but could not move into the end zone.

On and off the field unruly behavior occurred. Jones vehemently complained to the officials at halftime that the Spartans were roughing the Cardinals' passer. In the fourth quarter he rushed on the field during a row over a fumble recovery and

Home and Away

attempted to "throttle" Glassgow because of his rough treatment of Nevers. The "Emancipation day crowd," blacks, gave their solid backing to Slater, the "big guard of color," and at halftime, some fans, evidently blacks, broke down a gate on the west side of the field and stormed into the paddock reserved for blacks.

The game with the Cardinals was the first of seven that the Spartans would play over twenty-one days, three of them on separate road trips. It was an exacting schedule. Still undefeated, they played the Frankford Yellowjackets at Universal Stadium on the Wednesday night following their game against the Cardinals. From a suburb of Philadelphia, the Yellowjackets were coming off two good years in league play, finishing high in the standing in 1928 and 1929. Wittenburg and MacMillan knew little about the Yellowjackets but reported that "on paper" their backfield was fast and that their line was strong. On the field, though, they were neither fast nor strong. Playing before a crowd made small by rain, the Spartans, attired in their new "gorgeous purple" uniforms, dominated play, winning 39–7, even though Griffin, presaging his use later of a controversial strategy, started second-stringers.

Still undefeated and leading the league, the Spartans next played their first game on the road, meeting the Minneapolis Red Jackets in their home city. The Red Jackets, sometimes called the Millers, had entered the league in 1929, quickly becoming a doormat despite the play of Herb Joesting, an All-American back from the University of Minnesota. Playing at Nicollet Park, the teams slipped and slogged on the turf of a rain-soaked field, all the players becoming covered with mire. Joesting was the decisive player, running through the Spartans' right side of the line for crucial yardage resulting in his team's victory, 13–0. The Spartans, nonetheless, won the "hearts of hundreds of fans" by their fighting spirit.

Returning to Portsmouth on Monday evening, weary from the game on Sunday and from travel, the Spartans had only a few hours to prepare for the Tanks' appearance at the stadium on Wednesday night. They "limbered up" at Universal Stadium a day later. That night, at Snyder's invitation, the Tanks, having never played under lights, came to the stadium for a practice. Fans in both communities eagerly awaited the opening kickoff. At Ironton they perceived the game as a "battle of the century" between teams meeting at the Tournament of Roses. Virtually all the residents of Portsmouth were "living and talking" football.

Around seventy-five hundred fans bought tickets. Another twelve hundred, including the "hole in the wall gang," paid nothing to stand on the floodwall overlooking the field.[29] Officials held up the game for fifteen minutes while fans struggled to get to their seats, many caught in automobiles moving slowly on surrounding streets. The game they saw was different and exciting. Neale, resorting to an "old boxing

Portsmouth Is in the Big League

trick," had the Tanks take the field first and left them there waiting for the Spartans to come out for the kickoff. Emulating Rockne, Griffin started his second-stringers, later explaining that he wished to save his starters for important league games. Neale had a surprise in his starting lineup. Thirty-nine years old and inactive as a player for nearly twelve years, he boasted at the Elks Club in Ironton that he would play, catch a pass, and score a touchdown. McMahon bet him that he would not. True to his word, he commandeered a uniform in the locker room before the game, put it on, and placed himself in the lineup.

Griffin made a costly mistake in his strategy. The Tanks scored two touchdowns to go ahead 13–0 before the Spartans' first-stringers entered the game in the middle of the second quarter. They scored two touchdowns and a safety in the second half to claim the lead 15–13. Then late in the game, Molesworth threw a thirty-yard pass to Neale, setting up a field goal for a Tanks victory, 16–15. Reportedly, it was another field goal worth $10,000 to bettors on the Tanks. Besides catching the crucial pass, Neale played a good game at defensive end. McMahon, ignoring his failure to score a touchdown, paid the coach the wager. But Neale paid a price for his play. Years later, a teammate recalled that "Greasy played almost the whole game, but he was so sore when it was over that he had to stay in bed for a couple of days to recover."[30]

Again, but with more reason, Tanks fans were euphoric. Many saw the Tanks returning to their old glory. In a full-page story, Burke described the atmosphere of play as typical of Ironton: "Attending Ironton-Portsmouth football games is like sitting in a seething volcano. . . . It takes but a spark to ignite an explosion. . . . Ironton has more tricks in her bag than fleas on a dog's back. They've got a Tank team of old, scrappy, foxy and never beaten until the game ends." McCarthy joined Burke in celebrating the Tanks' triumph. He was not one to gloat, he insisted, but he had to say that the victory was a tribute to Neale, whose intelligent "pigskinners" played rings around the Spartans. Wittenburg agreed with the *Tribune* men, acknowledging that the Tanks were tricky and versatile and had outsmarted the Spartans. The Tanks did have one complaint about the game. Receiving 40 percent of the gate, they took $2,500 back to Ironton, a sum less, they contended, than what the Spartans had realized out of their visit to Beechwood. As a trophy, they received the "ghost" ball used by the Spartans in the first night game at Universal.[31]

Griffin found himself engulfed in a wave of rebuke following the Spartans' loss, made all the more frustrating because of his use of second-stringers and the Spartans' advantage in yardage gained, 213 to the Tanks' 104. Implying that Griffin was at fault, Wittenburg complained that the Spartans were playing individually and that they lacked versatility in their attack. Hundreds of fans, he said, insisted that Griffin had

Home and Away

to "mix 'em up," had to give the enemy something difficult to fathom. On the day following the loss, the Spartan directors had a meeting with Griffin, warning him that if the team did not improve, he would have to go.[32] Though explaining again that he had started his second-stringers to conserve strength for important league games, Griffin offered his resignation, which, for the moment, the directors refused to accept.

The Tanks' game marked the beginning of a downward course for the Spartans, with a few victories palliating the sting of defeats. They tasted the first of the losses in the South. Receiving a large guarantee, they traveled to Memphis to meet the Tigers, perhaps the strongest independent team in the South. At Memphis the *Commercial Appeal* and the *Press-Scimitar* portrayed the Spartans as the premier team of the NFL, their backfield as the "strongest quartet" in the league, their line as the heaviest. They drew a crowd of about seven thousand at Hodges Field. They did not live up to their reputation. They could not move the ball and resorted to "reckless" and "futile" passes in losing 20–6. According to the *Appeal*, the Spartans, showing no verve, "played . . . like it was just a business with them." Griffin, though acknowledging that the Tigers had "outfought and outplayed" the Spartans, railed against the "unfavorable officiating" and wanted to wager $500 that his team could beat the Tigers in a return game. Nothing came of his challenge.[33]

Returning to Portsmouth on Monday evening, the Spartans had to play the Bears in two days in a night game at the stadium. The Bears coming to Portsmouth were a different team from what they had been in the 1920s. Under co-coaches and owners George Halas and George Sternaman, they had been the only eleven in the league using the T formation. The T was beginning to creak late in the decade and Halas and Sternaman quarreled about the offense, so they turned the coaching over to Ralph Jones of Lake Forest College. Jones refurbished the T, splitting ends and backs to spread the defense and putting halfbacks in motion to confuse the secondary. Ironically, owing to an injury to the starting quarterback, Joey Sternaman, in the first game of the season, Carl Brumbaugh, who had made the Bears' roster against great odds, took over direction of the new T.[34] Fans in Portsmouth were eager to see Brumbaugh—reportedly to give him a "big hand"—and even more they wanted to see whether Red Grange could gallop ghostlike through the Spartans. They were curious, too, about the rookie Bronko Nagurski, whose powerful running complemented Grange's shifty gait. Grange aside, the Spartans and their fans were pessimistic about beating the Bears. In two weeks, the players had traveled twenty-eight hundred miles playing five games of a "suicide" schedule. They did not quarrel with the popular view that the Bears were four touchdowns stronger than they.

Portsmouth Is in the Big League

The game brought to the stadium about seventy-five hundred fans. Sizable delegations came from surrounding communities. Carr and a "bunch" of his friends came down from Columbus. The attendance proved, declared Wittenburg, that Irontonians were dealing in "banana oil" when they contended that Portsmouth had to depend on them for good crowds. The night was cold, and fans wore and used "artificial heat galore"—fur coats, topcoats, mittens, earmuffs, canned heat, bottled heat, all but hot bricks. Seemingly Griffin won a measure of vindication in his tactics and in the results. He "out-Rocknied Rockne" in keeping two reserves in the game all the time, and his men "stopped playing drop the handkerchief," completely outplaying the Bears except for the last few minutes of the game, said Wittenburg. Scoring in the second quarter after recovering Brumbaugh's fumble of a punt, the Spartans held the Bears scoreless until they pushed over a touchdown late in the fourth quarter; the Bears missed the extra point, and the Spartans won 7–6. The Bears did little on offense, and Lumpkin, who had two long runs called back by penalties, outshone Grange, who, asserted Wittenburg, was just another player that night. Griffin won laurels, too, outplaying the Bears' great center, George Trafton. For the moment, the "downtown coaches" were willing to make him mayor only a week after reproving him. One man who had refused to buy stock in the football corporation was now willing to take some shares. Wittenburg discerned in the Spartan victory, perhaps not in a serious vein, the triumph of the wild, pristine Scioto Countians over the corrupt urban mob; the players "from the city of gunmen and racketeers found too much light at the stadium."[35]

The win enabled the Spartans to remain in contention for the league title, a game behind the Packers. But facing them were two successive road games against tough opponents, the Cardinals and the Packers. The wear and tear of a difficult schedule showing, they arrived in Chicago with only seventeen players, leaving behind three injured linemen. The Cardinals, in contrast, had twenty-two men in uniform at Comisky Park and used twenty-one in the game. Griffin protested, to no avail, asserting that league rules permitted a team but twenty players in uniform. Playing before a crowd of eight thousand, the Cardinals, led by Nevers, overwhelmed the Spartans, 23–13. The Cardinals, "peeved" about the "dusting off" of Nevers in Portsmouth, sent three or four Spartans to the sidelines with injuries.[36] Lumpkin and Nevers engaged in several "verbal tilts" over rough play. The Spartans left Chicago reading consolatory words from Warren Brown, sports editor of the *Chicago Herald-Examiner*; he contended that until they incurred the injuries, the Spartans had fielded the best team seen in Chicago that year.

Returning to Portsmouth nursing their wounds, the Spartans had to prepare to

Home and Away

meet the Packers the following Sunday in Green Bay. Griffin had managed to shore up the roster slightly, acquiring on a hasty recruiting trip around Chicago Frank "Duke" Hanny, a tackle who played for Green Bay earlier in the year, and Gene Smith, a guard whom the Bears had released recently. Journeymen, they proved no sovereign remedy for the Spartans. At Green Bay, the Packers mauled the Spartans 47–13, the worst defeat in their history. Yet a reporter for the *Green Bay Gazette* wrote that the Packers had their "hands full" containing the Spartans' backs, especially Lumpkin.[37] Falling further behind the Packers in the league standings, the Spartans had to begin winning at once.

Wounded in body and spirit, the Spartans returned to Portsmouth determined, nonetheless, to redeem themselves on their home ground. It would not be an easy task. They had to face the New York Giants, a strong team led by Benny Friedman, an outstanding passer and All-American. Sponsoring the game on "Homecoming Day" was the Portsmouth Chamber of Commerce, which ran a half-page display advertisement in the *Times* urging residents of Portsmouth and throughout southern Ohio to support the team that was putting Portsmouth "on the map." Fans wanted to see the famous Friedman, and the Spartans were making brave talk about reviving themselves. About seven thousand fans were at the stadium. Ambivalent, they wanted the Spartans to win as Friedman displayed his wares to good effect. Protected by doubled-decked blankets against a raw west wind, they sat looking for the contradictory outcome of the game. Chilled spectators on the floodwall lit bonfires against the cold —appropriately it was Guy Fawkes Day. Perhaps the floodwallers felt greater discomfort in finding that new fences at the southeastern and southwestern corners of the field shielded more play from their view. Soon, said Wittenburg, they would have to go to Kentucky to see the games at the stadium. The fans had to be disappointed in the Spartans, the Giants winning 19–6. Obversely, they had to be satisfied in Friedman. The Spartans stopped the Giants reasonably well on the ground but could not contain Friedman, who passed for two touchdowns in the first quarter.

Assessing the game and the Spartans' slide—they had lost six of their last seven games—Wittenburg was certain that the grueling schedule was to blame. The Spartans, traveling thousands of miles to the north and south, had played twelve games in about seven weeks. Unfortunately, the Spartan directors, taking their first fling into the higher reaches of professional football, had to accept much of the schedule as offered them; perhaps, he wrote, they could exercise some control over it the next year. The directors knew that Wittenburg's views had merit. In the wake of the loss to Green Bay, hearing that there was friction in the ranks of the Spartans, they

Portsmouth Is in the Big League

had "huddled" with the players without Griffin present, asking them to express their opinions of or grievances against the coach. All insisted that they were satisfied with Griffin and gave him a unanimous vote of confidence. But they were weary of a schedule requiring them to "hop, skip and jump around the country without sufficient periods of rest." They were spending too much time on railroad cars at the expense of "breathing intervals" at home to polish teamwork and develop new plays. The meeting ended on a hopeful note, the players pledging their loyalty to the coach and the directors.[38]

Complaints and meetings could not alter the realities of the itinerary in front of the Spartans. A few days after the game with the Giants, the players boarded a car of the Chesapeake and Ohio for the beginning of a two-weeks trip through the East. They would play the Staten Island Stapletons first, lay over in Newark for a few days of practice, then go to Philadelphia to meet the Frankford Yellowjackets, next travel to Providence to play the Steamroller the following day, and finally retrace the rail to Newark for a game with the Tornadoes. Four days later, after returning to Portsmouth, they expected to confront the Tanks again. Neither Wittenburg nor MacMillan accompanied the Spartans, and fans read brief accounts of the games coming by wire services to the *Times* in secondhand reports on Griffin's telephone calls to Snyder.

They did not read of much success. Meeting the Stapletons, an ordinary team with an extraordinary player in Ken Strong, an All-American halfback from New York University, the Spartans managed to leave the field with a tie after trailing 13–0 in the third quarter. Because the laws of Pennsylvania prohibited play on the Sabbath, they then played the Yellowjackets on a Saturday. They had easily defeated the Yellowjackets at Portsmouth, but now the Yellowjackets had eight or nine men from the Minneapolis Red Jackets. The Jacket teams, then in disarray, were pooling players on days when only one team was playing.[39] Missing the attempt at extra point because of a bad snap from center, the Spartans fell 7–6.

Directly from the field at Frankford, the Spartans entrained to Providence to meet the Steamroller on Sunday. There inclement weather seemed to save them. A tremendous rainstorm that turned the field into a lake forced postponement of the game until Monday, and then the Steamroller management, piling up an increasing deficit each game and finding the field unplayable, canceled the game and disbanded the team for the season. The weary Spartans appreciated the respite. In the meantime, the Spartan directors, eager for their men to be fresh for a Thanksgiving Day game against the Tanks, managed to cancel the game with the Tornadoes. The Spartans then returned to Portsmouth well ahead of the date on their original itinerary.

Griffin was able to strengthen the Spartans out of the collapse of the Steamroller. He signed five Providence players to contracts, four linemen—Forrest "Jap" Douds, Warren McGurek, Al Graham, and Ray Smith—and a back known for his drop-kicking—Forrest "Frosty" Peters. Ever a nomad, Graham, a former Triangle, had played a few games for the Spartans in 1928. He, Peters, and Douds joined the Spartans, but for some reason McGurek and Smith did not. To keep the roster at twenty-two, the Spartans released several players who had only recently signed contracts.

The Spartans came home scheduled to meet the Tanks and then conclude the season in three games that would determine their standing and status in the NFL. While the Spartans had been traveling south, north, and east on their way to the close of their season, the Tanks were playing through their schedule and a rancorous dispute with the Spartans before their final appearance in Portsmouth.

At mid-season, the Tanks clearly were a better team than they had been in the closing games of 1929. McMahon had brought new talent to Ironton, Presnell had recovered from his injury and was running in his old form, and Neale was giving the team innovative and effective direction. The Tanks had won three of four games, mostly against strong teams, their one loss by only a point, and that later reversed. Before the season ended, they might restore their reputation and renew their usual records. They had yet, to course, to play some sturdy teams. And they faced problems in scheduling and mustering the dollars necessary for survival.

As sweet as their victory over the Spartans was, the Tanks came home in a crisis threatening their survival. Their next game gave it focus: McMahon, improvising the schedule, had just booked the Washington Olympians of Pennsylvania for the game. Supposedly the Olympians had recently claimed a semiprofessional championship of the state.[40] But few fans in Ironton knew of them, and the players, mostly from around Pittsburgh, had little regional or national reputation. And the gate for the game appeared as a microcosm of the Tanks' financial problems.

As McCarthy explained the problem in a lengthy editorial a few days before the game, it was one admitting a simple solution. The Tanks were losing money on practically every game and would go under if attendance at Beechwood did not pick up.[41] Fans had to make the Tanks' game with the Olympians a testimonial—they had to come out in large numbers to show their support for the team. The city had benefited tremendously from the favorable publicity that the "sterling" club had brought it—he did not number the specific benefits. But if the fans did not pay the

Portsmouth Is in the Big League

freight, if they were not at Beechwood for the game, the "jig was up." On the day of the game, he renewed his call for a large crowd, repeating his earlier warnings.[42] If his lectures had any effect, it was marginal. Reporters took no note of the size or enthusiasm of the crowd. Whatever the number, the fans could not have long remained interested in the game. The Tanks crushed the hapless Olympians, scoring touchdown after touchdown in winning 70–0.

As McCarthy harangued the community, McMahon continued to work on scheduling, managing to give the Tanks formidable opponents. With all the games to be played on the road, evidently he had the Tanks' treasury more in mind than the fans in Ironton. He did not have to work hard to arrange the Tanks' game the Sunday after the Olympians left town. After the Memphis Tigers defeated the Spartans, their manager, knowing of the Tanks' reputation as a strong, independent team— they had also defeated the Spartans—offered them a "lumpy" guarantee to come to play his men. Needing a good gate, McMahon accepted the offer. Burke readily endorsed his decision. He saw the game as an opportunity for the Tanks to spread their fame further.[43] He argued that if the Tanks were victorious, they would be on their way to the national championship. According to his view, since the Tigers had defeated the Spartans by a greater margin than any NFL team had, which was not true, the winner of the game in Memphis could reasonably claim the national title for all football. What partisans could do with comparative scores was wondrous. At Memphis, though not investing the game with cosmic significance, the *Commercial Appeal* and the *Press-Scimitar* gave the Tanks considerable play.[44] A reporter for the *Appeal* described the Tanks as "tougher" than any other eleven the Tigers had faced.

Traveling by rail on the longest road trip in their history, the Tanks left Ironton early on Saturday and stayed overnight in Memphis. About a hundred fans arrived in the city the next morning. At Hodges Field the Tanks gave a good account of themselves, holding the Tigers' leading backs, Tony Holm, who later joined the Spartans, and Bill Banker, to negligible yardage. "It was rather curious," said the *Appeal*, to see this unheralded team for the Midwest stop the thrusts of two of the best backs the South had produced."[45] According to a reporter for the *Scimitar* misspelling Ironton, the "stubborn Oronton team" contested every inch of the way."[46] For three quarters the Tanks held the Tigers scoreless but then yielded a touchdown in the fourth quarter and lost 7–0.

Searching for more opponents to give the Tanks good gates, McMahon found two tough big city elevens. Just before they went to Memphis, their "popularity increasing," the Tanks reportedly were receiving offers for games from enough teams to "fill a book," and McMahon and the football committee were discussing propos-

Home and Away

als to play two of the "best" teams in the nation. The reports did not come out of whole cloth. Holes in the Tanks' schedule permitted McMahon maneuver, and he was able to schedule games with the Giants and Bears, both to be played in Cincinnati at Redland Field.

The Tanks first played the Giants on Armistice Day, a Tuesday night, less than a week after the Giants had defeated the Spartans at Portsmouth. Led by Friedman, the Giants were playing well and would finish second in the league. The game created great interest among Tanks fans. The Tanks had met NFL teams in the past—the Canton Bulldogs in 1925, the Kansas City Cowboys in 1926, and the Spartans in 1930—but none had equaled the Giants of 1930. As many as one thousand Irontonians traveled to Cincinnati. The *Tribune,* ever the booster of the city, called on all Ironton fans to urge their friends in Cincinnati to attend the game; it was a "choice advertising" opportunity for Ironton. At Cincinnati supposedly football fans were interested in the game because promoters there were organizing a team for entry into the NFL. If the Giants regarded it as an exhibition game, the Tanks and their fans viewed it as they did any other, one to be played hard and won.

Held down by rain, the crowd of about five thousand, mostly cheering for the Tanks, saw a game that became embedded in Tanks lore. Despite the wet weather, Friedman and Presnell resorted to a passing attack, each throwing the ball more than twenty times. Leading 12–6 late in the fourth quarter, the Giants punted from their own thirty-three-yard line, and Presnell made a dazzling return to the Giants' twenty-seven, going out of bounds to stop the clock with but seconds to play. What happened then was the stuff of football legend in Ironton. Years later, Presnell remembered the dramatic ending of the game:

> The time clock for pro games was kept on the field then and I asked "Shorty" Davies, the timekeeper, how much time was left. He told me only three seconds [were] left so I knew we had time for only one play.
>
> I ran around behind the line of scrimmage, looking for an open man, dodging tacklers. Finally I saw Gene Alford down near the end zone waving his hands. I threw the ball and he caught it and stepped into the end zone to tie the score. That pass was the biggest thrill of my career.[47]

Bedlam broke loose in the crowd, but the Tanks had yet to win the game. The Tanks' place kicker, Clair Sloan, then kicked the extra point, making the Tanks the victors 13–12.

Tanks fans basked in the afterglow of the triumph. The *Tribune* published an

Portsmouth Is in the Big League

"extra" edition with a front-page account of the game and the Frank Merriwell finish. Burke, calling on his minute poetic skills, wrote a poem set to the melody "It Happened in Monterey," reading in part

> It happened in Cincinnati, not long ago.
> It happened in Cincinnati, in old Ohio
> Passes and thrusts and flashing plays
> As red as its wine
> Stole somebody's game away.[48]

Becoming more prosaic but still ecstatic, Burke gloried in Presnell's performance, saying that he had stolen the show in throwing more completed passes than Friedman had. Presnell, indeed, did, completing fourteen of twenty-even attempts for 203 yards, Friedman thirteen of twenty-two for 131 yards. A less partisan reporter for the *Cincinnati Commercial Tribune* wrote that Presnell had beaten Friedman at his own game.[49] At least one of the Giants' owners conceded that the Tanks were as good as any team in the NFL. In New York, though, sportswriters took little note of the game, treating it as an exhibition game; the *New York Times* gave it a few lines without commenting on the play by either eleven.[50]

Relishing the victory and contemplating a triumph over the Bears in ten days or so, Tanks fans and the *Tribune*, the everlasting cheerleader, gave scant attention to the game sandwiched between, a return contest with the Awnings in Akron. Attendance at Akron was slipping badly—the crowd for the Tanks' game was only about a thousand—but the Awnings were still a good team. Their only loss of the season had come at the hands of the Tanks, and they had not yet surrendered a touchdown. The Tanks, scoring the only touchdowns of the season against them, controlled play and won 13–0. Schlemmer of the *Beacon-Journal*, explaining that the Awnings were playing with many injured men, discounted the performance of the Tanks, saying that they were not a particularly brilliant team.[51]

Going home, the Tanks, along with their fans, prepared for the game with the Bears at Redland Field. Now the Tanks had the opportunity to defeat another NFL team, the third that season, and accordingly claim high rank in American professional football. They knew that the Bears, using their refurbished T, could run over them, but they also knew that they might stand well, as had the Spartans. Neale especially prepared the Tanks' defense to contain Grange. As they had for the Giants game, hundreds of Tanks fans journeyed to Redland Field. Businessmen underwrote their expenses by passing the hat, and all the Spartans went, expecting to "uncover

237

[the] magic of the Tanks' plays." Caught up in the excitement, McCarthy cheered the Tanks on, his exhilaration expressed in an editorial concluding with the exclamation, "Come on Tanks, let's go."[52]

The Tanks required little cheering at Redland, from either the editor or the "record" crowd of ten thousand, nearly all rooting for them. Neale, who had slipped a "bag of tricks in his left sock," left them unfurled. As Presnell had outpassed Friedman, now he outran Grange, showing him various "tricks" in eluding tacklers. Their line standing up "nobly" after "catching on" to the Bears' play, the Tanks held Grange and his teammates in check, and their offense, amassing 336 yards from scrimmage, doubled that of the Bears, the result a convincing win, 26–13. Almost immediately, Burke pronounced the Tanks "the best football team in the United States. That's the weighty title that rests on the capable shoulders of the Tanks." He came to his view with impeccable logic: the Packers had beaten the Cardinals, the Cardinals had whipped the Memphis Tigers, the Giants had defeated the Packers and Spartans, and the Tanks had beaten the Giants, Bears, and Spartans. He overlooked the Tanks' loss to the Tigers. The Tanks, in effect, had also bested the Spartans again. Spartan players had seen "plenty" of football at Redland but none of the Tanks' trick plays and, Burke asserted, had lost money betting against the Tanks. They departed Cincinnati awed by the "reckless manner" in which the Tanks had run roughshod over the Bears.[53]

Having won seven of their last eight games, three against NFL teams, two of them strong elevens, the Tanks could reasonably claim a high rank among the nation's independent teams. No other independent club had won three games against NFL teams. Offering them another opportunity for repute—but also standing in their way—were the Spartans, scheduled to play them on Thanksgiving Day in Portsmouth.

The game came about only after no little caterwauling among managers, sportswriters, editors, and fans. From late in September until well into November, they quarreled over the site of the game and the split of the gate. All cited statistics on recent attendance at Tanks-Spartans games, the prospects for a large crowd, fairness for the fans, competition with high school games, and more. At one point Joe Carr entered the dispute, seemingly supporting the Spartans, but eventually refused to take a definitive position. Finally, the Tanks agreed to go to Portsmouth, and the Spartans gave them a larger share of the gate.

The Tanks acceded to the decision in part because the Ironton High School Tigers were playing Lancaster in Ironton on Thanksgiving morning. But far from fearing

Portsmouth Is in the Big League

the competition for a crowd from the Tigers, they did not wish to damage attendance at the high school game. Though Shorty Davies coached the Tigers through much of the decade, they had been playing in the shadow of the Tanks.[54] They usually drew crowds of less than a thousand and, relative to the Tanks, received little attention from the *Tribune*. McCarthy once complained that "Ironton has never supported the school team."[55]

The Spartans and Tanks prepared to do battle for what reporters were calling the Ohio or midwestern championship. Sharp-tongued, Minego said that if the Tanks won, they would claim the "championship of the United States and Siberia." As many as a thousand fans turned out for the Spartans' practices. They exhaled "oohs and aahs" as Frosty Peters drop-kicked six field goals out of ten attempts from the forty-yard line, and they watched with curiosity the new plays that Griffin was running. Notwithstanding what they had seen of the Tanks against the Bears, the Spartans were confident of victory, encouraged especially by the recent acquisition of the players from Providence. A local wag declared that if the Spartans won, they would do so by "act of Providence."

The Spartans and their fans heard little from the Tanks' camp, except that they were practicing hard and that Neale would not play. McMahon nearly had to go looking for players to replace two Tanks, Red Martin and John Blackman. Celebrating the victory over the Bears, they were navigating a sailboat on the Ohio River when Martin fell out and almost drowned; fortunately, Blackman pulled him from the water and revived him. Hundreds of fans were buying tickets for the fray. They expected to see the "most bitterly contested inter-city tilt in history." Though the Spartans were a heavier eleven, the Tanks' fans took heart in their recent slide and their team's victories over the Giants and Bears. They urged the Tanks to buy mud cleats, believing that in 1929 the Spartans had used such cleats to great advantage on a wet field. Proving them to be farsighted, a snowstorm struck the Ohio Valley on the eve of the game.

The game came on the coldest Thanksgiving Day for which the local weather bureau had a record—about five degrees above zero.[56] Ice and snow covered the field, and the crowd, about forty-five hundred, sat in an arctic stadium swept clear of snow. No one stood on the floodwall. Everywhere, one saw a chopped sea of stocking caps, hoods, and scarves. In the stadium a prominent society matron clutched a hot water bottle as her husband swallowed hot roily coffee. "Overcome by the heat" despite the cold and prohibition, several men had to be carried out of the stadium. At halftime, Griffin invited reporters into the Spartans' dressing room, where hot bricks and charcoal stoves cut the biting cold. Supposedly the Tanks wanted to postpone the game until Sunday, but the Spartans, scheduled to play the Bears in Chicago, could not accommodate them.

On the slippery field, the heavier Spartans, Irontonians believed, held their traction better than the lighter Tanks, whose "famous speed" did them little good. Certainly the Spartans had the better of the going in the statistics and score. They outgained the Tanks on the ground 220 yards to 38. Stopped on the ground, the Tanks resorted to a passing game that netted 105 yards but no touchdowns. With Peters kicking two field goals, the Spartans won 12–0 in a rather uninteresting game. Thus the Tanks lost whatever claims they had to state and regional titles. Their share of the gate gave them a purse of $2,400, far less than they had been looking for.[57]

 The victory for the Spartans was but their second, along with two ties, in their last ten games. Their record now was six wins, seven losses, and two ties, in league play four wins, five losses, and two ties. They were in the lower third in the league standings and had yet to win a league game on the road. But with three games to play, they had the opportunity on paper to stand well at the end of the season. Unfortunately, two of their opponents were the league-leading Packers and the Bears, the latter still in contention for the league title.

They met the Bears in Wrigley Field, where about six thousand fans braved the frigid air of the grandstand. Griffin believed that the Spartans were in good condition. But they seemed "disorganized" in the first half. The line could not meet the Bears' charge, and Grange ran brilliantly. Brumbaugh reeled off some good runs, notably a "spinner" for nineteen yards. The Spartans played much better in the second half, even "shoving the Bears around." But their awakening came too late to avoid a loss, 14–6.

Next the Spartans played the Minneapolis Red Jackets at Universal Stadium. Snyder said that a large crowd would spell success "from every angle," and he and other Spartan directors, noting that no other teams, high school, collegiate, or professional, were playing in the Ohio Valley on the weekend, urged fans to come out to the stadium and support the team. The Red Jackets had already defeated the Spartans twice, once in Minneapolis and once in Frankford when nine Red Jackets were in uniform, mostly as starters, for the Yellowjackets. Their victories over the Spartans, under whatever the color of their name, did not translate into a good crowd on another wintry day. Only thirty-five hundred fans, the smallest home crowd of the season, came to Universal. No one was in the bleachers, only a handful of men stood on the floodwall, and eighteen people perched in trees. With Tiny Lewis run-

Portsmouth Is in the Big League

ning sixty yards on one play, Bennett sixty-eight on another, and Peters returning a punt for seventy yards, the Spartans demolished the Red Jackets 42–0. Apparently all the players were Red Jackets.

Fans took out of the victory hope that the Spartans might avoid another drubbing or even win glory in their final game of the season against the Packers at Universal. Undefeated in 1929 and now running neck-and-neck with the Giants for another title, the Packers had become the Spartans' principal kin in the league—though not always a friendly one. In their first two years of play, the Spartans had developed ties with the Packers as Lambeau pointed released players to Portsmouth. In 1929 the teams had become involved in an imbroglio over a proposed game in Portsmouth. Fans in Portsmouth could see in the relationship between Green Bay and the Packers a model to emulate. Green Bay "loved" the Packers, as South Bend "loved" Notre Dame. The Packers, though playing in the smallest city in the league, had survived despite the players' large salaries and substantial travel expenses.[58] They had weathered financial problems, attendance at their games was increasing, and their stadium was undergoing expansion. For a decade they had excelled on the field. What they were, the Spartans might become.

The Spartans expected a "mammoth" crowd, and local reporters created copy fanning interest in the game. They alerted fans to the arrival of the Packers at the railroad depot and their appearance at public workouts and used reverential language to describe the great Packer linemen, especially Cal Hubbard. Fans from every community in the Ohio Valley, they said, would be in the crowd. Carr and other luminaries from Columbus would also be there. Sportswriters from out-of-town newspapers—from Chicago, Milwaukee, Columbus, even New York—would be in the press box. All the Tri-State "graphite wielders," said Minego, would also be on hand. The Packers were looking for a large crowd, perhaps twenty thousand. They looked for the Spartans, their roster strengthened by the recent addition of new men, to give them a battle.[59]

The Packers were wrong about the crowd. It was about sixty-five hundred, still a good number for mid-December. They were right in expecting the Spartans to give them stiff opposition. Neither eleven mounting sustained offensive drives, they played to a tie, 6–6, a victory of sorts for the Spartans considering the beating the Packers had given them in Green Bay. Minego of the *Times* and Arthur Bystrom, the sportswriter for the *Green Bay Gazette*, had different views of the game. For Minego, it was a "hard clean" game; Bystrom, saying that there was "little love lost on either side," saw some "unnecessary piling on."[60] Minego thought that Spartans should have used a different defensive alignment against the Packers when they scored. Bystrom believed that Griffin had squandered an opportunity for a win: limited to twenty men in uniform, at halftime, dissatisfied with the play of Peters, the good drop-kicker, he had him get out of uniform and called Glasgow from the stands to take his place. In the fourth quarter, when the Spartans reached the Packers' twenty-three-yard line, he did not have Peters available to attempt the field goal. Bystrom acknowledged that the Spartans had played well, improving considerably since their visit to Green Bay. Ironically, their good play fed complaints that Griffin had given the Spartans inconsistent direction. Had they lost by a large margin, fans might have blamed the players as well as the coach.

For the Packers, the tie was as good as a win, giving them the league title by four percentage points. The game completed the Spartans' season. In league play they posted a record of five wins, six losses, and three ties. They finished eighth in the league, then numbering eleven teams. Their season's record was seven wins, eight losses, and three ties. Altogether, Minego thought, the Spartans had proved their entry into the league to be a success, and with a few changes—he did not enumerate them—they would become invincible.

As the season wound down in December, Spartans were taking up activities tying them to the community and creating continuity for the team. Father Lumpkin was holding his annual dance at Baesman's academy, with the Spartans as honored guests. Cy Kahl was planning to read law in a local attorney's office. Several were returning to work in the steel mills and shoe factories. Apparently believing that he would continue as the Spartans' coach, Griffin was planning to attend Rockne's school in 1931. He was also taking steps to ensure that the Spartans had clear title to Douds, the Steamroller having raised a question about which club had the right to his services. Snyder was meeting with each player, paying him, and asking whether he needed financial assistance or help in finding employment. Griffin and the directors were attempting to sign players to contracts before they left the city and reportedly had secured many signatures, among them those of Lumpkin and Bennett. Lumpkin, evidently receiving an offer from an independent team, said that he started his career in Portsmouth and intended to end it there—no other community could be as good as Portsmouth. Besides, he expected to appear on some wrestling cards in the city. Directors, fans, and reporters all rejoiced at the news that sportswriters in Green Bay and Chicago had placed Lumpkin on their all-star league teams. Converse to their efforts to sign veterans, the directors were preparing letters to send to three hundred young players around the nation inviting them to become candidates for the team in 1931.

Portsmouth Is in the Big League

The season at an end, Grimes wrote an editorial for his *Times* on where the Spartans had been and where they might be going.[61] Unfortunately, his column was more nearly an exercise in boosterism than a critical look at what a small town franchise could expect in what was becoming a big-city professional league. Not for many months, he lamented, would one hear the "whack of leather," the "resounding cheers" at the stadium. But the season was well worth remembering. Playing against the cream of professional elevens in the nation, the Spartans had done well, notwithstanding their low finish in the standings. They had only to drop some old players and obtain some new men to rise in the league. Fans should continue to support the Spartans and give credit to the businessmen who believed in them and the fans. And in a year of economic distress, these men were satisfied with what their franchise had accomplished and were optimistic about the future. Neither the editor nor the other directors had yet commented on whether the Spartans had earned their keep in 1930.

Just after the Spartans had defeated the Tanks on Thanksgiving Day, Charles Collett of the *Ironton News* had looked much more critically at professional football in Portsmouth and Ironton. Certainly at points, as he commented on football at Portsmouth, his words were sour grapes; but he set forth, in the main, an objective view of the professional game in both cities. He was skeptical about whether either community could support paid teams. As a small city, Portsmouth, he thought, could not sustain a franchise in the NFL any more than the larger cities of Newark and Minneapolis, which were abandoning their clubs in the league. The Spartans could not point to success either in their record or in attendance. They had finished near the bottom of the standings and had won but one game on the road, that against the Tanks by one point. Their crowds had not been uniformly good, a portent of coming problems. Fans in the Tri-State, he admitted, had supported them in their first year in the league as "something new" but would they soon see them as a novelty wearing thin and less worthy of their dollars? Could Portsmouth become another Green Bay, another small city mustering the material support necessary to keep a professional team competing on equal terms with the big city elevens in the NFL? He thought not.[62]

If the directors of the Portsmouth Football Corporation, if the journalists of the city, if the fans in the community feared that they could not, they did not seem apprehensive. Already they were looking forward to and planning for another season in the "big league."

Collett had a dark message of another sort for Ironton. Though he believed that the Tanks had won "more favorable mention" for Ironton in the past season than the Spartans had for Portsmouth, he was pessimistic about the future of professional football in the city. Even if the Tanks continued to be a "high type" team, they would find scheduling increasingly difficult. With good teams in larger cities such as Columbus, Akron, Canton, and Dayton disbanding, only Portsmouth in Ohio could give the Tanks a team that was a good draw. Thus the Tanks had met the Giants and Bears as imports—and at Cincinnati at that—and had traveled to Memphis to play the Tigers. They could not secure good opposition unless they joined a league, presumably the NFL, in 1931. He was skeptical about such a remedy. Columbus, Canton, and Dayton all had tried to make it in the big league, and all had failed. Moreover, it was not likely that the Ohio Valley could provide adequate support for Ironton and Portsmouth in the NFL—indeed even for one city; in any case, the cities would drain each other dry in competing for fans in surrounding communities.

If Collett sounded an alarm bell in the night, his readers in Ironton did not hear it. The Tanks' officials and followers were still aglow over their team despite the loss to the Spartans closing the season. McMahon hoped to schedule one more game with an NFL team, wishing especially to persuade the Cardinals to come to Ironton, but was unable to do so. Though their record, seven wins and three losses, was not as good as in the mid-1920s, the Tanks, argued Burke, had had, considering their opposition, the "greatest" season in their history, one affording the city "great advertising." He dismissed the losses to the Spartans as meaningless, saying that the Tanks "deserved" to win the first game and that they had lost the third game to "Old Man Winter," not to the Spartans.[63]

A few days after the Spartans' game, with many players preparing to leave the city, the Rotary Club held an "appreciation dinner" at the Marting Hotel for all the Tanks, bidding farewell for the year to the "greatest professional team ever assembled in the United States."[64] An "All-Star" orchestra donated its services. Bill Brooks addressed the guests, recounting the Tanks' history. The city manager and president of the Chamber of Commerce also gave "inspiring" talks, both praising the Tanks for giving the community "national advertising" and for serving as models of "clean living, true sportsmanship and an indomitable fighting spirit." After the ceremonies, all went to the Marlow Theater for a public "demonstration" and reception for the players. The Rotary president introduced Neale and the players to the attendees. Fans gave Neale a billfold with a hundred dollar bill in it. Neale praised the team and then announced what many people already knew—he had accepted the posi-

Portsmouth Is in the Big League

tion as head football coach at West Virginia University. No doubt his stint at Ironton had advanced his consideration for the post. At the conclusion of the program, fans and players attended the movie playing at the Marlow, *On the Level*, starring Victor McLaughlin and Fifi Dorsey.

In the following days, fans continued to talk about the Tanks and their season. Especially they began to compare the Tanks with the Notre Dame eleven of 1930, which had claimed the national collegiate championship. A sportswriter for the *Huntington Dispatch* asked Neale to discuss the subject. "I think," he said, "the Notre Dame team of this year could beat any pro team except the one I had at Ironton."[65] He went on to argue that Notre Dame's passing attack would succeed against any professional team except the Tanks, which had stopped Friedman, who could "hit a dime at upteen yards."

Seemingly fans could look forward to another good season in 1931. Unquestionably, the Tanks of 1930 had played well, and nearly all the players had assured fans and Tanks' leaders that they wished to return to the team. But late in December, with the public disclosure of the Tanks' financial status coming as economic conditions continued to worsen in the nation and the region, the fans had to become apprehensive about their team's fate. The figures on losses and profits for each game of 1930, though not corresponding in the aggregate with the reported deficit of $3,530 for the entire season, were dismal.[66] On only two games, the first with the Spartans and the one with the Bears, did the Tanks realize a profit, $1,300 on each game; on six games, they lost anywhere from one dollar—on the Thanksgiving Day game with the Spartans—to $2,100—on the game with the Chillicothe Eagles. On two games, they broke even. As reported in the *Tribune*, the accounting of the Tanks' ledger had to be confusing. The Tanks had lost $3,800 in operations, expenses running $30,000, largely for salaries; but taking into account $1,300 that they had not paid to the association for the use of Beechwood, the deficit was close to $5,000 for the season. Tangled in the books were a note for $3,000 held by a local bank against the association, a contribution of $2,500 from boosters, and a carryover of $800 from 1929. Any way the counting went, the Tanks were in trouble.

The Stadium Association, which "felt the depression," was ready to sever all connections with the Tanks, but reportedly a group of fourteen businessmen was willing to assume responsibility for the deficit and to take control of the team.[67] No one or no group, though, took any specific steps in the next few months to support or direct the Tanks in 1931. For the moment they seemed adrift. Presnell, not certain of what might happen, began to think about going over to the Spartans. Late in the spring of 1931, some boosters convened a public rally to consider the team's future.

Home and Away

One proposal surfaced calling for the Tanks to operate on a "cooperative" basis, as they had "several years ago," when players received no fixed salaries but only a share of the gate after all expenses had been met.[68] Virgil Perry, erstwhile coach of the defunct Armcos, expressed interest in the proposal and offered to serve as coach of the Tanks. Nothing concrete came of the meeting, and the Tanks appeared ready to become the subject of obsequies in August when Presnell, believing that his old team was about to quit the field, signed a contract to play for the Spartans.

Later that month, a reporter for the *Tribune* pronounced the Tanks virtually dead even as he wrote of unnamed boosters attempting to reorganize the team for play in 1931.[69] They believed that they could obtain many players who had been with the Tanks in 1930 and at much lower salaries. As they saw it, their great problem was scheduling good teams—teams that would draw well—on reasonable terms. Some proposed the creation of a "guarantee fund" to be raised through a public subscription. But they could see only the Spartans as a viable opponent. Teams in Columbus had never attracted large crowds in Ironton, and Akron had fallen off as a "paying center." A projected team at Charleston might draw well only in an initial game with the Tanks. About the only elevens in the Tanks' class were NFL clubs. To book them, the Tanks would have to offer guarantees far beyond the capacity of the community to bear. Again, nothing came of talk to salvage the Tanks. Apparently football fans would not see the "famous" Tanks in 1931.

11

Football Is the Salvation

THE SEMIPROFESSIONAL FOOTBALL TEAMS of Portsmouth seldom developed any appearance of continuity. Typically, after the conclusion of a season, the community did not know until late in the following summer whether the Smoke House or other teams would take the field in the fall; the promoters promised nothing. But with the rise of the Spartans, professional football in the city took on a permanent aspect, with reports of their activities and preparations for the coming season appearing in the *Times* and becoming the staple of daily conversations in public places as the seasons changed on the way to football weather. Meanwhile, up the river in Ironton, fans suddenly had before them the prospect, belated though it was, of again talking about the Tanks.

Midway through August of 1931, the Tanks were becoming a memory for Irontonians. They had lost money throughout the previous season, the Depression was worsening, and the problems of scheduling seemed insurmountable. No one, no group of businessmen had stepped forth to rescue them, and apparently they were beyond resuscitation. Then in mid-September, "out of the clear sky," as Burke reported it, a proposal surfaced for reviving the Tanks as a member of a Tri-State league, the other members to be teams from Ashland, Huntington, and Charleston. For Burke and many fans the report renewed the spirit. Ironton, said Burke, seemed "like home with no furniture . . . when the grid season roll[ed] around—and no Tanks."[1]

No one identified the provenance of the proposal, but early in October representatives from the cities met in Ashland and came to an agreement for the creation of a four-team circuit, the Tri-State League.[2] Representing the Tanks were Shorty Davies and Homer Edwards. Virgil Perry, Tiny Lewis, and Russell Smith spoke for Ashland; their team would be the Armcos. Intending to reorganize the Boosters, Johnny Stuart came from Huntington. Speaking for Charleston, which already had a team playing, the Trojans, were Jimmie Dugan and Russ Leader.

By their agreement, uncodified in a constitution or by-laws, the men called on member teams to conform to virtually no rules, and they designated no official to enforce rules. Still they made a start at developing some uniformity in conduct among the clubs. To curb expenditures, players would receive no salaries; rather, they would share in profits from gate receipts. Essentially, the teams became semi-professional clubs. The organizers wished to lay down eligibility regulations but did not do so because the Trojans then might have to revise their roster; reporters offered no explanation of the problems the Trojans might have faced. Scheduling would be fairly simple and symmetrical. Each team would play two games against each of the other elevens, one at home, one away. Then each team would meet the other teams for a third game, to be played at the field of the team that drew the larger crowd in the first two games. Such a schedule had some merit. A team could easily book nine games and have room left to play one or more nonleague opponents. If two teams had played closely contested games, a third encounter might draw well; conversely, if one team had won victories in each of the two games, a third game might attract few fans.

Play began in the second week of October. Coaching the Tanks was Davies. Perry was the Armcos' mentor. Stuart took the reins of the Boosters, and Dugan led the Trojans. All the teams could look to some experienced players to bolster their rosters. At least seven veterans joined the Tanks, including Bill Brooks, Evard Lee, Phony Smith, Clair Sloan, and Red Martin. At Ashland several old-line Armcos—Perry, Lewis, Ashby Blevins, Fayne Grone, and Layne Tynes—were ready to play for the new Armcos, as were several former Tomcats. Besides himself, Stuart had several former Boosters coming to his roster and Joe Gembis, who had played for the

Football Is the Salvation

Tanks in 1930. The Trojans had six players from West Virginia University and two from the University of Kentucky in their lineup.

At the outset the Trojans were favored to win the championship of the league, evidently because they had already won two games before league competition began, the other teams having played no games. But the Tanks soon controlled the race for the title, defeating the Trojans twice 3–0, the Armcos 7–0 and 13–7, and the Boosters 32–0 and 13–0. The Boosters were the doormat of the league and had to postpone one game for a few days because five players deserted the team. After two rounds of play, the Tanks had won six and lost none; the Armcos were at three wins, two losses, and a tie; the Trojans had won but one game while losing three and tying one; and the Boosters had lost five games and tied one.

Other than those involving the Boosters, the teams played closely contested games. But fans showed little interest in the league, crowds seldom exceeding a thousand, and sportswriters paid little attention to the games. Surely the Depression cut attendance. As one resident of Ironton, prosaically put it, "people just could not afford to go to the games anymore."[3] Players earned scarcely nothing beyond bruises for their play. The Stadium Association also suffered a fiscal battering. The Tanks were not on the "field on a large scale" and provided the association slightly over $400 in rental income, so it could not meet the expenses for operating the stadium, much less return any dividends to stockholders.

Because attendance and interest were low in the league and the Tanks held a commanding lead in the standings, the members decided not to complete the schedule after the second round of play. But the Tanks were not ready to mothball their uniforms. Briefly they entertained a proposal from the Cleveland Indians, an NFL club drawing poorly at home, to play a game at Redland Field. When the Indians refused to offer a flat guarantee to them, the Tanks decided not to play. Now the Tanks were truly at the end of their tether. Paradoxically, they ended play for all times in the kind of a league probably best suited for them—a league composed of teams from cities not much larger than Ironton, teams of no great repute demanding no guarantees. By their own admission, what had brought them down was their attempt to compete with elevens from much larger communities requiring guarantees beyond the means of Ironton. But fans and players alike might have found victories against teams of their own kind no source of pride and distinction. As it was, they could "remember with advantages what feats" the Tanks of old had recorded in the book of common memory.

Home and Away

 At Portsmouth the Spartans were preparing to create legends for the common memory. Through the late spring and summer of 1931, the Spartans' directors were organizing their team for play, rebuilding the roster and giving the team new leadership. Working with other owners, they were shaping the schedule. Their club a full-fledged member of the NFL, they were parties to decisions affecting all franchises. They were promoting the Spartans in the city and throughout southern Ohio as never before. And with the Depression worsening, they were taking steps to slash their budget.

They effected dramatic changes in the roster. They were acting in accord with the views of fans, reporters, and the editor of the *Times,* who, as the season ended in 1930, were saying that many players had "to go" and that the Spartans had to correct "weaknesses" in the lineup. With the directors supporting him, Griffin was soon negotiating contracts with a few select players already on the team but was withholding contracts from many men who had played in 1930 as he scoured the nation for new men. Early on he had a contract in hand from the ebullient Lumpkin, who was organizing and appearing on wrestling and boxing cards up and down the Ohio Valley. Lumpkin believed that wrestling was complementary to football. "This rassling racket," he declared, "put me in shape for football."[4] Chuck Bennett, who had played well, also appeared to be in the fold; Griffin had signed him to a contract before he returned home to Indiana at the close of the season. But then early in June, he notified the Spartans that he would not be returning to them, that he had accepted a position as coach of the football and track squad at La Porte High School. It was a bitter disappointment for the Spartans.

The Spartans did retain two other backs from 1931, Mayes "Chief" McClain, a burly fullback, and Cy Kahl, a halfback. A returnee shoring up the line was Forrest "Jap" Douds, the tackle from the Steamroller who had joined the Spartans late in the season of 1930 after his team disbanded for the year. For over six months, the Spartans and the Steamroller squabbled over the right to sign Douds before the Spartans finally agreed to turn over three players—all journeymen at best—to the eastern club and pay it $250 for a clear claim to Douds.[5] Another tackle staying with the Spartans was Vin "Slice" Schleusner, one of the several Iowa men whom Griffin had recruited.

The Spartans more than made up for the loss of Bennett in their acquisition of two backs, veritable "stars" in every sense of the word, one coming from the Tanks, the other directly out of college. With the Tanks apparently folding after the season of 1930, many of the players were looking around for new berths well before the new Tanks took the field. Among them was Glenn Presnell, whose abilities as a runner, passer, and kicker would have made him an adornment to any professional team in

Football Is the Salvation

the nation. Learning of his desire to continue playing, the Spartans offered him a contract—really two contracts—in mid-July. Because he was the football coach at Russell High School, one contract, conditional on whether the Tanks played, called for him to play for the Spartans in their first five games, all home games, if he could not or would not leave his coaching position; the other assumed that he would play all year and attend all practices.[6]

At Ironton, no one found fault with the Spartans' dealing with Presnell. Collett of the *News* even encouraged the Spartans, saying that the Tanks surely would not play in the fall. The Spartans, he said, had to draw Irontonians in large numbers to their games but could do so only if they signed Presnell. Collett hoped that they would even if he then had to root for an old rival. Presnell revealed that the Spartans had made him a "splendid" offer but asked for more time to consider his decision.[7] A delegation of Ironton fans called on him, urging him to sign with the Spartans; since they could not see him playing for the Tanks, they were eager for him to be in uniform from a team near at hand. Supposedly, he was also weighing an offer from the Brooklyn Dodgers. Early in August, he cast his lot with the Spartans. Resigning his position at Russell, he signed a contract with the Spartans for a salary reported at $4,200 a year.[8] People at Ironton and Russell expressed regret at his decision but wished him good fortune. Four other Tanks, all first-rate men, signed with the Spartans and played for them in 1931, linemen Bill Hastings, John "Popeye" Wager, and Gran "Buster" Mitchell and a back, Gene Alford.

Presnell proved to be a luminary for the Spartans and then the Detroit Lions even as a younger star and teammate eclipsed him, Earl "Dutch" Clark, who also joined the team in 1931. Clark, six feet, 183 pounds, had been a triple-threat tailback at Colorado College. In 1929, when Clark was a junior, Alan Gould of the Associated Press named him to his All-American team, a selection that scribes questioned because he came from a small college. When he left Colorado in 1931, he was determined to vindicate himself and Gould. He signed with the Spartans for $140 a game, learning later, though, that the Spartans had problems in making payments.

The Spartans also acquired several excellent linemen. By a trade, Clare Randolph, who, asserted Griffin, had "few peers as a pivot man," returned from the Cardinals. A newcomer to the Spartans was Grover "Ox" Emerson, a guard and tackle from the University of Texas. Though not big at 197 pounds, he soon became one of the premier linemen in the league. Maury Bodenger, George Christensen, and Harry "Irish" Ebding, respectively just concluding their play at Tulane, the University of Oregon, and St. Mary's, all proved their mettle as linemen with the Spartans and then later with the Detroit Lions. Sifting through applications from men who wanted to try out for the team, supposedly as many as a hundred, Griffin invited only twenty-six to come to the Spartans' opening practices in August.[9] After the third game, the Spartans intended to release six men and then soon reach the league limit of twenty players. All twenty-six had played collegiate football, and fourteen had been captains of their teams. At least four had played in the Dixie Classic or East-West All-Star game. As it turned out, altogether twenty-nine men were on the Spartans' roster at one time or another during the season's play. Of these only five had been Spartans in 1930.

Ironically, Griffin, who did much of the legwork in recruiting the new men for the Spartans, found himself cut. Especially after midseason in 1930, he had become the object of considerable reproach, fans and reporters alleging that he gave no consistency to the team's play, that he had created no deception in the offense, and that he had blundered badly in starting second-stringers against the Tanks in the second game of the season. The directors had stated their confidence in him when he offered to resign, but surely the common view of him lingered on. In any case, in the summer of 1931, the directors were looking for a replacement for him and found their man in George "Potsy" Clark, demoting Griffen to business manager.

Clark, a graduate of the University of Illinois, was then the head coach at Butler University, hardly one of the shrines of collegiate football.[10] Under Coach Bob Zuppke, he had quarterbacked the Illini to consecutive undefeated seasons in 1914 and 1915. He had no experience in professional football but brought to the Spartans the intellect and the intensity, discipline, and fiery spirit that might serve them well. He came at an annual salary of $5,000. Soon after the directors announced his appointment, Clark, who lived in Indianapolis, came to Portsmouth with his wife to meet the community. He addressed civic clubs—the Civitan and Kiwanis Clubs among others—and employees at the steel mills and shoe factories. Joining municipal officials, he spoke to a mass rally of fans at the Masonic Hall. He also made a flying trip to surrounding communities to meet various "dignitaries." To all his auditors, he struck the same theme: if the players did as they were told, if they fought, if they stayed in training, the Spartans would have a good season.[11] He spoke often of the need for mental power, teamwork, cooperation, and coordination.

Once in Portsmouth permanently in August, only about three weeks before the Spartans' opening game, Clark seemed to demonstrate that he was no poseur acting the part of a Rockne or martinet. At his very first practice, with five thousand enthusiastic fans looking on initially and then dwindling to several hundred as the session stretched out for three or four hours, he asserted his authority, revealing at once a steel will and a soft smile. First, he warned Mayes to stop his buffoonery.

Football Is the Salvation

Then, Lumpkin engaging in "too much horseplay," Clark banished him from practice, saying to all the spectators that he would not tolerate clowning.[12] Lumpkin apologized to Clark and the team the next day, and Clark, his authority vindicated, named him captain of the team. Clark, Presnell recalled decades later, cut several Spartans "because they would not be disciplined."[13] Determined to have the Spartans in good physical condition, he ran two sessions a day, one at 9:00 A.M., the other at 3:00 P.M. Holding court with fans, he proclaimed that practice was no "pat-on-the-back" affair. He smiled approvingly at a hard tackle, noting that "ettiket stuff" did not win football games. He gave special attention to the line, which had been vulnerable throughout the previous season. Seemingly, Clark had a good understanding of offensive play, developing especially quick-opening and wide-running plays from the single wing.

Clark added to his rigorous practices training rules truly for Spartans—or in part for boy scouts. Posting them at the locker room, he called on the players to get eight "regular" hours of sleep—twelve hours were too much—and to follow prescribed hours for eating—7:15 to 8:00 A.M., 12:00 to 12:15 P.M., and 6:00 to 8:00 P.M.[14] He warned them not to eat between meals. A player eating candy set in motion a train of unhappy consequences: he would develop bad teeth, the bad teeth would cause poor digestion, and the bad stomach would then result in poor health and a weak disposition. If a player smoked, he should do so only after meals; if he used alcohol, he was on a dangerous course. He should refrain from the use of foul language. If he lost his temper—he should not—he should sleep it off overnight or take a cold shower. He did not spell out in detail the penalties for infractions; probably they were extra exercises, small fines, or short suspensions. Clark called on "downtown coaches" to assist players in abiding by training rules; they should not, Clark declared, urge players to take just a little drink or two or ask them to smoke or keep late hours.[15] The downtown coaches could become his training police.

Summer saw Spartan leaders building a schedule for their team in a much more rational way than possible for sponsors of the old semiprofessional elevens of the community. After working in Chicago with officers from other clubs at the annual owners' meeting in July, Griffin and Clark returned to Portsmouth with fifteen league games for the Spartans. They would play two games, home-and-home, with seven of the nine other teams in the league. They would not meet the two teams at the farthest eastern and western points on road trips, the Steamroller and the Packers, thus cutting the burdens of travel. They did expect to meet the Packers in a home game closing the season. The schedule called for the Spartans to open the season with five consecutive home games; then they would play five straight games on the

253

Home and Away

road, the first four on an eastern swing for two weeks; and they would play four of their last five league games at home (a game originally scheduled at home against Cleveland was moved to Cincinnati). Altogether, the Spartans would go on three road trips, the eastern swing and two to Chicago. The schedule was somewhat less demanding of travel than that of 1930. Such scheduling comported with traveling realities of the day. Players traveling by bus or rail for two weeks might become weary, but if they had to play a schedule punctuated by one- or two-game road trips in a single region, they would spend even more time and miles on the road. Thus the club might save expenditures for food and accommodations.

By the fall of 1931 the Depression was truly becoming the Great Depression. Across the land, the decline of business activity continued, with the inevitable consequence of rising unemployment as downtown stores looked in vain for customers, industrial plants for orders. Financial collapse in Europe threatened to worsen conditions. Now the steel mills and shoe factories and retail establishments in Portsmouth began to lop off workers and otherwise cut expenses. The Portsmouth Football Corporation also slashed expenditures. Without disclosing the size of their budget, the directors asserted that they had shaved $37,000 from it but offered only a few details of where the cuts had come. Instead of each game costing management $2,800, as in 1930, the cost would be $1,900—enough to sustain a "high class of football" and to "meet any situation to perpetuate National League football in Portsmouth."[16]

The directors effected some savings by changing the Spartans' mode of travel. In 1930 the team had traveled by rail, sometimes in Pullman cars, to all road games. Now the Atlantic Greyhound Company remodeled a bus specifically designed to meet the players' needs and leased it to the corporation for all road trips.[17] Saving the Spartans $4,000, the bus also gained publicity for the city. Painted in the Spartan colors, purple and white, it bore the name of Portsmouth in huge letters—"real advertising" for the city, said Pete Minego. The directors may have cut expenditures slightly, too, through a new policy on payment for players' meals on road trips. Saying that the old practice of giving players a stated allowance for meals—$2.50 a day —had "drawbacks," the directors required them to submit receipts for all meals to the business manager for reimbursement. The business manager also attempted to reduce expenses for tape, rubbing alcohol, and other supplies for the locker room. Abandoning parsimony for a moment, the directors ordered new uniforms.

The directors also sought to strengthen the Spartans financially by vigorous marketing. In the summer, they conducted a traditional campaign for the sale of season tickets to local fans, evidently with a modicum of success despite the gloomy economic conditions. But they wanted to reach out to another market, the surrounding communities in Ohio, Kentucky, and West Virginia. Giving them support was Vaughan Talbott, president of the Chamber of Commerce. He persuaded members of the Retail Merchants' Association to join with Spartan players in promotional tours of Ironton, Ashland, Huntington, Jackson, Chillicothe, MacArthur, Waverly, and other communities, altogether twenty-six. On three separate days early in September, the merchants drove automobiles, as many as a hundred, each draped with a banner naming the driver's firm, in cavalcades to the communities.[18] There local dignitaries received the merchants and the Spartans in their uniforms. Then for thirty minutes, the players gave an exhibition at a field, going through their old and new plays and punting and passing. Little boys must have been bug-eyed. About five hundred Irontonians gave the Spartans a cordial welcome at Beechwood Stadium. Complementing the tours, the directors established ticket agencies in many of the communities. Surveying the results of the campaigns, they were optimistic, asserting that sales of tickets, six hundred more than the thousand sold in 1930, had virtually underwritten the season's expenditures before play began. But at season's end, they learned that they were living a fantasy.

 The Spartans opened the season against the Brooklyn Dodgers at Universal Stadium on a Sunday afternoon. Because their uniforms were largely yellow, the *Times* called the Dodgers the "Yellow Peril of the East." The Dodgers, having posted a record of seven wins and four losses in their first year in the league in 1931, seemed capable of making a good showing at Portsmouth. With a "sun-cooked" crowd of seven thousand looking on, the elevens played on fairly even terms for much of the game, but in the second quarter the Spartans scored two touchdowns on short runs to take the win, 14–0, seemingly an auspicious debut for Coach Clark. After the game, in accordance with league rules, Clark cut the roster to twenty-two, releasing among others McClain and Kahl.

The Spartans then rolled up four more wins at home, their defense permitting but nine points. Fans found two of the games to be especially interesting. When the Chicago Cardinals came to town, accompanying them was their owner, "Doc" Jones, who was still complaining about the Spartans' "rough" treatment of Nevers in 1930. More than eight thousand "football hungry fans" saw the teams meet at night in a fierce battle. For a while, the Cardinals, said Wittenburg, "threatened to turn into birds of prey," outplaying the Spartans through the first half; but in the second half, the Spartans, their "knives sharpened," turned the "cuisine fiasco" their way, coming off the field with a win, 13–3.

The largest crowd until then in the history of football in Portsmouth, nine thousand, came out to see the next game against the New York Giants. The fans anticipated seeing a strong team. Led by Benny Friedman, the Giants had won thirteen league games in 1930, including one over the Spartans in Portsmouth, and had finished second in the standings only four percentage points behind the champion Packers. Friedman, though, was not in the lineup at the outset of the season, having accepted a full-time coaching position at Yale. But fans were eager to see the Giants' rookie back, Chris Cagle, who had starred at West Point. The Giants came to the provinces, said Wittenburg, with a short punt formation serving as a hinge for their running attack. The Spartans yielded more than two hundred yards from scrimmage to the hinged attack but mounted a savage finish in the fourth quarter for a win, 14–6.

Attempting to build goodwill outside of Portsmouth, as the recent tour had, the Spartans dedicated their next game against the Cleveland Indians to Hoge Workman, a former high school star at Huntington and the old Boosters. Hundreds of fans from Huntington were in the crowd of about five thousand at Universal.[19] The Indians, a new team, had nine former Spartans on their roster. Their line, surprisingly, kept the Spartans at bay much of the game. But a former Tank, Gene Alford, playing an outstanding game, scored a touchdown for another Spartan victory, 6–0. The Spartans then concluded their home stand against the Frankford Yellowjackets in a game moved from Wednesday night to Thursday night because of a thunderstorm. The teams played on a field made muddy by the thunderstorm. It did not inhibit the Spartans' running game, and for the first time Dutch Clark appeared in the limelight, scoring two touchdowns as the Spartans vanquished the Yellowjackets, 19–0.

Unbeaten at home, the Spartans now faced five consecutive road games, four on an eastern swing against the Dodgers, the Stapletons, the Yellowjackets, and the Giants. Now they had the opportunity to convince football fans in the East that they were a good team; particularly they wanted play well in the "big city," New York. On a Friday morning following the game against the Yellowjackets, with a large crowd cheering them at the Union Station in downtown Portsmouth, twenty-two players, Clark, Griffin, Minego, and the driver boarded the "palatial" Greyhound bus, waved at the fans, and were on their way.[20] They listened to the radio for news of the outside world, played cards, read, and tried to nap as the bus lumbered eastward. Somewhere in Pennsylvania, Clark stopped the bus along an open field and discharged the players for a short practice before directing the bus on to Harrisburg for the night. The next day they reached New York City, took rooms at the Marseilles Hotel, and nervously meditated on the morrow's game with the Dodgers at Ebbets Field.

There, a crowd of fifteen thousand gathered to see the Ohioans challenge the

Football Is the Salvation

Dodgers—and defeat them 19–0. The Spartans made their mark with the fans and the reporters. Partisans of the Dodgers acknowledged the visitors' superiority. As the reporter for the *New York Times* portrayed them, the Spartans were marathon men: "Racing out eagerly on the gridiron at the start of the game, eleven young men from Portsmouth, Ohio, never stopped running at Ebbets Field yesterday until they had rolled up three touchdowns on the Brooklyn Dodgers." The Spartans' line "tore" the Dodgers apart, allowing them no first downs and opening wide holes for Clark, who ran "brilliantly" in scoring three touchdowns.[21] Clark, of course, delighted in showing his wares to the easterners, who had questioned his selection as an All-American. Spartans fans at Universal cheered as they listened to a play-by-play account of the game.

Remaining in the city, the Spartans prepared to meet the Stapletons a week later at Thompson Stadium on Staten Island. Clark put them through two workouts a day at a football field on 135th Street. The Stapletons were an ordinary team but they did have in their lineup Ken Strong, an outstanding runner and place-kicker. Also playing for them was McClain, who, smarting over his release by the Spartans, vowed revenge. About twelve thousand fans saw an exciting contest. The teams were locked in a tie at 7–7 going into the last few minutes of the game when Popeye Wager intercepted one of Strong's passes, the Spartans then scoring a touchdown from scrimmage. They scored again following another interception and won 20–7. Clark, who made several long runs, and Presnell scored touchdowns.

With a record of seven wins and no losses but tied with the unbeaten Packers, the Spartans faced the truly arduous segment of their road trip. They had to go to Philadelphia to meet the Yellowjackets on Saturday six days after playing the Stapletons and then return to New York to face the Giants the next day at the Polo Grounds. Minego depicted them as true Spartans, warriors ready to sacrifice pleasure for victory. Caring not a "rap" about Broadway and its dazzling lights, eschewing all thought of fleshly pursuits, the players voluntarily went to bed at 9:00.[22] Even the frolicsome Lumpkin was "staying put" at the hotel, demonstrating to the "kids" on the team the way to stay in condition. Sportswriters in New York, Minego asserted, were "chirping" about Presnell and Clark, and Stapleton reporters were praising Presnell as an open-field runner and field general. John Kieran, the erudite sports columnist for the *New York Times*, noted that college coaches and scouts were calling the Spartans a "powerful football team."[23]

The Spartans were performing well on and off the field, but Griffin was apprehensive about the club's revenue from the trip, especially from the game with the Giants. If the crowd reached forty thousand—some reporters predicted it would be

Home and Away

fifty thousand—the Spartans had a guarantee of $4,500, far below what they would receive if they had a percentage of the gate; but a team had to be in the league three years and "show something" before the Giants would agree, say, to a 40 percent cut for the visiting team. Despite his concern about the purse, Snyder said that if the Spartans defeated the Yellowjackets and Giants, he might send them home by Pullman.

Arriving in Philadelphia on Friday, the Spartans checked in at the Robert Morris Hotel and then, determined to live up to the praise of eastern writers, they worked out for two hours and practiced again on Saturday morning. That afternoon they met the Yellowjackets in rickety Baker Bowl, a small park but seemingly made cavernous by the crowd of five thousand. Clark kept several Spartans out of play because of minor injuries, saving them for the next day's game against the Giants. The game was mundane, punctuated by several Yellowjacket fumbles leading to a Spartan victory, 14–0, and a half-game lead over the Packers.

At the Marseilles on Sunday morning, players from the Giants, the Steamroller, and the Cardinals greeted Potsy Clark. Their friendliness did not mask the import of the game with the Giants coming a few hours later. If the Spartans won, they would remain undefeated and sustain their lead over the Packers. The Giants had begun the season with three wins and three losses, one to the Spartans, and then, with Friedman returning to guide them, appeared to be climbing into the race with a string of victories. Cutting a swath through the East, the Spartans drew the largest crowd of the season, and the largest that the Spartans ever played before—over thirty-two thousand—to the Polo Grounds despite an incessant rain. Among the fans was Mayor Jimmy Walker. Unfortunately, the Spartans caught Friedman and the Giants in their run of victories, four eventually, and lost 14–0. Friedman, said Arthur Daily of the *New York Times,* was the "direct cause" of the Spartans' fall, throwing three passes in the second quarter that led to two touchdowns. The Spartans threatened to score but once, in the first quarter, and then slogged ineffectually through a sea of mud. Friedman left the game after the Giants scored their second touchdown; the "Jewish star," complained the editor of the *Portsmouth Times,* was "rubbing it in."[24] He did not comment on Walker's departure in the rain at about the same time. Neither the Spartans nor their fans and reporters explained away their loss, as surely they could have, on the ground that the team was weary from the wear and tear of travel and the previous day's game at Philadelphia. The Packers having won, the Spartans fell a half-game behind them.

Notwithstanding the defeat, Snyder returned the Spartans to Portsmouth by Pullman, and the fans there crowned them with the victors' laurels. When their car

Football Is the Salvation

reached the edge of the city on Monday evening, the players detrained and joined a parade of three hundred automobiles led by the high school band. At the stadium ten thousand fans greeted them with a cheer lasting two or three minutes, long and loud enough that it could have "awakened Daniel Boone in Kentucky." Portsmouth and the Ohio Valley should feel "reflected glory" in a team that ventured into hostile country and won the "admiration of the East." Grimes editorially commended the Spartans for providing the community with "mighty fine football."[25] A group of directors and other admirers gave the players a banquet at the Mary Louise restaurant, an orchestra playing as all ate turkey.

The cheers were ringing hollow in a few days. Resting briefly in Portsmouth, the Spartans traveled on to Chicago to meet the Bears at Wrigley Field in another important game. Boarding their bus, they declared that they were ready for the battle. But they could not mount much offense, failing to take advantage of their few scoring opportunities; the Bears, led by former Spartans Brumbaugh and Molesworth, had, reported the *Chicago Tribune*, a "superior attack" and won 9–6.[26] Disheartened by the two consecutive losses, the Spartans and their fans returned to Portsmouth. The Packers had won again so the Spartans were a game and a half behind them. At least they could take heart from sharing a percentage of the good gate that the crowd of twenty-five thousand yielded.

Playing at home, the Spartans righted themselves for the moment. They met the Stapletons on Wednesday following the loss in Chicago, and with about thirty-five hundred fans on hand Presnell directed a passing attack giving them the win, 14–12. The close score concealed the substantial advantage the Spartans had in yardage gained from scrimmage. Then they played the Indians in a game originally scheduled for Cleveland but now moved to Redland Field, apparently because a group of Cincinnatians was contemplating acquisition of the Indians' franchise. About fifteen hundred Spartan fans were in the crowd of ten thousand, which left the "vast reaches" of the park unoccupied.[27] The game was fairly exciting, the Indians fighting hard before falling to the Spartans 14–6. With a record of ten wins and two losses, the Spartans were in a virtual tie with the Packers at nine and one.

But waiting for the Spartans in Chicago were the Cardinals. Clark was optimistic about the Spartans' chances, saying that his players were in good spirits. They traveled to Chicago on their bus, practicing at Indianapolis on Friday and going on to the city on Saturday. The next morning rain swept over Wrigley Field, but the field was fairly firm under an inch of mud.[28] That afternoon, the elevens met in a fiercely fought game. Tied at 13–13 at the end of the third quarter, each team scored a touchdown in the fourth quarter, but the Spartans missed the extra point and lost

20–19. Fights and arguments marred play. The officials ejected Douds for talking back to them and threatened to forfeit the game to the Cardinals. After the game, four policemen entered the clubhouse to prevent a fight between the officials and Spartans, who bitterly complained that they had been jobbed. It was a devastating loss for the Spartans, for the Packers defeated the Giants that day and the Yellowjackets in midweek and now led the Spartans by a game and a half with, they believed, but two games to play, one against the Dodgers, one against the Bears.

The Spartans, though, thought that the Packers had three games to play. As they understood the schedule, if they could beat the Bears at Portsmouth the next Sunday and should the Dodgers or Bears then defeat the Packers in the following weeks, the Spartans could earn a tie and force a play-off for the championship by beating the Packers at Portsmouth. But as they would learn, their game presumably scheduled with the Packers was really not scheduled.

In any case, first the Spartans had to beat the Bears—no easy task. The Bears had defeated them a few weeks earlier and were playing reasonably well. Grange was enjoying a good year, and Molesworth had strengthened their offense. Clark, seeking to muster all the strength he could for his team, announced that he was not suspending Douds for his ejection from the Cardinals' game, as he might have in accordance with his standing policy in such instances; after all, Douds had gotten a "raw deal" in Chicago and was simply asserting his rights in "sassing" the officials.[29] The Bears came to town and, with a "good" crowd on hand, met the Spartans on a rain-drenched field. Slow-footed in the mud, they could not score, and the Spartans made Presnell's field goal in the second quarter stand up for a victory, 3—0. The Packers also won at Brooklyn and declared themselves the champions.[30] Officially, though, the NFL owners, using won-loss percentages, awarded the title at a later date.

Nonetheless, the Spartans, with no league game scheduled the next week, awaited the outcome of the Bears-Packers game in Chicago, believing that they still had a chance to win the championship. But the Packers would not accept the Spartans' view. Lambeau told Bystrom of the *Green Bay Gazette* that the game at Portsmouth was only tentatively scheduled and that the Packers would not play there if they lost to the Bears. He was forthright: "We do not plan to put our title in jeopardy."[31] He might play the game, he said, if the Packers defeated the Bears. Griffin contested Lambeau's explanation. Neither team, he acknowledged, had signed a contract for the game, but they had agreed to play and, he said, Carr expected them to do so.

Arguing the Spartans' view at a meeting of the Exchange Club, Snyder explained that at the owners' meeting that summer the teams had scheduled the game but

Football Is the Salvation

that the Packers' management had then suggested that it be made tentative because of the prospect of bad weather in December.[32] At the time no one saw the Spartans as a contender for the championship. Now, said Snyder, the Packers were hedging. If they beat the Bears and thus clinched the title, probably they would come to Portsmouth, but if the Bears beat them, they might not want to face a possible loss there. According to Snyder, nearly all the owners in the league were calling on the Packers to play the game if it had a bearing on the title. Leland Joannes, president of the Packers, and Lambeau, confirming much of what Snyder had said, sent telegrams to him and the *Times* insisting that they had scheduled the game tentatively and that they would decide whether to play it after the Bears game. Perhaps expecting to lose to the Bears, the Packers' men lamented the "bad condition" of their squad. Snyder then wired Carr and all the owners calling on them to unite in requiring the Packers to commit themselves to playing the game. His plea was ignored.

Still hoping to meet the Packers, Spartan managers cast about for a game to keep the players in condition, to avoid a layoff that might turn them "stale." They talked to Shorty Davies about reviving the Tanks for a game, but the old warriors were beyond persuasion. Then Snyder and Griffin looked to the Safety Cab team of Columbus, supposedly one of the strongest semiprofessional teams in the city. A game with them, besides its physical benefits for the players, would enlarge the Spartans' coffers. Though the Cabs were willing to play, not many Spartan fans wanted to see them. The crowd was small, the score large, the Spartans scoring at will against the light and inexperienced cabmen to win 101–7.

On the same day, the Bears defeated the Packers 7–6. The Spartans rehearsed their refrain. They could become champions of the NFL if the Packers would play them, if the Spartans could win the game for a tie in league play, and if they could defeat the Packers again in a play-off. Clearly the odds were against the Spartans, but they wanted to roll the dice. The Packers would not gamble. Joannes would not agree to play, arguing, as he had before, that the teams had only tentatively scheduled the game and that they had not signed a contract for it. In response, the Spartan directors noted that they did not sign contracts for many of their games and that "tentatively" scheduled games had appeared on the "official league schedule." But for Lambeau's opposition, said Potsy Clark, the Packer players were willing to come to Portsmouth. He might have noted that even then the players were arranging a barnstorming tour of Wisconsin without the consent of management.[33] Carr would not support the Spartans' protest against the Packers' decision. The teams, he insisted, had arranged the game "after the regular schedule had been drawn up," and the Packers could cancel the game. He would not forfeit it to the Spartans. The Packers could claim the championship.

In an editorial, Grimes said the decision revealed the looseness and expediency at work in the NFL. Professional football, he argued, was no better than any other ragtag sport—wrestling, boxing, six-day bicycling.[34] The NFL had to suffer if it permitted teams to back out of agreements. Green Bay was more concerned about a paper championship than about integrity and the future of the league. The confusion surrounding the game was an indication of the sloppy way the league operated. Carr had to take a firmer grip and run the league in a businesslike manner. Bob Hovey, a sportswriter for the *Ohio State Journal,* agreed.[35] He called the Packers the "cheese champions," men who would not endanger their crown whatever fairness and equity required. Relations between the franchises, once cordial, now turned sour, the Spartans looking for revenge, the Packers for vindication.

The Packers' refusal to play could not have come at a worse time for the Spartans. Only two days after they beat the Bears, the *Times* ran a story and an editorial that stunned the community. According to the story, the directors of the football corporation had called a meeting of all stockholders to consider a matter of "vital importance"—that other men in another city had offered to purchase the franchise. Readers learned nothing more, nothing about why the directors would discuss an offer or about the men offering to buy.[36] The editorial suggested that financial problems lay at the heart of the matter but gave much more attention to questions about whether Portsmouth could or should support a professional franchise. What was the future for professional football in the city, Grimes asked. Was the city too small to compete with great cities like Chicago and New York? Was the widespread publicity for the city, the advertising derived from the Spartans, too great to be thrown away? Could the franchise realize a profit if attendance at home games remained at five or six thousand? Could the Spartans attract more fans to home games? Or should they become primarily a road team dependent on income from outside of Portsmouth? Could they substantially cut expenses and yet remain a first-class team? In the "final analysis," were there enough businessmen and boosters in the city who saw the franchise as a civic asset worthy of their financial aid for a year or so until it could stand on its own feet? The editor seemed to frame his questions so as to induce support for the Spartans, saying that "it seems that the football team is the only community project in which the entire city shows a deep interest—isn't it?"[37]

Covering the meeting of the stockholders, Wittenburg provided more specific

Football Is the Salvation

information on the Spartans' problems. Much to the surprise of stockholders and fans, who had assumed that the large crowds at Universal spelled financial success, Snyder presented a distressing financial report and said that losses were so high that the directors had to consider sale of the franchise to men who would move it unless they received some succor soon. Though average paid attendance at home games had increased by 531 per game over that of 1930, from 3,139 to 4,139, and though average receipts had increased by $86, $5,781 to $5,868, the Spartans had lost money on every game, anywhere from $151 on the Giants game to $3,167 on the Yellowjackets game.[38] Guarantees for the visiting teams, salaries for players, expenditures for game officials, police, and gatemen, and other expenses had always surpassed revenue. On the road, the Spartans had not done much better. Despite the large crowds for the Bears and Giants games, they had realized profits respectively of $472 and $137. For other road games, they had lost anywhere from $1,362 to $1,924. Expenditures for transportation, food, and accommodations and for salaries nearly always exceeded guarantees. Altogether, he estimated the loss for the year at $16,000, the loss for 1930 at $30,000. The unidentified group offering to buy the Spartans was willing to pay an amount that would nearly wipe out that loss. Unless the community could make $20,000 available almost immediately and $10,000 later, the Spartans had to leave Portsmouth.

Heeding Snyder's words, several men, probably directors or stockholders, called for Spartan fans to attend a "mass" rally to consider means for saving the team. More than seven hundred people jammed into the gymnasium at the high school to hear Snyder, the mayor, and the city manager—all with an interest in the use of the stadium—give speeches beseeching support for the Spartans.[39] All who spoke from the platform or floor agreed that the players, having not received any pay for the last two games, had to be paid before the franchise attempted to take care of other debts. No one offered specific proposals for raising money; but "enthusiastic football men" left the rally determined to save the Spartans. The Spartans' woes appeared incongruous in light of Carr's surprising declaration in December, as the Depression worsened, that the league had enjoyed its best season in history.[40]

As the corporation worried, Clark arranged a final game against the Charleston Trojans at Charleston, evidently in an attempt to pay the players at least some of their arrearage. The Trojans had played an abbreviated schedule in the abortive Tri-State League earlier in the season, losing two games 3–0 to the Tanks. Apparently Clark negotiated terms for the game without reference to the corporation. Whatever the guarantee was, the players, who would drive "their own machines" to Charleston, would receive all of it and 50 percent of the gate. He expected as many as six to seven hundred fans to travel to Charleston, but harsh weather cut that number to well under five hundred. Only a few hundred Trojan fans were in attendance. The Spartans had no trouble with the Trojans on a muddy field, "daubing" them 33–0. The Spartans concluded their season with a record of thirteen wins and three losses, eleven and three in league play.

Certainly the Spartans enjoyed a good season and good representation on several all-star teams. On the official All-NFL team, an outgrowth of a poll that Bystrom of the *Green Bay Press-Gazette* had originally conducted, were Dutch Clark and tackle George Christensen. Bill McKalip, Douds, and Presnell were on the second team.[41] Clark was named to teams chosen by the Associated Press and United Press. Lambeau also placed him on his all-star team. Potsy Clark also selected a team, naming Clark, Presnell, Lumpkin, and McKalip as all-stars.

As the Spartans were winning places on all-league teams, an ad hoc "Save the Spartans Committee" appeared in the community. Eighteen men, nearly all business and professional men, composed the committee; chairing it was Homer Selby, president of the Selby Shoe Company.[42] The members declared that fans had to show the "proper interest" in the team. At a public meeting attended by several hundred people, Selby issued a call to arms. The "pride and prestige of Portsmouth," he said, "was at stake" in saving the Spartans; if the fans did not do so, they would leave a "blot" on their community's history.[43] Fans and the club shared a moral obligation to pay the players for their last two games. To save the soul of Portsmouth, the committee and fans had to sell forty-five hundred shares of stock in the corporation, each with a par value of $10. Very soon, warned the committee, the club had to have $33,000 to $38,000 in working capital or it would fold. Subscriptions to stock in the right amount would assure retention of the Spartans for years. Potsy Clark had no doubt that the community could meet its responsibility. He delivered a "blood-stirring" talk, pointing out that Green Bay was not as large as Portsmouth and could not draw on a "territory" as large as the one around Portsmouth.

Attending the meeting were several Spartans who encouraged fans to buy shares. Their spokesman, Clare Randolph, praised them, saying that they had accorded all the players "splendid treatment." More than in any other community, residents had taken them into their homes, their family circles, their social life. They were loyal to the team, and the players deeply regretted the financial muddle. All the Spartans, he reported, wanted to remain in the city. Committee members profusely thanked the players and assured them that they would be paid—eventually. It would be nothing "short of a tragedy" to abandon them.

In mid-December the committee dispatched volunteers, their number evidently

Football Is the Salvation

in the hundreds, to seek out subscribers, who could pay cash or two dollars a month for shares. They scoured the business district and industrial sections looking in offices, stores, and shops for subscribers and then went to all parts of the city.[44] Supporting their labor, Vaughan Talbott directed thirty students at the International Business College—all volunteers—in preparing a list of ten thousand names for solicitation. Clerks, stenographers, and others in business establishments also worked on the list without pay. Despite the best efforts of the volunteers, by Christmas Eve they had found subscribers—879—to only 1,177 shares, a far cry from the 4,500 sought. Vaughan then announced that a new drive would begin in January.

Perhaps giving the drive greater urgency, if not success, was an official audit of the Spartans' books. Published in the *Times* two days before Christmas, it covered the period from January 15, 1930, to December 10, 1931.[45] In precise statistics, it amplified the report that Snyder had earlier given to the stockholders. The corporation had liabilities of $34,280 and assets of $6,561, giving it an actual liability of $27,719. Gross income from games came to $63,639; income from other sources, notably donations, raised that income to $64,001. Operating expenses for the year were $80,074, the result a net operating loss of $16,000. Guarantees to visiting teams accounted for expenditures of $19,000. Traveling expenses for road games amounted to $5,454, accommodations on the road $1,837. The greatest expense was players' salaries of $32,889, and unpaid salaries accounted for the large part of the corporation's debt of $16,562. The corporation owed players anywhere from $346 to $1,306 —the latter to Presnell. Apparently the player Clark had received all of his pay, but Coach Clark had $3,800 coming. The unpaid salaries were mostly $400, $500, and $600. Altogether, management owed Clark and twenty-one players $15,004. The corporation had five cents in the bank.

Initiated by a pep rally akin to an old-time tent revival, with speakers, including Joe Carr, calling on volunteers to save Portsmouth's "pride and honor," the new drive began early in January, the goal the sale of shares in the amount of about $23,000.[46] The campaign continued well into February but never gathered momentum. Counting the shares sold in December, two drives netted about $23,500 in pledges. A select committee then abandoned the drive, reporting that the football corporation had current obligations of $21,000 and needed far more working capital than the pledges, which inevitably would shrink, could provide. Though complaining that the community had failed "in the pinch," the committee said that anyone else could attempt to renew the solicitation.[47]

Almost immediately, Harry Snyder responded, saying that he would try to "rally" the corporation. He intended to secure "new blood" and "crystallize" sentiment for

Home and Away

a new drive.[48] Grimes was not optimistic about what Snyder could do, but he moved ahead. He sent letters to people who had subscribed to the stock in the two drives, urging them not to withdraw their money or pledges and painted a bright future for the Spartans. The deficit of 1931, he said, was half that of 1930. The team had risen from sixth in the standing to second and certainly would draw better crowds in 1932. He told subscribers that he had persuaded creditors to accept payments of debts in installments so the corporation could liquidate its debt gradually and not ruin its financial structure. He was also working with the players and Clark to effect a satisfactory settlement. As to the health of the league, a question that some stockholders had raised, he asserted that, despite the Depression, attendance was rising and various cities were clamoring for franchises. Subscriptions, he insisted, were not a donation; subscribers would receive dividends on their stock within a year.

Snyder elicited a good response from his letters to people who had purchased stock in the recent drive. Of the 1,420 shareholders, 428 responded to his letter. Only 5 canceled subscriptions.[49] Over a hundred increased their shares subscribed from one to five. Altogether, he raised over $6,000 in a few days. Several players accepted his offer for payment of part of their back salary in March and the rest in monthly payments. Confident that he could save the Spartans, he called for a mass meeting of all stockholders to nominate and elect new directors of the corporation. Soon he reported that 877 of the original 1,400 subscribers had renewed their pledges and that he was receiving more pledges. Encouraged by Snyder's seeming success, Clark announced that he would return to Portsmouth if the new "set-up" materialized as he expected.

At the mass meeting, held in March, all augured well for the Spartans. Joe Carr, delivering a cheerleading address, praised Spartan fans for giving Portsmouth its "greatest advertisement."[50] The community had done the pioneering work in creating the team and ought not now lose it. Other cities were knocking at the door for admission to the league, but he would not sacrifice a franchise that fans had struggled to sustain. By unanimous vote, the shareholders selected a committee to nominate new directors of the corporation. Soon thereafter, they elected the directors, nineteen in all, distinctly an elite in the community—two bankers, three executives from the steel companies, three from the shoe factories, three officers from other manufacturing firms, two downtown merchants, a public official, and others. Snyder, of course, was among them. Hardheaded businessmen, not ordinary fans, would direct the affairs of the Portsmouth Football Corporation. The directors then appointed an executive committee of seven directors to carry on the daily business of the corporation. They were *primi inter pares*, among them Homer Selby of the Selby Shoe

Football Is the Salvation

Company, Hugh Allen from the Wheeling Steel Company, Clarence Nodler of the First National Bank, and Snyder. Selby became president of the corporation, Snyder vice-president, Allen secretary, and Nodler treasurer.

Above all, the members of the executive committee had to translate pledges into cash. Otherwise, they could not take care of the players' arrearage and move on to a new season. They notified all subscribers that the first payment for their stock was due. Of nearly fifteen hundred, four hundred did not respond. The committee then decided to send out "flying squadrons" to seek payment.[51] Fortunately, enough subscribers did pay to enable the corporation to initiate monthly payments to the players. The directors also sent a contract to Clark, who signed it as coach and business manager. He was eager to sign old and new players but had to await the consent of the directors, who, in turn, were waiting on shareholders to make more payments on their subscriptions. Acknowledging that stockholders first had to make payments, Clark saw the Spartans serving as a therapeutic agent for a community in distress: "Depression or no depression . . . we must have relaxation. Football is the salvation Portsmouth has that other cities do not have." He was a good soldier, though; to cut expenses, he was willing to reduce the roster from twenty-two to twenty.[52]

The directors continued to liquidate the players' salaries, but not rapidly. They urged subscribers to redeem their pledges more quickly and in May employed collectors to call on them personally for payments.[53] Clark hesitantly began to talk to players about contracts for 1932 and came to terms with Dutch Clark and a "huge" tackle from the University of Nebraska; but he did not have the assurance of sufficient funds to take up wholesale signing of players.

At a rally of fans late in May, Selby seemed to commit the corporation to play for the coming season. He told fans that the Spartans had given Portsmouth more "real honest-to-goodness" advertising than his company had in its fifty-four years of operation in the city.[54] Clark sounded the same theme, saying that no one had heard of Green Bay until the Packers came into the NFL. Both men commented on the status of payments to players. Denying that proceeds from the sale of season tickets would be used to pay them, Selby insisted, nonetheless, that the corporation had to pay the players their salaries before August 1 or they would become free agents. For Clark, it was a matter of both expediency and equity. He wanted to retain twelve or fourteen of the old players and needed to sign them immediately or let them go to seek out berths with other teams. In the interest of fairness, the corporation also ought to pay players whom he did not intend to sign. He suggested that the directors borrow money in anticipation of subscribers' paying for their stock. He was confident of success on the field and in the box office. With a few additional players—and

Home and Away

many were available—the Spartans could win for years. And economic conditions, he was certain, would improve and permit professional football in the city to stage a comeback.

The collectors had some success in persuading subscribers to meet their obligations. They found, though, that many who had subscribed to more than one share were not paying, and the directors remained apprehensive about completing payments to the players.[55] If subscribers had doubts about whether the Spartans would play in 1932 and thus had hesitated to pay, the directors, who may have contributed to doubts about the issue by failing to issue affirmative statements for several weeks, clearly settled the question when in June they authorized Clark to sign players and decided to send Clark, Snyder, and Selby to the annual owners' meeting. The amount of cash and pledges they had in their treasury they did not reveal.

12

If We Had Scored Then

Erratic and loaded with the rhetoric of boosterism, the drives to save the Spartans, though falling far short of their goal, gave Portsmouth another season of professional football. The minimal reach of the subscription drives, economic conditions, and the size of their market gave no certainty of financial security, but they had prospects for a good season on the field that might vault them to the summit of professional football in the nation.

The Spartans began the season, more or less formally, when Snyder and Selby journeyed to Atlantic City in July to attend the annual NFL owners' meeting. They intended to work out a new kind of schedule for the Spartans. Before they left, they received a letter from Lambeau proposing that the Packers and Spartans meet twice in the fall. In view of what he apologetically called the "mixup" of 1931, he would let the Spartans choose a home date late in October or early in November while the Packers were on a road trip.[1] Snyder tentatively accepted the proposal, stipulating, though, that the teams should not play at the end of the season.

269

Believing that Sunday afternoon games outdrew midweek night games because out-of-town fans wanted more daylight to return home and that local fans wanted more free time in the evening, they resolved to ask for fewer night games—the Spartans had played five in 1931. They wanted three night games and five Sunday games.[2] They wished, too, to play more road games early in the season rather than opening the season with a string of home games, then going on the road for four or five games and waiting until November to play again at home. Snyder and Selby returned from the meeting with at best a half-loaf. The league was down to eight franchises, and the Spartans had a tentative schedule of eleven league games, six at home, five on the road. They would play one home game at night. But as in 1931, they had alternating long stretches at home, on the road, and at home, beginning with three home games, then five road games, and finally three home games. The Spartans played only five of the tentatively scheduled games on the dates originally called for but had to adhere to the pattern of home and road games. And they were not able to schedule the Packers as they wished; rather than playing the Packers at home late in October, they were to go to Green Bay early in October and then host the Packers late in the season. Eventually, they played seventeen games, five of them nonleague games.

Snyder and Selby left Atlantic City with one important success. They persuaded Jack and Wellington Mara, owners of the Giants, to agree to a change in the distribution of receipts for the Spartans-Giants game scheduled for the Polo Grounds. In 1931 the Spartans received no percentage of the gate derived from a large crowd of thirty-two thousand at New York, only a flat guarantee of $4,000. The Maras, who "appreciated" that crowd, were now willing to grant the Spartans 40 percent of the receipts for the fall game after deducting 25 percent of the gross receipts for rental of the Polo Grounds.[3] The pay-off, thought Minego, ought to fatten the Spartans' exchequer.

Once the Spartans seemed certain to play in the fall, Clark vigorously pushed old and new players to sign contracts. Collectively, the reports of signings said much about what professional football players did in the off-season, their aspirations, and their personalities. The effusive Lumpkin walked into the Spartans' office, barely looked at his contract, and, allowing that "things had changed in the economical situation," signed it with a flourish. Though a "flashy" lineman, Popeye Wager had little to say at his signing. When he agreed to terms, Randolph, who had recently passed the bar examination in Indiana, was driving a "picture film truck" between Parkersburg and Portsmouth. John "Jumpin' Jawn" Cavosie, who had played for Clark at Butler, spent his winter and spring in a lumber camp in Ironwood, Michigan, and

If We Had Scored Then

was as tough as the wood that he chopped but signed his contract in an exquisite hand. One of the best flankers in the league in 1931, Buster Mitchell did not hesitate to sign again with the Spartans because he liked Portsmouth. Another end, Harry Ebding, returned his signed contract to Clark from Oakland, California, where he had loafed during the off-season. Bodenger, the guard of great girth, returned to the Spartans, abandoning a business in New Orleans that was failing. The former coach of the Spartans, Harold Griffin, who had been working on a farm in Ross County to get into shape, signed a contract, believing that he could make a comeback as a center. "Ox" Emerson, who "gladly" returned to the Spartan yoke, spent the off-season driving a truck, a "four-ton baby," for his father, a contractor in Houston, Texas. Unsung Gene Alford, a halfback from Texas Tech and an old Tank, came virtually from a baseball field in Texas to Portsmouth, a signed contract in his hand, announcing, "Here I am." George Christensen, the "jovial Swede" from Oregon, signed his contract a few weeks before practices began, as did Bill McKalip. Also signing at about the same time after protracted negotiations with Clark was Presnell; the "pride of football" in Portsmouth and Ironton walked into the Spartans' headquarters with his contract, saying, "I know of no city where I would rather play than in Portsmouth."[4]

The roster Clark had constructed as the Spartans began practice in 1932 was similar to that of 1931. Altogether, he re-signed fourteen players from the team of 1931. He did not offer contracts to six players who were with the Spartans at the close of play that year. Three of them, Elmer Schwarz, Jap Douds, and Tony Holm, soon became Chicago Cardinals. Clark signed ten new men to contracts, six of whom played for the Spartans at one time or another in 1932. Probably the outstanding player among them was Leroy "Ace" Gutowski, who had been with the Giants in 1931 after starring as a halfback, quarterback, and fullback at Oklahoma City University. Unfortunately for the Spartans, apparently they had Bill Hewitt, an end and fullback from the University of Michigan, under contract, only to learn that Carr had upheld the Bears' claim to him; Hewitt became one of the premier players in the league in the 1930s.

As practices and the season approached, fans learned by bits and pieces about the Spartans. The directors, cutting the home schedule to five league games because of "economic conditions," lowered the price of a season ticket from $9 to $7.50. Snyder addressed four hundred fans at a rally and presented a "thumbnail" sketch of each of the players expected to report for practices. In his column, "Hot Shots," Minego chatted amusingly about the players. Dutch Clark, he said, would arrive in the city soon, looking for his headgear and a good place to eat. For all anyone knew,

Lumpkin, who had not been in touch with anyone recently, might be in Europe—he was "funny that way." Somehow, though, he was able to book four wrestling matches for the coming winter. Bob Armstrong, a holdover tackle, had brought an Eskimo pup to the city as a mascot for the team. Presnell was hunting for a house in Portsmouth. The directors were still attempting to collect payments due on purchase of stock, largely to settle the account with Potsy Clark. They did have sufficient funds to purchase new jerseys, purple with twelve-inch numerals on the back, stockings, and helmets for the team, but the players had to furnish their own khaki pants.[5]

Late in August, the players were drifting into the city in the annual "leather pilgrimage" signifying, as Minego saw it, the changing of the seasons. "Summer wanes," he wrote. "Autumn approaches, [the] acrid smoke of burning leaves penetrates the crisp atmosphere." On Labor Day, the players made their first public appearance as a team at the stadium; the white-clad Portsmouth High School band and seven thousand fans, many women in their summer finery, greeted them. For nearly two weeks, Clark sent the Spartans through signal drills and scrimmages, all the while deciding who among the thirty-five candidates would remain on the roster. He used three squads in scrimmages, the so-called regular team that played one of the other elevens for a half, the other for a half. A crowd of four thousand paying an admission fee of one dollar attended an intersquad game between the Blues and Grays.

Clark was ever tight-lipped about whom he would cut. In his new column, "Huddle Whispers," Minego declared that one could as well "borrow a thin dime from Jawn D. [Rockefeller]" as persuade Clark to reveal his preference among players competing for a position. About three days before the Spartans' first game, though he found it difficult to choose among the "many good players," he pared the squad to twenty-five, eight of them new men.[6]

The Spartans opened their season against an independent eleven, the Grand Rapids Maroons. On the morning of the game, Murray Powers, the new editor of the *Times*, succeeding Grimes, wrote his lead editorial as a call for the community to support the Spartans in the new season.[7] He argued that despite financial problems, professional football had become the city's favorite sport. The Spartans had many new potential stars, a good schedule, and reduced operating expenses. Fans should attend their games and boost them in every way possible, for they afforded the community great publicity. If fans had any complaints about the team, they should go to the management and not spread their talk to the four winds. On the sports page, Wittenburg urged fans to go out to the stadium on the first "Look 'Em Over Day" to see whether the new men were as good as the veterans. With Chuck Bennett, the former Spartan, and the "bald-headed Al Nesser" leading them, the Maroons gave the Spartans a battle for one quarter and then gave way, losing 33–0. Thus the Spartans were off to a satisfactory start. But despite the editor's call, they drew a small crowd, 2,256; receipts were slightly over $2,000, leaving the club in the red after the first game of a season that surely would test the community's ability and willingness to support professional football.

With the Giants coming to town for the opening league game, the Spartans had the opportunity to draw well and claim an important win. All signs indicated that a good crowd would appear at the stadium. Advance sales of tickets at the Spartans' headquarters were good, and inquiries from communities around Portsmouth about availability of seats were numerous. Among the "dignitaries" expected to attend were Carr, Tim Mara, and Sid Weil, president of the Cincinnati Reds.[8] Selby, disappointed in the crowd for the first game, urged local fans to demonstrate their loyalty to the team, noting that "now is the time to encourage the Spartans." Besides, the game would produce the "greatest array of talent" ever to appear at Portsmouth. Anticipating or hoping for an "immense crowd," the Spartans' managers planned to use two hundred men as ushers, patrolmen, ticket sellers, and so on.[9]

The Giants the Spartans faced, touted locally as a strong team, were not the Giants of 1931. Friedman had gone to the Dodgers, and his former teammates were a graying lot who would play through a disappointing season. They and the Spartans did draw a good crowd. Many Irontonians, their automobiles causing congestion around the stadium, came expecting to see Dick Powell, an erstwhile Tank, play for the Giants.[10] The teams played on even terms through much of the game, Clark's four-yard run for a touchdown giving the Spartans the edge, 7–0. Attendance was about 6,000, paid admissions 4,606. The Spartans' directors expressed delight over income from the game, but surely the guarantee to the Giants of $4,000 kept profits at the margin.

The Spartans next met the Cardinals at the stadium in a game marked by tense play. Now without Nevers, the Cardinals were not ordinarily a good draw, but reportedly demand for tickets was great. No one, though, publicly announced the size of the crowd. "Doc" Jones, the fiery owner of the Cardinals, accompanied his players to Portsmouth, intending, as usual, to protect them, especially, as it turned out, Joe Lillard, a rangy black halfback. Throughout the game, Jones saw his Cardinals and the Spartans playing as though they were in a boxing ring, usually with Lillard the subject, if not the victim, of conflict. Twice police came on to the field to quell fighting. On one occasion, Lumpkin threw a punch at Lillard, owing to what Wittenburg called a "misunderstanding." When Presnell threw the football to the referee follow-

Home and Away

ing a play, Lillard, fearing that Presnell intended to strike him, made a motion leading Lumpkin to believe that he intended to hit the Spartan. Lumpkin did only what he had to do—throw a punch at the Cardinal. Later, Jones, the "peppery, pugnacious Cardinal owner," dashed on to the field to protest the Spartans' "dusting" of his "colored" player as he punted.

Wittenburg and Minego employed language in their columns replete with racial allusions. Lillard was "Massa Lillard." Jones and Coach Jack Chevigny of the Cardinals flashed an "ace of spades" who trumped nearly every Spartan trick. Lillard was a "dark black cloud that hung over the Spartans' hopes."[11] He was the "Ethopian in the woodpile." But the reporter for the *Chicago Tribune* took no note of racial animus.[12] Almost incidental to the antics on the field was the game, which, despite the Spartans' clear dominance, ended in a tie, 7–7. The decisive play was incongruous with the fighting on the field. The Cardinals scored their touchdown on recovery of "one low punt from the toe of Jumping Jawn Cavosie, the ball striking big Pop Lumpkin where the Father got the paddle in his boyhood."

The game with the Cardinals barely over, the Spartans and their fans turned their attention to the coming game at Green Bay against the Packers. Since the Spartans had entered the league, the teams had met once, in 1930, but, of course, their rivalry was intense, inflamed not by the one game played but by the game not played in 1931. Fans in Portsmouth were still calling the Packers the cheese champions, and fans in Green Bay were vigorously defending their "real" champions. Through the week before the game, looking over his shoulder, Clark ran the Spartans in secret practices, complaining that many regulars had not played well against the Cardinals and had expended too much energy in fisticuffs, not in playing.

With Clark calling on his men to win "undying fame" for Portsmouth, they headed off to Green Bay by rail, taking the Norfolk and Western to Cincinnati, the New York Central to Chicago, and the Chicago and Northwestern to Green Bay. At Green Bay they faced the Packers at City Stadium and their six thousand fans, many reminding them of their decisive taunts about cheese champions and carrying signs reading, "They called us cheese champions."[13] A cold, raw wind and rain swept across the field throughout play. At Universal Stadium, three thousand Spartan fans gathered at a "football party" to hear T. J. Henderson read a play-by-play account of the game received via a wire service.

The fans cheered through three quarters as the Spartans led 10–7 but then fell silent as the Packers scored a touchdown and safety in the fourth quarter to win 15–10. Though their partisans—the coach, fans, reporters, and directors—all praised them for their battle and lauded the Packers for their sportsmanship and clean play,

If We Had Scored Then

the Spartans did not take the loss gracefully. Clark prompted their indignation by confronting Lambeau after the game in a "caustic verbal tilt," alleging that the officials had "handed" the game to the Packers by their incorrect calls. In his wake, fans and reporters recited a litany of complaints about the game: the officials had made bad calls, the Packers' backs were in motion throughout the game, the Packers had twenty-five men in uniform in defiance of the league rule permitting but twenty men on rosters, the Packers had "earned" but one touchdown, the Packer fans had rushed on to the field before the game ended. Perhaps the Spartans let go of their anger at the reception given them on their return to Portsmouth. A "rollicking, jubilant" crowd—reportedly "thousands"—gathered at the railroad station in a rainstorm and cheered the players as aerial bombs boomed overhead and a band played.[14]

The game at Green Bay was the first of eight consecutive road games the Spartans played on two separate trips. To cut expenses, on the eve of the second trip, the Spartans' management released two men—one was Griffin—reducing the roster to eighteen even though the league authorized an increase to twenty-two.[15] The journey had to be a grueling experience. Traveling entirely by the Greyhound bus for over two thousand miles, the Spartans were on the road for a month, playing seven games with a roster of seventeen and eighteen men. Years later Popeye Wager had that trip clearly in mind as he recalled the hardships of travel:

> It was tough. We had a small roster because we just could not pay more players. Other teams traveled by train, but we went by bus to save money. We would pack enough clothing for three or four weeks and take off. Potsy would stop the bus alongside the road and we would practice in a farmer's pasture. In New York we practiced in Central Park, but we did not have to practice much because we played a game every three or four days.[16]

The Spartans had to enjoy their game to live as they did on the road.

They did not begin their road trip on an auspicious note. Playing the Stapletons on Staten Island before a crowd of seven thousand, they managed only a tie, 7–7, fumbles halting their offense until finally in the fourth quarter they scored their lone touchdown on Cavosie's pass to Clark. Four days later, Snyder literally scheduling games on the run, they met the Stapletons again, this time drawing a crowd of five thousand. It was another closely fought encounter. Early in the game, Clark ran seventy-four yards for a touchdown; the Spartan fans at the high school gymnasium listening to Henderson's play-by-play description went "wild." The Stapletons narrowed the score to 7–6 going into the fourth quarter, and then Cavosie intercepted a lateral and ran forty yards for a touchdown, sealing the Spartans' victory, 13–6.

Snyder, scrambling for every dollar he could get, then had the Spartans meeting an independent team, the Paterson (New Jersey) Panthers, three days later. The Panthers, with thirty-five hundred fans cheering them on in the rain, gave the Spartans a stiff battle before falling 6–0 on Presnell's thirty-five-yard pass to Mitchell for a touchdown. The Spartans had a mere moment to celebrate the win, learning after the game that Armstrong, the big tackle, was leaving the squad to accept an engineering position with the national government in Memphis. A few days later, their number reduced to seventeen, the Spartans voted to finish the season at that count, adding, though, that they would not oppose the signing of a "real" tackle.[17]

From Paterson, the Spartans moved on to New York City to face the Giants on Sunday. Directors and players were looking for a large crowd at the Polo Grounds, from twenty-five to thirty-five thousand, one that would enable the Spartans to "ride high financially." But the Giants were not playing or drawing well, and paid admissions numbered only about twenty thousand. The crowd, said a reporter for the *New York Times*, did see "one of the most exciting" games ever played in the NFL.[18] Clark threw a "looping" pass to Lumpkin for a touchdown in the first quarter, and the Spartans held on to win 6–0, Clark batting down two passes in the fourth quarter to deny the Giants a touchdown. Though the Giants had the better of the going in yardage gained, the New York reporter thought that the Spartans were the "master of the situation." Minego attributed the Spartans' victory, in part, to the presence of Eddie Cantor, the vaudevillian and movie star, on the victor's bench, explaining that he had a reputation for sitting with the winners.

Remaining in New York, the Spartans prepared to meet the Dodgers at Ebbets Field. They took time off for a fishing trip off Long Island. Lumpkin, according to an amused reporter, caught a whale and threw it back.[19] Their financial status evidently still precarious, players urged Snyder to continue negotiations for games with independent teams. Perhaps they took heart at the good crowd, twenty-five thousand, turning out for their game with the Dodgers. The Dodgers, with Friedman now in their lineup, caught the Spartans by surprise with a "liberal" use of laterals in the first quarter that led to a touchdown. Then Clark, making the "celebrated Jewish gridder look like a dub," ran sixty-five yards for a touchdown in the second quarter, and Gutowski piled up twenty-seven yards in "fierce line-plunging" in a short drive in the fourth quarter for another score, finishing off the Spartans' victory, 17–7.

Departing New York after the win, the Spartans could look back on a successful eastern swing—four wins and a tie—and the praise of eastern sportswriters. In his daily column "Sports of the Times," John Kieran recounted his interview with Potsy Clark, portraying him as a dynamic and effective leader. A "neat, keen, trim little

If We Had Scored Then

fellow," Clark, asserted Kieran, deserved a better nickname than "Potsy," a sobriquet implying that he was slovenly.[20] Clark, still complaining about the Packers' refusal to play the Spartans in 1931, told Kieran that his team was better than the Packers and, always using their nicknames, showered compliments on nearly every Spartan player. He lauded the team for being well-drilled in the use of "double and single wingback stuff." According to Minego, eastern writers nearly ran out of superlatives in describing Clark as the last word as a coach and the Spartans as "deadly" in their tackling, "marvelous" in their blocking, "refreshing" in their spirited play.[21] Scribes from the *Mirror*, the *World-Telegram*, the *Herald-Tribune,* the *Times*, and the *Sun* had all punctuated their columns with words of praise for the Spartans.

Originally, Snyder had intended for the Spartans to return to Portsmouth after the eastern trip, remain there for a few days, and then go to Chicago to play the Bears. But seeing a chance to "make some money," he arranged for the team to go directly from New York, stopping at Columbus overnight, to St. Louis to meet the St. Louis Gunners three days after the game with the Dodgers. The players, told that the Gunners, a strong independent team, would pay expenses and a guarantee, voted for the game despite coming off the Dodgers game with various injuries and the arduous 979-mile trip by bus to St. Louis. They needed the "dough" when the wintry blasts came, explained the *Times*. After meeting the Gunners, they would travel to Chicago, practice for two days, and play the Bears on Sunday. And Snyder was talking about stopping in Dayton on the return trip from Chicago to play the Dayton Guards for "soft kale." If the Spartans "came through" all these games, Minego remarked, they were real "ironmen."

The Spartans "came through" reasonably well. At St. Louis, playing before a crowd of about three thousand shivering in the cold at Frances Field, they ground out a victory over the Gunners, 12–0. Far more important to them was the coming contest with the Bears. The Spartans were in second place in the league, the Bears in third place, with both trailing the Packers and in danger of falling out of the race if they lost another game. Several hundred fans from Portsmouth journeyed to Chicago for the game. They were in a crowd of about fifty-five hundred that saw a "gruelling battle" played on a slippery turf. Neither team mounted many drives except those resulting in the touchdowns, leaving them tied 13–13 at the final gun. Clark, the "blond flash," was brilliant; Grange did not play because of an ankle injury. The tie did not seriously damage either eleven. The Packers had posted eight wins, no losses, and a tie; the Spartans were at four wins, one loss, and three ties; the Bears had two wins, one loss, and five ties. (Ties were commonplace in the period. Relative to the number of teams in the league, eight, and the number of games played, forty-seven,

Home and Away

the ten tied games played by all teams in 1932 set a record—in 1929 twelve teams played ten ties out of seventy games. They derived largely from low scoring. From 1930 through 1932, scores were lower than in the mid-1920s, the average points a game falling from about twenty to sixteen. Defensive play, improving more rapidly than offensive play, generally contained the offenses, which had not yet integrated "wide-open" play and passing into their attacks.)[22] Because standings derived from only the percentage in wins and losses and ties did not count, the Packers had a percentage of 1.000, the Spartans were at .800, and the Bears had a mark of .667. If the Packers lost two of their last few games, either the Spartans or Bears could claim the title of the NFL.

At their return from Chicago—they did not stop in Dayton—the Spartans received an enthusiastic welcome from the community. Fans drove to Lucasville about ten miles north of Portsmouth and escorted them to the city. People lined the downtown streets for several blocks, and motorcycle officers and the high school band, aerial bombs exploding above them, led a parade from the Scioto bridge to the esplanade on Gallia Street. Dignitaries lauded the "boys," who readily admitted that they were weary from the journey—and with good reason. In five weeks, they had traveled 2,480 miles by bus—729 miles from Portsmouth to New York, 1,058 miles from New York to St. Louis, 284 from St. Louis to Chicago, and finally 409 miles from Chicago to Portsmouth. And they had not lost a game, winning five and tying two.

They had little time to rest on their laurels. The next weekend the Boston Braves would come to town. A new team in the league, the Braves were not an easy mark; they had two outstanding rookies in their lineup, Cliff Battles, who led the league in rushing, and Glen Edwards, a bruising tackle. Hinting that the Braves could be a formidable opponent, Minego referred to them as a "colorful" team. The Spartans could ill afford to lose to them, but a win would enhance their position in the standings, especially should the Packers falter.

More than winning was at stake, said Selby, who appealed to fans to come out in large numbers for the game. His words presaged a coming crisis for the franchise. The Spartans had returned from a "grueling and glorious trip," heralded on radio and in newspapers throughout the nation. Now they were scheduled to play three home games testing whether the city could sustain a "high class" franchise. On the road, he declared, the Spartans received guarantees sufficient to meet expenses. But at home, they had to pay the visitors, their own salaries, and many bills associated with staging games. The directors had held expenditures down as far as they could, but with no "angel" to support the team the fans had to step into the breach. They

If We Had Scored Then

would face the "acid test of sincerity" when the Spartans met the Braves. He had heard rumors that many fans would pass that game up in favor of the coming games with the Bears and Packers. But the Bears' and Packers' appearance in Portsmouth was contingent on a good crowd for the Braves. The corporation could not ask clubs to come to Portsmouth without knowing that it could pay them and the Spartan players who were risking their necks. In simple imploratory language, he called on all residents to come to the stadium: "Fans and friends, we are depending on your support."[23]

Fans did not respond wholeheartedly to Selby's appeal. About five thousand, a fair but not great number, were on hand at the stadium. Battles was good but Clark "great" in leading the Spartans to a victory, 10–0. The fans became "hilarious and delirious" at the announcement that the Bears had defeated the Packers. As Wittenburg calculated the standings, the Spartans were now within easy striking distance of the Packers and the championship. His editor, glorying in the news, declared in an editorial that the Packers were not a "miracle" team, that the Spartans now had a chance to put them in their place.[24] Amid the euphoria, the Spartans "dug into practice" for their next game against the Bears at home, seeing on the horizon a league title. Then came unsettling news. The gate from the Boston game had not been sufficient to pay the Braves their guarantee of $3,000, much less the Spartans' salaries.[25] The players threatened to strike, rumors floated around about the team's moving to a larger city, and the Spartan directors began talking to the Packers about playing them in Milwaukee. Fans were aghast. At a raucous meeting, the players decided to continue to play. Decades later, Presnell recalled that on that occasion and other payroll crises "we talked about not playing, but in the end we always played in the hopes of drawing a big enough crowd to get paid."[26] Dutch Clark helped quell the "mutiny," contending that the players had little to lose if they played, all to lose if they did not play. Players and directors met in conferences, laid their "cards on the table," and "cleared away the financial angle." Reminiscing years later, Clark spoke of the Spartans' chronic problems in meeting the payroll:

> My second year at Portsmouth, I got a raise, but the club kept running behind on paychecks. I would get provoked and say "Well, I'm going home." In fact, I didn't care whether I stayed or not. The ballplayers would have meetings over at the Elks Club, and they would say, "Shall we quit, or shall we play?" Everyone hung around the Elks Club, because they had slot machines and cards there, and things like that. Of course, Potsy would hear about those meetings, and he'd come in and scream. He would say, "If you quit now, you'll be quitting things the rest of your life!" A couple of times, the club was going to pay me but

Home and Away

> not pay the other guys. I said, "No, I don't get paid if the others don't." Frankly, I'd just as soon have gone home. But somebody always came through with the dough.[27]

Under such circumstances, Clark would need little cause to leave the Spartans.

Somehow, Clark recalled, the corporation was able to pay the players, who then continued to prepare for the Bears. Surveying the resolution of the problem, created, he said, because subscribers to stock failed to honor their pledges, Powers of the *Times* expressed relief, arguing in an editorial that otherwise fans, players, and the league would have suffered grievous damages.[28] Had games gone to Milwaukee or Chicago or had the players decided not to play, season ticket holders would have been left holding the bag and professional football in Portsmouth would have been dead. The NFL would also have been a casualty. Sportswriters who asserted that professional football was purely a commercial venture with little room for sentiment would have appeared to be correct. Worst of all, the relationship between the community and the players would have ended. Residents had idolized players, taken them into their homes, and wined and dined them. In no other community could the players have known such hospitality.

The crowd for the Bears game was good, at ten thousand the largest in the history of football in Portsmouth. Tackling and blocking vicious as it was, the fans, wrote Minego, would long be talking about the game. The reporter for the *Chicago Tribune* agreed, saying that the play held the interest of the fans until the final whistle.[29] Though outgaining the Bears from scrimmage, 291 yards to 136, the Spartans had to score a touchdown in the final quarter to gain a tie, 7–7. So eager for victory was Potsy Clark that he attempted to talk to his team on the field in the guise of the water boy. After the game, Halas proposed a one-game play-off of the tie game in Chicago, certain that such a contest would pack Wrigley Field. Snyder demurred because he expected Dutch Clark to be in Colorado coaching the basketball team at Colorado College. Eventually, the Spartans had to face that problem under more significant circumstances.

Neither of the two ties with the Bears directly affected the Spartans, though, of course, victories would have improved their percentage in wins and losses. Actually, the Spartans now had a measure of control over their rank in the standings. If they defeated the Packers at the stadium, their record for determining percentage would be six wins and a loss, or .857; the Packers' record would then be ten wins and two losses, or .833. All would then depend on the Bears-Packers game the following week at Chicago, the last of the season. If the Packers won, the Spartans would

280

If We Had Scored Then

finish as the champions; if the Bears won, they and the Spartans would end the season in a tie for first place, each with six wins and a loss.

As the game approached, Spartan managers looked forward to counting a huge crowd. Sports columnists for the *Times* were billing it as the "Championship Game," the contest for the national championship.[30] The headline on the front page of the *Times* on the day of the game read the "World Grid Title at Stake." "Public spirited" businessmen—operators of a cafeteria, owners of a hardware store, automobile dealers, a restaurateur, an insurance agent, and others—paid for a full-page display advertisement in the *Times* urging all residents to "Boost the Spartans," to "Cheer the Ironmen" in the game to decide the "World Championship." Believing the fervor for the game was running high in a "two hundred mile" radius, the directors expected a throng of twelve thousand or more to press into the stadium. At their request, municipal authorities had patrolmen ready to control traffic around Universal. Also at their request, a local unit of the Ohio National Guard, Battery B, agreed to patrol the fence around the field to deny "sneakers" free entry to the game. Anticipating an overflow crowd, the directors had three rows of temporary seats built in front of the box seats and erected temporary bleachers at one end of the field. To accommodate sportswriters from newspapers in Ohio, Kentucky, West Virginia, and Wisconsin, the largest number ever to cover a game in the Ohio Valley, they refurbished the press box.

Neither team was a decided favorite, and no one, except Potsy Clark, was predicting the outcome. Sports columnists saw the game hinging on the battle between the two backfields, the "best backfields" in the NFL, Clark Hinkle and Johnny Blood leading the Packers, Clark, Presnell, and Gutowski the standard-bearers for the Spartans. One writer narrowed the battle down to Clark and Gutoswski against Hinkle. Spartan fans compared the lines, worried because the Packers outweighed the Spartans seventeen pounds to a man on average.

On the day of battle, like Shakespeare's Henry V, Powers exhorted the Spartans in the name of a community taking to football "like a duck to water" and living it throughout the autumnal season.[31] The gates of the stadium opened early before noon on Sunday, and a great traffic jam developed on the surrounding streets. Soon more than fourteen thousand fans had pushed their way into Universal. Hundreds more lined the floodwall. The butcher, the baker, the candlestick maker, the rich man, the poor man all were at the game, said Wittenburg, all forgetting the Depression and their worries for the moment. Fans at home could listen to a broadcast of the game on WSAZ in Huntington.

Home and Away

In the Spartans' locker room emotions ran high. Coach Clark was tense but ready for the fray, remembering the loss at Green Bay. He and Lambeau had argued heatedly about the officiating, and Lambeau had declared that the Spartans could use their own officials at Portsmouth but still could not beat his Packers. Clark responded that his Spartans, his "ironmen," would demonstrate their strength in defeating the Packers without using substitutes. "Talk is cheap," said Lambeau. True to his word, when Clark sent his starting eleven on to the field, he set his oath before them: "I am going to start eleven men and the only way you're going to come off the field is we have to carry you off."[32] Playing on a dry but windswept field, the Spartans made Clark's word good. Like a trained boxer, Wittenburg wrote, they "crossed, feinted and struck" the mighty Packers. They blocked a punt in the first quarter and went on to score a touchdown, then added touchdowns on Clark's running in the third and fourth quarters to win 19–0. The Packers had a slight edge in yardage gained from scrimmage but could not turn it into touchdowns.

The community exulted in the victory, more for its own sake than for the lead in the standings that it gave the Spartans over the Bears and Packers. After the game, fans crowded into restaurants and hotel lobbies to celebrate. Powers declared in his lead editorial that many years would pass before the memory of the game faded. For the community, the victory went beyond its "wildest dreams," a "great day for Portsmouth."[33] The story of the victory without substitutes did, in fact, become a part of local lore, long enshrined in the community's memory as "the day we beat the Packers." And the game had material benefits, too; the directors were "well pleased" with the financial results.

For the Packers the day lived long as one of humiliation. The Packers acknowledged that the Spartans played an "inspired" game; but Lambeau and Dr. Webber Kelly, a Packers director, explained the loss as a result of an extended road trip that had worn out the players. Kelly and another director, Andrew Turnbull, publisher of the *Green Bay Press-Gazette*, attributed the defeat, in part, to poor officiating that demoralized the players. Conceding that the Spartans were "smart," sportsmen, and well coached, the Packers players and management complained bitterly about the home crowd's behavior, intended, they thought, to intimidate the team. "The mood of that crowd was ugly," said Hinkle years later; "when we got off the team bus, they threw oranges and eggs at us."[34] At the time, Kelly was appalled: "In all my connection with professional football, I never have seen a crowd so unsportsmanlike and insulting as the crowd in Portsmouth. From the moment the Packers arrived at the field until the time they left, they were subjected to a barrage of epithets and collection of abuse which would have taken the heart out of any team. The unfortunate

If We Had Scored Then

attitude was not confined to the male fans, but was general among the women as well."[35] After the game about five hundred fans circled the Packers' bus and razzed the players, reminding them that they were "cheese champions."

The victory moved the Spartans into first place, awaiting the outcome of the Bears-Packers game to be played the following week in Chicago. If the Packers won, the Spartans would claim the league title; if the Bears won, they and the Spartans would complete the schedule in a tie and, presumably, would meet for the championship.

In the meantime, Spartan players and officials were attempting to exploit the team's position as the front-runner in the NFL and prospective champion. Acting independently of management, Lumpkin arranged for the Spartans to play the Giants in a game at Lexington, Kentucky, on the Saturday following their win over the Packers. He had been organizing a barnstorming tour for the team in the South after the regular season.[36] The Giants were coming to Lexington at the behest of alumni of the University of Kentucky who wished to use the game to raise money for a fellow alumnus and Giants back, John "Shipwreck" Kelly, then suffering from heart disease. Charity games of that sort were commonplace in the day. The Spartans had a guarantee of $1,000 and were to receive 40 percent of the gate. The Spartans expected to play the Giants, move on to Maysville for the night, and then drive to Columbus on Sunday to meet the Mendel Tailors in a game arranged by Snyder. Scratching everywhere for chicken feed, Snyder was also considering proposals for games with teams in Des Moines, Memphis, and St. Louis and had scheduled yet another encounter with the Bears to be played as a charity game for the Veterans of Foreign Wars late in December. Because of an ice storm, the Spartans did not play the Giants at Lexington on Saturday, the game being moved to the following Tuesday. Nor did they go to Columbus to meet the Tailors, the weather and a dispute over the gate canceling the date. They waited impatiently, instead, in Portsmouth for news of the Bears-Packers game. Late on Sunday they learned that the Bears had defeated the Packers, 9–0, at snow-covered Wrigley Field. Now they and the Bears shared first place, each with six wins and a loss; the Bears had played to six ties, the Spartans to four.

Even as Snyder and Halas began to consider arrangements for a play-off game the following Sunday, Lumpkin took the Spartans to Lexington to meet the Giants on Tuesday. The game was a mistake for everyone. A crowd of merely three hundred was on hand to see the teams play on the ice-covered field at the University of Kentucky. The Spartans played poorly, losing 18–0, in four shortened quarters. And the charitable alumni took a beating at the box office, turning over little if any money to Kelly.

283

Neville Dunn, a sports columnist for the *Lexington Herald*, complimented the crowd for sticking out the game and the teams for playing it when they could have been home "hugging the fire place."[37] It was "sportsmanlike" for the teams to play, he said, when they could make no money, had no alma mater to love, no coach to die for, no sweetheart to play for.

Probably even before the end of the regular season, Halas and Snyder had agreed to a play-off game for the championship of the league. Never before in the history of the NFL had teams ended scheduled games in a tie, but the owners had always "understood" that a play-off game would follow should that happen. Both clubs needed the money from a game. The Bears, who had always turned a profit, were in the red in 1932 by $18,000 as the Depression cut attendance throughout the league. And, of course, the Spartans were hanging on to solvency by the skin of their teeth. Apparently no one seriously questioned that Chicago would host the game. Obviously the city provided a tremendously larger market than did Portsmouth, and the Bears had much greater prestige than the Spartans. Perhaps Portsmouth, which had drawn a crowd of fourteen thousand for the Packers game, would have been as satisfactory a location as Chicago, especially in view of the problems in staging the game there.

The urgent question was the site of the game in Chicago. In the season's final and crucial game against the Packers, the Bears had drawn only five thousand spectators at Wrigley Field on the snow-swept, frozen field, with the temperature at zero. Snow continued in the hours after the game, and the temperature remained at an arctic level. Halas, fearing that again only a small crowd would brave the elements, proposed that should the frigid weather continue the game be moved indoors, to the Chicago Stadium, where the Bears and Cardinals had played an exhibition game in 1930. Carr and Snyder gave their consent to the proposal, and Bill Veeck Sr., owner of Wrigley Field, agreed to release the Bears from a contract requiring them to play all home games there.[38] As late as Wednesday a ground crew was preparing Wrigley for the game.[39] Then on Thursday, three days before the game, after "huddling" with Clark, who had arrived in Chicago with the Spartans, and feeling the wintry blasts still striking the city, Halas decided to go to the stadium.[40] According to the *Chicago Tribune,* players on both team gave their "unanimous" consent to the decision.[41]

Opened in 1929 on the near west side as a hockey and boxing arena, the Chicago Stadium could accommodate about sixteen thousand spectators.[42] Beyond seating capacity, it was hardly a suitable site for a football game. At its greatest length, the field for play was barely eighty yards long, fifty yards wide. As it turned out, a punt

If We Had Scored Then

could reach the ceiling rafters, and the cement floor below obviously required a protective covering. Fortunately, only a few days before the game, a circus had given a benefit performance for the Salvation Army necessitating the spreading of about six inches of dirt over the floor.[43] Halas had tanbark, wood shavings, and sod to cover the dirt. Though affording protection to the players, the surface was so loose that they could not get traction or quickly change directions while running.

To render the stadium even remotely receptive to football, the Bears and Spartans had to force the field into its inflexible confines. They laid out the field sixty yards from goal line to goal line, with yard markers lined out every five yards, the thirty-yard line becoming in effect the midfield stripe. Surrounding the arena was a twelve-foot wooden fence running straight down the sidelines and in arc through the corners at the end zones, which thus became half-moon in their shape. Because the fence directly abutted or even was in the end zone, the goal post—only one went up—was placed on the goal line. Despite the reduction of the field to about forty-seven yards in width, the fence was only about fifteen feet from the sidelines.

Obviously the teams had to play under rules dictated by space. Halas, Snyder, and Clark learned from the example of the Bears-Cardinals game played at the stadium in 1930, a charity contest intended to raise funds for distribution to the unemployed in Cook County.[44] Kickoffs in 1930 came from the goal line; now they would come from the ten-yard line. As in 1930, players could not attempt drop-kicks or place-kicks for field goals. In 1930, to make the field theoretically one hundred yards long from goal line to goal line, after a team received a kickoff, it had to move the ball back twenty yards, and after reaching the midfield stripe it had to move it back another twenty yards. The Bears and Spartans set the rule aside. Evidently rules in 1930 and 1932 governing punts were about the same. With the rafters of the stadium ninety-four feet above the playing surface, Halas and Clark did not expect punted balls to reach them. In the event that they did, as with touchbacks, the ball would be placed at the ten-yard line. As a matter of fact, during the pregame practice, a Portsmouth punter struck the organist perched on a rafter with a punt, and during the game Dick Nesbitt of the Bears punted a ball nearly straight up into a rafter. The wooden fence along the sidelines called for an improvised rule of lasting import, one not employed in 1930. Ordinarily, following a play, the ball was placed where the play ended, and when a play went out-of-bounds, the ball went to a point one yard from the sideline. To reduce the danger of players colliding with the fence, the stadium rule called for the ball to be moved fifteen yards in-bounds, with the loss of a down, following an out-of-bounds play, thus creating an imaginary hash mark.[45] No rules could deal with the odor left by the circus. One spectator complained that it "was a little too aromatic, what with the horses and elephants that had traipsed around there a few days before the game."[46]

The Bears and Spartans faced the same conditions. Howard Roberts, a sportswriter for the *Chicago News,* and Lou Diamond of the *Chicago Times* thought as a lighter team the Spartans reduced the advantage that the heavier Bears would have had on a frozen field.[47] But the Spartans entered the game under two distinct handicaps. Before the season began, Dutch Clark had accepted the position of head basketball coach at his alma mater, Colorado College, with the understanding that he would take up his duties as soon as the Spartans had played out their schedule. The president of Colorado insisted that Clark, who already was disenchanted with the Spartans, meet his contractual obligation; Clark complied and did not come to Chicago. Lumpkin declared, nonetheless, that "we'll beat them without Clark." Additionally, because of injuries and expenses, the Spartan management brought only sixteen players to Chicago instead of the twenty-two permitted under league rules. Few substitutes would be available to spell weary players.

On the eve of the game, Roberts prophesied that it would drive professional football in a profound way. The Bears and Spartans, two "great" teams with the "finest" players from the collegiate ranks, could give fans an exciting, well-played game. It would, he said, test Grange's assumption that large crowds would attend night games.[48] Like most sports columnists, he believed that the heavier Bears would eventually overpower the Spartans in a high-scoring contest, the shortened field giving the offense an advantage over the defense.

The Bears ran from the T, the Spartans in their usual single wing, with an unbalanced line to the right, in a tense, hard-fought, low-scoring game decided in the end by a controversial play. Contrary to Roberts's prediction, seemingly the compression of the stadium field made the Bears' and Spartans' defenses even stronger. Pass receivers had less room in which to maneuver, and the overhanging mezzanine may have inhibited passing. In the first half, the Spartans had at least a slight edge over the Bears. Twice they came close to the Bears' goal line only to be turned back. Late in the second quarter, they reached the Bears' six-yard line on fourth down. Over fifty years later, Presnell still regretted but did not lament what happened: "Our favorite play was a fake end run where I would plant my foot and cut off tackle. We ran that on fourth down. Just as the hole opened, I tried to plant my foot, slipped and fell. If we had scored then, it might have been a different game."[49]

The second half saw the Bears wearing the Spartans down but unable to score. Then five minutes into the fourth quarter, Gutowski threw a pass from deep in

If We Had Scored Then

Spartan territory. Nesbitt intercepted it and returned the ball to the seven-yard line before a Spartan defender knocked him out-of-bounds. On the first play from scrimmage, actually second down because the ball was brought in-bounds fifteen yards, Nagurski smashed six yards through the Spartan line, then lost one on third down. The Spartan line massed, expecting Nagurski to charge again bull-like on fourth down. And as before, Brumbaugh handed the ball off to Nagurski, who ran forward but then retreated a step or so and lobbed a short pass to Grange in the end zone for a touchdown. Potsy Clark stormed on to the field in protest, arguing that Nagurski had not been five yards behind the line of scrimmage when he threw the pass, as required by the rules. Bobby Cahn, the referee, refused to reverse the call, and the touchdown stood.[50] The Bears forced a safety later in the quarter and won 9–0. Just after the game, Emerson, the Spartan guard, complained to sportswriters that Nagurski "wasn't five yards back of the line! It was an illegal play! He wasn't five yards back!"[51] Emerson had the same memory of the play more than sixty years later.[52] Wager was still insisting decades later that he had his hands on Nagurski near the line of scrimmage when he passed.[53] Interestingly, Wittenburg, who called the contest the "Tom Thumb" game because of the dimensions of the field, took no note of the alleged infraction in his story, and not until late in the week did more Spartan players raise the issue, and then only in mutters.[54]

The game did not prove a sovereign remedy for the Bears' and Spartans' financial ills. About twelve thousand spectators were in attendance, and gross receipts were approximately $15,000.[55] With each winning player receiving $240 and each losing player $175, and with operating expenses of the game to be met, neither club cleared enough to escape a drenching in red ink for 1932. Returning to Portsmouth, the Spartans received an obligatory reception in their honor, a "football party" attended by three hundred fans. Momentarily, they and their fans took consolation from a report in the *Times* saying that league officials regarded the Bears and Spartans as co-champions—that the game in Chicago was not a title game. According to Powers, the publicity director of the league issued the announcement without saying anything about the game at the stadium.[56] Why, asked Powers, had the league owners led fans and players to believe that it was a title game, not the "synthetic affair" that it was. Though pleased that someone had recognized the truth, he saw the so-called play-off game as a sad commentary on the "looseness" of the NFL. But at their annual meeting two months later, the owners formally awarded the championship to the Bears.[57]

At that meeting, the owners gave clear expression, as they never had before, to the experience of one game—the play-off game—adopting three new rules that moved professional football in a different direction, giving greater strength to the offense.[58] Citing in ambiguous language the rules of collegiate football, they approved a rule moving the ball on out-of-bounds play ten yards in-bounds to hash marks without charging a down to the offensive team. The change reduced the inflexibility of play calling at the sideline. Obviously taking note of the disputed pass at Chicago, the owners voted for a rule permitting a forward pass from anywhere from behind the line of scrimmage. Halas, reminiscing on his life in professional football, asserted that it was a fundamental force in changing the game.[59] The owners also adopted a rule placing the goal posts on the goal lines, a proposal they had rejected in 1932. Taken together, these changes dramatically increased scoring and significantly reduced the number of ties. Later in 1933, George Preston Marshall, owner of the Boston Braves, arguing that play-off games created great interest among the fans, the "masses," persuaded the owners to organize eastern and western divisions of the NFL, the winners of the divisions to play each other for the league championship.[60]

The Spartans still had a few games to play beyond their regular season. They journeyed to Redland Field the day after Christmas to meet the Bears again, the fourth time in the year, in a game scheduled earlier by Snyder. Before a meager crowd of two thousand, the teams played their third tie, 6–6. Then fifteen Spartans prepared for Lumpkin's barnstorming tour. They knew, they said, that they could not easily find off-season employment so they would play football as long as possible, even under straitened circumstances. They first met the Dallas Rangers in Dallas early in January, with a crowd of about five thousand in attendance. Playing the first half under rules of 1932, the second half by rules from the 1920s, the Spartans defeated the Rangers 21–0. Lumpkin starred, giving the fans a "glimpse" of the way fullbacks played in the NFL. Presnell passed with accuracy. A week later, they ended the season with a win in Oklahoma City over the Oklahoma Chiefs, 13–7, before a crowd of three thousand. Playing for the Chiefs was Grange, perpetually a barnstormer. The players then scattered to the four winds. Presnell, McKalip, Christensen, and Ebding played on an all-star team that met the Packers in a charity game at Kansas City in January. Several could read press clippings about their selection to all-pro teams. Clark and Lumpkin were named to the official All-NFL first team, Christensen and Bodenger to the second team. Clark, Lumpkin, and Emerson had berths on the first team selected by the United Press, Christensen and Presnell on the second team.

13

The League Wants Larger Cities

IF THEIR SEASONS OF 1931 and 1932 meant anything, the Spartans of 1933 could look forward to another successful year. They had come tantalizingly Sisyphean-close to league championships in each year, a yard here and there, a point now and then separating them from the prize. If the directors and coach could sustain the roster of 1932, surely the players could post a good record; they were not graybeards—not one was yet thirty years old—and presumably the experience of 1932 would serve them well. Probably the directors were as concerned about keeping them paid and on the field as they were about their performance.

At the tag end of the season in 1932, Spartans fans were becoming apprehensive over a report that Potsy Clark was looking for another coaching berth.[1] Undoubtedly, he was concerned about the stability of the franchise. Certainly his record at Portsmouth might commend him to colleges or other professional clubs seeking a new mentor. Reportedly, he did receive some offers. If the directors proffered him a contract at that time, he kept them and fans waiting

Home and Away

in the wings. Not until well into the spring of 1933 did he accept a contract, again at a salary of $5,000.

That spring, the *Times* columnists, anticipating the coming season, were peppering their readers with reports about the players. They especially continued to find Father Lumpkin a colorful figure. Football player and sometime wrestler and boxer, he had written or taken credit for writing a limerick:

> A lonesome fellow named Pratt,
> Sat down near a mule for a chat;
> When he woke up in bed
> A day later he said,
> Well, I sure got a kick out of that.[2]

He was the subject of an old chestnut in one of Minego's columns. Asked about the state of his mind during an examination for insurance, he replied, "Oh, just leave that blank." The players had taken up a variety of activities in the off-season. Several remained in athletic pursuits. Lumpkin, George Christensen, and Andy Rascher were all appearing on wrestling cards in and around Portsmouth. Maury Bodenger was a physical education instructor in a Jewish boys' camp. Gene Alford was playing minor league baseball in Texas, and Dutch Clark was coaching basketball at Colorado College. Others were preparing for a life out of sports. Presnell was taking a graduate course in education at the University of Nebraska, and Ox Emerson was a student at the University of Texas. Clare Randolph had already hung up his shingle as a lawyer. A few were simply in catch-as-catch-can employment. John Cavosie was working in a lumber camp in Montana, "cutting little trees out of big trees." "Popeye" Wager was driving a truck delivering film.

Once Clark signed his contract, he set himself to the task of building the Spartans' roster. He, the directors, and the fans all were concerned about whether Dutch Clark would be in uniform again. At the close of the season in 1932, he had left the Spartans to take up his coaching duties in Colorado while his teammates met the Bears for the championship. At the time, he had also said that he might quit professional football altogether for basketball. Coach Clark was in touch with him throughout the spring attempting to persuade him to remain with the Spartans. Then in June he signed a contract to become the head football coach at the Colorado School of Mines. And he also took on Bill McKalip as a line coach. No problems attended the signing of Lumpkin. Before Clark took his leave, he walked into the Spartans' office and signed, declaring that he started with Portsmouth and would end with Portsmouth. "Football players get better treatment in Portsmouth," he told Potsy

The League Wants Larger Cities

Clark, "than in any other city in the loop and under present conditions you should not have any trouble signing any of the old boys or new ones." Whether by "present conditions" he meant the state of the franchise or national affairs he did not specify. Lumpkin and fans believed that if Clark did not return to the Spartans, the fullback might become a halfback, "lugging" the ball more often and running as a blocking back less often.

Lumpkin was correct on the matter of signing players old and new. Of the seventeen "ironmen" on the roster at the close of the season, Clark decided to offer contracts to fifteen; all signed with the exception of Clark and McKalip. Eventually, including old players, new men who signed contracts, and men who tried out without contracts, Clark had twenty-seven candidates for the team at the outset of practices. At one point in the summer, he had expected at least forty men to be on hand. But as many as nineteen who said that they would be reporting for practices—many who had not signed contracts—did not report. Minego believed that "evil influences" were at work, that other clubs were tampering with the prospective players.[3] All of the thirteen old players signing contracts survived Clark's cuts. Nine new players were on the roster for at least one or two games, eight for the entire season. Probably the outstanding men among them were Ernie Caddel, a halfback from Stanford, Elmer "Dutch" Schaake, a hard-running fullback out of the University of Kansas, and John Schneller, a tough guard from the University of Wisconsin.

Attending the owners' meeting in Chicago in July, Clark, Selby, and Snyder—Snyder in particular—arranged a schedule similar in structure to those of 1931 and 1932. The Spartans would play twelve league games, beginning with three games at home, four on the road—three on an eastern swing—come home for one game, go on the road for two more, and conclude the season with two home games. Surprisingly, with two minor exceptions, they were able to adhere to the proposed schedule. Powers editorially applauded it, saying that it would end the "stove league" speculation on what teams the Spartans would be playing and again turn Portsmouth into a "football mad" community.[4] Wittenburg seconded his editor. Snyder, he believed, had not fared as well in previous years when the "big city dudes" had snookered the small town. But now, like little Jack Horner in the corner, he had obtained juicy meat in getting four good home games. In fact, though, the schedule had five "good" home games.

Certainly the Spartans would be playing in a different kind of league. The Stapletons had withdrawn from the league, and three new clubs had entered—the Philadelphia Eagles, the Pittsburgh Pirates, and the Cincinnati Reds. Now ten teams in two divisions, the eastern and western divisions, composed the league. Along with the

Home and Away

Pirates, Packers, Bears, and Cardinals, the Spartans were in the western division but would play four teams in the eastern division. Of special interest to the Spartan directors were the Reds, whose admission they supported. Powers argued that games between the Spartans and Reds would stimulate interest in professional football in southern Ohio, resulting in good attendance at Portsmouth and Cincinnati.[5] Powers, though, did not approve of the Spartans' support of Carr, whom the owners returned to the presidency of the league; he would continue, Powers feared, the loose administration of the league that had damaged the Spartans in the past.

Divining the signs around them, Spartan managers were sanguine about the coming season. They believed that they had a good team going into a good schedule. Economic conditions in the city seemed to be improving in the wake of the New Deal. They had to be optimistic on learning that employment in the local steel plants, now fifty-four hundred, had reached the highest point since the end of the war, and they could take heart, too, as they read Wittenburg's columns asserting that interest in football in Portsmouth was at an unprecedented level. Anticipating an increase in attendance of 30 percent, they had a new bleacher erected to accommodate three thousand spectators and had a new box office built at the entrance to the stadium. So that the crowd could more easily hear the loudspeaker, they installed a five-foot horn in the speaker system. They hoped to attract more fans by other means, arranging for a local drum corps to entertain the crowd at all games. They ordered new uniforms, staying with the Northwestern purple of the past but changing the solid purple stockings to ones with white stripes.

The Spartans opened practices early in September on a buoyant note. Players reporting from out of town were optimistic and in good spirit. Buster Mitchell was "raring" to go. Because he wanted to "mingle" with his "old buddies," Emerson had willingly left his good business in Houston. Lumpkin infused all with his Brobding-nagian spirit and imbibition. A bartender asking him what size glass he wanted when he "angled" into a "suds emporium" (Prohibition had ended) to "blow off foam," Lumpkin demanded the "biggest glass you have," received a mug with 118 ounces of beer in it, and promptly "sluiced his way through the amber fluid."

Physically as well as emotionally, players arrived in the city ready to practice. At signing men, Clark, a stickler for conditioning, instructed them to begin a training program—to play baseball and tennis, to box, wrestle, swim, or row, and to run two or three miles a day. He wanted them to work out under the boiling sun because he expected the first two or three games to be played in hot weather. Whether or not they followed his regimen, apparently nearly all were in good condition when practices began. Clark put them through rigorous sessions from the start, allowing no respite for "leg-weary" players. Often in scrimmages, he had two teams, the veterans and the rookies, playing each other. The rookies were "good, bad, and indifferent" in their play; the bad and indifferent were soon released. Among those who performed well and made the squad were Caddel, Schaake, Schneller, Raney Hunter, and "Big Jim" Bowdoin. Schaake, thought Minego, ran as a halfback "a la Dutch Clark." Indicative of interest in the Spartans, good crowds, one nearly three thousand, came out for the scrimmages, paying ten to twenty-five cents for admission to sessions at the stadium.

 The Spartans began the season with a nonleague road game against the Indianapolis Indians, a newly organized independent team. Playing essentially a practice game but receiving a guarantee and a percentage of the gate, which was not substantial, the Spartans toyed with the Indians, beating them 19–0. Their true opening game was against the Cincinnati Reds at Universal. The Reds, a fledgling team, worked their "hearts off" in practice, seeking to give the Spartans a "surprise."[6] Their labor was in vain. Before a crowd of five thousand, hundreds from out of town, sweltering in the heat, the Spartans dispatched the Reds 21–0, their veterans and rookies seemingly working well together.

The Spartans' first real test came the next week when the Giants came to Portsmouth. The Giants, rebuilding after a poor season, had acquired Ken Strong from the Stapletons and Harry Newman, an excellent passer who had starred at the University of Michigan. Newman, the Giants correctly believed, could exploit the new rule permitting passing from any point from behind the line of scrimmage. In various ways, the Spartan managers attempted to fan interest in the game. They arranged for the players of both teams to appear in a downtown parade, riding in automobiles preceded by the high school band. They managed to get Presnell and Newman on a radio program aired by WLW in Cincinnati, then a station commanding a national audience with its power of fifty thousand watts and its so-called clear channel; the adversaries shared with listeners their views on the art of the forward pass. The Spartans also sent passes to the game to nearly every football coach in the Tri-State.[7]

The game drew a crowd of about seven thousand, good-sized but not as large as those coming to "crucial" games in 1931 and 1932. With Bodenger leading them on defense and Presnell on offense, the Spartans won 17–7. Bodenger nearly scored after intercepting one of Newman's passes, and Presnell ran fifty-five yards from scrimmage for a touchdown. In rushing and passing yardage, the Spartans outgained the Giants 303 yards to 138. Nonetheless, Steve Owen, the Giants' coach, ascribed his team's defeat, in part, to the officials' bad calls. Giving the Giants one of

Home and Away

but three losses that they would suffer in capturing the championship of the eastern division, the Spartans seemed on their way to a banner season.

The Spartans closed their home stand with the Cardinals in a game that nearly became a free-for-all, a clear reminder of the rough play in their contest of 1932. Joe Lillard, the black star, was still playing for the Cardinals, a potential lightning rod for more trouble. The irascible Dr. Jones had sold the Cardinals to Charles Bidwell. Saying that the players needed "verbal" encouragement against the tough Cardinals, the Spartans' managers called on fans to flock to the stadium. Lumpkin was out with injuries for the first time since 1929—the trainer was covering him with 443,542 yards of tape—so the Spartans expected a close game. Their fans, remembering the game of 1932 and looking for a point or so to decide the contest, came to Universal in good numbers, about seven thousand.

The game was indeed close, the Spartans winning 7–6, a "delicious victory morsel." As in 1932, the play and the score became almost incidental to the wrangling and fighting on the field. Both teams were "pugnacious" throughout the game. Pup Graham, now with the Cardinals, cudgeled Spartans on several occasions and continuously threatened to "erupt pugistically." The contentious play reached a crescendo late in the fourth quarter when Emerson and Walt Kiesling, a Cardinal guard, engaged in a spirited boxing and wrestling joust. Excited spectators rushed on to the field, and "American bobbies," clubs in hand, followed them to quell the hubbub. Belligerent fans in the stand argued among themselves and staged several set-tos.[8] If Dr. Jones had still owned the Cardinals and been present, surely he would have been a combatant.

Lillard was not expected to be at the center or the object of any scuffling, but the editor of the *Times* implied that racial prejudice was at work throughout the game. Local sportswriters did not hesitate to use racial allusions in describing Lillard. He was the "dark menace," the "ebony hued bird in the Red Bird covey" who "darted and swooped about the Universal gridiron as unerringly as a falcon and as dangerously as an eagle." Fortunately for the Spartans, Emerson blocked his attempt to drop-kick the extra point, thus preserving the Spartans' victory, 7–6.

Distressed by what he saw at Universal, Powers used a lead editorial to reprove the Cardinals and Spartans. Professional football, he wrote, had long had a questionable reputation because of rough play and poor sportsmanship. Recently, though, young men had elevated its reputation by their obvious love of the competition and willingness to rely on the game for a living. But Sunday the teams had given critics of the sport ample material for complaining about its roughness and squinted sportsmanship. If the Cardinals and Spartans could not play a clean game, if their

The League Wants Larger Cities

lines could not charge without slugging, if they could not tackle cleanly, perhaps they should not play each other again in the city. Many residents had come to know the Spartan players as a "fine group of college men" but now were disappointed by their behavior on the gridiron. By their conduct, the Spartans and Cardinals had shortchanged the fans. In venting their personal feeling and racial prejudices, they had given a "distinctly inferior brand of football" to the "people who paid hard-earned money for their tickets."[9] Fans wanted to see good football; they could take in alley-fighting and boxing matches at other times. Harsh as his words were, they did not elicit protests or apologies from any quarter in the community.

Undefeated in three games at home, the Spartans prepared for a long road trip to Green Bay and to the East for league games that would test their mettle. They also expected to play some nonleague games on the eastern swing. Before leaving for Green Bay, they took a midweek side trip to Huntington to play the Mendel Tailors. They drew a good crowd, three thousand, and "clowned" around after piling up an insurmountable lead, eventually winning 45–0. They returned to Portsmouth for a day and then boarded their Greyhound bus for the journey to Green Bay, with a small group of fans driving their automobiles to the city.[10] At Green Bay, the Spartans met a Packer squad destined for a poor season but still fuming over the loss to the Spartans in 1932. On a rain-swept field, with a small crowd of three thousand in the stands, the Packers decisively outplayed the Spartans for a victory, 17–0. The gate was not good for either team, especially for the Packers, then in the throes of a financial crisis occasioned by a civil suit brought against them by a fan injured in a fall from wooden bleachers at City Stadium.

From Green Bay, the Spartans returned to Portsmouth and then began the long eastern swing. They were on the road for nearly four weeks playing three league and two nonleague games. First they played the Boston Redskins, formerly the Braves, at Fenway Park before a big crowd of twenty thousand. As the reporter for the *New York Times* described the game, the Spartans won it on the right arm and right leg of Presnell, who passed for a touchdown and kicked two field goals for a win, 13–0.[11] The Spartans were then in second place in the western division, a half game behind the undefeated Bears. Three days later, they played the Eagles at Baker Bowl. In front of a small crowd of thirty-five hundred, Presnell again led the Spartans' attack, his passing, running, and kicking accounting for three scores in the victory, 25–0.

The Spartans met sterner opposition or eased up in their next game, a midweek "exhibition tilt" against the Presidents of Shenandoah, a coal-mining town in northeastern Pennsylvania. They received a guarantee of $500 and a share of the gate, which evidently was satisfactory. A crowd of sixty-five hundred tested the capacity

Home and Away

of the stands to see the visitors' "million dollar backfield." The teams fought to a tie, 7–7, the Spartans coming out of the contest with five men sidelined by injuries.[12] They had two more games tentatively scheduled for the next four days, one against an eleven in Bridgeport, Connecticut, the other against a team in Paterson, New Jersey. Unforeseen circumstances, luck, or good sense prevailing, the Spartans or their opponents canceled the games. The Spartans did go on to Staten Island the following Sunday to play the Stapletons in an exhibition game. Local fans, perhaps recalling other games between the teams, turned out in a fairly large number, about six thousand, and saw Presnell again decide the issue, scoring a touchdown with an intercepted pass to give the Spartans the win, 14–7.[13]

Crossing the Narrows and going on to Manhattan, the Spartans prepared to meet the Giants the next Sunday in a crucial game for both teams. They had expected to play the Dodgers in midweek, but the teams' officials, unable to agree on the split of the gate, canceled the game. For the Spartans, the Giants game was memorably unhappy. Through three quarters, the home crowd of fifteen thousand sitting cheerlessly at the Polo Grounds, they dominated play, Presnell's eighty-one-yard run and a field goal giving them the lead, 10–0, going into the fourth quarter. The Giants, wrote Allison Danzig of the *New York Times*, had met their master in "attack, defense, kicking, blocking and passing."[14] Then in the fourth quarter, Presnell went to the bench with an injury, and the Giants, playing like tigers and with Newman leading them, scored two touchdowns in six minutes and won 13–10. Never before had the Spartans lost a game after entering the fourth quarter ahead by a touchdown or more. Snyder attributed the defeat to an official's bad call, but his complaint fell on deaf ears in New York and Portsmouth. Measured by the record—three league wins and a loss—the Spartans had enjoyed a successful road trip, but that hardly assuaged the pain of the loss at the Polo Grounds. Fortunately, the Bears lost their first game that day; the Spartans remained a half game behind them at five wins and two losses.

Returning to Portsmouth, the Spartans could not conceal the pall of defeat from the fans gathered to greet them. And they could not hide their injuries—Cavosie with a twisted ankle, Presnell a sore shoulder, Gutowski a discolored eye, Emerson a sprained ankle.[15] But with the Packers coming to the stadium for an important game, they could not dwell long on dark thoughts. Playing before a large crowd, nine thousand, the teams fought on even terms, the Spartans reportedly demonstrating "smart" football. In the third quarter, Presnell threw a short pass to Caddel for a touchdown, and the Spartans made it stand up for the win, 7–0. Either bearing in mind Powers's recent strictures or wary of the fourth official, evidently the

The League Wants Larger Cities

Spartans avoided roughhouse tactics, and the home crowd, though animated, did not offer insults to the visitors, as it had in 1932. Lambeau thought that the game was the cleanest and best officiated of the season.

Having defeated the Packers, the Spartans had a record of six wins and two losses and were half a game behind the Bears in the western division, their record at six wins, a loss, and a tie. They were in position for a run at the championship, for next they faced the Reds, seemingly easy prey, and then the Bears in two consecutive games, one in Chicago, one in Portsmouth. Going into the game at Redland Field, the Spartans were confident of victory, Presnell recalled years later.[16] Spartan fans, taking Norfolk and Western cars to Cincinnati, saw the game as a lark. They were more interested in taking lunch and dinner at the new Union Station in Cincinnati, a marvelous rendering of art deco.

Probably their lunches turned acidic at Redland. In a crowd of seven thousand, the largest in the short history of professional football in Cincinnati, they saw the Reds turn two Spartan fumbles in the second quarter into a touchdown and a field goal for a lead of 10–0. The Spartans threatened the Reds' goal line throughout much of the second half but could score only one touchdown. The Reds halted them with interceptions and a fumble recovery at their own two-yard line and won 10–7. Usually forgiving, fans of the Spartans denounced them for their "apathetic," "amateurish" play. On their return to Portsmouth, the players were a "sickly looking bunch of big league football players" who would have preferred "sneaking" through the city to facing their fans.[17] Presnell later blamed the loss on overconfidence. Clark exercised more forbearance than the fans, simply noting that fumbles and a sluggish start were costly. The Bears also lost that Sunday, 3–0 to the Giants, leaving the Spartans still half a game back.

Clark knew that it would be inappropriate for him to scold the players. They still had two games with the Bears, and they were not likely to make a good showing if they saw that everyone's hand was against them. If they won the first contest, they would take over first place but would have to defeat the Bears in the second game to capture the championship of the western division. Clark did not, of course, let them off easily in their preparations for the Bears. He had them go through two strenuous practices each all week before the first game, giving special attention to shutting down the Bears' aerial attack. The Spartans did improve their play and led the Bears 14–10 with about five minutes to play, the crowd of ten thousand at Wrigley ready to accept their team's first loss at home in 1933. Then the Bears recovered a blocked punt, and Nagurski ran twenty-nine yards from scrimmage for the touchdown that defeated the Spartans 17–14. They ascribed their loss primarily

Home and Away

to the "brilliant" play of Bill Hewitt. The "battered" Spartans were "deeply grieved" and "bitterly disappointed."[18] They were out of the race for the title and had lost three of their last four games, each by three points, two in the last quarter.

Despite or because of the loss, Clark was in a "lenient mood" and had the Spartans go through light drills before their return game against the Bears in Portsmouth. They did work rigorously on ways to blunt Hewitt's defensive charges. Regaining their composure, the Spartans were "full of fight," determined to make the Bears pay for the victory a week earlier. Their fans, also confident, came to Universal in large numbers, about seven thousand. On a soggy field, the Bears won again. Hewitt continued to be a "source of annoyance," and the Bears' "aerial bombs" produced two touchdowns for the victory, 17–7. Probably equally annoying to the Spartans was the failure of their managers to pay them after the game. At about this time, the directors began to force the players to accept shares of stock in lieu of payments in cash. The practice said much about the financial exigencies of the corporation.

The Spartans could still clinch second place in the western division if they defeated the Pittsburgh Pirates in the final game of the season. Somewhere along the line, Snyder, looking to expand the Spartans' following, arranged for the team to play it at Red Bird Stadium in Columbus as a charity affair for local newsboys. Probably the hand of Joe Carr, a resident of Columbus, was at play. Season ticket holders could use their tickets for admission. Hundreds of dyed-in-the-wool fans expected to come to Columbus. The Spartans practiced at Aquinas High School on Saturday and looked forward to playing before a big crowd the next day. But an ice storm struck Columbus, covering the field with six inches of snow and ice. Art Rooney of the Pirates and Snyder called the game off but discussed playing it the next Wednesday or Sunday. Snyder believed that the weather would still prevent play on Wednesday, and Spartan players complained that they had already made plans for a barnstorming tour in the South and Midwest to begin the following Sunday. They were already in a contentious mood, having not received their pay for the Bears game. Snyder finally agreed to cancel the game.[19]

Thus the Spartans ended their season on an unhappy note. With six wins and five losses, they finished second in the western division. But they could look at three losses by three points and speculate on what might have been if they had scored from the one-yard line against the Giants in New York, if the Bears had not blocked a punt in Chicago, if they had not fumbled against the Reds in Cincinnati, or if Dutch Clark had been in the lineup. Ironically, Clark would soon be talking to the Spartan people about returning to the team.[20] He had found coaching at the Colorado school to be "irksome" and saw no future there, especially with the collapse of the conference to which his team belonged. He knew, too, that the Spartans, seeing him as a "draw," were eager for him to return.

The Spartans could take a measure of solace in the composition of the several all-star teams selected at the end of the season. Potsy Clark named Emerson and Presnell to his mythical eleven. Grange placed Presnell, Christensen, and Emerson on his all-pro team; the United Press had the same men and Ebding on its team; and the official All-NFL squad included Presnell.[21] Fans took pride in learning later that Presnell led the league in rushing yardage and finished second to Newman in passing yardage.

The game with the Pirates canceled, the Spartans were nearly ready for their barnstorming tour. Lumpkin served as their press agent and business manager. For a while, they considered beginning it in Portsmouth, meeting an Ironton team coached by Shorty Davies, but they and Davies could not come to a satisfactory arrangement. Then Lumpkin "hopped into his pet rod" and like a carnival barker drove off to North Carolina and Tennessee to announce the coming of the Spartans. For about three weeks, the players were on the road picking up "soft alfalfa," as the *Times* put it, playing before crowds ranging from two hundred to five thousand in Johnson City, Charlotte, Omaha, Lincoln, and Oklahoma City; they won four games and tied one, the scores usually lopsided—44–23, 40–6, 42–7.[22] At the close of the tour, Caddel, Ebding, and Presnell joined an all-star eleven on the Pacific Coast to play the Bears in exhibition games for charity. The Bears defeated the all-stars in games at Los Angeles and San Francisco, 21–7 and 23–0.

As the Spartans completed the tour, their directors and fans were discussing whether the franchise would remain in Portsmouth. Early in December, Naylor Stone, sports editor of the *Cincinnati Post*, had first broached the subject. The Reds, he reported, had gone through a "lean year" at the ledger, and a group of St. Louis men wished to acquire their franchise. He added ominous news: "And this may be the last year Portsmouth will have the Spartans. Columbus and Indianapolis want in the league and are talking terms with owners of the Spartans. They say a crowd of 7,000 is tops in Portsmouth. The league wants larger cities."[23] In light of later reports, certainly fans in the city knew throughout December that their Spartans were under the auctioneer's gavel. As evidenced by their failure to pay the players after the second Bears game, the directors were again facing financial problems, if not a crisis. Clark, all knew, was looking at other berths, among them the positions of head coach at Yale and Dartmouth. On New Year's Day in 1934, Minego noted in his column that local fans were awaiting the directors'

decision about the Spartans. Snyder had been in Pittsburgh, Detroit, and New York talking to individuals and groups interested in the Spartans' franchise, and everyone knew that he was eager to place the team on a solid footing in 1934.

Rumors about the fate of the Spartans flew about for the next few weeks. One had several businessmen in Detroit "not adverse" to taking over the franchise "bag and baggage."[24] Groups in other cities evidently also had their eyes on the Spartans. In an interview with Wittenburg, Snyder revealed that "capitalists" in New York City were eager to acquire them.[25] The directors, he said, could not continue on financial tenterhooks as in the past; unless local individuals or groups could offer substantial backing, they had to sell the club. They did not want to sell, but a city the size of Portsmouth could hardly support a franchise in the NFL. The fans were admirably loyal, but their number was simply too small to provide guarantees of $4,000 and $5,000 to the Bears and Packers, as well as a share of the gate. The Spartans received similar guarantees in other cities but where the crowds were much larger. The size of the city, he argued, not the Depression, was the problem. According to Snyder, losses in the ledger had a pronounced effect on the quality of play. If the Spartans had sufficient local support, the morale of players would rise, and, of greater importance, management could sign leading collegiate players because nearly all preferred living in small communities. The Spartans had lost such players as Hewitt and Jack Manders of the Bears because the corporation could not offer them salaries that were sufficiently high and certain. Moreover, Clark would not long remain under such precarious conditions; indeed, already he had offers from other league teams. Snyder did not explain away the Spartans' success on the field and signing of some excellent football players.

Following Snyder's statements, the directors and fans "huddled" to discuss the Spartans' problems, but no one offered a realistic solution. Though he expected to become the business manager of the franchise if it moved east, Snyder insisted that he preferred that it remain in Portsmouth.[26] Charlie Bidwell, the new owner of the Cardinals, opened the door to a means of staving off losses when, at 4:00 in the morning, he called Snyder offering to buy Dutch Clark at a remarkably high price; neither Snyder nor the other directors would consider such a measure, a holding step at best. Reportedly, several eastern businessmen were about to purchase the franchise and locate it in Newark.[27] Shortly thereafter, Snyder spent a few days in New York City, returned to Portsmouth, and announced that he would go to New York again, stay a few more days, and return to Portsmouth with something "definite" to say about the situation.

But Snyder said nothing for nearly two months. Then late in March, the death

The League Wants Larger Cities

watch for the Spartans truly began. Snyder had gone to Detroit, and there a syndicate headed by George Richards, owner of WJR, the largest radio station in the city, and several other moguls offered to buy the Spartans. Snyder had conferred with Carr and arranged a meeting of the Spartan directors to consider the proposal.[28] The directors met a few days after Snyder returned from Detroit and accepted the offer subject to the stockholders' approval at a meeting to be held in about two weeks. Snyder did not publicly reveal the selling price but did say that the Detroit people intended to retain Clark as coach and nearly all the players, who were the principal assets of the corporation.

At Snyder's announcement, no one in the community called for a mass rally to consider means of saving the Spartans or for a subscription drive. Fans seemed resigned to seeing the franchise go. In Minego's view, the "old guard" had given up the cause long before Snyder brought the "news from Ghent," but only after a prolonged effort. "'Twas a battle, fellows, a battle."[29] At least the loyal fans could say that for a season or so they had seen great football. Now, some lamented, they would have to go to Cincinnati to see "big time" football. Halas, though, held out the possibility of his Bears coming to Portsmouth to play the Reds. Some fans saw the prospect of lower-level professional football in the city. According to Minego, one group approached Lumpkin with a proposal that he organize a semiprofessional team for the community. He preferred to play in Detroit. Perhaps, said Minego, the city would return to Tri-State football. It was not as "flossy" or as colorful but was a "thousand times cheaper." Fans now began to give their attention to the question of what Spartans would go to Detroit. Minego believed that the Detroit men would effect "radical" changes and that some of the Spartans, having slowed down "precipitously," would not play in the "big show."[30]

The directors did not expect the stockholders' meeting to be the scene of any controversy. It was not. Contrary to a story floating around that had the Detroit syndicate ready to pay $60,000 for the franchise, Snyder told the hundred people in attendance, eighty of them stockholders, that the offer was $10,000 for the team and equipment. The terms and the financial state of the football corporation, he said, required a sale. He provided details on what the corporation would do with the money from the proposed sale. It would use $3,000 to pay players' salaries left unpaid after the Bears game, $3,300 for federal taxes due, and $1,058 to complete the guarantee of $4,000 for the Bears. The remainder would go to pay a few commercial bills and part of $6,000 for notes held by local individuals.[31] For years a rumor had Richards personally giving the corporation another $5,000 to meet all of its debts. Apparently players did not receive full payment of their salaries; men who had accepted shares of stock instead of cash still had unredeemed shares fifty years later.

The historical record, argued Snyder, gave no hope of relief. Every year they were in the league, the Spartans had lost money—$27,000 in 1930, $16,000 in 1931, $5,000 in 1932, $14,000 in 1933. He revealed, for the first time, that early in December the directors had approved extending an option to a group of New York businessmen to buy the franchise. Then when the Detroit men tendered a better offer, they rescinded the option. He assured everyone that the sale would not affect the lease on Universal, unencumbered as it was. Of course, the lessee stood to lose money if the Spartans were not playing there. He concluded his presentation with an endorsement of the proposal to sell. Selby and Clark concurred, insisting that it was in the best interest of the players and the stockholders. On the subsequent ballot, shareholders adopted the resolution to sell forty-nine to thirty-one. What motivated the thirty-one to cast negative votes the reporter did not explain. They represented, though, a distinctly minority voice in shares represented, accounting for but 83; those voting for the sale held 1,541 shares.

Less than a week later, at a luncheon in Detroit, Richards and three other men on the Detroit board signed the final papers for the sale. Noting the contract with the old Spartans board, Minego pointed out that the twenty-one members of the Detroit syndicate, many of them automobile magnates, had personal resources valued at $50 million.[32] Soon, except for the players, the Spartans had no legacy left. In July, after giving some thought to calling the team Tigers, long used by the baseball team in the city, Richards conducted a contest through his radio station for another name. Lions won. The Spartan colors also disappeared. Resolving to make the Lions the "best dressed" team in the league, the Detroit men chose blue and silver as their colors—silver pants, blue jerseys, and silver helmets; they ordered all players to wear white laces in their shoes. Annoyed at what he saw as pretentious nonsense, all Minego could write was "Oh piffle."[33] The last formal obsequies in the burial of the Spartans came in August 1934. At a meeting of the stockholders at the Selby auditorium—virtually no one was there—A. A. Wing, secretary of the Portsmouth National Football League Corporation, declared the corporation dissolved.

As the corporation moved to and through the sale of its franchise, local fans felt great ambivalence about what was happening to the Spartans—and would for many years. Many fans, as attested by their failure to mount a campaign to rescue the franchise for the city, accepted its demise as a financial exigency, as no reflection on their commitment to the team and professional

The League Wants Larger Cities

football. Others, still lamenting the loss of the Spartans sixty years later, recalled that they had suffered a "blow," a "devastating injury."[34] They felt a generalized resentment, blaming no one in particular. Certainly they did not find fault with the players. Rather, they wished them well and followed their careers in football as closely as they could. According to a contemporary observer, faithful fans bought radios enabling them to pick up the Lions games on WJR.[35]

For a few years, they could hear the names of many former Spartans. Of the Spartans who played in Portsmouth in 1933, eleven became Lions in 1934, with Potsy Clark again coaching them.[36] Dutch Clark also joined the new team. He was a prize, almost worth the price of the old franchise. The Detroit men also coveted Presnell but did not land him easily. At the conclusion of the Spartans' barnstorming tour early in 1934, he accepted a position as an assistant coach at West Virginia University, fully intending to begin a new career in football. Then Richards invited him to Detroit, there hosting him in sumptuous style and offering him a "great deal."[37] Carr urged him to accept the offer, and he did.

The former Spartans gave fans in Detroit and Portsmouth something to cheer about. In 1934 the Lions won ten games and lost three, finishing second to the undefeated Bears. Then in 1935 they captured the championship of the western division and with Presnell, Clark, and Gutowski leading them won the league title with a victory over the Giants. The Lions continued to post good records in the 1930s but did not win any more division titles. Gradually, of course, the old Spartans left the team. Lumpkin and Bodenger played for only one year. At the conclusion of the season in 1935, Mitchell departed. Presnell, Randolph, and Schneller all hung up their togs after 1936, as did Ebding and Emerson following the season of 1937. The remaining Spartans—Clark, Gutowski, Christensen, and Caddel played their final games for the Lions in 1938. Now fans in Portsmouth cheered old Spartans in memory alone.

EPILOGUE

Three American Cities and Their Paid Football Teams

WITH THE DEMISE of the Spartans in Portsmouth, an unusual epoch in American football came to an end. For fifteen years, teams in three relatively small cities on a short course of the Ohio River had been sovereigns of play in the Ohio Valley and had reached, or nearly reached, the pinnacle nationally in their levels of competition. The Tanks became the strongest independent professional eleven in the state, one of the strongest in the nation, with the Armcos not far behind them at one point, and the Spartans had come within a few points of claiming the championship of organized professional football two consecutive years. No other set of small cities in the nation at a stone's throw from one another could claim a comparable record in the 1920s.

Though all enjoyed successes, the Tanks, Armcos, and Spartans had different origins and represented different ideals and aspirations. At Ironton, the Tanks grew organically and spontaneously out of the ordinary life of the community and sought at the outset no special niche in its affairs. Men simply wanted to play football. But as they won game after game, they became a source of pride for working-class people, businessmen, and professional men, who turned them into emotional property em-

304

Three American Cities and Their Paid Football Teams

blematic of the intrinsic worth of the community. Especially businessmen and journalists, like eternal whippoorwills, sang night and day of the Tanks as an instrument "advertising" the community. They never explained, though, what the advertising meant to the city, never calculated the sum of the economic or emotional benefits, with the result that they had to look eventually at the sobering numbers of reality. Before they did so, the boosters were willing to turn the city inside out for the wherewithal to support the Tanks. For a season, the community responded, subscribing to stock for a covered grandstand and giving recruits employment in the school system. And the crowds at Beechwood, averaging about three thousand from 1926 through 1929, were large, considering the population of the city. Eventually, though, the community simply could not sustain the Tanks in a new world of competition.

At Ironton, businessmen and journalists embraced the Tanks as and after they became winners. At Portsmouth, the Smoke House offering no great victories, businessmen took it upon themselves to create a winning team, one that, of course, "advertised" the community. Initially, they turned to shoe factories and steel mills, not the public schools, to provide employment for Spartan recruits. As in Ironton, the football team became a symbol of civic progress, indeed the means to the construction of a public monument to sports. The business leaders sought to emulate the success of another small city franchise, the Packers, but the Depression, though perhaps not as corrosive as in large industrial centers, had its effects. As Dutch Clark later noted, the people in Portsmouth were "nice" but did not "have the money."[1] More fans came out to watch scrimmages, he complained, than paid their way into some of the games. In a bittersweet ending, they saw their Spartans survive in another city under another name. Though Clark probably was correct about the fans' stringency, a fact of the Depression, attendance at the Spartans' home games in 1932 and 1933 averaged about 7,000 a game. In 1930 and 1931 crowds averaged 5,800 and 6,250. Probably Snyder was close to the mark in attributing the Spartans' continuing funding problems to the small size of Portsmouth that placed the city at a competitive disadvantage with the larger league cities.

The Tanks, at least at first, came on to the gridiron for the purpose of play, the Spartans for the pride of the community. But the Armcos were born out of a policy of a steel company, not out of a community. Only sporadically did Ashland view the Armcos as a "town team"; only infrequently did the Armcos go to the community for sustenance. The Armcos did draw on average larger home crowds—thirty-two hundred—than did the Tanks through four years late in the 1920s, but they had the advantage of playing in a city with a population half again as large as that of Ironton. Additionally, they had in the mill workers a built-in constituency. At their passing,

305

Epilogue

an Armco executive remarked later, no one proposed a heroic effort at resuscitation and few in the mills or community shed tears.[2]

Though displacing hometown men, the latter-day Tanks and the Spartans became adoptees of Ironton and Portsmouth. Editors and sportswriters portrayed them as full participants in the life of the communities. They walked the streets, worshiped at churches, joined local clubs, and had personal relations with residents. Father Lumpkin was a conspicuous example in Portsmouth. Some lived in rooming houses, but many stayed in homes of families, broke bread with them, occasionally married their daughters, and shared the gossip of the day with them. Glenn Presnell exemplified many Tanks. He liked Ironton when he first visited it and at the end of his career as a player and coach returned to live near the city. Grover Emerson long remembered Portsmouth as a community of "cordiality" and "hospitality."[3] At Ashland, in contrast, sportswriters seldom described the Armcos as at one with the community. They seemed detached from everyday existence there, their lives tied to the team and the steel mill.

Similarly, down through the years the Tanks and Spartans were enshrined in the public memory of Ironton and Portsmouth while the Armcos disappeared from view at Ashland. At Ironton the organizers of the annual Ironton Sports Day periodically honored former Tanks. On occasion the local historical society displayed Tanks' memorabilia in its museum. The public library gave space to Tanks' programs and other ephemera. Appropriately, Beechwood Stadium, where the Tanks played, eventually became the Tanks Memorial Stadium. At Portsmouth, the public library maintained a file on the Spartans. A community-wide committee chose Presnell and the Spartans (and the Shoe-Steels) as subjects for one of the huge murals painted on the floodwall of the city. Universal Stadium became the Spartan Municipal Stadium. Meanwhile, the Armcos languished in the common memory, few materials in the public library or elsewhere marking their place or play in the community, no organization preserving their history. The park where the Armcos played, named for the company at its opening, remained Armco Park down through the years without reference to the football team that once played there.

But no matter their connection with the communities, the Tanks, the Spartans and their predecessors, and the Armcos all played for the crowd, giving people a rich taste of expectations, disappointment, and exhilaration.

APPENDIX

Seasonal Records of Teams, 1919–1933

The scores in the tables below come from the newspapers of Ashland, Ironton, and Portsmouth. Nearly all figures on attendance are estimates of reporters and managers of teams. In a few cases, when the figures are specific, the reporters or managers were reporting actual ticket sales. Frequently, no one reported figures on attendance.

Table 1. Tanks, 1919   2 Wins, 1 Loss, 1 Tie

Date	Site	Tanks	Opponent		Crowd
November 4	H (Home)	9	New Boston Tigers	0	250
November 11	A (Away)	0	Ashland Playhouse	7	—
November 17	H	0	Ashland Playhouse	0	1,000
November 28	H	12	Portsmouth N. & W.	0	—

Appendix

Table 2. N. & W., 1919   Wins, 2 Losses, 2 Ties

Date	Site	N. & W.	Opponent		Crowd
September 28	H	12	Camp Sherman	0	—
October 5	A	0	Columbus Chippewas	14	—
October 19	H	6	Camp Sherman	0	—
October 26	H	6	Ashland Playhouse	0	—
November 4	H	18	Columbus All-Stars	0	500
November 11	H	0	Chillicothe	0	—
November 17	H	40	Fort Thomas	0	—
November 24	H	0	Wellston Eagles	0	—
November 28	A	0	Ironton Tanks	12	—

Table 3. Tanks, 1920   5 Wins, 1 Loss, 1 Tie

Date	Site	Tanks	Opponent		Crowd
October 10	A	0	Morris Harvey	14	—
October 24	A	6	Smoke House	6	—
November 6	A	13	Marshall	0	—
November 8	H	77	New Boston Tigers	0	—
November 15	H	13	Nitro	0	—
November 26	H	26	Lombards	0	1,500
November 29	H	14	Smoke House	0	(?)3,000

Table 4. Smoke House, 1920   3 Wins, 4 Losses, 3 Ties

Date	Site	Smoke House	Opponent		Crowd
October 3	A	0	Jungle Imps	24	—
October 10	H	0	Chillicothe	9	—
October 17	H	13	Catlettsburg	7	600
October 24	H	6	Ironton Tanks	6	—
October 31	H	6	Wellston Eagles	6	700
November 7	H	7	Columbus Maroons	7	—
November 14	H	66	Ashland Bulldogs	0	—
November 25	H	14	Columbus Oakwoods	0	—
November 29	A	0	Ironton Tanks	14	(?)3,000
December 12	H	0	Wellston Eagles	10	—

Seasonal Records of Teams

Table 5. Tanks, 1921   7 Wins, 2 Ties

Date	Site	Tanks	Opponent		Crowd
October 2	H	6	Jackson Bearcats	0	—
October 16	H	34	Charleston West Side	0	400
October 23	H	7	Ashland Tigers	0	1,500
October 30	H	0	Smoke House	0	1,800
November 13	H	21	Lombards	7	—
November 20	A	14	Smoke House	0	4,000
November 27	H	0	Wellston Eagles	0	—
December 4	H	19	Morris Harvey	14	—
December 11	H	7	Wellston Eagles	6	

Table 6. Smoke House, 1921   3 Wins, 3 Losses, 2 Ties

Date	Site	Smoke House	Opponent		Crowd
October 2	H	0	Ashland Tigers	0	—
October 9	A	3	Circleville	6	—
October 16	H	6	Jackson Bearcats	0	—
October 23	A	50	Chillicothe Majestics	0	—
October 30	A	0	Ironton Tanks	0	1,800
November 6	H	27	Asheville	7	—
November 20	H	0	Ironton Tanks	14	4,000
December 4	H	0	Wellston Eagles	14	—

Table 7. Tanks, 1922   8 Wins, 1 Tie

Date	Site	Tanks	Opponent		Crowd
October 1	H	13	Columbus Olympians	6	781
October 8	H	19	Athens	0	—
October 15	A	18	Huntington Boosters	7	2,000
October 22	H	76	Williamson	0	—
October 29	H	40	Jackson Bearcats	0	1,000
November 5	A	7	Huntington Boosters	7	2,500
November 12	H	38	Lancaster	0	1,000
November 26	H	45	Washington Court House	0	—
November 30	H	12	Huntington Boosters	10	3,000

Appendix

Table 8. Smoke House, 1922   5 Wins, 3 Losses, 1 Tie

Date	Site	Smoke House	Opponent		Crowd
October 1	A	19	Washington Court House	14	—
October 8	H	0	Chillicothe Sunnybrooks	0	—
October 15	H	0	Washington Court House	6	—
October 22	A	0	Huntington Boosters	9	—
October 29	H	44	Chillicothe Sunnybrooks	0	500
November 12	A	0	Chillicothe Sunnybrooks	28	—
November 19	H	13	Jackson Bearcats	6	—
November 26	H	53	Williamsport	0	—
December 3	H	32	New Boston Strollers	0	—

Table 9. Tanks, 1923   10 Wins, 1 Loss

Date	Site	Tanks	Opponent		Crowd
September 30	H	46	Ironton Eagles	0	—
October 7	H	18	Columbus Seagraves	0	2,147
October 14	H	7	Columbus West Side	6	—
October 21	H	40	Smoke House	0	2,000
October 28	A	7	Huntington Boosters	0	1,600
November 4	H	7	Logan Wildcats	0	1,100
November 11	H	6	Huntington Boosters	12	2,600
November 18	H	31	Cincinnati Saints	0	1,000
November 25	A	21	Smoke House	6	3,000
November 29	H	20	Cincinnati Harrisons	0	2,500
December 9	H	26	Huntington Boosters	0	2,000

Table 10. Smoke House, 1923   5 Wins, 2 Losses, 1 Tie

Date	Site	Smoke House	Opponent		Crowd
October 7	H	13	Washington Court House	0	—
October 14	H	2	Columbus Seagraves	0	—
October 21	A	0	Ironton Tanks	40	2,000
October 28	H	64	Lancaster	0	—
November 4	A	0	Chillicothe Athletic Club	0	—
November 11	H	27	Wellston Eagles	7	—
November 18	H	17	Chillicothe Athletic Club	7	—
November 25	H	6	Ironton Tanks	21	3,000

Seasonal Records of Teams

Table 11. Tanks, 1924   11 Wins, 1 Tie

Date	Site	Tanks	Opponent		Crowd
September 21	H	38	Ironton Panthers	0	500
September 28	H	25	Columbus Jungle Imps	6	1,000
October 5	H	7	Murray City Tigers	0	—
October 12	H	31	Louisville Brecks	0	2,700
October 19	H	14	Cincinnati Potters	3	2,500
October 26	H	19	Akron Silents	0	1,800
November 2	A	6	Huntington Boosters	0	3,000
November 9	H	44	Smoke House	0	2,800
November 16	A	7	Cincinnati Potters	3	3,300
November 23	H	12	Covington C.A.C.	0	1,500
November 27	H	21	Huntington Boosters	0	2,600
November 30	A	0	Smoke House	0	624

Table 12. Smoke House, 1924   2 Wins, 3 Losses, 1 Tie

Date	Site	Smoke House	Opponent		Crowd
October 5	A	7	Wellston Eagles	6	—
October 19	H	27	Wellston Eagles	0	—
October 26	H	0	Columbus Jungle Imps	10	—
November 2	H	6	Columbus Clothiers	23	—
November 9	A	0	Ironton Tanks	44	2,800
November 30	H	0	Ironton Tanks	0	—

Table 13. Armcos, 1925   4 Wins, 6 Losses, 1 Tie

Date	Site	Armcos	Opponent		Crowd
September 27	H	0	Columbus Clothiers	3	2,000
October 4	H	48	Ohio State Stoves	0	—
October 11	H	0	Columbus West Side	21	—
October 18	A	6	Ironton Tanks	21	3,500
October 25	H	13	Columbus West Side	0	—
November 1	H	6	Middletown Armcos	0	3,000
November 8	H	0	Ironton Tanks	9	3,500
November 15	H	6	Columbus Bobbs	0	—
November 22	A	6	Cincinnati Potters	20	5,000
November 29	H	0	Huntington Boosters	0	—
December 6	A	0	Huntington Boosters	7	1,500

Appendix

Table 14. Tanks, 1925   9 Wins, 1 Loss, 2 Ties

Date	Site	Tanks	Opponent		Crowd
September 27	H	29	Chillicothe	0	2,000
October 4	H	35	Columbus Bobbs	0	—
October 11	H	15	Cincinnati Potters	6	3,000
October 18	H	21	Ashland Armcos	6	3,535
October 25	A	12	Huntington Boosters	0	3,000
November 1	H	19	Columbus Wagner -Pirates	5	2,000
November 8	A	9	Ashland Armcos	0	3,500
November 15	H	0	Huntington Boosters	0	1,650
November 22	H	7	Dayton Koors	7	2,200
November 26	H	0	Canton Bulldogs	12	3,000
November 29	A	9	Cincinnati Potters	0	6,000
December 14	H	24	Dayton Koors	6	—

Table 15. Smoke House, 1925   1 Win, 1 Loss

Date	Site	Smoke House	Opponent		Crowd
October 11	H	30	Wellston Eagles	0	—
October 18	A	0	Huntington Boosters	34	—

Table 16. Presidents, 1926   8 Wins, 3 Losses

Date	Site	Presidents	Opponent		Crowd
September 26	H	7	Ironton Panthers	0	—
October 3	A	6	Xenia Tiltons	0	500
October 10	H	20	Xenia Tiltons	7	—
October 17	H	34	Columbus Wagner -Pirates	0	1,500
October 24	H	12	Portsmouth Merchants	0	—
October 31	H	12	Chillicothe Merchants	0	—
November 7	A	0	Ironton Tanks	9	2,500
November 14	H	12	Columbus Bobbs	0	—
November 21	H	31	Cincinnati Friars	0	500
November 28	H	0	Middletown Armcos	6	1,800
December 5	A	0	Ironton Tanks	33	2,200

Seasonal Records of Teams

Table 17. Armcos, 1926   6 Wins, 3 Losses, 2 Ties

Date	Site	Armcos	Opponent		Crowd
September 26	H	6	Dayton Koors	0	3,000
October 3	H	30	Columbus Bobbs	0	—
October 10	H	13	Cincinnati Potters	0	1,500
October 17	H	20	Middletown Armcos	0	2,500
October 24	H	0	Ironton Tanks	2	5,000
October 31	H	20	Columbus Tigers	0	—
November 7	H	45	Oorang Indians	0	3,000
November 14	A	0	Cincinnati Potters	0	3,000
November 21	A	0	Ironton Tanks	7	4,000
November 28	H	0	Dayton Triangles	3	—
December 5	A	0	Cincinnati Potters	0	2,100

Table 18. Tanks, 1926   11 Wins, 1 Loss, 1 Tie

Date	Site	Tanks	Opponent		Crowd
September 19	H	27	Columbus All-Stars	0	—
September 26	H	27	Middletown Armcos	0	2,000
October 3	H	39	Columbus Wagner -Pirates	0	—
October 10	H	23	Dayton Koors	0	—
October 17	H	47	Cleveland Indians	0	2,500
October 24	A	2	Ashland Armcos	0	5,000
October 31	H	27	Akron Silents	0	1,000
November 7	H	9	Portsmouth Presidents	0	2,500
November 14	H	15	Kokomo American Legion	0	1,800
November 21	H	7	Ashland Armcos	0	4,000
November 25	H	0	Kansas City Cowboys	0	—
November 28	A	0	Cincinnati Potters	28	8,000
December 5	H	33	Portsmouth Presidents	0	2,000

Table 19. Tanks, 1927   6 Wins, 2 Losses, 3 Ties

Date	Site	Tanks	Opponent		Crowd
September 18	H	7	Columbus Bobbs	0	850
September 25	H	0	Middletown Armcos	0	—
October 2	H	25	Toledo Boosters	7	—
October 16	H	14	Shelby Blues	0	—
October 23	A	0	Ashland Armcos	0	4,700
October 30	H	27	Akron Indians	0	—
November 6	A	18	Portsmouth Shoe-Steels	0	3,500
November 13	H	7	Ashland Armcos	7	3,500
November 20	H	0	Portsmouth Shoe-Steels	7	3,800
November 24	H	0	Middletown Armcos	8	—
November 27	A	14	Logan Wildcats	0	—

Appendix

Table 20. Armcos, 1927   7 Wins, 1 Loss, 3 Ties

Date	Site	Armcos	Opponent		Crowd
September 25	H	22	Dayton Koors	6	2,000
October 2	H	30	Cleveland Panthers	0	—
October 9	H	16	Middletown Armcos	6	3,000
October 16	H	0	Dayton Triangles	0	3,500
October 23	A	0	Ironton Tanks	0	4,700
October 30	H	7	Canton Bulldogs	0	2,000
November 6	A	9	Middletown Armcos	16	3,000
November 13	A	7	Ironton Tanks	7	3,500
November 20	H	6	Canton Bulldogs	0	2,000
November 27	H	14	Kokomo American Legion	0	—
December 4	H	7	Portsmouth Shoe-Steels	6	3,195

Table 21. Shoe-Steels, 1927   7 Wins, 4 Losses

Date	Site	Shoe-Steels	Opponent		Crowd
September 25	H	13	Columbus Clothiers	0	—
October 2	H	0	Columbus Bobbs	12	1,500
October 9	H	6	Springfield Bulldogs	0	1,500
October 16	H	8	Logan Wildcats	6	1,000
October 23	H	26	Martins Ferry	7	—
October 30	A	12	Cincinnati Guards	19	5,000
November 6	H	0	Ironton Tanks	18	3,500
November 13	H	13	Hocking Valley	7	800
November 20	A	7	Ironton Tanks	0	3,800
November 27	H	32	Columbus Bobbs	0	—
December 4	A	6	Ashland Armcos	7	3,195

Table 22. Spartans, 1928   9 Wins, 3 Losses, 2 Ties

Date	Site	Spartans	Opponent		Crowd
September 16	H	20	Columbus Bobbs	12	2,000
September 23	H	54	Springfield Bulldogs	7	1,203
September 30	H	13	Middletown Armcos	0	1,853
October 7	H	31	Columbus Mendel Tailors	6	—
October 14	A	0	Ashland Armcos	13	4,000
October 21	H	0	Ironton Tanks	0	5,000
October 28	A	0	Cincinnati Guards	13	5,200
November 4	H	35	Logan Wildcats	0	—
November 11	A	0	Ironton Tanks	0	4,000
November 18	H	60	Wabash Athletic Club	0	—
November 25	H	13	Columbus Tigers	0	1,200
November 29	H	19	Ashland Armcos	0	3,000
December 2	A	7	Middletown Armcos	0	—
December 9	A	0	Ironton Tanks	14	3,575

Seasonal Records of Teams

Table 23. Armcos, 1928   8 Wins, 4 Losses

Date	Site	Armcos	Opponent		Crowd
September 23	H	13	Logan Wildcats	0	—
September 30	H	6	Cincinnati Guards	0	—
October 7	A	13	Middletown Armcos	0	1,500
October 14	H	13	Portsmouth Spartans	0	4,000
October 21	H	7	Dayton Triangles	10	2,500
October 28	H	7	Ironton Tanks	6	4,760
November 4	H	13	Canton Rogers Jewelers	0	—
November 11	A	14	Middletown Armcos	0	6,000
November 18	H	26	Columbus Tigers	0	—
November 25	A	0	Ironton Tanks	3	3,000
November 29	A	0	Portsmouth Spartans	19	3,000
December 2	A	0	Cincinnati Guards	20	7,000

Table 24. Tanks, 1928   7 Wins, 1 Loss, 3 Ties

Date	Site	Tanks	Opponent		Crowd
September 30	H	52	Columbus Bobbs	0	1,500
October 7	H	47	Cleveland Panthers	0	—
October 14	A	0	Akron Awnings	0	8,691
October 21	A	0	Portsmouth Spartans	0	5,000
October 28	A	6	Ashland Armcos	7	4,760
November 4	A	7	Cincinnati Guards	0	8,000
November 11	H	0	Portsmouth Spartans	0	4,000
November 18	A	13	Middletown Armcos	0	—
November 25	H	3	Ashland Armcos	0	3,000
November 29	A	19	Akron Awnings	0	8,600
December 9	H	14	Portsmouth Spartans	0	3,575

Table 25. Spartans, 1929 12 Wins, 2 Losses, 1 Tie

Date	Site	Spartans	Opponent		Crowd
September 15	A	0	Green Bay Packers	14	5,000
September 22	H	7	Chillicothe Eagles	0	2,500
September 29	H	32	Middletown Armcos	0	2,500
October 6	H	79	Detroit Tigers	0	—
October 13	H	0	Ironton Tanks	3	6,200
October 20	A	6	Cincinnati Guards	6	4,100
October 27	A	19	Ashland Armcos	0	6,500
November 3	A	20	Ironton Tanks	0	7,206
November 10	A	15	Akron Awnings	6	8,000
November 17	A	22	Middletown Armcos	0	1,000
November 24	H	38	Ironton Tanks	0	3,500
November 28	H	25	Cincinnati Guards	0	2,500
December 1	H	19	Ashland Armcos	0	4,000
December 8	H	30	Chillicothe Eagles	7	2,500
December 15	H	44	Columbus Mendel Tailors	0	—

Appendix

Table 26. Tanks, 1929   5 Wins, 6 Losses

Date	Site	Tanks	Opponent		Crowd
September 22	H	39	Columbus Mendel Tailors	0	—
September 29	H	6	Chillicothe Eagles	0	—
October 6	H	78	Toledo Boosters	0	—
October 13	A	3	Portsmouth Spartans	0	6,200
October 20	H	2	Ashland Armcos	7	6,200
October 27	A	7	Akron Awnings	5	12,000
November 3	H	0	Portsmouth Spartans	20	7,206
November 10	A	0	Cincinnati Guards	5	—
November 17	A	0	Ashland Armcos	7	3,500
November 24	A	0	Portsmouth Spartans	38	3,500
November 28	A	3	Akron Awnings	7	6,000

Table 27. Armcos, 1929   8 Wins, 2 Losses, 1 Tie

Date	Site	Armcos	Opponent		Crowd
September 22	H	79	Fort Wayne Pyramids	0	3,000
September 29	H	22	Canton Bulldogs	0	—
October 6	H	14	Chillicothe Eagles	6	—
October 13	A	34	Middletown Armcos	0	—
October 20	A	7	Ironton Tanks	2	6,200
October 27	H	0	Portsmouth Spartans	19	6,500
November 3	H	32	Kokomo American Legion	0	—
November 10	H	48	Cleveland Panthers	0	—
November 17	H	7	Ironton Tanks	0	3,500
November 24	A	0	Middletown Armcos	0	2,000
December 1	A	0	Portsmouth Spartans	19	4,000

Table 28. Spartans, 1930   7 Wins, 8 Losses, 3 Ties; League 5 Wins, 6 Losses, 3 Ties

Date	Site	Spartans	Opponent		Crowd
September 14	H	13	Newark Tornadoes	6	4,000
September 24	H	12	Brooklyn Dodgers	0	6,000
September 28	A	7	Ironton Tanks	6	6,000
October 5	H	0	Chicago Cardinals	0	6,500
October 8	H	39	Frankford Yellowjackets	7	—
October 12	A	0	Minneapolis Red Jackets	13	2,000
October 15	H	15	Ironton Tanks	16	7,500
October 19	A	6	Memphis Tigers	20	6,500
October 22	H	7	Chicago Bears	6	7,500
October 26	A	13	Chicago Cardinals	23	8,000
November 2	A	13	Green Bay Packers	47	9,000
November 5	H	6	New York Giants	19	7,000

Seasonal Records of Teams

Table 28. *(cont.)*

Date	Site	Spartans	Opponent		Crowd
November 9	A	13	Staten Island Stapletons	13	5,000
November 15	A	6	Frankford Yellowjackets	7	3,500
November 27	H	12	Ironton Tanks	0	4,500
November 30	A	6	Chicago Bears	14	6,000
December 7	H	42	Minneapolis Red Jackets	0	3,500
December 14	A	6	Green Bay Packers	6	6,500

Table 29. Tanks, 1930   7 Wins, 3 Losses

Date	Site	Tanks	Opponent		Crowd
September 28	H	6	Portsmouth Spartans	7	6,000
October 5	H	14	Chillicothe Eagles	0	2,500
October 12	A	3	Akron Awnings	0	7,000
October 15	A	16	Portsmouth Spartans	15	7,500
October 26	H	70	Washington Olympics	0	—
November 2	A	0	Memphis Tigers	7	3,000
November 11	Redland	13	New York Giants	12	4,000
November 16	A	13	Akron Awnings	0	—
November 23	Redland	26	Chicago Bears	13	10,000
November 27	A	0	Portsmouth Spartans	12	3,300

Table 30. Spartans, 1931   13 Wins, 3 Losses; League 11 Wins, 3 Losses

Date	Site	Spartans	Opponent		Crowd
September 13	H	14	Brooklyn Dodgers	0	7,000
September 23	H	13	Chicago Cardinals	3	8,000
September 30	H	14	New York Giants	6	9,000
October 7	H	6	Cleveland Indians	0	5,000
October 15	H	19	Frankford Yellowjackets	0	5,000
October 18	A	19	Brooklyn Dodgers	0	15,000
October 25	A	20	Staten Island Stapletons	7	12,000
October 31	A	14	Frankford Yellowjackets	0	5,000
November 1	A	0	New York Giants	14	32,500
November 8	A	6	Chicago Bears	9	25,000
November 11	H	14	Staten Island Stapletons	12	3,500
November 15	Redland	14	Cleveland Indians	6	10,000
November 22	A	19	Chicago Cardinals	20	5,000
November 29	H	3	Chicago Bears	0	—
December 6	H	101	Columbus Safety Cab	7	—
December 13	A	33	Charleston Trojans	0	1,000

Appendix

Table 31. Spartans, 1932   9 Wins, 3 Losses, 5 Ties; League 6 Wins, 1 Loss, 4 Ties

Date	Site	Spartans	Opponent		Crowd
September 18	H	33	Grand Rapids Maroons	0	2,256
September 25	H	7	New York Giants	0	6,000
October 2	H	7	Chicago Cardinals	7	—
October 9	A	10	Green Bay Packers	15	6,000
October 16	A	7	Staten Island Stapletons	7	7,500
October 20	A	13	Staten Island Stapletons	6	5,000
October 23	A	6	Paterson Panthers	0	3,500
October 30	A	6	New York Giants	0	20,000
November 6	A	17	Brooklyn Dodgers	7	25,000
November 9	A	12	St. Louis Gunners	0	3,000
November 13	A	13	Chicago Bears	13	5,000
November 20	H	10	Boston Braves	0	5,000
November 27	H	7	Chicago Bears	7	10,000
December 4	H	19	Green Bay Packers	0	14,000
December 13	Lexington	0	New York Giants+	18	500
December 18	A	0	Chicago Bears	9	12,000
December 26	Redland	6	Chicago Bears+	6	2,000

+ Non-league game.

Table 32. Spartans, 1933   9 Wins, 5 Losses, 1 Tie; League 6 Wins, 5 Losses

Date	Site	Spartans	Opponent		Crowd
September 10	A	19	Indianapolis Indians	0	—
September 17	H	21	Cincinnati Reds	0	5,000
September 24	H	17	New York Giants	7	7,000
October 1	H	7	Chicago Cardinals	6	7,000
October 4	Huntington	45	Columbus Mendel Tailors	0	3,000
October 8	A	0	Green Bay Packers	17	3,000
October 15	A	13	Boston Redskins	0	20,000
October 18	A	25	Philadelphia Eagles	0	3,500
October 22	A	7	Shenandoah Presidents	7	6,500
October 29	A	14	Staten Island Stapletons	7	6,000
November 5	A	10	New York Giants	13	15,000
November 12	H	7	Green Bay Packers	0	9,000
November 19	A	7	Cincinnati Reds	10	7,000
November 26	A	14	Chicago Bears	17	10,000
December 3	H	7	Chicago Bears	17	7,000

Abbreviations

ABJ	*Akron Beacon-Journal*
AI	*Ashland Independent*
CCT	*Cincinnati Commercial Tribune*
CD	*Columbus Dispatch*
CE	*Cincinnati Enquirer*
CG	*Charleston Gazette*
CN	*Chicago News*
CP	*Cincinnati Post*
CPD	*Cleveland Plain Dealer*
CR	*Canton Repository*
CT	*Chicago Times*
CTr	*Chicago Tribune*
DDN	*Dayton Daily News*
DH	*Dayton Herald*
DJ	*Dayton Journal*
DSG	*Daily Scioto Gazette* (Chillicothe, Ohio)
GBG	*Green Bay Press-Gazette*
HD	*Huntington Dispatch*
IN	*Ironton News*
IR	*Ironton Register*
IT	*Ironton Tribune*
LCJ	*Louisville Courier-Journal*
LH	*Lexington Herald*
MCA	*Memphis Commercial Appeal*
MI	*Morning Irontonian* (Ironton)
MJ	*Middletown Journal*

Abbreviations

MNS	*Middletown News-Signal*
MS	*Morning Sun* (Portsmouth)
NYT	*New York Times*
OSJ	*Ohio State Journal* (Columbus)
PS	*Press-Scimitar* (Memphis)
SN	*Springfield News*
TB	*Toledo Blade*
WHR	*Waverly Herald Republican*
WS	*Wellston Sentinel*

Notes

For Chapters 2 through 13, the citations below refer primarily to sources bearing on the organization of teams, their recruiting of players and preparations for important games, their financial condition, their relationship to their communities, and conditions affecting their games. Only occasionally do they refer to sources detailing play of games.

Prologue

1. *A History of Ashland, Kentucky, 1786 to 1954* (Ashland, 1954), 7; Arnold Hanners, *Ashland Past: A Pictorial History* (Ashland, 1976), 5.

2. *Fourteenth Census of the United States: 1920, Population,* 3 (Washington, D.C., 1922), 384.

3. *Fifteenth Census of the United States: 1930, Population,* Pt. 1 (Washington, D.C., 1932), 929.

4. *Story of the Glorious Past: One Hundred Years* (Ironton, 1949), 2–16; Phillip Gene Payne, "Modernity Lost: Ironton, Ohio, in Industrial and Post-Industrial America" (Ph.D. dissertation, Ohio State University, 1994), 50–52

5. *Fourteenth Census of the United States: 1920, Population,* 3:773.

6. Payne, "Modernity Lost," 50–51.

7. *Fifteenth Census of the United States: 1930, Population,* Pt. 2 (Washington, D.C., 1932), 492.

8. *History of Scioto County, Ohio, 1986* (Dallas, 1986), 8–10; Portsmouth Area Chamber of Commerce, "History of Portsmouth," 1963.

9. *Fourteenth Census of the United States: 1920, Population,* 3:774.

10. *Fifteenth Census of the United States: 1930, Population,* Pt. 2, 494.

Chapter One

1. Benjamin G. Rader, *American Sports: From the Age of Folk Games to the Age of Spectators* (Englewood Cliffs, 1983), places American football in its social setting and traces its changes. The best and most detailed history of the game is Allison Danzig, *The*

Notes to Pages 7–11

History of American Football: Its Great Teams, Players, and Coaches (Englewood Cliffs, 1956). Parke H. Davis, *Football: The American Intercollegiate Game* (New York, 1911), looks at the early history of American football in a comprehensive but confusing way. Interesting and useful is John Allen Krout, *Annals of American Sport* (Toronto, 1929). See also A. M. Weyand, *American Football: Its History and Development* (New York, 1926); and Alexander M. Weyand, *The Saga of American Football* (New York, 1955).

2. Krout, *Annals of American Sport,* 237.

3. Descriptions of rule changes may be found in Rader, *American Sports,* 142–44; Danzig, *History of American Football;* and Davis, *Football.*

4. For a description of American athletic clubs, see Rader, *American Sports,* 55. Useful for their connection with American football is Bob Braunwart, ed., *Professional Football Researchers Association 1989 Annual* (North Huntingdon, Pa., 1969), 3–10. See also David S. Neft et al., eds., *Pro Football: The Early Years* (New York, 1978), 11.

5. Bill Barron et al., eds., *The Official NFL Encyclopedia of Pro Football* (New York, 1977), 11.

6. For the pioneering account of this rivalry and the origins of professional football, see J. Thomas Jable, "The Birth of Professional Football: Pittsburgh Athletic Clubs Ring in Professionals in 1892," *Western Pennsylvania Historical Magazine* 62 (April 1979): 131–74.

7. On this competition, see Marc S. Maltby, "The Origins and Early Development of Professional Football, 1890–1920" (Ph.D. dissertation, Ohio University, 1987), 178–275, and Bob Carroll, *The Ohio League, 1910–1919* (North Huntingdon, Pa., 1997). Particularly interesting for the professional football in northeastern Ohio is the reminiscence of one of the managers of the Canton Bulldogs, Jack Cusack, *Pioneer in Pro Football* (Fort Worth, 1963). On Cusack, see also Bob Curran, *Pro Football's Rag Days* (Englewood Cliffs, 1969), 5–31.

8. Several histories describe the early evolution and leading figures of professional football. Perhaps the best account is Maltby, "Origins and Early Development of Professional Football." See also Harold Classen, *The History of Professional Football* (Englewood Cliffs, 1963); Myron Cope, ed., *The Game That Was: The Early Days of Pro Football* (New York, 1970); Howard Roberts, *The Story of Pro Football* (New York, 1953); Robert Smith, *Pro Football: The History of the Game and the Great Players* (New York, 1963); Harry A. March, *Pro Football: Its Ups and Downs* (New York, 1934); and Robert W. Peterson, *Pigskin: The Early Years of Pro Football* (New York, 1997).

9. For a different definition, see Bob Carroll, "Semi or Pro?" *Coffin Corner* 19 (Late Winter 1996): 20–21.

10. On this point, see Rader, *American Sports,* 58, 134–35.

11. Quoted in "Evil to Be Stamped On, Says Yale News of Pro Football," *NYT,* December 2, 1921.

12. "Pro Elevens Hurt Sport, Says Stagg," *NYT,* November 2, 1923. Stagg's statement came in a letter "to all friends of college football." Both the *Morning Sun* and *Irontonian* noted Stagg's complaints in their editorial columns of November 2, 1923.

13. Carroll, *Ohio League,* 56. See also Phil Dietrich, *Down Payments: Professional Football, 1896–1930 as Viewed from the Summit* (North Huntingdon, Pa., 1995), 85–86.

Notes to Pages 11–18

14. Bob Carroll, *Bulldogs on Sunday 1922* (North Huntingdon, Pa., N.d.), 6–7.

15. "Griffith Sees End of Pro Football," *NYT*, December 18, 1925.

16. "N.C.A.A. to War on Pro Football," *NYT*, December 16, 1925; Minutes, Proceedings, Twentieth Annual Convention, N.C.A.A. Archives, NCAA, Overland, Kansas..

17. Krout, *Annals of American Sport*, 257.

18. Rader, *American Sports*, 134–35.

19. Quoted in Foster Rhea Dulles, *America Learns to Play: A History of Popular Recreation, 1607–1940* (New York, 1940), 352.

20. One may find an excellent description of the single wing in Jim Campbell, "The Power and the Glory—Single Wing Football," *Coffin Corner* 14 (September 1992): 18–20.

21. Quoted in Ron Fimrite, "A Melding of Men All Suited to a T," *Sports Illustrated* 47 (September 5, 1977): 90–100.

22. Danzig, *History of American Football* , 59.

23. For a good description of the nature of play in the 1920s, see Bob Carroll and Bob Gill, eds., *Bulldogs on Sunday 1919* (North Huntingdon, Pa., N.d.), 14–15.

24. Brief comments on equipment and uniforms are in Neft et al., eds., *Pro Football*, 13; Barron et al., eds., *Official NFL Encyclopedia of Pro Football*, 554–59; and Danzig, *History of American Football*, 88–89.

Chapter Two

1. "Ironton High School Scored Its First Win over Portsmouth in 1915," *IR*, October 9, 1949.

2. For a summary of early football in Ironton, see C. Robert Barnett, *The Spartans and the Tanks* (North Huntingdon, Pa., 1983), 4–5; and C. Robert Barnett and Linda Terhune, "When the Tanks Were Tops," *River Cities Monthly*, 1 (September 1979): 14–20.

3. Charles Collett, "An Old Story." The "Old Story" was one of a series of accounts of the Tanks that Collett, publisher and editor of the *Ironton News*, wrote in the 1950s in his continuing column "Soliloquy." It is undated, as is the entire series, but probably appeared sometime in 1956 (photocopy in author's possession). No issues of the *News* are generally available; the files were lost in the flood of 1913. Ritter Collett, son of Charles Collett, provided me with photocopies of the series.

4. *MI*, November 5, 1919.

5. Program, "Ironton Sports Day, 1988," June 23, 1988.

6. Quoted in Barnett, *The Spartans and the Tanks,* 4; Barnett and Terhune, "When the Tanks Were Tops."

7. Jack Coins, "Tanks Copped 85, Lost 17, Tied 15," *IT*, October 19, 1949.

8. Barnett, *The Spartans and the Tanks*, 4; Barnett and Terhune, "When the Tanks Were Tops."

9. This figure came from a search of *The Official Roster of Ohio Soldiers, Sailors and Marines in the World War, 1917–1918*, 18 vols. (Columbus, 1926).

10. *The Owl: Patriotic Edition* (Ironton High School Yearbook, 1918).

11. Identification of these occupations came from a reading of the original schedule

Notes to Pages 18–28

of population of the census of 1920 for Ironton, "Fourteenth Census of the United States: 1920—Population, City of Ironton." See also Phillip Gene Payne, "Gridiron in Ironton: Semi-Professional Football in a Small Ohio Town, 1919–1931" (Master's thesis, Ohio State University, 1990), 19.

12. Payne, "Gridiron in Ironton," 11.

13. Barnett, *The Spartans and the Tanks*, 4; *MI*, December 6, 1919.

14. "How the Tanks Were Named," Tanks' Program, 1924, Pro Football Hall of Fame.

15. *PT*, October 22, 1919.

16. *PT*, September 7, 1919.

17. *PT*, September 17, 18, 1919.

18. *Portsmouth, Ohio Directory, 1920* (Columbus, 1920); "Fourteenth Census of the United States: 1920—Population, City of Portsmouth."

19. Coins, "Tanks Copped 85"; Barnett, *The Spartans and the Tanks*, 4.

20. Barnett, *The Spartans and the Tanks*, 16; "A Large Crowd Saw the Tanks Battle Ashland," *IR*, November 14, 1919; "Tanks vs. Ashland," *MI*, November 16, 1919; "Tanks and Ashland Tie," *MI*, November 18, 1919.

21. "Challenge Is Accepted," *MI*, September 28, 1919.

22. "Lombards Accept Tanks Challenge for a Decision," *IR*, November 20, 1919; "Tanks Play Lombards Sunday," *MI*, November 20, 1919.

23. *PT*, October 17, 1919; October 20, 1919.

24. *PT*, October 26, 1919.

25. *PT*, November 19, 1919.

26. *IR*, November 27, 1919.

27. "Tanks Beat N. & W. Eleven," *MI*, November 29, 1919; *PT*, November 28, 1919. A spectator who later became a teammate of Davies with the Tanks asserted that on that day Davies was the best runner he ever saw. Interview by Carl Becker with Lincoln G. DeLong, July 14, 1993.

28. "Tanks Beat N. & W. Eleven"; "Fumes," *IR*, December 1, 1925; interview by Carl Becker with Harold Rolph, July 15, 1993; Paul Miller to Carl Becker, June 2, 1993.

29. "N. & W. Wants Second Game," *MI*, November 30, 1919; *PT*, December 1, 1919. According to Barnett and Collett, the Tanks and the N. & W. team met twice in 1919, playing to a scoreless tie a week after the Tanks had lost to the Playhouse eleven (Barnett, *The Spartans and the Tanks*, 16; Collett, "An Old Story"). But on that weekend, the Tanks and the Playhouse played a scoreless game, and the N. & W. defeated Fort Thomas ("Tanks and Ashland Tie," *MI*, November 18, 1919; "A Large Crowd Saw the Tanks Battle Ashland," *IR*, November 18, 1919; *PT*, November 17, 1919). Somehow, the second game between the Tanks and Playhouse has been transposed into a second game between the Tanks and the N. & W. eleven.

30. "Football Team to Represent City Underway; Davies & Brooks Are Promoters," *IR*, August 27, 1920.

31. "How The Tanks Were Defeated," *MI*, October 10, 1920.

32. "To Tackle Tanks," *PT*, October 23, 1920; "Tanks Here Sunday," *PT*, October 23, 1920; "Tanks Play N. & W. Team Here Today," *PT*, October 24, 1920.

33. "Catlettsburg Has Cancelled Game," *IR*, October 28, 1920.

34. *MI,* November 21, 1920.

35. "Crow Instead of Turkey for Gang from Lombards," *IR,* November 17, 1920.

36. "Fear of Tanks Now Admitted," *IR,* November 11, 1920; "Smoke House Team Will Gladly Play Ironton Tanks on Any Neutral Field," *PT,* November 11, 1920.

37. "News Writer Gets His Signals Twisted," *PT,* November 14, 1920.

38. The details of the agreement appear piecemeal in at least eight issues of the *Times* and *Irontonian* running from November 12 to November 21.

39. *PT,* November 27, 1920; November 28, 1920.

40. *PT,* November 28, 1920.

41. This description of the crowd and game comes from five accounts in the *Times, Irontonian,* and *Register* appearing on November 29 and November 30.

42. "Tanks Rumbled over Portsmouth 14 to 0," *IR,* November 30, 1920; Collett, "Soliloquy, 2nd in Series," *IN,* n.d.

43. *MI,* November 30, 1920; "A Clean Cut Victory," *IR,* November 30, 1920; "Ironton Still Chirping," *PT,* December 30, 1920.

44. For this view, see Maltby, "Origins and Early Development of Professional Football," 139–41; and Payne, "Modernity Lost," 268.

45. Payne, "Modernity Lost," 267–68.

Chapter Three

1. "Lombard Has Bright Array of Collegiate Stars on '21 Eleven," *IR,* September 10, 1921.

2. "Tanks Have Fine Bunch," *MI,* September 17, 1921.

3. "Tanks Will Rumble Loud and Long on Gridirons This Year," *IR,* September 12, 1921.

4. "Tanks Have Fine Bunch."

5. "Shorty Davies Leg Is Broken," *MI,* September 9, 1921; "Tanks Sign New Halfback," *MI,* September 27, 1921.

6. "Fumes," *IR,* September 19, 1921.

7. "Park Rights Divided Up," *MI,* September 29, 1921; *PT,* October 1, 1921.

8. "Tanks Wins Opener from Jackson 6–0," *IR,* October 2, 1921; "Fumes," *IR,* September 20, 1921.

9. "Tanks Boosters Day Meets with Popular Approval," *IR,* October 18, 1921.

10. "Arrange Prelim for Portsmouth Game," *IR,* October 23, 1921.

11. Interview by Carl Becker with Lincoln DeLong. Jim Thorpe received $250 a game from the Canton Bulldogs in 1915. For a brief commentary on salaries of professional players, see Neft et al., eds., *Pro Football,* 12.

12. "Great Tank Machine Humbles Charleston," *IR,* October 17, 1921.

13. "'Boosters Day' Next Sunday at Beechwood for Tank Team," *IR,* October 17, 1921.

14. "Tanks Boosters Day"; "Tanks Already in Need of Boosters' Day," *PT,* October 19, 1921; "Tanks in Fine Shape for Meeting with Ashland," *MI,* October 22, 1921.

15. *PT,* October 25, 1921.

Notes to Pages 38–48

16. "One Touchdown Won for Tanks from Ashland Tigers," "Fumes," *IR*, October 24, 1921; "Tanks Continue Winning Rampage," *MI*, October 25, 1921.

17. *IR*, October 28, 1921.

18. "First Call Issued for Smoke House," *MS*, August 26, 1921; "Smoke House Eleven Will Hold First Practice Tuesday Night," *MS*, September 11, 1921.

19. "Speaking of Pure Bunk," *PT*, October 21, 1921; "Portsmouth Here Strong," *MI*, October 28, 1921.

20. "800 Fans to Invade Cannonville, *PT*, October 26, 1921; "Big Grid Battle Will Be Fought Today between Tanks and Smoke House," *MS*, October 30, 1921.

21. *IR*, November 3, 1921.

22. "Sunday's Game as Seen by the Portsmouth Times," *MI*, November 2, 1921.

23. "Peeved Because Team Was Clearly Outplayed, Ironton Tanks Are Rapping Officials," *PT*, November 2, 1921.

24. *IR*, November 4, 1921.

25. "Decide upon Officials for Smoke House–Tank Game Sunday," *MS*, November 21, 1921.

26. "Smoke House Getting in Shape for Tanks," *MS*, November 15, 1921.

27. "Lombards Can't Play Either Is Portsmouth Wail," *IR*, November 16, 1921.

28. "Tickets for Sunday's Football Game on Sale," *MS*, November 16, 1921; "Thousands Will Be in Attendance at the Tank-Portsmouth Game," *IR*, November 17, 1921.

29. "Special Train Secured, Band Follows Tanks," *IR*, November 14, 1921.

30. "Fist Fights Enliven Game," *PT*, November 21, 1921.

31. "Ironton Won Easy Victory from Portsmouth," *IR*, November 21, 1921.

32. "Portsmouth Proves Very Easy for Tanks," *MI*, November 22, 1921.

33. "A Cheap Squeal," *WHR*, November 24, 1921.

34. Quoted in "Rules Commission of Football Decides Game Could Not Be Forfeited and Clearly Indicates That 'Welchers' Have No Leg to Stand On," *IR*, November 22, 1921; and "High Football Authorities," *MI*, November 22, 1921.

35. "Disregarding Iron-Bound Eligible List Tanks Import College Stars and Beat Smokehouse Eleven, 1 to 0," *PT*, November 21, 1921; "Smoke House to Play Two More Games," *MS*, November 21, 1921.

36. "Gamblers Take over Tanks and Engineered Deal Whereby Three Ringers Joined Them to Beat Portsmouth," *PT*, November 21, 1921.

37. This section derives from twelve issues of the *Portsmouth Times* published from November 21 through November 25. Shannon at Morris Harvey is mentioned in the "Miscellaneous Records of the Intercollegiate Athletic Program of Morris Harvey College—1910/11–1947/48" and in the "Roster of Students, 1921–22, Morris Harvey College Annual Catalogue," in Archives, University of Charleston.

38. "Legal Action Likely [to] Be Taken," *MT*, November 23, 1921; "Tanks Retain Local Attorney to Get Their Portion of Gate Receipts," *PT*, November 22, 1921; "To Begin Legal Proceedings for Receipts," *PT*, November 22, 1921.

39. "Ironton Manager Comes after Team's Portion of Sunday's Receipts; He Returns Empty-Handed," *PT*, November 25, 1921.

Notes to Pages 48–57

40. "Ironton Scribe Says Jackson Eleven Was Afraid of Locals," *MS*, December 1, 1921.

41. "Diamond Dust," *HD*, November 23, 1921.

42. "Ironton Manager Comes after Team's Portion of Sundays Receipts"; "Portsmouth Still Whining," *MI*, November 24, 1921.

43. "Speed vs. Speed in Saturday's Game Backfields Indicate," *IR*, December 1, 1921; "Fans Won't Miss Football Test of Season," *IR*, December 2, 1921; *IR*, December 3, 1921.

44. "Tanks Come after Money; Whistle for It," *PT*, December 6, 1921; "Portsmouth Says Tanks," *MI*, December 7, 1921; "Puts It Up to the Tanks," *PT*, December 5, 1921; "Wellston Wants $450," *PT*, December 8, 1921.

45. "Hughes Says Team Has Yellow Streak," *PT*, December 12, 1921.

46. "Tanks Win Title in Hard Struggle with Wellston," *IR*, December 12, 1921; "Tanks Win from Wellston, 7 to 6," *MI*, December 13, 1921.

47. For this view of the crowd and the fighting during and after the game, see "Tanks Defeat Wellston, 7 to 6," *PT*, December 12, 1921; "Ironton Fans Beat up Four Wellston Men and Then Hold Big Crowd at Bay with Their Guns," *PT*, December 12, 1921; "Wellston Passes up Tanks," *PT*, December 12, 1921; "Portsmouth Times Sidelights," *MI*, December 13, 1921.

48. "Portsmouth Takes Wellston Loss as Bitter Pill," *IR*, December 13, 1921.

49. "The Football Controversy," *PT*, December 9, 1921.

50. "The Football Controversy," *IR*, December 10, 1921; "The Football Controversy," *MI*, December 10, 1921.

51. *IR*, December 15, 1921.

52. "Suppress the Gamblers," *PT*, December 21, 1921.

53. "Fumes," *IR*, November 23, 1921.

Chapter Four

1. "Fumes," *IR*, September 2, 1922.

2. "Celts of Cincinnati Likely to Be Booked," *IR*, September 8, 1922; "Heavy, Fast Line and Speedy Backfield Object of Tanks," *IR*, September 13, 1922.

3. "Olympian A. C. of Columbus Has Wealth of Great Stars," *IR*, September 27, 1922; "Tanks Face Strong Opposition in Game with Capital City Eleven," *MI*, September 28, 1922.

4. "Both Teams Ready for Football Opening," *IR*, September 30, 1922; "Fumes," *IR*, September 30, 1922.

5. "Tanks Show Great Form in Defeating the Columbus Olympic Team," *MI*, October 3, 1922. Barnett has the score as 22–13 (*The Spartans and the Tanks*, 16).

6. Collett, "Soliloquy, 4th in Series," *IN*, n.d.

7. "Tanks Show Wonderful Form and Defeat Athens Eleven 19 to 0," *MI*, October 10, 1922.

8. "Week End Will See Both High School and Tanks Playing on Foreign Fields," *MI*,

Notes to Pages 57–63

October 11, 1922; "Tanks Roll over Local Footballers Piling up Score of 18 to 7," *HD*, October 16, 1922.

9. "Tri-State Region Agog over Tanks Game at Huntington," *MI*, October 13, 1922; "Huntington Eleven Expects to Mar Tank Record," *IR*, October 14, 1922; "Huntington Is in Glorious State over Battle with Tanks Sunday," *MI*, October 14, 1922.

10. "Tanks Roll over Local Footballers"; "Tanks Won Hard Battle from Huntington, 18–7," *IR*, October 16, 1922.

11. "Jackson to Be Accompanied by a Big Crowd of Fans," *IR*, October 28, 1922.

12. "Portsmouth Runs out of Game with Tanks, Big Red Plays Huntington up There," *IR*, October 30, 1922; "Portsmouth Admits Superiority," *MI*, October 31, 1922; "Oh Mercy, This Is Awful; Tanks Pass up River City," *PT*, October 31, 1922.

13. "Cheap Chirp from Cannonville," *PT*, October 31, 1922.

14. "Tanks Face Much Stronger Team"; "Huntington Expects Hardest Game of Career Sunday," *IR*, November 1, 1922.

15. "Bleacher to Be Erected on Athletic Field at Beechwood," *IR*, November 2, 1922; "Four Thousand May See Tank Game at Huntington," *IR*, November 4, 1922; "Tank-Huntington Game Greatest Contest Yet Staged," *IR*, November 4, 1922.

16. "Huntington All Worked up over Game with Tanks," *IR*, November 4, 1922.

17. "Huntington Boosters Battle Ironton to 7–7 Draw in League Park Game," *HD*, November 6, 1922; "Brilliant Game Says Ridgley in Comment Today," *IR*, November 6, 1922.

18. "Tanks and Huntington Battle to 7–7 Tie," *IR*, November 6, 1922.

19. "Columbus Eagles Club Plays Tanks Sunday at Park," *IR*, November 16, 1922; "Portsmouth Cancels; Columbus Eagles Are Booked for Sunday's Game," *MI*, November 16, 1922.

20. "Sputterings from a Two-Story Town," *PT*, November 23, 1922.

21. "Zanesville Cancels Game with Tanks at Eleventh Hour," *MI*, November 19, 1922; "Local Interest Added When Tank Players Go into Jackson Lineup," *IR*, November 20, 1922.

22. "Local Interest Added When Tank Players Go into Jackson Lineup"; *IR*, November 20, 1922; "Fumes," *IR*, November 22, 1922.

23. "Washington Independents Will Play Tanks Sunday," *MI*, November 23, 1922.

24. "Three Thousand Expected to See Thanksgiving Day Game," *IR*, November 28, 1922; "Boosters Claim to Be Equal of Tanks," *MI*, November 29, 1922.

25. "Thousands of Fans Will Witness Today's Tilt with the Huntington Team," *MI*, November 30, 1922.

26. "Huntington Nosed Out in Sensational 12–10 Game on Ironton Grid," *HD*, December 1, 1922.

27. Collett, "Soliloquy, 4th in Series."

28. "Wellston Draws Fangs of Jackson Bearcats," *WS*, December 1, 1922; "Terrible Tanks Running out of Game with the Coal Barons Is Wellston Cry," *IR*, December 2, 1922.

29. *IR*, December 5, 1922.

30. Collett, "Soliloquy, 4th in Series."

328

Notes to Pages 63–74

31. "Mighty Tanks Met Their First Defeat of Year Sunday," *IR*, December 11, 1922.

32. "Smoke House Aggregation Organizes for Grid Season," *MS*, August 31, 1922.

33. *PT*, October 27, 1922.

34. *PT*, November 27, 1922.

35. "Tanks Deserve Financial Support of Ironton This Season," *MI*, September 12, 1923.

36. Ibid.

37. "Tanks Take Their First Workout This Afternoon," *IR*, September 22, 1923; "Tanks Hold Their First Workout," *MI*, September 23, 1923.

38. "Tanks Will Be in Prime Condition for the First Game," *IR*, September 26, 1923; "Football Blowoff Will Draw Largest Crowd in History," *IR*, October 5, 1923.

39. "Football Blowoff Will Draw Largest Crowd in History."

40. "Columbus West Side A. C. Grid Team to Play Tanks Sunday," *MI*, October 10, 1923.

41. Ibid.; "All Tri State Looks Forward to Tanks–West Side Game," *IR*, October 12, 1923.

42. "Tanks Playing Good Game, Won 7–6 Victory from Columbus," *MI*, October 16, 1923; "Tanks Come from Behind to Win," *IR*, October 16, 1923.

43. "Ironton Beats West Side A. C.," *OSJ*, October 16, 1923; "Journal Was Misinformed," *MI*, October 17, 1923.

44. "Journal Was Misinformed."

45. *IR*, October 17, 1923.

46. "Ironton-Portsmouth Road Will Be Kept Hot for Gridiron Classic Sunday," *MI*, October 19, 1923; "Smoke House out to Duplicate Victory of P. H. S. over Ironton by Fray with Famous Tanks This Afternoon," *MS*, October 21, 1923.

47. "Portsmouth Game Drew Largest Paid Attendance," *IR*, October 22, 1923.

48. "Boosters Ready for Tank Battle," *HD*, October 25, 1923.

49. "Tanks: Won 7–0 Victory over Huntimgton in Great Game," *IR*, October 28, 1923; "Fumes," *IR*, October 28, 1923; "Tanks Aerial Attack Carried Boosters off Their Feet Sunday Afternoon," *MI*, October 30, 1923.

50. "Tanks Wanted in Columbus," *MI*, November 6, 1923.

51. "Huntington Assembling Powerful Machine to Battle Tanks Sunday," *MI*, November 7, 1923; "Boosters Prepare to Tackle Tanks," *HD*, November 7, 1923; "Formidable Huntington Team Here to Down Tanks Today," *MI*, November 11, 1923; "Great Strength Has Been Added to Huntington Eleven," *IR*, November 11, 1923.

52. "Boosters Loading up for Game with Ironton Tanks Sunday," *MI*, November 8, 1923.

53. "Formidable Huntington Team."

54. "Tanks Getting Ready for Grid Tilt Sunday," *MI*, November 15, 1923; "Tanks Will Receive Acid Test against Queen City Eleven Sunday," *MI*, November 16, 1923; "Big Red Eleven Defeats Cincinnatians," *IR*, November 19, 1923.

55. *PT*, November 17, 1923.

56. "Smoke House Eleven to Meet," *MS*, November 20, 1923.

57. "Ackroyd Says Team out to Win," *MS*, November 23, 1923.

58. The description below of the game comes primarily from "Tanks Have No Trouble Winning from Columbus at River City Sunday," *MI*, November 27, 1923. See also Barnett and Terhune, "When the Tanks Were Tops," 17.

59. "Tanks Have No Trouble."

60. *PT*, November 26, 1923.

61. "Tanks Have No Trouble."

62. "West Side Humiliated on Portsmouth Field," *IR*, November 26, 1923.

63. "Poor Old Portsmouth," *IR*, November 26, 1923.

64. "Turkey Day Football Menu Best Ever Offered Local Fans," *MI*, November 28, 1923; "Tanks Smash Way to Grid Title of Southern Ohio," *MI*, December 1, 1923.

65. "Fumes," *IR*, December 1, 1923.

66. "Tanks Play Huntington at Beechwood Next Sunday," *IR*, December 3, 1923; "Tanks and Huntington at Beechwood Park Sunday Afternoon," *MI*, December 4, 1923.

67. "Tanks Play Huntington."

68. "Fumes," *IR*, December 6, 1923.

69. "Season's Biggest Game Will Be Staged at Park This P.M." *MI*, December 9, 1923.

70. "Duke Ridgley Pays Tribute to the Tanks," *IR*, December 12, 1923.

71. "Tanks and Boosters Settle Championship Feud at Ironton Today," *HD*, December 9, 1923; "Tanks Push Boosters into Mud and Win the Title Game," *HD*, December 10, 1923.

72. "Listen to Portsmouth Squawk; Boosters a 'Home' Team Sunday," *MI*, December 11, 1923.

73. *IR*, December 10, 1923.

74. "Tanks Play for Dinner," *MI*, December 30, 1923; "Real Program Arranged for Tanks Dinner," *IR*, December 30, 1923; "Big Red Eleven Chalks up Real Post Season Victory," *IR*, January 4, 1924.

75. "Ball Benefit Game to Be Arranged by Committee Soon," *IR*, December 11, 1923; "How Would You Like to Be a Tank? Players Given $290 Check Last Evening," *MI*, December 23, 1923.

76. Peterson, *Pigskin*, 91.

Chapter Five

1. "Football Fans Are Awaiting Opening Kick-Off," *MI*, August 31, 1924.

2. "Tanks Bring Strong Teams to City," *MI*, September 12, 1924; "Tanks to Use Diversified Attack This Season," *IR*, September 17, 1924.

3. "Sports of All Sorts," *AI*, September 14, 1924; "Ashland-Ironton Tanks Will Be Name of This Year's Grid Eleven," *AI*, September 15, 1924.

4. "Tanks Are 'Ironton Tanks,'" *MI*, September 16, 1924.

5. "Fence Climbers to Be Prosecuted," *MI*, September 26, 1924.

6. "Murray City–Tank Game Should Be Best of Whole Schedule," *MI*, September 21, 1924.

Notes to Pages 84–92

7. "Tanks Win from Padded Murray City Eleven," *MI*, October 7, 1924.

8. "Brecks Snowed under by Ironton Eleven," *LCJ*, October 13, 1924.

9. "Going to Show Tanks Something New, Potters Declare," *MI*, October 14, 1924.

10. "Potters Give Tanks Terrific Battle but Big Red Won," *IR*, October 20, 1924; "Notes on the Game," *MI*, October 21, 1924; *CE*, October 20, 1924.

11. For comments on the Silents, see Phil Dietrick, *The Silent Men* (North Hunting-don, Pa., N.d.), passim; Dietrich, *Down Payments*, passim; Maltby, "Origins and Early Development of Professional Football," 68.

12. "Tanks Will Have Chance at Semi-Pro Championship," *MI*, October 22, 1924.

13. "Tanks Defeat Akron Silents: Become State Champs," *IR*, October 27, 1924; "Semi-Pro Champions of Ohio," *MI*, October 28, 1924; "Notes on the Game," *MI*, October 28, 1924.

14. "Akron Silents Lose to Ironton Tanks," *ABJ*, October 27, 1924.

15. "Jungle Imps Cross Smoke House Goal Line; Won 10–0," *PT*, October 27, 1924.

16. "Portsmouth Is Recruiting for Players to Oppose Tanks," *MI*, November 6, 1924.

17. *PT*, November 10, 1924.

18. "Solomon Will Not Play with Tanks against Potters Sunday," *MI*, November 14, 1924.

19. "Member of Tank Team Expresses Self," *MI*, November 14, 1924.

20. "Tank Team Is Addressed by Booster Who Asks for a Little Consideration from a Civic Standpoint," *IR*, November 13, 1924. Though the letter appeared in the *Register* a day before the player's letter to the *Irontonian*, the "Booster" obviously knew what the player would be saying.

21. "Tanks Won 7–3 Decision from Potters in Flashy Game," *IR*, November 17, 1924.

22. "Tanks Playing Best Game of Year, Romp Away with Huntington Team," *MI*, November 28, 1924.

23. "Huntington Boosters Are Crushed Again by Ironton Tanks," *HD*, November 28, 1924.

24. "What Team Will Tanks Play Sunday?" *MI*, November 29, 1924.

25. "Tanks Are Ready to Defeat Anything Portsmouth May Offer Them," *MI*, November 30, 1924.

26. "Tanks and Portsmouth Play Scoreless Tie," *IR*, December 1, 1924; Collett, "Soliloquy, 6th in Series."

27. "Tanks and Cleveland Bulldogs May Play Sunday," *MI*, December 7, 1924; "Tanks Will Not Meet Cleveland Team," *MI*, December 8, 1924.

28. "Tanks Turn in Uniforms," *IR*, December 3, 1924.

29. "Ashland's Greatest Football Eleven," *AI*, August 31, 1924.

30. For a brief description of Armco in Ashland, see Carl Becker, "Armco Incorporated" and "John Butler Tytus," in Bruce E. Seely, ed., *Iron and Steel in the Twentieth Century: Encyclopedia of American Business History and Biography* (N.p., 1994), 18–23, 435–37; and Christy Borth, *True Steel* (N.p., 1941), 261–63.

31. See John McGill, *Kentucky Sports* (Lexington, 1978), 84; "People Make the Difference," *MJ*, July 11, 1975; Interview by Carl Becker with Harold Nicholson, May 23, 1995.

331

Notes to Pages 93–104

32. "The Sportsman's Corner," *AI*, August 27, 1925; "Tank Question Still Pending," *MI*, August 27, 1925.

33. Quoted in "Ashland Ready to Receive the Tanks with Open Arms," *MI*, August 25, 1925.

34. "$25,000 Park to Be Biggest in Tri-State," *AI*, September 6, 1925.

35. On this subject, see "Sonny Winters to Meet with Local Business Men Monday," *MI*, August 29, 1925; "Arguments over Tanks and 'Shorty' Davies Continue in Sports Realm," *MI*, August 30, 1925; *AI*, August 28, 1925.

36. "Fumes," *IR*, August 25, 26, 1925.

37. "Sonny Winters to Meet with Local Business Men Monday"; "Tanks, Fans and Merchants Will Meet This Evening," *MI*, September 1, 1925; "Reception Tonight Will Give Idea of Strength of Season's Tanks," *IR*, September 1, 1925.

38. "Board of Education Requests Resignation of Shorty Davies," *IR*, September 5, 1925; "Resignation of 'Shorty' Davies Requested by School Board," *MI*, September 5, 1925. The minutes of the Board of Education of the Ironton City School District do not refer to the request.

39. "He Must Choose," *MI*, September 5, 1925.

40. "Ironton and Coach Charlton Davies," *AI*, September 6, 1925.

41. "Shorty Davies Resigns as Athletic Director," *MI*, September 6, 1925.

42. "Ironton High and Semi-Pro Football," *AI*, September 10, 1925.

43. "A Natural Complaint," *MI*, September 11, 1925.

44. Bob Gill, *Down in the Valley: A True Story of the Ohio Valley League in the 1920s* (North Huntingdon, Pa., 1993), 3–6.

45. "West Side Athletic Club from Columbus Will Oppose Armcos Sunday," *AI*, October 9, 1925.

46. "Diamond Dust," *HD*, October 9, 1925; "The Sportsman's Corner," *AI*, October 9, 1925.

47. "The Fault with Professional Football," *AI*, October 14, 1925.

48. "Business Men Pledge Support to Armco Team," *AI*, October 15, 1925.

49. "Retail Merchants Meet Today to Go over Tank Drive Report," *MI*, September 19, 1925.

50. "Red Machine Given Action Thru Scrimmage," *IR*, September 21, 1925.

51. "Tanks Play Greatest Game to Defeat Potters," *IR*, October 17, 1925; "Tanks Win Brilliant Game from Potters," *MI*, October 18, 1925.

52. "Tanks Crush Armco Team, Start Early Drive for 21–6 Victory," *MI*, October 20, 1925.

53. "Ashland Conquers Middletown in Thriller" *AI*, November 2, 1925; "Armco Blues Lose First Game in Two Years to Fast Ashland Crew," *MJ*, November 2, 1925.

54. "Boosters Have Crack at Gridiron Honors If They Can Beat Tanks," *HD*, October 21, 1925; "Boosters Plan to Pass Tanks to Defeat Sunday," *IR*, October 23, 1925.

55. "Terrible Tanks Go Abroad Sunday, Playing Huntington," *IR*, October 20, 1925.

56. Gill, *Down in the Valley*, 7; "Wagner Pirates Have Many College Stars," *MI*, October 30, 1925; "Wagner Pirates Oppose Tanks," *IR*, October 30, 1925. Gill argues that

332

Notes to Pages 104–118

the Pirates did not meet strong competition in Columbus because the many semiprofessional teams there diffused the pool of talent.

57. "Wagner Pirates Lose," *CD*, November 2, 1925.

58. "Armcos Trying to Sign Jim Thorpe," *IR*, October 30, 1925; "Tanks to Turn Heavy Guns on Armco Team," *MI*, November 6, 1925; "Tanks and Armco Will Present Strongest Fronts Today," *MI*, November 8, 1925.

59. "Armco to Meet Strong Bobbs-Chevrolet on Local Field Today," *AI*, November 15, 1925; "Shorty Still with Armco," *MI*, November 15, 1925.

60. "Damnable Rumors," *AI*, November 17, 1925.

61. "Cincinnati Swamps Ashland Armcos by 20 to 0," *AI*, November 23, 1925; "So Easy! Armco Soft Picking," *CE*, November 23, 1925.

62. Articles on the controversy appeared in the *Ohio State Journal* on November 12, 15, 17, and 18, 1925.

63. "Diamond Dust," *HD*, November 11, 1925.

64. "Boosters Coming after Tanks' Title Today," *MI*, November 15, 1925.

65. "Koors Pull Comeback on Ironton Tanks," *DJ*, November 23, 1925; "Forward Pass Enables Koors to Tie Ironton," *DH*, November 23, 1925. The *Herald* estimated the crowd at three thousand.

66. "Notes on the Game Today," *MI*, November 26, 1925.

67. "Tanks Are Under-Dogs in Pre-Game Gossip," *MI*, November 25, 1925.

68. "A Sunday Editorial," *IR*, November 29, 1925.

69. One may find figures on attendance in the NFL in the 1920s in Carroll et al., eds., *Total Football*, 1593–96.

70. "Tanks Closed Season Sunday in Blaze of Glory, 24–6," *IR*, December 14, 1925.

71. "Tanks Banquet Following Game of Sunday Will Long Be Remembered by Participants," *IR*, December 14, 1925.

72. "To Seek $125,000 for Municipal Athletic Field," *PT*, October 9, 1925; "Civic Clubs Back Proposal for $125,000 Athletic Field," *MS*, October 9, 1925.

73. "Smoke House 11 May Disband," *MS*, October 24, 1925.

Chapter Six

1. "Presidents, Panthers Clash Here Sunday," *PT*, September 20, 1926.

2. Bob Gill, "Rosters of Armcos, Tanks, Presidents, Shoe-Steel and Spartans," typescript in author's possession.

3. "Double Attraction on Labold Field Sunday; Football Will Be Mixed with Diamond Game," *PT*, September 25, 1926.

4. "Presidents Win at Xenia," *PT*, October 4, 1926.

5. "Local Grid Teams Propose Merger for Peerless Winner," *MS*, October 12, 1926.

6. "Local Football Merger Plans Meet Disapproval of Teams," *MS*, October 13, 1926; "Elevens Oppose Merger; Will Settle Field Dispute Tonight," *PT*, October 13, 1926.

7. "Presidents and Merchants Sign Contracts for Game," *MI*, October 21, 1926; "Merchants to Battle Sunday; And They Don't Mean Maybe," *PT*, October 22, 1926.

Notes to Pages 118–128

8. "Football Today," *MS,* October 17, 1926.

9. "Tanks Set Nov 7 Portsmouth Date," *MS,* October 21, 1926.

10. *PT,* October 22, 1926; "Portsmouth Accepts Terms of Tanks: Mussolini Had Nothing on This Bunch," *IT,* October 27, 1926; "Local Club Is Guaranteed $400," *PT,* October 29, 1926.

11. "Sportsman Corner," *AI,* August 10, 1926.

12. Ibid.; "First Call for Practice Issued to Armco Grid Candidates," *AI,* August 9, 1926; "Armco Football Eleven to Be One of Strongest in Tri-State," *AI,* August 15, 1926.

13. "Sportsman Corner," *AI,* August 4, 1926.

14. Interview by Carl Becker with Louis Ware, May 23, 1995.

15. Gill, "Rosters."

16. "Armco Getting in Trim for Sunday Game with Koors," *AI,* September 22, 1926.

17. "Armco Football Eleven to Be One of the Strongest."

18. "Business Men Pledge Support to Armco Football Team," *AI,* August 20, 1926.

19. "Hot Weather Football Prospects," *AI,* August 22, 1926.

20. "Sales Meeting to Be Held Tonight," *AI,* September 9, 1926.

21. "Ashland Ready for Invasion of Columbus," *AI,* October 3, 1926.

22. "Armco Blues Lose Battle at Ashland," *MNS,* October 18, 1926.

23. "Mass Meeting Will Consider Stadium Plans," *IT,* January 5, 1926.

24. The list of members appeared in "Stadium Boosters Will Meet Tonight," *IT,* April 16, 1926, and "New Stadium Committee Will Meet Monday Night," *IT,* April 18, 1926. For a view of the members, see Payne, "Gridiron in Ironton," 75–77.

25. "Corporation Organized to Build Beechwood Stadium," *IT,* April 20, 1926; "Stadium Association Gets Twenty-Year Lease on Grounds," *IT,* May 14, 1926.

26. "Stock Subscriptions for Stadium Is $26,000," *IT,* May 4, 1926.

27. Collett, "Soliloquy, 8th in Series," *IN,* n.d.

28. Payne, "Gridiron in Ironton," 77–78.

29. Barnett, *The Spartans and the Tanks,* 7.

30. The *Ironton Tribune* described the controversy in murky detail: "Agreement Is Reached on Personnel of Tank Eleven," September 29, 1926; "Wagner Pirates Rank at Top of Columbus Football Heap," October 1, 1926. Providing a much clearer picture was the *Independent:* "Contract Mailed to Tank Players," October 1, 1926. Gill mistakenly lists five Tanks opposing Lambert; there were three at the outset (*Down in the Valley,* 33).

31. *CD,* October 4, 1926.

32. "Tanks Defeat Cleveland Indians by 47–0 Count," *IT,* October 18, 1926.

33. "Tanks Won Ashland Regatta by Two Lengths," *IT,* October 25, 1926.

34. "Lambert Having Trouble Seeking Tank Opposition," *IT,* October 18, 1926.

35. "Presidents in Tip-Top Shape for Gridiron Battle with the Tanks in Ironton Sunday," *PT,* November 5, 1926.

36. "Ironton Stadium Is Mecca for the Local Grid Fans Today," *MS,* November 7, 1926.

37. *PT,* November 8, 1926; "Ironton Admits Presidents Good," *MS,* November 9, 1926.

38. One may read of Thorpe and the Indians in Robert L. Whitman, *Jim Thorpe and*

Notes to Pages 129–138

the Oorang Indians: The N.F.L.'s Most Colorful Franchise (Defiance, Ohio, 1984), 43–87. See also Bill Baron et al., eds., *The Official NFL Encyclopedia of Pro Football* (New York, 1982), 19.

39. "Armcos Overwhelm Oorang Indians by 45–0 Count," *AI*, November 8, 1926.

40. Collett, "Soliloquy, 8th in Series."

41. "Perry's Team Praised at Annual Banquet of Armco," *AI*, December 4, 1926.

42. "Cincinnati Potters and Ashland Fight to Scoreless Tie at Redland," *AI*, December 26, 1926; "Tie Tilt," *CE*, December 6, 1926.

43. Nine clubs, all but one in a metropolitan area, constituted the league. The NFL sought to hamstring the new league by increasing the number of its franchises. Support for the league was minimal, and it folded after one season, the Philadelphia Quakers winning the championship (Baron et al., eds., *Official NFL Encyclopedia of Pro Football*, 114).

44. *IT*, November 24, 1926.

45. Quoted in Barnett, *The Spartans and the Tanks*, 7–8.

46. "Tank Special Train Leaves for Cincinnati Sunday Morning," *IT*, November 27, 1926.

47. "Says Panthers Would Draw Well Here," *PT*, November 9, 1926.

48. "A Football Surprise," *PT*, November 10, 1926.

49. "Presidents Meet Worthy Foe in Scrappy Middletown Armco Eleven Here Next Sunday," *PT*, November 23, 1926; "Middletown Armco Eleven Plays Here Next Sunday," *MS*, November 23, 1926.

50. "Armco Blues Win over Portsmouth Team by Lone Touchdown," *MJ*, November 29, 1926; "Armco Blues Winner of Sunday Game," *MNS*, November 29, 1926.

51. "Ironton Tanks Agree to Meet Presidents," *MS*, November 25, 1926.

52. "Local Big Red Squad Will Drill Overtime for Tanks," *MS*, November 28, 1926; "Presidents Are Preparing for Tanks' Clash," *MS*, November 30, 1926.

53. "Reinforced Presidents Get Final Workout," *PT*, December 4, 1926.

54. "Presidents to Don War Togs for Drill Tonight," *MS*, December 2, 1926; "Presidents Are Set for Tank Battle," *PT*, December 3, 1926.

55. "Presidents Enjoy Grid Feast Sunday," *MS*, December 7, 1926.

56. "Fumes," *IT*, December 8, 1926.

57. "Steps Taken for Organization of Professional Grid League," *IT*, December 6, 1926; "Move to Form Pro League," *MI*, December 17, 1926.

58. Collett, "Soliloquy, 8th in Series"; "Stadium Assoc. to Hold Annual Meeting Tonight," *IT*, December 15, 1926.

59. "Winters Team Wins Benefit Game 2 to 0," *IT*, January 2, 1927.

Chapter Seven

1. "Stadium Association to Take over Tank Football Team," *IT*, January 7, 1927; "Ironton Stadium Company to Take over Tanks Team," *MS*, January 8, 1927.

2. "W. A. 'Bill' Brooks Named 1927 Manager of Tanks," *IT*, January 9, 1927.

Notes to Pages 138–149

3. Minute Book, Board of Education, Ironton, Ohio, February 11, 1927; "Shorty Davies Elected I.H.S. Athletic Director," *IT*, February 12, 1927.

4. "Precipitate Action," *IT*, February 17, 1927.

5. "Concord Needed," *IT*, February 20, 1927.

6. "Fumes," *IT*, February 19, 1927.

7. "Fumes," *IT*, April 12, 1927.

8. "Fumes," *IT*, June 19, 1927; "Prospects Bright for Tank and Tiger Teams," *IT*, July 31, 1927.

9. "Fumes," *IT*, September 11, 1927.

10. Gill, "Rosters."

11. "The Tank Team to Continue on Profit Sharing Basis," *IT*, September 27, 1927.

12. "Stirring Appeal Made for Support of Tanks," *IT*, September 27, 1927.

13. "'They Cannot Pass,' Spirit of Tank Players," *IT*, September 27, 1927; "Brooks Quits as Manager of Ironton Tanks," *MS*, September 29, 1927.

14. *IT*, September 29, 1927.

15. "Drive Will Be Launched to Fill Stadium at Tanks' First Game," *IT*, August 21, 1927.

16. *IT*, October 3, 1927; "Boosters Beaten by Tanks, 25–7," *TB*, October 3, 1927.

17. "Tanks Disband; Cancel Sunday's Game," *IT*, October 5, 1927; "Famous Ironton Tanks Disband," *MS*, October 6, 1927.

18. "Tanks Back: Agree with Stadium Association," *IT*, October 8, 1927; "Ironton Tanks Settle Differences," *MS*, October 9, 1927.

19. "Support the Tigers," *IT*, October 9, 1927.

20. Collett, "Soliloquy, 10th in Series," *IN*, n.d.

21. "Winters Quarter for Armco Eleven," *AI*, August 7, 1927; "Public Asked to View Prospects of Perry's Team," *AI*, September 5, 1927.

22. Interview with Louis Ware.

23. "Perry Announces Lineup for Opening Game with Dayton Koors," *AI*, August 31, 1927.

24. "Armco Not to Enter League," *AI*, September 16, 1927.

25. "Perry's Men Face Hard Battle at Armco Field This Afternoon," *AI*, October 2, 1927.

26. Such writers as Grantland Rice, Ring Lardner, and Arch Ward turned out "daily paeans to the feats of athletes" (Rader, *American Sports*, 199).

27. "Steelmakers and Tanks to Clash in Valley Classic Sunday," *AI*, October 18, 1927.

28. "Both Tanks and Armcos Holding Secret Practices for SundayÕs Game," *AI*, October 21, 1927.

29. "Fumes," *IT*, January 18, 1927.

30. "Ohio Valley Championship to Be Settled Sunday," *AI*, November 29, 1927.

31. "Football Players Look with Favor on Plan to Sign Up Thorpe," *MS*, September 22, 1927.

32. "Thorpe to Be in City Today," *MS*, September 3, 1927.

33. "Players Respond Enthusiastically to Thorpe's Acceptance as Grid Coach," *MS*, September 9, 1927.

Notes to Pages 149–158

34. *PT,* September 13, 1927.

35. Gill, "Roster."

36. "Bulldogs Drop Close Game to Thorpe's Team," *SN,* October 10, 1927; *PT,* October 10, 1927.

37. *PT,* October 28, 1927.

38. "Thorpe Prepares Locals for Battle Sunday," *PT,* October 25, 1927.

39. "Guardsmen Win over Portsmouth," *CE,* October 31, 1927.

40. *PT,* October 27, 1927; *IT,* October 28, 1927; "Tanks Cancel the Season's Dates with Shoe-Steels," *MS,* October 28, 1927.

41. *IT,* October 28, 1927; *PT,* October 29, 1927.

42. *PT,* November 3, 1927.

43. *IT,* November 9, 1927; "Tanks Commence Loading up for Sunday Contest," *AI,* November 9, 1927.

44. "The Tanks-Armcos Game Ends in 7–7 Tie," *IT,* November 14, 1927.

45. "Figures Show Much Smaller Attendance at Second Armco-Tank Contest," *AI,* November 15, 1927.

46. "Ah, More Football," *IT,* November 17, 1927.

47. "Tell It to the Wide World, Shoe Steels Beat Tanks, 7–0," *PT,* November 21, 1927.

48. "Portsmouth Wins," *IT,* November 22, 1927.

49. "Now Is the Time," *IT,* December 1, 1927.

50. "About Town," *IT,* December 3, 1927.

51. "The Football Situation," *IT,* December 4, 1927.

52. "Stadium Association Will Now Take Management of Tanks," *IT,* December 22, 1927.

53. Interview by Carl Becker with Glenn Presnell, December 22, 1995.

54. "Tanks to Split Sum of $6,000," *MS,* December 3, 1927; "Tank Players Should Have Merry Christmas," *IT,* December 18, 1927.

55. "Valley Championship up for Decision at Armco Park Today," *AI,* November 23, 1927; "Thorpe Outfit Will Play Here," *AI,* November 29, 1927.

56. "Notre Dame Full Back May Join Creasy," *MS,* December 1, 1927; "Shoe Steels Have the Most Powerful Football Team in History of Peerless City," *MS,* December 4, 1927; "Green Bay Stars to Join Shoe Steels for Championship Battle with Armco Team," *MS,* December 3, 1927.

57. "Notre Dame Full Back May Join Creasy."

58. "Steelmakers to Stick by No 'Loading Up' Policy," *AI,* November 30, 1927.

59. "Stuart Sprints Ball with Punt to Turn Tide for Armco 7–6," *AI,* December 5, 1927.

60. Interview with Louis Ware.

61. "One Point Defeat at Ashland Ends 1927 Season for Locals," *MS,* December 6, 1927; McGill, *Kentucky Sports,* 89.

62. "Armco Banquet Closes Season," *AI,* December 5, 1927.

Notes to Pages 159–169

Chapter Eight

1. Certificate of Death, 45552, Vol. 5766, Jacques Creasy, Ohio Historical Society, Columbus, Ohio.

2. *PT,* August 11, 1928.

3. "Optimistic Letter from Jean," *PT,* August 17, 1928.

4. *PT,* August 28, 1928.

5. "Portsmouth Assured Professional Grid Team This Season," *MS,* August 21, 1928; *PT,* August 23, 1928. Dr. Frank Coburn was secretary, and Graf became the treasurer. The directors were Vaughan A. Talbott, Grimes, Thomas Williams, Earl Cunningham, Father L. P. Falver, Peter Warsaw, and Edward Leach.

6. *PT,* August 22, 1928.

7. *PT,* August 23, 1928; "Coach Jean Assumes Charge of Grid Team," *MS,* August 23, 1928.

8. "Grid Players to Report Next Saturday," *MS,* September 1, 1928.

9. "Will Ask for Bond Issue to Build Stadium on Labold Field," *MS,* August 28, 1928; "New Stadium to Be World War Memorial," *MS,* September 20, 1928.

10. *PT,* September 7, 1928; "'Spartans' Favored as Name of Portsmouth's Professionals," MS, September 7, 1928.

11. *PT,* September 7, 1928.

12. *PT,* September 24, 1928.

13. *PT,* September 25, 1928.

14. *PT,* October 1, 1928.

15. *PT,* October 8, 1928.

16. "Perry to Stress Action in Armco Football Eleven," *AI,* August 21, 1928. For a brief description of Jones's offense, see Howard E. Jones and Alfred F. Wesson, *Football for the Fan* (Los Angeles, 1929), 28–29.

17. "Armco Has Record Sale of Tickets," *AI,* August 31, 1928.

18. "Perry to Stress Action in Armco Football Eleven."

19. Interview with Louis Ware.

20. "Armco Has Record Sale of Tickets," *AI,* August 13, 1928.

21. "Football Heads Draw up Dates," *AI,* August 28, 1928.

22. "Steelmen Play Strong Cincinnati Soldiers Here Today in Second Game," *AI,* September 30, 1928.

23. "Armco Blues Lose to Ashland, 13–0," *MJ,* October 8, 1928.

24. "Busy Week in Portsmouth as Spartans Prep for Ashland," *AI,* October 11, 1928.

25. *PT,* October 15, 1928; "Steelmakers Turn Back Portsmouth 13–0 in Colorful Contest," *AI,* October 15, 1928; "News Carries Weird Account of Armco-Spartan Skirmish," *AI,* October 15, 1928.

26. Barnett, *The Spartans and the Tanks,* 8.

27. I derived these figures from a reading of the McMahon Letters, Archives, Pro Football Hall of Fame, Canton, Ohio.

28. Glenn Presnell to Nick McMahon, March 15, 1928, ibid.

Notes to Pages 169–179

29. Barnett, *The Spartans and the Tanks*, 8. For a biographical sketch of Presnell, see Barnett, "Glenn Presnell," in David L. Porter, ed., *Biographical Dictionary of American Sports: Football* (New York, 1987), 479–80.

30. Quoted in Barnett, *The Spartans and the Tanks*, 8; Interview by Carl Becker with Glenn Presnell, October 19, 1992.

31. Quoted in Barnett, *The Spartans and the Tanks*, 9; Interview by Carl Becker with Harold Rolph, July 19, 1993.

32. "The Faithful Brooks," *IT*, August 31, 1928.

33. "The Tanks," *IT*, August 31, 1928.

34. "Tanks Have Material for Greatest Team Ever," *IT*, September 2, 1928.

35. "Have a Care," *IT*, September 26, 1928.

36. "'Big Red' Opens Sunday," *IT*, September 30, 1928.

37. "Panthers Lose to Tanks, 47–0," *CPD*, October 8, 1928.

38. *IT*, October 12, 1928; "Tanks and Akron Battle to Scoreless Tie in Thrilling Game," *IT*, October 15, 1928.

39. "Awnings Tie Ironton 0–0," *ABJ*, October 15, 1928.

40. "Perry Leaves Town with Armco Team," *AI*, October 23, 1928; "Armco Team Goes into Hiding for Sunday Game," *IT*, October 24, 1928.

41. "Armco Wins," *IT*, October 30, 1928.

42. *IT*, November 3, 1928; *IT*, November 5, 1928.

43. "Let's Be Fair," *IT*, November 14, 1928.

44. *IT*, November 1, 1928; "Ironton Tanks Outplay Blues; Score Ends 13–0," *MNS*, November 20, 1928.

45. Gill, *Down in the Valley*, 97.

46. "Steelmakers Overcome Bulldogs 13–0 with Little Trouble," *AI*, October 11, 1928; "Ashland Hangs First Defeat on Rogers," *CR*, November 5, 1928.

47. "Middletown Has Booster Parade," *AI*, November 9, 1928.

48. "Ashland Outplays Armco Blues to Grab 14–0 Victory," *MNS*, November 13, 1928.

49. "To Renew Hostilities," *IT*, November 20, 1928.

50. "Armco Invades Tanks Stronghold for Clash Today," *AI*, November 25, 1928.

51. "Sunday's Game," *IT*, November 27, 1928.

52. *PT*, November 30, 1928.

53. "Big Surprise Turned in by Guards," *CE*, December 3, 1928.

54. "Armco Banquet Held at Gibson," *AI*, December 3, 1928.

55. "Awnings No Match for Tank Gridders," *ABJ*, November 30, 1928; "Tanks Carry Fight to Akron and Win 19–0," *IT*, November 30, 1928; "Fumes," *IT*, December 2, 1928.

56. "Portsmouth Turned Back in Title Game," *PT*, December 10, 1928.

57. "Armco Next on Spartans Menu for Sunday," *MS*, September 28, 1928.

58. *PT*, November 2, 1928; "Fumes," *IT*, November 16, 1928.

59. *PT*, December 5, 1928.

60. "Spartans Will Wind up Season Sunday in Ironton; Will Banquet Monday Night," *MS*, December 5, 1928.

61. "Spartans Scattered," *PT*, December 12, 1928.

Notes to Pages 180–193

62. "Winding It Up," *IT,* December 12, 1928.

63. *PT,* December 6, 1928. The report on the Tanks' financial condition did not appear in the *Tribune.*

Chapter Nine

1. "Portsmouth Football Association Names Additional Directors, Elects New Officers," *MS,* April 5, 1929.

2. "Plan Ohio Pro League for Buckeye Football," *AI,* July 5, 1929.

3. "Boosters of Spartans Eleven Hold Enthusiastic Meeting," *MS,* June 27, 1929.

4. "Lumpkin Rejoins Spartans Team," *MS,* August 20, 1929.

5. "Fumes," *IT,* July 7, 1929.

6. "Lumpkin Rejoins Spartans Team"; *PT,* August 21, 1929.

7. For an account of Brumbaugh's career, see Carl Becker, "A Darned Good Quarterback," *Timeline* 11 (September–October 1994): 12–27.

8. *PT,* August 21, 29, 1929.

9. *PT,* September 2, 1929.

10. *PT,* September 14, 1929; "Green Bay Team Is Strong Outfit for Spartan Opener," *MS,* September 10, 1929.

11. "Packers Whip Portsmouth, 14–0," *GBG,* September 16, 1929; *PT,* September 16, 1929; "Spartan Eyes Turned on Chillicothe," *MS,* September 7, 1929.

12. "Coach Griffin to Play Sunday," *MS,* September 21, 1929.

13. *PT,* October 1, 1929.

14. *PT,* October 6, 1929.

15. "Greatest Team in Midwest Tackles Tigers," *PT,* October 5, 1929; "Spartans Meet Real Opposition on Labold Field Today," *MS,* October 6, 1929.

16. "Tanks Open Season with Tailors at Beechwood Today," *IT,* September 22, 1929.

17. "Sunday Will Be Deb Rowan Day at Beechwood," *IT,* September 24, 1929.

18. "Ironton Beats Boosters, 78–0," *TB,* October 7, 1929.

19. *PT,* October 9, 1929; "Tanks, Portsmouth Test Strength Today at Labold Field," *IT,* October 13, 1929.

20. "Spartans-Tanks Ready for Grid Classic Today," *MS,* October 13, 1929.

21. "Victory Sunday and Tanks Get State Grid Title," *IT,* November 29, 1929; Interview by Carl Becker with Glenn Presnell, November 29, 1994.

22. *PT,* October 16, 1929; "Ashland Eleven in Crucial Battle This Week," *AI,* October 16, 1929. The *Times* quoted Collett.

23. Interview with Presnell, November 29, 1994.

24. This description comes from *PT,* October 14, 1929; "Punts and Passes," *PT,* October 14, 1929; *PT,* October 16, 1929.

25. *PT,* October 16, 1929.

26. "Freelance Sports," *AI,* October 15, 1929; "Ashland Sports Writer Says Only Clean Football Allowed," *MS,* October 17, 1929.

Notes to Pages 193–206

27. "Ashland Offered Franchise in National Professional Football League," *AI,* July 2, 1929.

28. "Armco and Tanks Heads Disagree," *AI,* July 3, 1929.

29. For a description of Armco social policies, see Borth, *True Steel,* 239–50, and Carl Becker, "George Matthew Verity," in *Iron and Steel in the Twentieth Century,* ed. Seely, 452–59.

30. "Plan Ohio Pro League for Buckeye Football," *AI,* July 25, 1929.

31. "Armco Has Fine Prospects for Great Eleven," *AI,* September 8, 1929.

32. "Ashland Armco Pro Eleven, Trounces Bulldogs, 22–0," *CR,* September 30, 1929.

33. "Let's Be Sportsmen," *IT,* October 20, 1929.

34. "Fans Urged to Buy Tickets Here for Ashland Game," *MS,* October 23, 1929; *PT,* October 26, 1929.

35. "The Lady in the Grandstand," *PT,* October 28, 1929.

36. McGill, *Kentucky Sports,* 95.

37. "Stadium Association Directors Reply to Candidates' Attack," *IT,* October 22, 1929.

38. Quoted in Barnett, *The Spartans and the Tanks,* 9.

39. Collett, "Soliloquy, 11th in Series," *IN,* n.d.

40. Dietrich, *Down Payments,* 182.

41. "Awnings Lose Great Fight with Ironton," *ABJ,* October 28, 1929.

42. "Moments We Like to Live over Again," *PT,* November 4, 1929.

43. *PT,* November 18, 1929.

44. "Armco and Tanks Play Today for Tenth Time," *AI,* November 17, 1929.

45. "Awnings Are Beaten by Portsmouth 15–6," *ABJ,* November 11, 1929.

46. "Tanks-Spartans Play for State Title Today," *IT,* November 24, 1929.

47. *PT,* November 21, 1929.

48. "Tanks Are Beaten, baffled, Routed by Portsmouth Spartans," *IT,* November 25, 1929; *PT,* November 29, 1929; *MS,* November 26, 1929.

49. "Spartans Annex State Graduate Football Championship," *MS,* November 29, 1929.

50. "Tickets for Spartans-Armco Game Go on Sale Tuesday," *MS,* November 30, 1929.

51. *PT,* November 29, December 2, 1929; "Green Bay Game up to Fans," *MS,* December 3, 1929.

52. "Green Bay Game up to Fans."

53. "Hitch Develops in Plans for Green Bay Contest Here," *MS,* December 7, 1929.

54. "Green Bay Game Will Be Played," *MS,* December 8, 1929.

55. Ibid. The leading historian of the Packers does not look at the issue: Larry Names, *The History of the Green Bay Packers, Book I: The Lambeau Years, Part I* (Wautoma, Wisc., 1987).

56. "Call off Green Bay Game," *MS,* December 11, 1929; "Packers Leave for Memphis Tonight; Cancel Ohio Game," *GBG,* December 13, 1929.

57. "Tickets for Final Game Spartan Season Selling for Dollar," *MS,* December 12, 1929.

341

Notes to Pages 206–222

58. *PT,* December 11, 1929; "Curtain Will Drop on Spartan Season Today," *MS,* December 15, 1929.

59. Interview by Carl Becker with Grover Emerson, November 12, 1993.

60. "Recreational Group Casts Favorable Vote on Stadium Project," *MS,* October 27, 1929.

61. *PT,* November 6, 1929; "Stadium Bond Issue Loses," *MS,* November 6, 1929.

62. Ordinance 4626, November 21, 1929, in Municipal Archives, Portsmouth, Ohio.

63. *PT,* November 2, 1929.

64. "Tank Manager of 1930 Will Be Named Soon This Week," *IT,* December 22, 1929.

65. Interview by Carl Becker with Glenn Presnell, April 11, 1995.

66. Barnett, *The Spartans and the Tanks,* 11.

67. McGill, *Kentucky Sports,* 93.

Chapter Ten

1. "Professional Football to Be Discontinued by Armco This Fall," *AI,* July 9, 1930; "Ashland Armco Will Not Put Grid Team on Field This Fall," *IT,* July 9, 1930.

2. "Ashland Armco Will Not Put Grid Team on Field This Fall."

3. "Spartans Apply for Berth in National Pro Grid League," *PT,* January 7, 1930.

4. Neft et al., eds., *Pro Football,* 14.

5. Minutes of the Executive Committee, NFL, January 25, 1930, Pro Football Hall of Fame, Canton, Ohio.

6. "Spartans Must Collect \$2,500 at Once or Lose Franchise,' *MS,* April 8, 1930.

7. Portsmouth City Ordinances, Ordinance 38, March 20, 1930, City Building, Portsmouth, Ohio.

8. "Tiny Lewis, Ashland Backfield Ace, Signs to Play with Spartans," *PT,* July 11, 1930.

9. "Twenty-Five College Gridiron Stars Signed for Spartan Football Squad," *PT,* June 13, 1930.

10. "Spartan Stockholders Organize," *PT,* July 23, 1930.

11. "Stadium, Only Skeleton of Real Self When Whistle Blows, Will Seat 8,000," *PT,* August 28, 1930.

12. "Spartan Squad Lines up for Initial Practice," *PT,* September 3, 1930; "Spartans to Play Tag in Mound Park Today," *PT,* September 8, 1930.

13. "Chirps from the Press Box," *PT,* September 15, 1930.

14. "Victory by Spartans Dedicates Stadium," *PT,* September 15, 1930; "Spartans Not Extended in Taking First Game of Year from Newark," *IT,* September 15, 1930.

15. "\$85,000 Cost of Spartans through 20-Game Schedule," *PT,* September 21, 1930; "Spartans Draw \$3,000 in Pay Every Time They Take Field," *IT,* September 22, 1930.

16. "Huge Crowd to See Spartans-Dodgers Play," *PT,* September 24, 1930.

17. "As The Moon Played Peekaboo," *PT,* September 25, 1930.

18. Record Crowd Puts Approval on Night Game," *PT,* September 25, 1930.

19. "Tulsa Center Signs to Play with Tanks," *IT,* April 22, 1930; "'Greasy' Neale to Coach Tanks This Year," *IT,* May 19, 1930.

Notes to Pages 223–237

20. William Gudelunas, "Alfred Earle 'Greasy' Neale," Porter, ed., *Biographical Dictionary of American Sports,* 420–22.

21. Quoted in Barnett, *The Spartans and the Tanks,* 11.

22. "The Opening Game," *IT,* September 28, 1930.

23. "Hard Work Is Neale's Recipe for Tank Success," *IT,* September 14, 1930.

24. "Tanks Will Win, Says Johnny, but Just Watch the Powell-Lumpkin Rivalry," *IT,* September 24, 1930.

25. "Tanks, Spartans Ready for Today's Battle," *IT,* September 28, 1930.

26. "Sunday Is Booster Day for Tanks," *IT,* October 1, 1930.

27. "Gembis Gives Tanks 3–0 Win over Akron," *ABJ,* October 13, 1930.

28. "Spartans in Good Shape for Sunday's Game," *PT,* October 2, 1930; "Spartans to Uncover New Offense against Cardinals," *PT,* October 4, 1930. For a description of the C, see Danzig, *History of American Football,* 54–55; supposedly it was effective for passing.

29. "Spartans Get It Where Chicken Got Ax," *PT,* October 16, 1930; "Spartan 'Million Dollar' Backfield Has No Scoring Punch," *IT,* October 17, 1930.

30. Quoted in Barnett, *The Spartans and the Tanks,* 12.

31. "Spartan 'Million Dollar' Backfield Has No Scoring Punch"; "A Great Victory," *IT,* October 19, 1930.

32. Barnett, *The Spartans and the Tanks,* 12.

33. "Spartans Will Bring 24 Men," *PS,* October 14, 1930; "Tigers Meet Spartans in Local Week End Grid Feature," *PS,* October 18, 1930; "Tigers Oppose Portsmouth Professionals Here Today," *MCA,* October 19, 1930; "Return Game of Spartans-Tigers Looms after Dispute," *PS,* October 20, 1930.

34. "Red Grange to Gallop at Stadium Tonight," *PT,* October 22, 1930; "Brumbaugh Will Get Big Reception Tonight," *PT,* October 22, 1930.

35. "Spartans Stop Red Grange to Beat Bears," *PT,* October 23, 1930; "Bears' Claws Clipped and Tail Twisted," *PT,* October 23, 1930.

36. "On the Sidelines," *PT,* October 28, 1930.

37. "Packers Trounce Portsmouth 47 to 13," *GBG,* November 3, 1930.

38. "Do Tell," *PT,* November 9, 1930.

39. David S. Neft et al., eds., *The Football Encyclopedia* (New York, 1994), 83.

40. "Tanks Prepare for Invasion by Penn Staters," *IT,* October 21, 1930.

41. "Tanks Need Help," *IT,* October 23, 1930.

42. "This Is the Day," *IT,* October 26, 1930.

43. "Grid Chatter," *IT,* November 2, 1930.

44. "Tigers and Ironton, Ohio 11 Clash at Hodges Field Today," *MCA,* November 2, 1930; "Tigers Revamp," *PS,* November 3, 1930.

45. *MCA,* November 3, 1930.

46. "Memphis Tiger Eleven May Be Idle Sunday," *PS,* November 3, 1930.

47. Quoted in Barnett, *The Spartans and the Tanks,* 13.

48. "About Town," *IT,* November 12, 1930.

49. "Presnell and Tanks Lauded by Cincinnati Tribune," *IT,* November 13, 1930; "Ironton Tanks Show Friedman How to Pass and Wallop Giants," *CCT,* November 12, 1930.

Notes to Pages 237–250

50. "Ironton Beats Giants," *NYT*, November 13, 1930.

51. "Ironton Tanks Whip Awning Outfit, 13–0," *ABJ*, November 17, 1930.

52. "Tanks at Cincinnati," *IT*, November 23, 1930.

53. "Bears Take Football Lesson from Tanks," *IT*, November 24, 1930.

54. According to Presnell, the high school team had little standing in the community. Interview by Carl Becker with Glenn Presnell, August 6, 1997. Ritter Collett, a boy in Ironton at the time, has expressed a similar view. Interview by Carl Becker with Ritter Collett, August 4, 1997.

55. "Support the Tigers," *IT*, October 9, 1927.

56. "Winter Blocks Tank Attack; Spartans Win 12–0," *IT*, November 28, 1930; "Booting Tanks off Throne," *PT*, November 28, 1930; "Spartans Flash Brilliant Play; Crush Tanks," *PT*, November 28, 1930; "Ironton Says Sloppy Field Cause of Defeat," *PT*, December 1, 1930.

57. "Spartans Flash Brilliant Play; Crush Tanks," *PT*, November 28, 1930; "Winter Blocks Tanks' Attack, Spartans Win, 12–0," *IT*, November 28, 1930.

58. "Record Crowd for Title Game," *PT*, December 10, 1930.

59. "Between Goal Posts," *PT*, December 12–13, 1930.

60. "Green Bay Wins Pennant as Spartans Tie," *PT*, December 15, 1930; "Spartans Tie Bay in Final Game of Year," *GBG*, December 15, 1930.

61. "The Curtain Falls," *PT*, December 21, 1930.

62. "Ironton Scribe Dips Pen into Tri-State Football," *PT*, December 2, 1930.

63. "Tanks Will Not Play Again This Year," *IT*, November 30, 1930.

64. "Meet The Tanks at the Marlow Tomorrow Night," *IT*, November 30, 1930; "Fans Bid Tanks of 1930 Farewell at Big Party," *IT*, December 2, 1930.

65. "How Would the Tanks Compare with Notre Dame," *IT*, December 8, 1930.

66. "Ironton Stadium Operated at Loss during Past Year," *IT*, December 18, 1930.

67. "Business Men Will Back Ironton Tanks Next Year," *PT*, December 18, 1930; "Business Men Will Probably Back Tanks of '31," *PT*, December 18, 1930.

68. "Tank Mass Meeting to Be Held Next Tuesday," *IT*, June 7, 1931.

69. "Lack of Good Teams at Reasonable Prices Kills Tanks Schedule," *IT*, August 16, 1931.

Chapter Eleven

1. "Ironton Tanks May Take Field Again This Fall," *IT*, September 13, 1931.

2. "Tri-State Grid Loop Is Formed," *HD*, October 4, 1931; "Trojans Entered in League of Tri-State Grid Teams," *CG*, October 4, 1931.

3. Quoted in Barnett, *The Spartans and the Tanks*, 14.

4. "Sparks from the Sports Anvil," *PT*, June 21, 1931.

5. "Cleveland Admitted to National Grid League," *PT*, July 13, 1931.

6. "Two Separate Contracts Are Mailed to Glenn Presnell," *PT*, July 21, 1931; "Spartans Offer Contract to Presnell," *IT*, July 22, 1931.

Notes to Pages 250–262

7. "Presnell Calls for Conference," *PT,* July 23, 1931.

8. "Presnell Resigns at Russell; Signs with Spartans," *IT,* August 2, 1931; "Presnell, Tank Star, Is Signed by Spartans," *PT,* August 2, 1931.

9. "26 Players Are Asked to Report to Spartans," *PT,* July 26, 1931.

10. A good biographical sketch of Clark may be found in Bob Carroll, "Potsy Clark: A Success Story," in *Coffin Corner* 7 (March–April 1985): 5–8.

11. For Clark's various appearances, see "Luncheon Clubs to Hear New Coach for Spartans," *PT,* July 26, 1931; "Spartan Admirers to Meet New Coach Tonight," *PT,* July 28, 1931; "Potsy Clark Scores Big Hit with Grid Fans," *PT,* July 29, 1931.

12. "Fans Impressed with Clark's Bunch of Huskies," *PT,* August 31, 1931.

13. Barnett, *The Spartans and the Tanks,* 22.

14. "Spartans Will Observe Rules," *PT,* September 12, 1931.

15. "Real 'Downtown' Coaches," *PT,* August 3, 1931.

16. "Slash Budget for Operating Team," *PT,* July 26, 1931.

17. "Sparks from the Sports Anvil," *PT,* June 14, 1931.

18. "Spartans to Go on Parade in Surrounding Towns Two Days Next Week," *PT,* August 25, 1931; "Spartans Plan Three Day Trip," *PT,* August 20, 1931.

19. "Cleveland Indians to Meet Spartans Next," *PT,* October 4, 1931.

20. "27 Persons Hop Bus for East," *PT,* October 16, 1931.

21. "Portsmouth Beats Brooklyn, 19 to 0," *NYT,* October 19, 1931.

22. "Sparks from the Sports Anvil," *PT,* October 29, 1931.

23. "Sports of the Times," *NYT,* November 1, 1931.

24. "A Pat on the Back," *PT,* November, 3, 1931.

25. Ibid.

26. "Spartans Lack Scoring Punch; Bears Win," *PT,* November 9, 1931; "Bears Win, 9–6; Johnsos Kicks Field Goals," *CT,* November 9, 1931; "Bears Win 9 to 6 in Clash with Spartan Pros," *CN,* November 9, 1931.

27. "Race Tightens a Spartans Win, Bays Lose," *PT,* November 16, 1931.

28. "Cards Plow to 20–19 Victory over Spartans," *CT,* November 23, 1931.

29. "Jap Douds Is Reinstated by Potsy Clark," *PT,* November 27, 1931.

30. "Packers Capture Third Grid Title," *GBG,* November 30, 1931; "Packers Clinch National Championship," *GBG,* November 30, 1931.

31. "Portsmouth Game December 13 May Be Played, Hint," *GBG,* December 4, 1931.

32. "Green Bay Game 'Up in Air': Snyder Explains Situation," *PT,* December 2, 1931.

33. "Barnstormers to Play Two Grid Battles," *GBG,* December 10, 1931.

34. "Green Bay Afraid?" *PT,* December 8, 1931.

35. "Green Bay 'Pikers' Cheese Champ," *PT,* December 8, 1931.

36. "Stockholders Meet Tonight," *PT,* December 2, 1931.

37. "The Spartans?" *PT,* December 2, 1931.

38. "Spartans Face Large Deficit as Season Ends," *PT,* December 3, 1931.

39. "Spartans to Hold Mass Meeting in Selby Gym Tonight," *PT,* December 9, 1931; "700 Persons Attend Football Mass Meeting," *PT,* December 10, 1931.

40. "Banner Year for Pro Game," *PT,* December 11, 1931.

Notes to Pages 262–273

41. Barnett, *The Spartans and the Tanks*, 31.

42. "Fate of Spartans to Be Decided at Meeting Tonight," *PT,* December 16, 1931.

43. "Fate of Spartans in Lap of Football Fans," *PT,* December 17, 1931.

44. "Fans Rallying to Save Spartans for City," PT, December 18, 1931.

45. "Audit of Football Corporation Books Complete," *PT,* December 23, 1931.

46. "Big Spartan Pep Rally to Be Held Tonight," *PT,* January 12, 1931; "Drive to Save Spartans in Full Blaze," *PT,* January 12, 1932.

47. "Fans Regret Drive to Save Spartans Failed," *PT,* February 13, 1932.

48. "Committee Decides to Abandon Spartan Drive," *PT,* February 12, 1932.

49. "Plan 19 Directors for New Spartans Organization," *PT,* February 23, 1932; "600 Stockholders Have Joined New Spartan Group," *PT,* February 23, 1932.

50. "Appoint Spartan Nominating Committee," *PT,* March 2, 1932.

51. "Spartan Directors Select Executive Committee," *PT,* March 13, 1932.

52. "Potsy Eager to Sign Players," *PT,* April 25, 1932.

53. "Sparks from the Sports Anvil," *PT,* May 2, 1932; "Spartans Employ Collectors to Round up Cash," *PT,* May 26, 1932.

54. "Potsy Clark to Retain 12 of Last Year's Squad," *PT,* May 25, 1932.

55. "Spartan Solicitors Are Still at Work," *PT,* June 16, 1932.

Chapter Twelve

1. "Dicker for Two Green Bay Tilts," *PT,* June 5, 1932.

2. "Spartans to Ask for Seven Home Games This Season," *PT,* May 22, 1932.

3. "Sitting on Cake of Ice Discussing Grid News," *PT,* July 14, 1932; "Hot Shots on Cold Weather Pastime," *PT,* July 24, 1932; "Giant Contracts Are Tucked Away," *PT,* July 31, 1932.

4. "Popeye Wagers, Flashy Center, Signs Contract," *PT,* June 22, 1932; "Randolph, Spartans Roving Center, Signs Up," *PT,* August 14, 1932.

5. "Plan Only Five Home Contests," *PT,* August 14, 1932; "Fans Get Low Down on Spartans," *PT,* August 17, 1932.

6. "Huddle Whispers," *PT,* September 9, 1932.

7. "Spartans Launch New Season," *PT,* September 18, 1932.

8. "Giants and Spartans Will Tangle in Loop Opener," *PT,* September 25, 1932; "Huddle Whispers," *PT,* September 25, 1932.

9. "Fans Set for Giants Game," *PT,* September 24, 1932; "Huddle Whispers," *PT,* September 25, 1932.

10. "Huddle Whispers," *PT,* September 26, 1932.

11. "Cardinals Handcuff Spartans to 7–7 Tie Score," *PT,* October 3, 1932.

12. "Cardinals Tie, 7–7," *CTr,* October 3, 1932.

13. "Spartans Drop Heart Breaker to Green Bay, 15–10," *PT,* October 10, 1932; "Huddle Whispers," *PT,* October 13, 1932.

14. "Fans Accord Spartans Great Reception Despite Downpour," *PT,* October 11, 1932.

346

Notes to Pages 274–284

15. "Griffin and Roberts Released by Spartans," *PT*, October 12, 1932; "Spartans off on Long Trip," *PT*, October 13, 1932.

16. Quoted in Barnett, *The Spartans and the Tanks*, 23–24.

17. *PT*, October 28, 1932.

18. "Touchdown in Opening Quarter Gives Spartans Victory over Football Giants," *NYT*, October 31, 1932.

19. "Spartans Got Seasick on Deep Sea Jaunt; Lumpkin Got Whale, Threw It Back," *PT*, November 4, 1932.

20. "Sports of the Times," *NYT*, October 30, 1932.

21. "Huddle Whispers," *PT*, November 8, 1932.

22. The departure of several very weak defensive teams from the NFL in 1931 and 1932, notably the Red Jackets and Yellowjackets, may have had a slight effect on scoring because it resulted in a greater parity among the remaining teams.

23. "Spartan Organization Issues Appeal to Fans," *PT*, November 18, 1932.

24. "Just Another Team," *PT*, November 21, 1932.

25. "Spartans Will Play Final Game Here," *PT*, November 23, 1932.

26. Interview by Carl Becker with Glenn Presnell, November 10, 1993.

27. Quoted in Cope, ed., *The Game That Was*, 89.

28. "Playing the Game," *PT*, November 25, 1932.

29. "Cardinals Lose; Bears Tie Portsmouth," *CTr*, November 28, 1932; "Spartans and Bears Hug to Draw," *PT*, November 28, 1932.

30. "Packers Are Here for Championship Game Sunday," *PT*, December 3, 1932.

31. "The Big Day," *PT*, December 4, 1932.

32. "Potsy Clark Used Only 11 Players to Avenge Old Grudge against Lambeau," *PT*, December 12, 1932; Barnett, *The Spartans and the Tanks*, 24; Interview with Glenn Presnell, November 29, 1994.

33. "A Great Day," *PT*, December 5, 1932.

34. Quoted in Barnett, *The Spartans and the Tanks*, 24.

35. "Green Bay Howls in Pain," *PT*, December 9, 1932.

36. "Barnstorming Trip Is Planned," *PT*, November 23, 1932; "Giants, Spartans May Meet Again; Team Is Going to Lexington," *PT*, December 5, 1932.

37. "Snapshots," *LH*, December 14, 1932.

38. "Bears Play Title Game in Stadium," *CN*, December 15, 1932; "Bears to Play Title Game in Stadium," *CN*, December 16, 1932.

39. "Spartan Mentor in Town, Plans to Scout Bears," *CT*, December 14, 1932; "Presnell to Lead Spartans' Attack against the Bears," *CT*, December 15, 1932.

40. "Bears Battle with Spartans Moved Indoors," *CTr*, December 16, 1932; "To Play Tilt Under Roof," *PT*, December 16, 1932.

41. "Bears Find Stadium Perfect as Grid," *CTr*, December 17, 1932.

42. One may read of the various athletic events held in the stadium in Robert Markus, "And, Now, the End Is Near," *CTr*, April 1, 1994. Markus referred to the Spartans as the Clippers.

43. Various contemporary and secondary sources describe the physical arrangements for the game. See, for example, "Bears to Play Title Game in Stadium"; C. Robert Barnett,

Notes to Pages 284–288

"The Spartans Live on (in Detroit)," *Coffin Corner* 2 (October 1980): 6+; Carl Becker, "The 'Tom Thumb' Game: Bears vs. Spartans, 1932," *Journal of Sport History* 22 (Fall 1995): 216–27; Howard Roberts, *The Chicago Bears* (New York, 1947), 92.

44. For explanations of the rules of the charity game, see "Bears and Cards Renew Rivalry in Indoor Charity Game," *CN*, December 15, 1930; "Charity Gets $20,000 If Pro Game Fills Stadium Tonight," *CTr*, December 15, 1930; "10,000 See Bears Win Stadium Game, 9–7," *CTr*, December 16, 1930.

45. Contemporary sources stated that the ball came in-bounds fifteen yards. See, for example, "Bears Annex Pro Title on Tabloid Grid," *CN*, December 19, 1932; and "Spartans Bow to Bears on Tiny Gridiron," *PT*, December 19, 1932. But later accounts had the ball coming in ten yards: Rudolph Unger, "In 1932 Bears Broke Ground Indoors," *CTr*, January 10, 1986; and Jim Murray, "It Was Most Noteworthy Game Ever," *Los Angeles Times*, February 11, 1986.

46. Quoted in Richard Whittingham, *The Chicago Bears: An Illustrated History* (Chicago, 1979), 82.

47. "Bears to Play Title Game in Stadium"; "Bears and Spartans Clash for Pro Grid Title Tonight," *CT*, December 1, 1932.

48. "Spartans and Bears on Edge for Title Game," *CN*, December 17, 1932.

49. Quoted in Barnett, *The Spartans and the Tanks*, 26; Interview with Presnell, November 10, 1993.

50. "Bears Win, 9–0: Pro Football Champions," *CTr*, December 19, 1932. See also George Halas, with Gwen Morgan and Arthur Veysey, *Halas by Halas: The Autobiography of George Halas* (New York, 1979), 169; and Roberts, *Chicago Bears*, 93.

51. Quoted in Roberts, *Chicago Bears*, 96.

52. Interview with Grover Emerson.

53. Barnett, *The Spartans and the Tanks*, 27.

54. "Spartans Bow to Bears on Tiny Gridiron"; "Sports," *PT*, December 21, 1932.

55. "Bears Win 9–0: Pro Football Champions"; "Chicago Bears Win Pro Football Title," *NYT*, December 19, 1932. The *Portsmouth Times* reported that "exact" paid admissions were 9,623 and that Annie Oakleys numbered several hundred ("Sports").

56. "League Says Spartans Co-Champs," *PT*, December 23, 1932; *PT*, December 25, 1932.

57. Minutes, Annual Meeting, NFL, February 25–26, 1933, Pro Football Hall of Fame, Canton, Ohio.

58. Murray asserted that the game may have been the "greatest" of all times for "sheer" significance. He cited "firsts" to support his argument: the first title game played indoors, and the first game played on an artificial surface ("It Was Most Noteworthy Game Ever") In fact, though, professional teams played in Madison Square Garden in 1902 and 1903 in "World Series" games. See Baron et al., eds., *Official NFL Encyclopedia of Pro Football*, 12. The rules changes coming out of the game were more important, of course, than the "firsts."

59. Halas, *Halas by Halas*, 70; George Vass, *George Halas and the Chicago Bears* (Chicago, 1971), 94.

Notes to Pages 288–299

60. Minutes, Annual Meeting, July 8–9, 1933, Pro Football Hall of Fame, Canton, Ohio.

Chapter Thirteen

1. "Clark Seeking Grid Coachship," *PT*, December 3, 1932.
2. "Sparks," *PT*, March 12, 1933.
3. "Thayer Arrives; Schaake on Way," *PT*, September 8, 1933.
4. "A Good Schedule," *PT*, July 13, 1933.
5. Bert Bell and Lud Wray owned the Philadelphia franchise; the Eagles' name derived from the symbol of the National Recovery Act of the New Deal. Art Rooney controlled the Pirates, and Sid Weil owned the Reds.
6. "Cincinnati Reds Expect to Give Spartans Surprise," *PT*, September 14, 1933.
7. "Spartans and Giants Will Stage Parade," *PT*, September 23, 1933; "Sparks," *PT*, September 23, 1933.
8. A lengthy account of the game appeared in "Spartans Clip Wings of Chicago Cardinals," *PT*, October 2, 1933.
9. "It Doesn't Pay," *PT*, October 2, 1933.
10. "Spartans Off for Green Bay," *PT*, October 6, 1933.
11. "Portsmouth Wins at Boston," *NYT*, October 16, 1933; "Presnell's Arm and Toe Trim Boston," *PT*, October 16, 1933.
12. "Spartans Play Exhibition Tilt," *PT*, October 20, 1933; "Spartans and Shenandoah Scrap to Draw," *PT*, October 23, 1933; "Portsmouth Plays 7–7 Tie," *NYT*, October 23, 1933.
13. "Portsmouth Downs Stapletons by 14–7," *NYT*, October 20, 1933.
14. "Thrilling Comeback in Final Period Wins for Giants," *NYT*, November 6, 1933; "Spartans Blow 10 Point Lead to Lose Game," *PT*, November 6, 1933.
15. "Bruised and Battered Spartans in Home Port," *PT*, November 8, 1933.
16. Barnett, *The Spartans and the Tanks*, 28.
17. "Sparks," *PT*, November 20, 1933.
18. "Spartans Drop Game in Final Minutes of Tilt," *PT*, November 27, 1933; "Bears Beat Spartans, 17–14; Score as Finish Nears," *CTr*, November 27, 1933.
19. "Snow Prevents Charity Game," *PT*, December 12, 1933; "Charity Game Entirely Off," *PT*, December 13, 1933.
20. "'Dutch' Clark Asks Spartans for Old Post," *PT*, December 23, 1933.
21. "Sparks," *PT*, December 12, 17, 1933; "Four Spartans Placed on United Press All-Pro Team," *PT*, December 18, 1933; "Presnell Only Spartan Selected by Coaches of National Pro Loop," *PT*, December 28, 1933.
22. One may follow the course of the tour in the following articles: "Spartans Win Road Contest," *PT*, December 17, 1933; "Spartans Pile up Big Score," *PT*, December 18, 1933; "Spartans Play in Lincoln," *PT*, December 21, 1933; "Spartans Won Two Contests," *PT*, December 26, 1933; "Spartans Tied in Rough Game in Oklahoma City," *PT*, January 1, 1934.

349

Notes to Pages 299–306

23. *CP*, December 2, 1933; "Last Season for Purple Spartans In Portsmouth?" PT, December 3, 1933.

24. "Sparks," *PT*, January 7, 1934.

25. "Spartans' Fate Is Uncertain, Say Directors," *PT*, January 9, 1934.

26. "Sparks," *PT*, January 12, 1934.

27. "Sparks," *PT*, January 16, 1934.

28. "Spartan Squad to Play under Detroit Colors," *PT*, March 23, 1934.

29. "Sports Gossip," *PT*, April 8, 1934.

30. "Sports Gossip," *PT*, March 25, 1934.

31. "Sports Gossip," *PT*, April 3, 1934; "Spartan Stockholders Approve Club's Sale to Detroit for $10,000," *PT*, April 6, 1934.

32. "Sports Gossip," *PT*, April 13, 1934.

33. "Sports Gossip," *PT*, July 29, 1934.

34. Interview by Carl Becker with Jim Secrist, October 14, 1993.

35. Interview by Carl Becker with Louis Chabody, September 24, 1994.

36. The players were Bodenger, Caddel, Christensen, Ebding, Emerson, Gutowski, Lumpkin, Mitchell, Presnell, Randolph, and Schneller.

37. Interview by Carl Becker with Glenn Presnell, November 15, 1993.

Epilogue

1. Cope, *The Game That Was,* 70.

2. Interview by Carl Becker with Harold Nicholson, May 23, 1995.

3. Interview with Grover Emerson.

Bibliography

Records of teams were not kept or not extant so newspapers of the 1920s constitute the bulk of sources for this study. The newspapers in Ironton, Portsmouth, and Ashland were often cheerleaders for their teams, but they provided detailed coverage of many games and subjects bearing on the teams of the communities. Frequently, unfortunately, reporters loaded their stories with allusions that only readers close to the scene might understand, and sometimes they did not complete a story running over several weeks—for instance, a campaign to raise funds for a team. Though limited in quantity of information, interviews with men who played at Ironton, Portsmouth, and Ashland in the 1920s and the fans who saw them proved fruitful for understanding an issue or game. One collection, the McMahon letters, provided an interesting account of the way in which a manager attempted to recruit players late in the 1920s. Other primary sources, cited in the notes, were bits and pieces of limited value. For the general demographic character of the three cities, the printed summaries of the censuses of 1920 and 1930 are useful. City directories and the original schedules of population for 1920 provide some identifying detail on men who were playing in the opening years of the 1920s. The minute book of the Board of Education for the Ironton City School District yields some information of the relationship between the Tanks and the Ironton school district.

The relatively sparse secondary sources on American football say little about semiprofessional and independent professional teams. In the largest body of literature, the publications of the Professional Football Researchers Association, one will find articles and booklets that touch peripherally on such teams. Of course, one must look at the evolution of collegiate and professional football down to the 1930s to understand the background against which men played semiprofessional football. Listed below are titles of books and articles serving that purpose. Several typescripts proved useful for this work, notably one that Bob Gill has produced, a construction of the rosters for the Tanks, Armcos, and Portsmouth teams in the period from 1926 through 1930. In his master's thesis and doctoral dissertation, Phillip Gene Payne offers a provocative view of the relationship between the Tanks and a community looking for evidence that it was a worthwhile place to live.

Bibliography

Newspapers

Akron Beacon-Journal, 1924–30
Ashland Independent, 1919–31
Canton Repository, 1927–29
Charleston Gazette, 1931
Chicago News, 1930–32
Chicago Times, 1930–32
Chicago Tribune, 1930–32
Cincinnati Commercial Tribune, 1930
Cincinnati Enquirer, 1924–30
Cincinnati Post, 1930
Cleveland Plain Dealer, 1927–28
Columbus Dispatch, 1925–27
Daily Scioto Gazette (Chillicothe, Ohio), 1920
Dayton Daily News, 1925–27
Dayton Herald, 1925–27
Dayton Journal, 1925–27
Frankfort State Journal, 1924
Green Bay Press-Gazette, 1929–31
Huntington Herald Dispatch, 1922–31
Ironton News, 1956
Ironton Register, 1919–25
Ironton Tribune, 1925–34
Lexington Herald, 1932
Louisville Courier Journal, 1924
Memphis Commercial Appeal, 1930
Middletown Journal, 1925–29
Middletown News-Signal, 1925–28
Morning Irontonian (Ironton), 1919–25
Morning Sun (Portsmouth), 1921–30
New York Times, 1925–30
Ohio State Journal (Columbus), 1919–29
Portsmouth Times, 1919–34
Press-Scimitar (Memphis), 1930
Springfield News, 1927–28
Toledo Blade, 1927–29

Waverly Herald-Republican, 1921
Wellston Sentinel, 1922.

Interviews

Burns, Russell, October 14, 1993
Chabody, Louis, September 21, 1994
Collett, Ritter, August 4, 1997
De Long, Lincoln G., July 14, 1993
Emerson, Grover, November 12, 1993
Horrigan, Joe, November 12, 1993
Nicholson, Harold, May 23, 1995
Presnell, Glenn, October 19, 1992; June 13, November 10, 15, 1993; November 29, 1994;
    April 2, 11, May 24, July 25, September 22, 1995; August 6, 1997
Rolph, Harold, July 15, 1993
Snead, Ralph, July 14, 1993
Secrist, James, October 14, 1993
Thuma, James, October 14, 1993
Ware, Louis, May 23, 1995

Records of National Football League, Archives, Pro Football Hall of Fame

The National Football Constitution and By-Laws, 1926
Minutes, NFL Owners' Meeting, April 23, 1927
Minutes, Annual Scheduled Meeting, NFL, July 27–28, 1929
Minutes of Executive Committee, NFL, January 25, 1930
Minutes, NFL Owners' Meeting, July 12–13, 1930

Government Records

Fifteenth Census of the United States: 1930, Population. Pt. *1.* Washington, D.C., 1932.
Fifteenth Census of the United States: 1930, Population. Pt. 2. Washington, D.C., 1932
Fourteenth Census of the United States: 1920, Population. Pt. 3. Washington, D.C., 1922
"Fourteenth Census of the United States: 1920—Population, City of Ironton."
"Fourteenth Census of the United States: 1920—Population, City of Portsmouth."

Bibliography

Ironton City School District, Minute Books, 1924–30.
Ordinance Books, City of Portsmouth.

Miscellaneous

Ashland Armco Association, Program, 1927.
Ironton High School *Owl,* Patriot Edition, 1918.
Souvenir Stadium Dedication, Beechwood Stadium, Thanksgiving, 1926.

Books

Ashland Centennial Committee. *A History of Ashland, Kentucky, 1786 to 1954.* Ashland, 1954.

Barnett, C. Robert. *The Spartans and the Tanks.* North Huntingdon, Pa., 1983.

Barron, Bill, et al., eds. *The Official NFL Encyclopedia of Pro Football.* New York, 1982.

Betts, John Rickards. *America's Sporting Heritage, 1850–1950.* Reading, Mass., 1974.

Braunwart, Bob, ed. *Professional Football Researchers Association, 1989 Annual.* North Huntingdon, Pa., 1989.

Carroll, Bob. *Bulldogs on Sunday 1922.* North Huntingdon, Pa., n.d.

———. *The Ohio League, 1910–1919.* North Huntingdon, Pa., 1997.

Carroll, Bob, and Bob Gill, eds. *Bulldogs on Sunday 1919.* North Huntingdon, Pa., n.d.

Carroll, Bob, et al., eds. *Total Football: The Official Encyclopedia of the National Football League.* New York, 1997.

Classen, Harold. *The History of Professional Football.* Englewood Cliffs, 1963.

Cope, Myron, ed. *The Game That Was: The Early Days of Pro Football.* New York, 1970.

Curran, Bob. *Pro Football's Rag Days.* Englewood Cliffs, 1969.

Cusack, Jack. *Pioneer in Pro Football.* Fort Worth, 1963.

Danzig, Allison. *The History of American Football: Its Great Teams, Players, and Coaches.* Englewood Cliffs, 1956.

Davis, Parke H. *Football: The American Intercollegiate Game.* New York, 1911.

Dietrich, Phil. *Down Payments: Professional Football, 1896–1930, as Viewed from the Summit.* North Huntingdon, Pa., 1995.

———. *The Silent Men.* Akron, n.d.

Dulles, Foster Rhea. *America Learns to Play: A History of Popular Recreation, 1607–1940.* New York, 1940.

Gill, Bob. *Down in the Valley: A True Story of the Ohio Valley League in the 1920s.* North Huntingdon, Pa., 1993.

Bibliography

Green, Jerry. *Detroit Lions: Great Teams' Great Years.* New York, 1973.

Halas, George, with Gwen Morgan and Arthur Veysey. *Halas by Halas: The Autobiography of George Halas.* New York, 1979.

Ironton Centennial Commission. *Story of the Glorious Past: One Hundred Years.* Ironton, 1949.

Jones, Howard H., and Alfred F. Wesson. *Football for the Fans.* Los Angeles, 1929.

Krout, John Allen. *Annals of American Sport.* Toronto, 1929.

Leckie, Robert. *The Story of Football.* New York, 1963.

McGill, John. *Kentucky Sports.* Lexington, 1978.

March, Harry A. *Pro Football: Its Ups and Downs.* New York, 1934.

Mrozek, Donald J. *Sports and American Mentality.* Knoxville, 1983.

Names, Larry D. *The History of the Green Bay Packers, Book I: The Lambeau Years, Part I.* Wautoma, Wisc., 1987.

Neft, David S., et al., eds. *The Football Encyclopedia.* New York, 1994.

————, eds. *Pro Football: The Early Years.* New York, 1978.

Noverr, Douglas A., and Lawrence E. Ziewacz. *The Games They Played: Sports in American History, 1865–1980.* Chicago, 1983.

Perrin, Tom. *Football: A College History.* Jefferson, N.C., 1987.

Peterson, Robert W. *Pigskin: The Early Years of Pro Football.* New York, 1997.

Porter, David, ed. *Biographical Dictionary of American Sports: Football.* New York, 1986.

Rader, Benjamin. *American Sports: From the Age of Folk Games to the Age of Spectators.* Englewood Cliffs, 1983.

Roberts, Howard. *The Chicago Bears.* New York, 1947.

————. *The Story of Pro Football.* New York, 1953.

Smith, Robert. *Pro Football: The History of the Game and the Great Players.* New York, 1963.

Vass, George. *George Halas and the Chicago Bears.* Chicago, 1971.

Weyand, Alexander M. *The Saga of American Football.* New York, 1955.

Weyand, A. M. *American Football: Its History and Development.* New York, 1926.

Whitman, Robert L. *Jim Thorpe and the Oorang Indians: The N.F.L.'s Most Colorful Franchise.* Defiance, Ohio, 1984.

Whittingham, Richard. *The Chicago Bears: An Illustrated History.* Chicago, 1979.

Articles in Journals

Barnett, C. Robert. "The Spartans Live On (In Detroit)." *Coffin Corner* 2 (October 1980): 6+.

Bibliography

Barnett, C. Robert, and Linda Terhune. "When the Tanks Were Tops." *River Cities Monthly* 1 (September 1979): 14–20.

Becker, Carl M. "A Darned Good Quarterback." *Timeline* 11 (September–October 1994): 12–27.

———. "The 'Tom Thumb' Game: Bears vs. Spartans, 1932." *Journal of Sport History* 22 (Fall 1995): 216–27.

Braunwart, Bob, and Bob Carroll. "The Columbus Panhandles." *Coffin Corner* 1 (October 1979): 1–7.

———. "The Columbus Panhandles—Last of the Sandlotters." *Coffin Corner* 1 (1979): 38–43.

Bussert, Joel. "The Case for Benny Friedman." *Coffin Corner* 15 (Winter 1993): 18-20.

Campbell, Jim. "John Alexander: Pro Football Pioneer." *Coffin Corner* 16 (Early Spring 1994): 3–10.

———. "The Power and the Glory—Single Wing Football." *Coffin Corner* 14 (September 1992): 18–20.

Carroll, Bob, "Potsy Clark: A Success Story." *Coffin Corner* 7 (March–April 1985): 5–8.

———. "Semi or Pro?" *Coffin Corner* 19 (Late Winter 1996): 20–21.

Fimrite, Ron. "A Melding of Men Suited to a T." *Sports Illustrated* 47 (September 5, 1977): 90–100.

Gill, Bob. "Just Staten out on the Island." *Coffin Corner* 16 (Summer 1994): 3–10.

———. "Mini-bios Again, Three Coaches." *Coffin Corner* 14 (November 1992): 18–19.

———. "The Ohio Valley in 1924." *Coffin Corner* 17 (Early Summer 1995): 6–9.

———. "Requiem for the Nighthawks." *Coffin Corner* 14 (November 1992): 5–8.

Jable, J. Thomas. "The Birth of Professional Football: Pittsburgh Athletic Clubs Ring in Professionals in 1892." *Western Pennsylvania Historical Magazine* (April 1979): 131–47.

Klosinski, Emil. "Move Over Gipp, Thorpe . . . Make Room for Bowser." *Coffin Corner* 14 (September 1992): 21–24.

Maltby, Marc S. "The Early Struggles of Professional Football: Evansville, Indiana, 1920–1922." *Coffin Corner* 14 (September 1992): 5–10.

Nikitas, Thomas S. "The Ironton Tanks, 1919–1939." *Coffin Corner* 1 (1979): 19.

Patterson, Jimmy. "A Man of Many Jackets." *Coffin Corner* 14 (April 1993): 3–5.

Plack, Joe. "1923 Football Rules Revisited." *Coffin Corner* 14 (November 1992): 17+.

Presar, Steve. "Present at the Creation: Dayton's Triangles and the National Football League." *Miami Valley History: A Journal of the Montgomery County Historical Society* 2 (1990): 19–29.

Walker, Jim. "Glenn Presnell." *Coffin Corner* 4 (August 1982): 7–8.

Unpublished Materials

Gill, Bob. "Rosters of Armcos, Tanks, Presidents, Shoe-Steels and Spartans."

"Ironton 'Fighting Tigers' Football History, 1910–1996."

Maltby, Marc S. "The Origins and Early Development of Professional Football, 1890–1920." Ph.D. dissertation, Ohio University, 1987.

McMahon Letters (manuscript), Archives, Pro Football Hall of Fame, Canton, Ohio.

Payne, Phillip Gene. "Gridiron in Ironton: Semi-Professional Football in a Small Ohio Town, 1919–1931." Master's thesis, Ohio State University, 1990.

———. "Modernity Lost: Ironton, Ohio, in Industrial and Post-Industrial America." Ph.D. dissertation, Ohio State University, 1994.

Portsmouth Area Chamber of Commerce. "History of Portsmouth." July 1963.

Index

Abel, Theodore, 61
Achroyd, Sam, 63, 64, 66, 69, 74
Adams, Dewey, 84, 119, 128
Ahrends, George, 162
Aichu, Walter "Sneeze," 156, 158, 161, 172
Akron Awnings, 171, 177, 198–99, 209, 202, 226, 237
Akron Indians, 152
Akron Silents, 85, 126–127
Alexander, William, 168
Alford, Gene, 236, 251, 256, 271, 290
Allen, Campbell, 106, 119, 127
Allen, Hugh, 267
Alvis, Dick, 211
Alvis, Ralph, 76
amateurs' view of profesional football, 10–12
American football: athletic clubs; defensive play, 8–9, 14; equipment, 14–15; intercollegiate play, 7; offensive formations, 12–13, Ohio Clubs, 9; origins, 6
American Rolling Mill Company (Armco), 2; Great Depression, 212–13; welfare capitalism, 92
Andrews, L. W, 135, 137
Archoska, Jules, 165
Armstrong, Bob, 272, 276
Arnil, Paul, 206
Asheville Athletic Association, 41, 42
Ashland, Ky.: economy 2; origins, 2; population, 2
Ashland Armcos, 92, 102, 103, 105, 126, 129, 133, 147, 153, 154, 156–57, 167, 171–72, 176–77, 197, 201; Armco Park, 93; attendance, 305; banquets, 130, 150, 170; coercion of employees to buy tickets, 165–66; composition of team, 184; Employees Association and founding of team, 92–93; Employees

Association eliminates team, 212–13; Employees Association and entry into leagues, 145, 193; outlook for 1928, 176–77; recruiting, 98–120; rumors, 105–6; scheduling, 98, 121, 166; status in community, 98–9 100, 121–22, 132, 164, 193–94, 211–13, 305–6
Ashland Bulldogs, 28
Ashland Playhouse, 20
Ashland Independent, 2
Ashland Refining Company, 2
Ashland Tigers, 35, 38
Ashland Tomcats, 106, 213
Ashme, Johnny, 225
Athens, 62
Atlantic City Americans, 188

Ball, Nate, 26, 36, 79
Banker, Bill, 235
Battles, Cliff, 278, 279
Beckleheimer, Herman, 42, 44
Beechwood Park, 20, 26
Bell, Bert, 349 n. 5
Bennett, Chuck, 184, 187, 191, 199, 219, 241, 242, 250, 276
Betterton, T. Lee, 100
Bidwell, Charles, 294, 300
Bingham, W. J., 107
Birmingham (Toledo) Boosters 142, 190
Black, Brady, 157, 172, 164, 167, 168, 201, 213; Armcos as "solid citizens," 146; "high plane" in semiprofessional football, 167; limits of Armcos, 146; rough play, 193; Tanks' loading-up, 153
Blackman, John, 239
Bland, Edward, 168
Blevins, Ashby, 38, 45, 46, 47, 55, 60, 98, 248
Blood, Johnny, 187, 281

Index

Bloodgood, Pete, 131
Bodenger, Maury, 251, 271, 288, 290, 293, 303
Boston Braves, 278
Boston Redskins, 295
Bowdoin, Jim, 293
Briggs, 71
Britton, Earl, 147
Bronson, Bill, 169
Brooklyn Dodgers, 255, 257, 276
Brooks, Bill, 17, 18, 23, 25, 28, 30, 31, 34, 35, 40, 51, 61, 72, 74, 75, 78, 90, 91, 96, 103, 110, 111, 124, 125, 138, 139, 170, 244, 248; to attend West Virginia Wesleyan, 34; crying, 23, 72, 108; resigns as manager, 139, 142; scheduling, 27–28
Brown, Warren, 160, 183, 188
Bruenfield, Roscoe, 168
Brumbaugh, Carl, 185, 191, 197, 199, 206, 231, 240, 259, 287
Brumberg, A. J., 73
Bryan, Robert, 243
Buckeye League, proposed, 183
Bullman, Gale, 103
Burke, Pete, 25, 55, 62, 65, 66, 71, 76, 78, 89, 111, 124, 136, 138, 139, 144, 147, 170, 172, 177, 178, 185, 189, 196, 199, 202, 220, 226, 229, 237, 244; explanation for Tanks' play, 209–10; revival of Tanks, 248; satirizes Slavics on Birmingham Boosters, 190; Spartans' opening game, 219; Tanks best by comparitive scores, 238
Bystrom, Arthur, 241, 242, 260, 264

Caddel, Ernie, 291, 293, 296, 299, 303
Cagle, Chris, 256
Cahn, Bobby, 287
Calac, Pete, 11, 92, 109
Camp, Walter, 100
Camp's *Annual Football Guide,* 168
Camp Sherman, 21
Canton Bulldogs, 11, 109, 151, 156, 195
Canton Jewelers, 174
Canton Repository, 110, 174–75
Cantor, Eddie, 276
Carnegie Report, 1929, 12
Carr, Joe, 107, 214, 219, 231, 238, 260, 261, 265, 273, 284, 292, 298; attends public rally for Spartans, 265; prohibits game between Spartans and Packers, 229
Catlettsburg Legion, 27–28
Catlettsburg, Ky., 1
Cavosie, John, 240, 270, 274, 275, 296
Centre College, 18, 26

Ceredo, W.Va., 1
Chamberlain, Guy, 102
Charles, Winston, 152
Charleston Trojans, 248
Charleston West Side Athletic Club, 37
Charlesworth, David, 133, 134
Chevigny, Jack, 27
Chicago Bears, 230–31, 259, 260, 277, 288, 297, 298
Chicago Cardinals, 195, 204, 227, 231, 274–75, 294
Chillicothe, Ohio, 1
Chillicothe Athletic Club, 27, 73
Chillicothe Eagles, 187, 190, 195, 206, 226
Chillicothe Majestics, 39
Chillicothe Merchants, 119
Chillicothe Paint Streeters, 101, 102
Chilton, M. M., 87
Chinn, Lonnie, 45, 46, 47, 51
Christensen, George, 251, 263–64, 271, 288, 290, 299
Christensen, Koester, 224
Cincinnati Celts, 25
Cincinnati Football Association, 67, 72
Cincinnati Friars, 132
Cincinnati Harrisons, 67, 72, 77
Cincinnati Home Guards, 150–51, 173, 176–77, 196, 203
Cincinnati Potters, 84–85, 102, 130
Cincinnati Reds, 273, 293, 297, 299
Cincinnati Saint Aloysius, 72
Circleville, Ohio, 39
Clark, Earl "Dutch," 216, 251, 257, 258, 263, 271, 275, 276, 277, 279–80, 281, 282, 286, 288, 298, 303; accepts coaching position in Colorado, 290; explains failure of Spartans, 305; on payment of salary, 279
Clark, Ernest, 17
Clark, George "Potsy," 256, 260, 261, 264, 267, 268, 271, 272, 274, 281, 282, 285, 290, 291, 292, 297, 299, 300, 303, 345; meets community, 252; hired as Spartans' coach, 252; "Football is the salvation," 296; ironman vow, 282; practices, 252–53; seeking another position, 289; training rules, 253; unpaid salary, 265
Cleveland Bulldogs, 89, 90
Cleveland Indians, 125–26, 256, 259
Cleveland Panthers, 131, 132, 146, 171, 200
Cloran, M. A., 177
Coal Grove, Ohio, 1
Coburn, Frank, 162, 338 n. 5
Cochran, Jerry, 107, 128, 140, 145

360

Index

Coins, Jack, 17
Collett, Charles, 91, 144, 192, 198, 251, 323 n. 3; editorial on Spartans and Tanks, 243–44
Columbus All Stars, 21–22, 125
Columbus Bobbs Chevrolets, 102, 122, 132, 140, 150, 156, 162–63
Columbus Chippewas, 26
Columbus Jungle Imps, 27, 83, 87
Columbus Maroons, 29, 64
Columbus Mendel Tailors, 164, 190, 206, 283, 295
Columbus Oakwoods, 29
Columbus Ohio Stoves, 99
Columbus Olympians, 55–56
Columbus Panhandles, 25
Columbus Rochester Clothiers, 87, 99, 149
Columbus Safety Cabs, 261
Columbus Seagraves, 67, 70
Columbus Tigers, 128, 175, 176
Columbus Wagner-Pirates, 29, 68, 104, 116, 117, 118, 125
Columbus West Side, 62, 68, 75, 83, 99, 103
Covington Catholic Athletic Club, 89
Crawford, Harry, 67
Creasy, Jack, 69, 148, 151, l52, 153, 155, 156, 157, 158; activities for Shoe-Steel, 149; death, 159
Cunningham, Earl, 181, 338n
Cusack, Jack, 322n
Cushing, Yabby, 94

Daily, Arthur, 258
Dallas Rangers, 288
Dandalet, Tom, 98, 99
Danzig, Allison, 296
Davies, Charlton "Shorty," 23, 25, 27, 31, 34, 55, 61, 70, 74, 75, 78, 82, 83, 85, 89, 90, 93, 98, 101, 102, 105, 125, 136, 138–39, 155, 170, 173, 223, 239, 248, 261; to attend West Virginia Wesleyan, 34; controversy over coaching Armco, 94–97; Merriwell-like run, 27; recruiting Tanks, 139; resigns as Armcos' coach, 119
Davis, Mae, 211
Davis, Paul, 194
Dayton Guards, 277
Dayton Koors, 109, 122, 146
Dayton Triangles, 47, 109, 129, 146, 172
Dazell, Bob "Chic," 167
De Lat, Leonard, 133, 134
Delong, Lincoln, 37
Dempsey, John, 75
Detroit Lions, 302

Detroit Tigers, 187–88
DeVoss, Harold "Heckie," 115, 162
DeWeese, Everett, 109
Diamond, Lou, 286
Doage, Walter, 19, 27, 29
Doerr, Harry, 27, 39, 42, 43, 45, 46, 47, 48, 51, 112, 216
Douds, Forrest "Jap," 234, 242, 250, 260, 264, 271
Drennon, Ralph, 194
Dugan, Jimmy, 248
Duluth Eskimos, 195
Dunn, Joe "Red," 156
Dunn, Neville, 284
Durfee, Jim, 192
Dutcher, William, 107

Ebding, Harry "Irish," 251, 271, 288, 299, 303
Eby, Bryan, 208
Edwards, Glen, 278
Edwards, Homer, 124, 248
Eichenlaub, Ray, 22, 30, 40, 41, 42, 78, 192
Elliott, Wallace "Doc," 147, 196
Emerson, Grover "Ox," 251, 270, 287, 288, 290, 294, 296; view of Portsmouth, 306
Englebrecht, Clarence, 115
Enright, Rex, 156
Essaman, Walter, 49, 50
Evans, Myles, 129

fanettes, 31, 108
Falver, L. P., 338 n. 5
Faurot, Don, 168
fence thieves, 56, 83
Finsterwald, Russell, 192
Fort, Jake, 170
Fort Thomas, 22
Fort Wayne Pyramids, 195
Frankford Yellowjackets, 228, 233, 256, 258, 347 n. 22
Frecka, Kermit, 101, 104, 124, 153, 155, 156, 186
Freutel, Dug, 77
Friedman, Benny, 155, 232, 236, 237, 256, 258, 273, 276
Friel, Bill, 22
Fries, Dan, 39, 63, 115
Funderberg, Roscoe, 115, 116, 134, 148
Fyock, Dwight, 167

Gableman, William, 160, 162, 179
Gates, C. G. "Gatling Gun," 98, 99
"Gee Whizzers," 147
Gembis, Joe "Dynamite," 223, 248

Index

Gillen, Roy, 222
Glass, "Dutch," 98
Glassgow, Willis, 216, 222, 228, 242
Glockner, Adolph, 183
Gordy, Minos, 100
Gorrill, Paul "Flop," 142
Gould, Alan, 251
Graf, Howard, 160, 162, 163, 173, 178 , 338 n. 5
Graham, Al "Pup," 152, 163, 202, 234, 294
Grand Rapids Maroons, 273
Grange, Harold "Red," 11, 147, 230, 23l, 237, 238, 240, 277, 287, 288, 299
Green Bay Packers, 156, 187, 232, 241–42, 274, 281–83, 296; complain about Spartans fans, 282–83
Griffin, Harold "Tubby," 179, 183, 191, 196, 205, 208, 214, 216, 219, 220, 221, 223, 225, 228, 230, 231, 234, 239, 240, 242, 250, 253, 256, 260, 261, 271; costly strategy against Tanks, 229; cuts Molesworth, 218; ejected from game, 187; grievances against, 233; installs "C" formation, 227; mistake in substitution, 242; recruiting, 184, 186, 216; rebuked by directors, 230; replaced as coach of Tanks, 252
Griffith, John, 11
Grimes, H. Coleman, 160, 162, 188, 203, 208, 259, 262, 266, 338 n. 5; on construction of stadium, 217–18; editorial on Spartans, 243; financial report, 262
Grone, Fayne, 248
Grow, Lloyd, 169
Gutowski, Leroy "Ace," 271, 276, 281, 286, 296, 303

Haggerty, Frank, 168
Halas, George, 185, 214, 230, 280, 282, 283, 284, 285, 301
Haley, Russell, 63, 64
Hall, Art, 44, 45, 47
Hamilton, Don, 30, 40, 41, 42, 78
Hammond, Art, 44, 46,
Hatcher, George, 89, 97, 99, 101, 105, 106, 135, 121–22; reports change in name of Tanks, 82
Hathaway, Russell, 151, 161, 163, 179, 183
Haynes, 157
Heald, Bill, 29
Heffelfinger, William "Pudge," 8
Heisman, John, 13
Henderson, T. J., 222, 274, 275
Henry, Ola, 63
Henry, Walter, 66, 96

Henry, Wilbur "Fats," 109, 110
Herman, Martin, 148
Hewitt, Bill, 271, 298, 300
Hinkle, Clark, 281, 282
Hocking Valley, 153
Hogan, Paul, 148
Hollisey, Ray, 161
Holm, Tony, 235, 270
Hook, Charles, 100, 204
Horchow, Joseph, 162
Houser, Ken, 89, 90
Hovey, Bob, 262
Hubbard, Cal, 187, 241
Hubert, Pooley, 165, 189, 191
Hudson, Tom, 66, 198
Huffman, Iolas, 58
Hughes, E. O., 49, 50
Hughes, Wilbur "Squimby," 26
Hunter, Raney, 293
Huntington Boosters, 61–62, 71–72, 86, 89, 103, 106, 108, 248
Hurth, Bret, 162

Indianapolis Indians, 293
Ironton, Ohio: early football teams, 16–17; economy, 3–4; origins, 2; population, 4
Ironton American Legion, 111–12
Ironton Eagles, 67
Ironton High Tigers, 144, 239, 344 nn. 54–55
Ironton News, 4
Ironton Panthers, 83, 115
Ironton Register, 4
Ironton Stadium Association, 123; control of Tanks, 124, 137–38; funding covered grandstand, 123–24; prepare to abandon Tanks, 245; proposal for Ohio Valley League, 135; sale of season tickets, 140
Ironton Tanks, 20–23, 26–28, 42–48, 69–72, 74–75, 77, 86, 89–91, 102–5, 108–9, 111, 125–29, 131, 134, 147, 152–56, 171, 176–78, 198–99, 200–203, 225–26, 229, 239; attendance, 305; banquets, 63, 79, 112, 244; benefit game, 151; collegiate spirit, 91; controversy over Davies as coach, roster, 125; controversy over strength of Tanks, 107; demise, 249; demise and revival, 143; dispute with Lombards on use of Beechwood, 36; dispute with Smoke House on use of ringers, 44–48, 50–52; dispute with Wellston on scheduling and fighting during and after game, 49–50; employment of players, 189–90, 220–21; fighting during and after game with Spartans, 191–92;

362

Index

financial conditions, 37–38, 52, 56, 65, 66, 79–80, 91, 96, 101, 133, 136, 140–41, 156, 179, 180–81, 210, 234–35, 240, 245; entry into NFL, 111; name, 18; occupation, 18; origins, 17; public rally to save, 245–46; pre-game atmosphere, 30–31, 74, 127, 134, 191; rank among independents, 238; recruiting, 101, 163, 168–69; roster, 83, 124, 140, 224; scheduling , 26, 28, 29–30, 35–36, 55, 56–57, 58, 65, 66–68, 82, 118, 125, 175, 238; status in community, 24, 32–33, 36–37, 38–39, 52, 66, 78–79, 114, 164, 210–11, 226, 301, 304–5; vignettes of players, 78–79

Ironton Tanks Memorial Stadium, 306

Ironton Tribune, 4

Jackson, Ohio, 1

Jackson Bearcats, 35, 36, 48, 57, 64

Jean (Gean, LeJean), Walter, 152, 157, 160; dismissed as coach, 163; portrait, 161; recruiting, 161

Jessen, Ernie, 206

Joannes, Leland, 261

Joesting, Herb, 253

Johnson, Newton, 137

Jones, David "Doc," 227, 255, 273, 274, 294

Jones, Howard, 165

Jones, Ralph, 185, 230

Joseph, Chal, 153, 154, 156, 161, 199

Kahl, Cy, 242, 250, 255

Kansas City Cowboys, 130–31

Karow, Marty, 147

Kaylor, Harry, 192

Kelly, John "Shipwreck," 282, 283

Kelly, Webber, 214

Kemerer, Paul, 154

Kenova, W. Va., 1

Kieran, John: interview with Potsy Clark, 276–77; sees Spartans as "powerful team, 257

Kiesling, Walt, 294

Kinderdine, George "Hobby," 153, 154, 156, 163, 202

Knieff, Pat, 189, 192

Knox College, 67

Koeper, Kenneth "Dum Dum," 82, 98

Kokomo Legion, 128, 156, 200

Koors, Carl, 109

Kotal, Eddie, 156

Kresky, Joe, 194

Kriss, Howard, 201

Kurtzhalz, Walter, 82, 98

Labold Field: bidding for construction of stadium, 215–16; bond issue for stadium, 162; proposals for stadium, 183, 207–8

Lambeau, Earl "Curly," 161, 184, 204–5, 241, 260, 261, 297

Lambert, James, 55, 56, 57, 60, 61, 62, 66, 67, 68, 72, 83, 84, 85, 86, 89, 96, 101, 102, 109, 110, 118, 124, 125, 127, 130, 133

Lancaster, Ohio, 60, 73

Lane, Frank, 84, 111, 177

Lardner, Ring, 336 n. 26

Lawrence County Board of Education, 197

Layne, A. J., 74

Leach, Edward, 162, 338 n. 5

Leader, Russ, 248

Lee, Evard, 176, 248

Lewis, Loren "Tiny," 194, 196, 197, 201, 205, 216, 240, 248

Liberty, 12

Lillard, Joe, 273, 274, 294

Lions Club, 199, 203

Lockland Athletic Club, 61, 62

"loading-up," 22

Logan Wildcats, 71, 150, 154, 166, 173

Lombard College, 67

Lombards, 16, 20, 21, 24, 25–26, 28–29; status in community, 36

Lough, Dana, 139

Louisville Brecks, 84

Lumpkin, Roy "Father," 187, 191, 197, 199, 205, 207, 219, 231, 242, 250, 257, 264, 270, 271, 275, 276, 286, 288, 290, 291, 292, 294, 299, 303; barnstorming, 283; in the community, 306; personality, 184–85; vows to knock Presnell out, 192

MacMillan, John, 222, 226, 233

Mahl, George, 135

Mahrt, Al, 109

Manders, Jack, 300

Maners, Roy, 77

Mara, Jack, 270

Mara, Tim, 214, 273

Mara, Wellington, 270

Marshall, George Preston, 288

Marshall College, 28, 42

Martin, Homer, 70, 72, 98

Martin, "Red," 239, 248

Martins Ferry, 150

Massillon Maroons, 195

Mayer, Emil, 153, 154, 161

Index

McCarthy, Charles, 96–97, 138, 142, 147, 154, 169, 170, 172, 196, 199, 225, 226, 229, 234–35, 238; counsels fans on behavior, 175–76, 195; defense of Presnell, 173–74; praise for Presnell as example for youth, 280; praise for Presnell's play, 176; response to Black, 153; on improving Tanks, 155; congratulates Tanks 180; view of Tanks' future, 143–44

McClain, Mayes "Chief," 250, 255, 257

McCormick, T. G., 162

McGurek, Warren, 234

McKalip, Bill, 264, 271, 290

McKinney, Dick, 58, 60, 63

McMahon, Nick, 37, 143, 151, 154, 155, 173, 178, 180, 188, 189, 191, 196, 198, 201, 202, 209, 220, 229, 234, 235, 236, 239, 244; recruiting, 168, 189, 223, 224; scheduling, 189, 224

McMillan, Alvin "Bo," 103

McNeal, John, 93, 105, 119

McNulty, Leroy, 98, 99

McWhorter, "Pup," 83

McWilliams, "Bunk," 98, 99, 165, 197, 200

Meck, E. N., 141

Memphis Commercial Appeal, 230, 235

Memphis Tigers, 205, 230, 235

Meyers, Denny, 224

Michalske, Mike, 187

Middletown Armcos (Blues), 92, 103, 122, 125, 133, 140, 146, 152–53, 154, 166–67, 174, 187, 195, 204

Midwestern Football League, 140

Millbrook Park, 21

Miller, Edgar, 47, 50

Miller, H. E., 177

Miller, J. C., 130

Mincher, Jerry, 103, 134

Minego, Pete, 49, 50, 63, 75, 132, 147, 178, 179, 239, 241–42, 254, 256, 257, 270, 271, 272, 274, 276, 277, 280, 290, 291, 293, 299, 301, 302

Minneapolis Red Jackets, 228, 233, 240–41, 347 n. 22

Mitchell, "Buster," 251, 271, 292, 303

Mittendorf, Earl, 89

Mittendorf, Ralph, 17

Mittendorf, Waldo, 17

Mohr, "Dutch," 35

Molesworth, Keith, 161, 163, 164, 178, 179, 191, 197, 199, 224, 259, 260

Molster, Dudley, 19

Montgomery, Orville, 63, 71

Moore, John, 139

Morning Irontonian , 4

Morning Sun, 5

Morris Harvey, 26, 48

Mullbarger, Joe, 129

Murdock, Ethel, 91, 112

Murray City Tigers, 83, 112

Murray, Jim, 348 n. 45, 348–49 n. 58

Nagurski, Bronislaw "Bronco," 230, 287, 297

National Collegiate Athletic Association, 11

Neal, R, E., 107

Neale, Earle "Greasy," 11, 220, 224, 226, 238; compares Tanks with Notre Dame, 245; resigns as coach of Tanks, 245; play against Spartans, 229; training rules, 225

Nemecek, Andy, 89, 90, 91

Nesbitt, Dick, 285, 287

Nesser, Al, 273

Nesser brothers, 21

Nevers, Ernie, 227, 231, 255, 273

Newark Tornadoes, 233

New Boston, Ohio, 1

New Boston Strollers, 64

New Boston Tigers, 28

Newman, Harry, 293, 296

New York Giants, 232, 236, 237, 256, 257, 258, 273, 276, 293, 296

New York Times, comment on Spartans, 257

Niemic, Johnny, 194, 196

Nitro, W.Va., 28

Nodler, Clarence, 267

Norfolk and Western (N. & W.) team, 22; origins, 19; occupations, 19; schedule, 21; status in communty, 25

Norfolk and Western Railroad, 4

Norris, Earle, 68, 70, 71, 72, 75, 77, 81, 83

North, "Hootie," 41

Ohio State Journal, 60, 107

Ohio Valley League, 139

Oklahoma Chiefs, 288

Oorang Indians, 128–29

Oosterbaan, Bennie, 155

Owen, Steve, 293

Paterson Panthers, 276

Paul, Floyd, 107

Paul, J. R., 66

Paul, William, 197, 198

Perry, Virgil, 89, 106, 121, 122, 130, 147, 153, 158, 246, 248; accepts position as Armcos' coach, 119; broken jaw, 176; conducts practices , 120, 176; recruiting Armcos, 144,

364

145; attends Rockne grid school, 165; wide-open attack, 165; attends Warner grid school, 145, 164

Petcoff, Boni, 129, 164, 165

Peters, Forrest "Frosty," 234, 239, 240, 241, 242

Pfau, Jake, 69, 86, 115, 134, 156, 161

Poole, Clarence "Concrete," 91, 124, 166

Pope, Harry, 22, 48, 49, 68, 91, 93

Pope, Virgil, 22, 48, 82, 90, 101, 108

Portsmouth, Ohio: economy, 4–5; origins, 4; population, 5

Portsmouth Football Association, 162, 183, 179, 217

Portsmouth Merchants, 116, 117, 118, 119

Portsmouth National Football League Corporation, 217

Portsmouth Presidents, 116–19, 126–28, 131–36, 141–42; dispute with merchants over use of Labold, 116–17; origins, 115; occcupations, 115; practices, 116; prospects after season, 148; status in community, 135

Portsmouth Shoe-Steels, 148–52, 151–52, 153–54, 156–57; outlook for 1928, 158; origins, 148–49; composition, 150–51

Portsmouth Smoke House, 29, 31, 40, 42, 63–64, 69–70, 73–74, 86–87, 90–91; origins, 26–27; scheduling, 29, 63; status in the community, 33, 39, 53, 65, 77, 86, 92, 112–13

Portsmouth Spartan Municipal Stadium, 306

Portsmouth Spartans, 163–64, 178, 187–88, 191–92, 196–97, 199–200, 206, 225–28, 230–34, 239–42, 255–60, 277–78, 280–83, 293–98; on all-star teams, 264–99; attendance, 305; banquets, 179, 207, 259; barnstorming, 288–99; eastern swing, 256, 295; fans condemn play against Reds, 297; financial conditions and subscription drive, 188, 200, 206, 220–21, 254, 257–58, 262–67, 273, 278–79, 299–300; first night game, 221–22; fishing trip, 276; naming, 162; in New York, 257; entry into NFL, 208–9, 213–14, 215; origins 160; off-season activities, 179–80, 242, 270–71, 290; practices, 186–87, 218, 292; publicity tours, 221–52; receptions, 258, 278, 287; recruiting, 186, 252, 257; relationship with Packers, 241; roster, 216–18, 291; sale of season tickets, 162, 179, 183–84, 217, 254–55; sale of team, 300–302; scheduling, 186, 253–54, 269–70, 291; status in the community, 186–87, 206–7, 305; threatened strike, 279; travel conditions, 275; uniforms, 163, 186–87, 218, 223, 279, 292

Portsmouth Spartans-Bears playoff game, 1932: Chicago Stadium, 285; disputed pass, 287; gate, 287; rules, 285; resultant rules, 288

Portsmouth Spartans-Packers, proposed game, 204–5

Portsmouth Times, 5

Powell, Dick, 189, 211, 224, 225, 227

Powers, Murray, 272, 281, 287, 291; censures Spartans and Cardinals for rough play, 294–95; on threatened strke, 280

Presnell, Glenn, 155, 172, 174, 177, 191, 195, 199, 201, 202, 209, 224, 236, 237, 245, 257, 264, 270, 272, 273, 274, 276, 281, 286, 288, 290, 293, 295, 296, 297, 299; resigns as coach, 223; fans criticize, 173; performance against Giants, 236; view of Ironton, 306; on payment of salaries, 279; signs with Lions, 302; signs with Spartans, 250–51; decision to become a Tank, 169; explanation for Tanks' play in 1929, 234

Press-Scimitar, 230–35

Progler, Pick, 36

Providence Steamroller, 233, 250

Purdy, Pid, 156

Putzek, August, 18, 19, 20, 23, 27, 29, 32, 116

Pyle, C. C. "Cash and Carry," 131, 132

Quinn, Bob, 19

racial allusions in reporting, 274, 294

Randolph, Clare, 185–86, 191, 197, 227, 251, 270, 290, 303

Rascher, Andy, 290

Raskowski, Leo, 194, 197

Read, A. C., 8

Rectanus, S. R., 130

Rezzonico, Art, 61

Ridgley, Duke, 48, 57, 72, 79, 89, 99, 103, 126; professional football in the Ohio Valley, 108; proposal for an Ohio Valley league, 208

Richards, George, 301, 302

Rice, Grantland, 336 n. 26

Ringers, 11

Robb, Harry, 109

Roberts, Fred, 216

Roberts, Howard, 286

Roberts, Jim, 98, 100, 106, 121, 145, 158, 165

Rockne, Knute, 13

Roebuck, "Tiny," 189, 211

Rolph, Harold, 169, 189, 210, 211

Rooney, Art, 349 n. 5

Ross, F. O., 195

Index

Russell, Ky., 1

Sacksteder, Norbert, 109
Saddler, Raymond, 51
St. Louis Gunners, 277
Salt, Benton, 42
Salt, Vic, 30
Schaake, Elmer "Dutch," 291, 293
Schachlerter, Bill, 35, 36, 42, 47, 48, 49, 51
Schlemmer, James, 171, 177, 202, 230
Schleusner, Vincent, 185, 250
Schneller, John, 291, 293
Schubert, A. C., 66
Schwab, Mattie, 93
Schwarz, Elmer, 270
Scott, H. R. "Doc," 37, 40, 45
Selby, Homer, 266, 268, 270, 278, 279, 291
Selby Shoe Company, 148
semiprofessional football: evolution to profes-
    sional football in Ironton and Portsmouth,
    182; organization of a team, 19; scheduling,
    132–33; state in 1920s, 76
Shannon, Earle "Red," 45, 46, 47, 48, 61, 71
Shea, Jim, 177
Shelby Blues, 144
Shelton, Kemper, 71
Shenandoah Presidents, 295
Shields, Jake, 115
Shipp, Fred, 151
Shoemaker, Pat, 116
Slater, Fred "Duke," 227–28
Sloan, Clair, 223, 236, 237
Smith, Carl, 107
Smith, Farrar "Phony," 170, 248
Smith, Gene, 232
Smith, Olen, 101, 124, 126, 129, 156, 166
Smith, Ray, 234
Smith, Russell, 92, 93, 115, 116, 129, 196, 204,
    248; recruiting, 160, 194; scheduling,
    194–95
Snowday, Roger, 82
Snowday, Terry, 66, 70, 82, 84, 85, 86, 89
Snyder, Harry, 216, 242, 258, 260, 261, 266, 268,
    270, 276, 277, 280, 283, 284, 285, 291, 298,
    300, 301, 302
Solomon, Moses, 87, 112
Springfield Bulldogs, 150, 163
Stagg, Amos Alonzo, 11
Stanford, Ralph, 209
Staten Island Stapletons, 233, 257, 259, 275, 296
Sternaman, George, 230
Sternaman, Joey, 230
Stewart, Hubert "Doc," 20, 23

Stinchcomb, Pete, 71, 144
Stoch, Herb, 102, 108
Stone, Naylor, 299
Strong, Ken, 233, 257
Stuart, Johnny, 121, 135, 157, 248
Stuber, Abe, 147, 153, 175

Talbott, Vaughan A., 221, 265, 338 n. 5
Talbott, Vaughan H., 221, 222
Taylor, Harry, 50, 51
Taylor, Jimmy, 75
Taylor, Paul "Horsemeat," 200
Tays, Jimmy, 173
Thomas, Frank, 168
Thomas, W. C., 42, 47
Thorpe, Jim, 104–5, 110, 129, 148, 152, 153, 154;
    goal for Steels, 149; conducts practices,
    149; refusal to coach, 157
Thuma, A. L., 66
ties, 277–78, 347 nn. 11–12
Toledo Boosters, 190
Tri-State, 1
Tri-State League, 248; finances, 249; former
    Tanks, Armcos and Boosters on teams,
    248; requirements for members, 248; sea-
    son shortened, 249
Tobin, Paul, 45
Trafton, George, 231
Turnbull, Andrew, 282
Tuttle, Clyde, 107
Tynes, Lane, 90, 91, 248

Van Nostrand, Rhoades, 115
Veeck, Bill, Sr., 281
Verity, George, 175
Vidt, C. E., 170

Wabash Athletic Club, 176
Wager, John "Popeye," 224, 251, 257, 270, 275,
    290
Walker, "Dixie," 116
Walker, Jimmy, 258
Walter, Jack, 115, 118, 133, 148; proposed Ohio
    Valley league, 134
Ward, Arch, 336 n. 26
Wardaman, Bill, 93
Ware, Louis, 120, 157, 164, 165
Warner, Glenn "Pop," 7–12
Warsaw, Peter, 338 n. 5
Washington Court House Independents, 61, 63,
    68, 70
Washington Olympians, 234
Waverly Herald Republican, 44

Index

Weaver, Jim "Red," 38, 103, 104, 106, 108–9, 121, 133

Weil, Sid, 273, 349 n. 5

Wellston, Ohio, 1

Wellston Eagles, 32, 48, 49–50, 62, 73, 86, 112

Welsh, Jim, 189

Whittaker-Glessner Mill, 5, 101, 148

Wieteki, Frank, 35, 37

Williams, Henry, 13, 45

Williams, Thomas, 338 n. 5

Williamson, W.Va., 57

Williamsport, 64

"Willson, Mr.," 103

Wing, A. A., 303

Winters, Lingrell "Sonny," 89, 90, 95, 96, 102, 103, 104, 110, 111, 124, 125, 126, 135, 136, 138, 142

Witt, Roy, 184

Wittenburg, Lynn, 200, 201, 214, 218, 219, 222, 229, 231, 232, 233, 255, 256, 262, 272, 273, 274, 281, 282, 287

Workman, Brad, 57, 58

Workman, Hoge, 256

Wray, Lud, 349 n. 5

Wykoff, Howard, 103

Xenia Tiltons, 33, 116

Yale Daily News, 10

Young, Dick, 167, 172, 178, 179, 186, 190, 191–92, 197

Zanesville Mark Greys, 29, 60

Zelt, Albert, 82

Zuppke, Bob, 7, 252